MONGOLIA

IN THE

TWENTIETH

CENTURY

A publication of the Northeast Asia Seminar

Rediscovering Russia in Asia
Siberia and the Russian Far East
Edited by Stephen Kotkin and David Wolff

Mongolia in the Twentieth Century
Landlocked Cosmopolitan
Edited by Stephen Kotkin and Bruce A. Elleman

MONGOLIA

IN THE
TWENTIETH
CENTURY

Landlocked Cosmopolitan

Edited by
Stephen Kotkin
and
Bruce A. Elleman

M.E.Sharpe
Armonk, New York
London, England

Library of Congress Cataloging-in-Publication Data

Mongolia in the twentieth century : landlocked cosmopolitan /
edited by Stephen Kotkin and Bruce A. Elleman.
p.   cm.
Includes bibliographical references and index.
ISBN 0-7656-0535-X (cloth : alk. paper)   ISBN 0-7656-0536-8 (pbk. : alk. paper)
1. Mongolia—History—20th century.   I. Kotkin, Stephen.
II. Elleman, Bruce A., 1959– .   III.Title : Mongolia in the 20th century.
DS798.75.M653   1999
951′.705—dc21   99-44518
CIP

Printed in the United States of America

The paper used in this publication meets the minimum requirements of
American National Standard for Information Sciences
Permanence of Paper for Printed Library Materials,
ANSI Z 39.48-1984.

BM (c)   10   9   8   7   6   5   4   3   2   1
BM (p)   10   9   8   7   6   5   4   3   2   1

For Nicholas Poppe (1897-1992),
Owen Lattimore (1900-1989),
and Nicholas V. Riasanovsky

Scholars, Teachers, Mentors

Contents

About the Editors and Contributors

Stephen Kotkin is associate professor in the history department at Princeton University. Author of *Steeltown, USSR: Soviet Society in the Gorbachev Era* (1991) and *Magnetic Mountain: Stalinism as Civilization* (1995), he is currently writing a book on the Ob River Basin, 1500-2000.

Bruce A. Elleman is assistant professor at Texas Christian University, where he teaches Chinese, Russian, and Japanese history. Author of *Diplomacy and Deception: The Secret History of Sino-Soviet Diplomatic Relations, 1917-1927* (1997), he is currently writing a military history of modern China.

Christopher P. Atwood is assistant professor of Mongolian history in the Central Eurasian Studies department at Indiana University. He is completing a book, tentatively entitled *Between Two Revolutions:Young Mongols and Vigilantes in Inner Mongolia's Interregnum Decade, 1921-1931.*

Tsedendambyn Batbayar is Director-General, Department of Policy Planning and Coordination, Ministry of External Relations, Mongolia. He has written *Modern Mongolia* (Ulaanbaatar, 1986) and *Mongolia and Japan in the First Half of the Twentieth Century* (Ulaanbaatar, 1998). His current research interests include Mongolia's Asia-Pacific security and foreign relations.

Elena Boikova is a Senior Researcher at the Institute of Oriental Studies, Russian Academy of Sciences, Moscow. Her publications include the *Bibliography of Mongolian Studies in Russia in 1992-1997* (Moscow, 1997), and she is currently writing a book on modern Mongolian intellectuals.

J. Boldbaatar is the Head of the Department of History, National University of Mongolia, and a member of Mongolia's Constitutional Court. His publications include *Historical Overview of Mongolia's State and Legal Traditions* (Ulaanbaatar, 1997), and he is currently researching Mongolian political history.

Elizabeth Endicott is associate professor in the history department at Middlebury College. She is the author of *Mongolian Rule in China: Local Administration in the Yuan Dynasty* (1989), and coauthor of *The Modernization of Inner Asia* (1991). She is currently working on a book manuscript detailing the 1910 Moscow Trade Expedition to Moscow.

Tom Ginsburg received his J.D. and Ph.D. (specializing in Jurisprudence and Social Policy) from the University of California at Berkeley. He has worked for the Asia Foundation in Mongolia. In 2000 he was appointed Assistant Professor of Law at the University of Illinois at Urbana-Champaign.

A. Hurelbaatar is a professor at the Institute of Mongolian Language and Literature, Inner Mongolia Normal University, Höhhot. His publications include "The Transformation of the Inner Mongolian Pastoral Economy: The Case of Hulun Buir," *Culture and Environment in Inner Asia*, vol. 2. He participated as a researcher on the MacArthur project on the Environment and Cultural Conservation in Inner Asia at Cambridge University, and is currently doing field work in Aga Buriat Autonomous District in Russia.

Mei-hua Lan received her Ph.D. in Inner Asian and Altaic Studies from Harvard University in 1996. She is an associate professor in the Department of Ethnology, National Chengchi University, Taipei, Taiwan.

Yeshen-Khorlo Dugarova-Montgomery received her Ph.D. from the College of Oriental Studies, Leningrad University, and has served as a staff researcher in the Department of Linguistics of the Buriat Institute of Social Science (Ulan-Ude). Her publications include *Glagol'nyi vid v sovremennom mongol'skom iazyke* (Verbal Aspect in Modern Mongolian) (Novosibirsk: Nauka, 1991).

Robert Montgomery received his Ph.D. in Russian history from Indiana University in 1995, and is currently the Slavic Acquisitions Coordinator of the Indiana Research Library. His publications include "Buddhist Monastic Education in Prerevolutionary Buriatia," *East/West Education*, vol. 17, no. 1-2 (1996).

Nakami Tatsuo is a professor at the Institute for the Study of Languages and Cultures of Asia and Africa, Tokyo University of Foreign Studies. He has edited *The Bordered Red Banners Archives, Ch'ien-lung Period* (1993), and coauthored *Inner Asia: a World History from a Regional Perspective*, volume 6 (1992).

David Sneath is an Assistant Lecturer in the Department of Social Anthropology, University of Cambridge, and a Research Fellow of the Mongolia and Inner Asia Studies Unit. He is coauthor of *The End of Nomadism: Society, State and the Environment in Inner Asia* (1999), and author of a forthcoming book *Changing Inner Mongolia: Pastoral Mongolian Society and the Chinese State*.

Guudain Tumurchuluun entered the MPR's foreign service in 1978 and is currently the Director of the Center of Foreign Policy Studies, Ministry of External Relations, Mongolia. His research interests include geopolitics, security, and foreign relations.

Acknowledgments

Financial support for the conference on which this volume is based was furnished by the U.S.-Japan Program as well as Princeton University's Woodrow Wilson School, Center for International Studies, Department of History, and Department of East Asian Studies. The editors would like to especially thank Princeton University's Council on Regional Studies and its former director, Gilbert Rozman, for substantial financial and logistical support.

We are also grateful to the American Museum of Natural History for permission to reproduce some of J.B. Shackelford's photographs from the Museum's 1922 and 1925 Central Asiatic Expeditions, reported in Roy Chapman Andrews' *On the Trail of Ancient Man.*

Midway through the editing stage, David Wolff, one of the conference organizers, had to leave the project. His work as co-editor was very graciously and ably performed by Bruce Elleman, with the ever-present and unflagging assistance of his spouse Sarah Paine. Christopher Atwood provided indispensable advice and contacts in Mongolia, as well as major editorial assistance, photographs from the Mongolian Central Party Archives, maps, and tremendous linguistic insight.

Patricia Kolb, Elizabeth Granda, and Ana Erlic of M.E. Sharpe maintained a strong interest in the book project over the years, and helped ensure that it came to fruition.

Trudy de Goede, reference librarian at the University of Texas at Arlington, helped determine the copyright status of the photographs used in this book.

To all the participants, including those whose papers did not end up in the present volume, the editors extend our heartfelt gratitude.

Note on Transliteration and Abbreviations

Except for the names of a handful of famous individuals, the transliteration system used for Russian is the Library of Congress system minus the diacritical marks. For Chinese, the *pinyin* system has been used, except for those names which have entered into common usage by another romanization, for example: Sun Yat-sen, Chiang Kai-shek, etc. In the case of Chinese names, the family name is usually placed first. For Japanese language, the Modified Hepburn system has been used throughout. For Mongolian language, the editors have elected to use the Mongolia Society system (as presented in *Mongolia Studies* No. 21, 1998). In order to avoid confusion, the editors have elected to use the old spelling—Sükhebaatur—when referring directly to the leader of the 1921 Mongolian revolution, while using the new spelling—Sükhbaatar—when referring to the names of cities, squares, and streets named in his honor.

The term *Outer Mongolia* refers to the northern portion of Greater Mongolia that roughly corresponds to modern-day Mongolia and is used prior to 1924, when the *Mongolian People's Republic (MPR)* was founded. *Soviet Russia* is used to refer to the Bolshevik state prior to 1922, while *Soviet Union (USSR)* is used after 1922. Other frequently used abbreviations include the *Moscow Trade Expedition (MTE)*, the *Mongolia People's Revolutionary Party (MPRP)*, and the *Inner Mongolia Autonomous Republic (IMAR)*.

List of Photographs

List of Tables

List of Charts

List of Maps

Preface

The fifteen years from 1980 to 1995 saw a succession of dramatic changes on the Mongolian plateau, changes that suggest historical trends reaching far beyond the political frontiers of the Chinese and Russian empires. In the early 1980s, as the nightmare of the Cultural Revolution lifted and China rejoined the world economic system, Inner Mongolia opened up to both foreigners and eventually to other Mongols; the Mongols there began to rediscover their ethnic past, a process that continues to gather momentum. In 1990, the disintegration of Soviet-bloc Communism as a separate world-system produced a democratic, market-based regime in the former Soviet satellite of Mongolia. In 1991, the Republic of Buriatia, no longer Soviet or socialist, openly asserted the once repressed questions of its Stalinist past in the sprawling and contentious Russian Federation that emerged from the wreckage of the Gorbachev regime. In all three Mongol regions, boundaries loosened, economic goods were privatized, and the state either renounced the promotion of a single ideology or else became uncertain as to what its ideology meant.

Despite the dramatic and unpredictable transformation of these two independent Communist bloc systems, these changes transformed the Mongolian plateau as a single trend, moving in uneven progress from south to north. This impression of a single historical movement is all the stronger given the memories of an almost mirror image progression earlier in the twentieth century, when revolutionary party rule, rigid boundaries, and Leninist-style bureaucratic nationalism swept in jerky progress from north to south, from Buriatia in 1920, to Mongolia in 1921, and finally to Inner Mongolia in 1947. These historical patterns suggest that a synoptic view of the twentieth century on the Mongolian plateau can provide insights not only on to the Mongolian experience but also on to the historical experience of other peoples of Northeast Asia. Just as the theme of the first half of the twentieth-century in Eurasian, and hence Mongolian, history was the ruthless building of state power, the theme of the final part of that century seems to be the privatization of that same power, with uneven consequences for the people involved.

These and other issues of the transnational history of the Mongols in the twentieth century were addressed at an international meeting of Princeton University's Northeast Asia seminar in February 1995. The present volume offers a selection of the presentations from that symposium, as well as some that were solicited afterward. No effort has been made to achieve comprehensiveness or a single point of view. Scholars of diverse interests, but all with recent archival or field experience pertaining to the Mongols and Mongolia, were brought together under the assumption that, properly staked out, the cosmopolitan region of Northeast Asia lends coherence to efforts at understanding its history and present circumstances.

Yet to write a wide-ranging volume on Mongolia that views the entire Mongolian plateau—Mongolia proper, Inner Mongolia, and Buriatia—as in some sense an interconnected whole, is to face the problem of names. Not just the problem of what to call the area itself ("Mongolian plateau" as used above is itself a delicate compromise straddling the bombastic "Greater Mongolia" and the bloodless "areas traditionally inhabited by Mongols"), but even the simple problem of how to spell the names of persons and places in the area. Virtually all the names in use in Mongolia have two or three forms in English, none of which has become decisively at home. Since 1924, for example, the capital of Mongolia proper, written according to a transcription of the modern Cyrillic Mongolian spelling (itself adopted only in 1946) has been "Ulaanbaatar," meaning "Red Hero," but the Russian version, dating from 1924-46, spells it Ulan-Bator. As late as the 1970s, this major city often appeared in textbooks and travel books as "Urga," the traditional Russian name for the city, which was derived from a Mongolian term Örgöö, meaning "palace tent." This term was used in Mongolia for the political center of Outer Mongolia only during a few decades in the eighteenth century.

The diversity of spellings represents in visible form the fact that Mongolia's story has been told exclusively in European languages, almost entirely by non-Mongols, and largely on the basis of non-Mongolian written sources. Even Chinggis Khan, Mongolia's great hero and the one figure who raises this small nomadic nation in the world's attention above the obscure Inner Asian ranks of the Kyrgyzstans and the Tannu Tuvas, has had to see his story told to the world under strange spellings mediated by Persian and French: Genghis, Jenghiz, and even Gibbon's version Zingis. The original Mongolian Chinggis was heard by the Turks, who served as key mediators of the Mongolian imperium in the west, as Chingiz. Ch- was the correct initial consonant, as was -i- (the unwritten but understood) initial vowel in the Arabic-script Persian spellings. Yet a common Persian shorthand convention of omitting the three diacritical dots that distinguish ch- from j-, and a mistaken reconstruction of the unwritten short vowel, led the eighteenth-century French pioneers in Middle Eastern history to read his name not as Chingiz, but as Jenghiz or Genghis.

Such appropriation of the great conqueror has not stopped only at his name. Chinggis Khan, who was born in the heart of Mongolian tribal society and was far more a genuine son of his people than Napoleon was of France, Stalin of Russia, or Sun Yat-sen of China, has proven to be a magnet for those seeking an assumed racial identity. From Harold Lamb's vision in *Genghis Khan: The Emperor of All Men* of Chinggis Khan as a displaced Aryan, with blue-grey eyes "that did not slant," to the Baltic German adventurer Baron Ungern-Sternberg's belief that his self-proclaimed descent from the Inner Asian conqueror made his savage antics welcome in Mongolia, to the Japanese legend, widely touted in Inner Mongolia during World War II, that the great Mongol was actually the romantic hero Minamoto Yoshitsune escaped to Mongolia to avoid his brother's envy, and finally to the Maoist adoption of Chinggis Khan as a model for Chinese revenge on the Moscow revisionists, the Mongols have seen their national founder repeatedly woven into the mythology of others. Widely known among Russians, Chinese, and other world powers, thanks to their unique history of world conquest, the Mongols have lacked the contemporary cultural presence to challenge external readings of either themselves or their greatest hero.

This Persianized, Frenchified "Genghis Khan" has come back to transform the way the Mongols themselves see their national hero, and that too is a symptom of how Mongolia's interaction with the outside world has played a unique role in its modern history. The Mongols have been remarkably adept at exploiting the outside world's fascination with their founder. The trend began with the 1911 restoration of Mongolian independence: within a year, the Buriat Mongolian scholar, Tsyben Zhamtsarano, a free-lance Mongol nationalist who worked as a translator in the Russian consulate, began serializing a translation of French author Leon Cahun's 1877 potboiler about the conquests of "Genghis Khan" in one of Mongolia's first journals, the *New Mirror* of 1912. The Chinese government originally sponsored the construction of the mausoleum of Chinggis Khan in 1963 as an episode in the Sino-Soviet rivalry, but the Mongols of Inner Mongolia took this mausoleum, built in the Ordos region to house what the Mongols had venerated for centuries as the personal effects of the great Khan, as a rallying point of Mongol identity and an object of a truly religious devotion. Since the democratization in Mongolia proper and the liberation from stifling Marxist-Leninist nomenclature, "Chinggis Khan" appears with monotonous regularity: Lenin Avenue was changed to Chinggis Khan Avenue, one of Ulaanbaatar's newest luxury hotels is the Chinggis Khan Hotel, and Mongolia's most exportable liquor brand is, of course, Chinggis Khan vodka.

Thus, just as the confusing multiplication of names for Mongolian people and places highlights the difficulty Mongols have experienced in defining and exporting their own history to the outside world, their openness in responding to the way outsiders see Mongolian history highlights the unexpected cosmopolitanism of Mongolian history in the twentieth century. Despite its isolated position, one of a small fraternity of "sandwich" countries which are entirely contained between other powers (Moldova, Nepal, Bhutan, and tiny Liechtenstein are some other members in this unfortunate club), Mongolia has shown an unusual eagerness to engage with the outside world. Chinggis Khan's memory has helped his descendants in their struggle to penetrate the consciousness of powers far beyond the imperial borders of China and Russia, and while using the mythology of Mongolia to elevate its profile in world affairs, at the same time the Mongols have quietly resisted the restrictive definitions of outsiders.

In this sense, as Stephen Kotkin and David Wolff noted while organizing the scholarly conference, Mongolia truly is a "Landlocked Cosmopolitan," a country where the primacy of foreign policy is unquestioned, yet where the overriding aim of foreign policy is to preserve its separate national life. Although the Mongols of Inner Mongolia and Buriatia have not played a part in the diplomatic world of Asia, as have the Mongols of independent Mongolia, they have stood out among other national minorities in China and Russia by their willingness to stake the future of their nationality on the assimilation of modernizing ideologies. Whether it is the Khorchin and Kharachin nationalists of Eastern Inner Mongolia, or the Buriat intelligentsia in Siberia, the Mongols of the twentieth century have had remarkably little use for the purely isolationist strategy of national survival, the sort of policy promoted by influential Tibetans in both China and British India, and by the Afghan, Tajik, and Uzbek peoples of Central Asia in the Tsarist era. Once again, however, this primacy of assimilating foreign culture is not for its own sake, but primarily a means for preserving the Mongolian and Buriat nationalities as competitive and modern entities within the larger Chinese and Russian spheres.

As a result of these constant interactions, the writing of Mongolian history must always address the problem of perspective, not only in the matter of names, but more fundamentally in the sources of information and the perspectives of the authors. The aim of the papers presented here is to cross political boundaries and to open the doors between disciplines and areas of specialization, so that the anthropology of Inner Mongolia and history of Japanese diplomacy, or the socio-linguistics of Buriatia and political science of contemporary Mongolia, can began to build a common terminology by pooling insights concerning these multiple Mongolian versions of the great transformation of twentieth-century Eurasia. Perhaps, in the far future, scholars of Mongolia may reach a common agreement on how to spell Chinggis/Chingis/Genghis/Jenghiz Khan/Qan's name. The result will not be to synthesize a single modal historical experience for the whole region, but to illustrate that the view of the historian cannot be limited by state boundaries, however solid they may appear. Precisely because the building of centralized states has been such a vitally important phenomenon in modern history, transnationalism as a perspective is not an "add-on" but an essential foundation of historical understanding. That, in a nutshell, is the credo of the Northeast Asia Seminar.

Christopher P. Atwood

MONGOLIA
IN THE
TWENTIETH
CENTURY

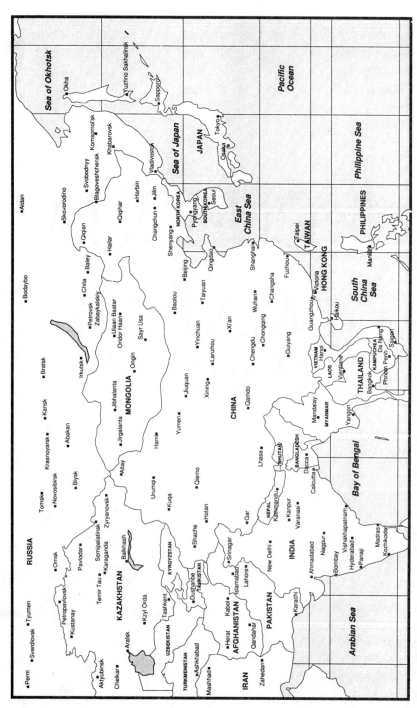

Map: East Asia

Introduction

In Search of the Mongols and Mongolia: A Multinational Odyssey

Stephen Kotkin

World history, according to Hidehiro Okada, was born in the thirteenth century, when what he called the only two "historically minded" civilizations, those of the Mediterranean and China, were brought into direct contact by the Mongols. Having conquered China and secured a stronghold near the Mediterranean on the Black Sea, the Mongols are said to have not merely facilitated unprecedented cultural and economic exchange throughout Eurasia, but to have given form to the major Eurasian peoples, including the Russians, Turks, Persians, Indians, Tibetans, Chinese, and Koreans. Around Eurasia's maritime periphery, meanwhile, Okada surmises that the ensuing "age of great navigations," alleged to have been begun by the Japanese in 1350 and the Portuguese in 1415, constituted a "response" to the Mongols' continental domination.[1]

Only the most unabashed enthusiasts of the imperial history of the Mongols would endorse these claims made by Okada. In fact, while noting the many forms of enduring Mongol influence, most scholars more often find themselves attempting to explain how a people who forged the world's most extensive land empire declined to virtual political oblivion, becoming the objects of imperial rule. So tenuous a connection do the Medieval exploits of empire-building seem to have with the twentieth-century subjugation of a tiny landlocked nation and related minority communities in adjacent states that Mongolia's modern history appears utterly discontinuous, if not a complete inversion.

Yet Okada's attempt to recapture for the Mongols historical influence over the basic internal structure of their powerful overlords, Russia and China—while pointedly passing over the Mongol relationship with a third regional colonizer, Japan—remains instructive. His thought experiment has the virtue of revealing usually unspoken fantasies of certain Mongolists, not to mention some Mongols, and more importantly, of highlighting the need to examine the history of twentieth-century Mongols and Mongolia in terms of the *longue durée* of Eurasian geopolitics, especially the shifting Russian-Chinese-Japanese triangle in Northeast Asia. That examination, as Okada insists, must not degenerate into a one-way search for the influence of outsiders on the Mongols, however weak the latter may have become.

Even if the medieval Mongols did not initiate world history, the travails of their successors in modern Mongolia (understood in the broadest sense) offer many insights into fundamental issues of today's world—from the Russian advance in Asia and the demarcation of the vast Sino-Russian frontier to the fate of pastoral nomadism when assaulted by modernity in its Communist and post-Communist guises; from Japanese attempts to conquer the Asian mainland to the relative weight of the cultural and the political in shaping a people's identity; from the spread of Chinese settlement across large parts of Asia to the conditions under which buffer nations are formed and preserved, or engulfed and nearly eradicated.

Over the course of the twentieth century in Northeast Asia, Mongols and interested outsiders alike have pursued their dreams and fashioned their identities in the sparsely inhabited steppe-desert. From the images of the mysterious "secret land" and the "grand world empire" of the khans, to the "geopolitical pivot" of Eurasia, and finally to the "exotic backwater" forced into modernity, Mongolia's heritage has been continually reshaped, and to an extent remains up for grabs among state builders on all sides of the border. To appreciate this enduring fascination with the cosmopolitan, landlocked Mongols, as well as the set of experiences and historical lexicon available to would-be rulers, some sense of the trajectory of Mongol studies will be given.

Russian Matrix

Modern scholarship on the Mongols began in the multinational Russian empire. Russian attention toward Mongol peoples focused first on the tsar's own subjects, including the Kalmyks of the lower Volga and the Buriats of eastern Siberia, and formed part of the expanding empire's efforts to study and master the Orient.[2] Beginning in 1833 the Mongolian language was taught at the University in Kazan, then Russia's main center for training Orientalists. Around mid-century a rival center developed at St. Petersburg University, which acquired an oriental languages department to complement the city's research-oriented Asian Museum (founded in 1818). St. Petersburg soon eclipsed Kazan.[3]

With Russia's acquisition of the Amur basin from China and the founding of Vladivostok in 1860, as well as the subsequent Russian penetration into Manchuria, Russia took greater notice of the Mongol subjects of China. The Russian Geographical Society organized several scientific expeditions to Outer and Inner Mongolia, both of which were under Chinese rule.[4] Siberian traders promoted further explorations, as did the Russian government's political ambitions in the Far East—symbolized and stimulated by Russia's construction of the Transsiberian and the Chinese Eastern Railroad (CER) in the 1890s.

In retrospect, the establishment of a Russian consulate in Urga (Ulaanbaatar) in 1858 can be seen as marking the onset of a successful thrust into the extensive Mongol lands claimed by China. This Russian advance was greatly spurred by the 1911 revolution in China, and not long diverted by the chaotic revolutionary and civil war years 1917-21 in Russia. By that time, Russia had come to hold a preeminent place as arbiter of Mongol affairs. A combination of the Russian empire's tradition of German-inspired scholarship, the diversity of a realm that stretched across Eurasia, and Russia's turn to a forward policy in Asia during the second half of the nineteenth century furnished a unique matrix for collecting and disseminating knowledge about the Mongols.

Chinese study of the Mongols provides an important contrast.[5] Among outsiders the Chinese have had the longest direct contact with the Mongols—experience that produced generations of interpreters expert in Mongol languages (the Manchu rulers of China even took their script from the Mongols). Under the Qing, Mongol Studies were advanced by Zhang Mu (1805-49), who wrote an investigation of "Mongolian Pastures," and Tu Ji (1856-1921), who employed ancient chronicles to rewrite the history of the Yuan. Wang Guowei (1877-1927) edited Chinese accounts of travels to Mongolian lands, and Ye Dehui (1864-1927) prepared the first modern edition of the thirteenth-century *Secret History of the Mongols,*which had been transliterated long ago into Chinese. Taking advantage of their experience as subjects and then overlords of the Mongols, Chinese scholars seemed well on their way to matching their Russian counterparts.[6]

But this early development did not grow into a mature tradition for a number of reasons. Unlike some Qing functionaries, Chinese scholars never fully learned Mongolian languages, instead working with Qing dynasty imperial records (Zhang Mu) or translated and transliterated texts (Tu Ji, Wang Guowei, Ye Dehui). No less consequentially, Chinese Mongol studies took shape as part of the Qing's project to map and classify the frontier regions. Individual scholars and the entire enterprise became closely tied to the Manchus and imperial rule, a circumstance that would come to discredit practitioners and the practice alike. Ye Dehui and Wang Guowei both fiercely opposed the 1911 revolution, whose circumscribed character enabled them to continue working. During the 1926-27 Nationalist revolution, however, Ye Dehui was executed as a counter-revolutionary and Wang Guowei committed suicide in despair.[7]

After the debacle of the nationalist triumph, Chinese Mongol Studies might have recovered and advanced, yet the Chinese lacked the impetus of a colonial context, of a search for an Asiatic "other" with which to define themselves.[8] It is not necessary to "apologize" for Russian condescension toward and mistreatment of "Asiatics" to recognize that in comparison with the Chinese, the Russians managed to encourage a sense of Mongol identity, record Mongol history, and not merely destroy but also preserve artifacts of Mongol culture, as part of a project to define the ethnic and national categories of Asia and Europe. Of course, not all non-Russians have enjoyed such "beneficial" effects of Russian imperialism. But the Mongols did—an outcome for which Russian competition with the Chinese was indirectly responsible.

Among Russian Mongolists Aleksei M. Pozdneev (1851-1920) stands out. A professor at St. Petersburg, and then founder and director of the Oriental Institute in Vladivostok in 1899, Pozdneev's two volumes (of a projected seven) on Mongolia and the Mongols, based on his 1892-93 travels to the area and published in 1896-98, inaugurated the attempts to bring Mongolian history up to the present.[9] Expeditions to Mongol regions by outside observers were then rare, although in Mongolia, as elsewhere in Asia, Russian efforts soon caught the attention of the British. Co-belligerents alongside the Russians in the imperial "Great Game" for influence across the Asian continent, British observers produced a spate of travel books with such titles as "Unknown Mongolia" and "With the Russians in Mongolia," the latter indicating unequivocally who had beaten her majesty's empire to the punch.[10] From the outset, study of the Mongols took place as part of grandiose political projections and Great Power imperial rivalry.[11]

Where Pozdneev led the way, other scholars and officials of Russia, and then the Soviet Union, followed. In 1921 there appeared what became the new standard work in Russian on Mongolia. It was written by Ivan Maiskii (1884-1975), a trade official (and later ambassador to Great Britain) who spent eighteen months in Outer Mongolia during the Russian civil war.[12] Maiskii's partisan eyewitness account of the Mongolian parallel to the "October revolution," and the resultant formation of a Mongol state between Russia and China, long colored subsequent treatments of twentieth-century Mongol history, whether written in support or denial of the view that Mongols had had their own revolution.[13]

In tracing the expanding enterprise of Russian Mongol studies from Pozdneev to Maiskii, it is important to keep in mind that in Russia the study of the Orient was often carried out by non-Slav subjects of the Russian empire. In the case of Mongolian studies, a critical role was played by the Buriat intelligentsia. Russified enough to have acquired a university education and a political vocabulary of nations, progress, and modernity, yet different enough to have retained a sense of their "Mongolness," the Buriats assisted Russian specialists and administrators in language and alphabet reform, Buddhist and Tibetan studies, as well as the study of Mongol law, literature, ethnography, and history, sometimes attaining the status of leading scholars in their own right.[14]

No doubt the most prominent Buriat intellectual was Tsyben Zamtsarano (1880-1940), who taught Mongolian language and culture in St. Petersburg (later Petrograd), the imperial metropole, before the 1917 revolution. In 1921, with Russian assistance he founded the Mongol Scientific Committee, which in 1961 became the Mongolian Academy of Sciences on the Soviet model. Behind Zamtsarano and the Mongol Scientific Committee stood a half century of Buriat-Russian interaction that helped make possible the pivotal Russian role in Mongol affairs. In sharp contrast, Beijing never tried to make similar use of its Mongol subjects. And Tokyo had no such option, until much later, when through conquest it unsuccessfully sought to replace China as the Middle Kingdom in Asia.

Scholarship and Service

Political developments in Russia after 1917 furthered the formidable Russian investment in the study of Mongolia, but they also eventually abetted the self-subversion of Russia as the singular arena of Mongol studies. No one better encapsulates these interrelated trends of consolidation and displacement than Nicholas Poppe (1897-1992).

Like many protagonists in this story, Poppe was born in Asia, more precisely, Shandong Province, China. His father, a graduate in Oriental Studies at St.

Petersburg, served as secretary of the Imperial Russian consulate in Tianjin and then in Qiqihar, Mukden, and Harbin (where he was murdered by a burglar in 1913). As a baby Nicholas spoke Chinese, but moved back to Russia and, like his father, studied at Petrograd University. Although his studies were interrupted by war service and the subsequent general dislocation, Poppe earned a degree in oriental languages in 1921, and began working at the Asian Museum of the Academy of Sciences and at Petrograd (later Leningrad) University.[15]

In 1925, at age twenty-eight, Poppe precociously became a professor at Leningrad University, the same year that the Asian Museum was remade into the Institute of Oriental Studies, where he also worked, cataloguing Mongolian manuscripts. The next year Poppe formed part of a select group sent by the Mongolian Commission of the Academy of Sciences to Mongolia. "Ulaanbaatar was a typical Chinese town," he recalled of his first trip. "There were numerous Buddhist temples and monasteries, Chinese shops and restaurants, and only a few Russian-style houses."[16] All this would soon change.

Through an unusual set of circumstances the talented Poppe rose quickly. After the Russian Pole Wladislaw Kotwicz (1872-1944) emigrated to take a post at Lwów University in newly independent Poland in 1923,[17] Kotwicz's student (and Poppe's teacher) Boris Vladimirtsov (1884-1931), who had briefly studied in Paris (with Paul Pelliot [1878-1945]) and in London, became the head of Mongol studies in the Soviet Union by virtue of holding the leading position in the Leningrad Academy of Sciences.[18] Following Vladimirtsov's death at age forty-seven, Poppe took over the Mongolian Department of the Soviet Union's Institute of Oriental Studies, amid an impressive constellation of linguists, enthnographers, geographers, and historians studying the diverse peoples of Eurasia.[19]

On the basis of the aforementioned *Secret History of the Mongols*, as well as various chronicles and law codes analyzed and published by nineteenth-century scholars, Vladimirtsov had cut a wide swath, putting forth a general theory of nomadic "feudalism" and attributing the advent of epics to the steppe "aristocracy." By contrast, Poppe and his generation were discouraged from grand visions, or even from comparative linguistics. Such approaches were thought to hint at a political movement supporting pan-Mongolism and pan-Turkism, both feared as dangerous to the Soviet state. Poppe concentrated on a Yakut grammar, Buriat dialects, and then a Khalkha (Mongolian) grammar, analyzed separately. Scholarship was encouraged and funded by state authorities, who also made plain their stake in the outcomes.[20]

During the Stalinist 1930s, the state's involvement in scholarship became more heavy-handed. Poppe recoiled at the devastation of innumerable purges while worrying about becoming a victim himself. Looking back, he remembered having suffered "all kinds of ideological obstructions," yet he concluded that by and large his work "proceeded satisfactorily."[21] Poppe assisted the Soviet army in the demarcation of the Mongolia-Manchukuo border with Japan in 1939, but claimed to have refused to serve as a translator in the winter war of 1939-40 against Finland (beloved site of his childhood summer retreats before the 1917 revolution).

A sense of genuine patriotism sometimes overlapped with Communist endeavors, and sometimes did not.

After the 1941 Nazi invasion of the USSR, Poppe was evacuated from Leningrad to the Kalmyk republic, and then closer to the Caucasus, which fell under German occupation. By his own account he served the occupiers as a translator, and in 1943, when the Germans were forced to retreat, Poppe left with them. He was posted to the Wannsee Institute just outside Berlin, an intelligence unit answerable to the SS, as a specialist on Soviet minority nationalities, and assigned the task of composing an encyclopedic work on the history and culture of Siberia, which he claimed never to have finished.[22] Poppe moved with the Wannsee staff during its evacuation to Graz, Austria, sought and received a transfer back to Berlin to the East Asian Institute, but was again evacuated when the latter shifted to Marienbad (Marienské Lázne).

With the German defeat, Poppe approached British intelligence, received an invitation to Cambridge, but then was refused a visa, evidently for his wartime work in Germany. Similar reasons apparently lay behind the withdrawal of an invitation to teach at Harvard. Supposedly sought by the Soviet authorities (for allegedly having instigated the turn of the Kalmyks to the Germans), Poppe finally departed Frankfurt on a U.S. military plane in May 1949 to begin a new life in America. Living under an assumed name for a time, he wrote a series of reports for the U.S. State Department on Soviet academic life, especially on the course and impact of Stalin's purges.

A linguist of esoteric languages, his services were deemed useful by yet another powerful patron of scholarship: in the fall of 1949, Poppe was asked to join the faculty at the University of Washington, Seattle. He became a member of Washington's Far Eastern and Russian Institute—a unique combination for an American university that his own life personified.[23] For almost two decades Poppe led the Institute's distinguished program in Mongolian and Altaic studies.

Despite his emigration to the United States, Poppe's collaboration with German scholars of the Orient continued.[24] He became especially close to the leading German Mongolist, Walther Heissig (b. 1913), who was born in Vienna and taught for many years at the University of Bonn, leading a research seminar on the peoples of the steppes.[25] Heissig's most accessible publication characteristically involved an instructional dialogue about what we know of the Mongols and how we know it. He swept the reader through a tour of ancient manuscripts uncovered in Russia, Persia, and China, as well as archaeological discoveries made in the sands, along the way dispelling the erroneous notion that the Mongols, as a nomadic people, had failed to record their own history.[26]

Heissig learned Mongolian and first collected manuscripts while working in the Japanese puppet state of Manchukuo established in the 1930s. As a German consular official, he enjoyed favorable access to Japanese-controlled territories throughout Asia, as did his Hungarian contemporary, Lajos Ligeti, another Mongolist oriented toward Inner Mongolia. For a brief period, the Japan-Germany-Hungary–Inner Mongolian "revisionist" axis formed an opposed pole to the Soviet-Buriat-Kalmyk-Outer Mongolia matrix discussed above, and provided a privileged space for conservative-minded scholars who saw Mongolia as another place to document the unwanted assault of modernity on "tradition."[27]

Avowedly anti-modernist, if not reactionary, Heissig embodied the kind of painstaking scholarship with source materials that prerevolutionary Russia had emulated, and that Poppe admired and practiced. Joining forces with the younger Heissig, Poppe asserted membership in an international circle of classically oriented scholars, seemingly above politics, disdainful of modern tendencies, and utterly devoted to the specialized knowledge of their arcane subjects.[28] Heissig's ability to transmit the joy and achievements of Mongol studies to a wide audience set him off from Poppe, but the German's commitment to scrupulous scholarship, within a conservative ethos, provided an important clue into the ease with which Poppe undertook his wartime work under the Nazis. Another clue lay in Poppe's disapproving attitude toward Soviet Communism.

In 1955, from the dual perspective of insider and outsider, Poppe composed an overview of Mongol Studies in the USSR, published in Russian for a Munich-based émigré journal.[29] He noted that prerevolutionary Russia had held a distinguished monopoly on Mongol studies, pointedly citing an impressive 1935 bibliography that listed more than 2,400 books and articles in Russian.[30] From experience he observed that the dependent status of Outer Mongolia had afforded unique access for Russians, and that the founding of the Buriat and Kalmyk autonomous republics inside the USSR had heightened interest still further. The construction of rail lines as well as the advent of auto transport also helped.

Then politics "intervened," however. Poppe asserted that prior to 1930 there had been little direct political interference in Soviet academic circles, and that under the Soviet regime a sizable number of serious publications on the Mongols were issued, but he emphasized that with the arrests of the 1930s, books, papers, and scholarly archives were confiscated, never to see the light of day. (Poppe did not say how he escaped arrest.) From 1937 through the war, not much scholarly activity on Mongolia seems to have been conducted, and in his opinion the few immediate postwar publications were often restatements of previously published research. He added that little note was taken of foreign scholars, except to denounce them—an especially inexcusable offense against the cosmopolitan ethos essential to serious scholarship.[31]

Stalin had died two years before Poppe composed his historiographical overview, but in Poppe's opinion a recovery of the Soviet community of Mongol scholars from the state's devastation was not visible. In the mid-1950s, the achievements of the 1920s and early 1930s, built on strong pre-revolutionary foundations, seemed to Poppe an archaeological ruin. Never again would Russia dominate the world of Mongol studies—such was his implied message. Indeed, his own emigration to the United States by way of Germany seemed to signal the end of Russian preeminence, and the self-inflicted nature of that downfall.

A retrospective of Soviet Mongol studies from within the USSR, not surprisingly, painted a picture of a robust community of scholars, at least by the 1960s, stretching back continuously to 1917. Poppe's name was conspicuously absent, blunt retribution for his "defection."[32] The contrast with Poppe's historiographical assessment could scarcely be more stark, underscoring how Communism partitioned the international community of scholars on the Mongols, as in other areas of inquiry.

Soviet scholars, although read by their counterparts abroad (including Poppe), remained largely unable to participate in conferences held outside the Soviet bloc or to obtain many foreign works, while non-Communists were forbidden from doing field work in Mongolia. To an extent, Hungarians formed something of a bridge between eastern and western Mongol studies, and Soviet-dominated Mongolia was eventually reopened to non-Communist specialists, beginning with the First International Congress of Mongolists in Ulaanbaatar in 1959. But dividing lines and antagonistic feelings were not easily overcome.

As for Nicholas Poppe, having transferred the skills and perspective he acquired in Russia to the United States, while continuing to draw on strong German connections, he helped implant a tradition of Mongol studies among Americans. Yet upon his retirement from the University of Washington in 1968, he was not replaced. "The inglorious end of Mongolian and Altaic comparative linguistics, which I had organized, was a severe blow to me, " Poppe wrote in his bittersweet memoirs.[33] But his legacy endures, through his publications and his students, one of whom was Hidehiro Okada and another, Robert Rupen.

Romance and Geopolitics

Mongolia, as viewed through its relationship to Russia, and with the aid of the philological lens supplied by Germanophile scholars such as Poppe, constitutes but half a picture. One must also examine the view from the Chinese side, and for that there is perhaps no better place to turn than the life of Owen Lattimore (1900-1989), who was born in Washington, D.C., capital of a then rather isolationist America but a city that was destined to play a defining role in world affairs.

In 1901 Lattimore moved abroad when his father, a physician and missionary, took a post teaching English in Shanghai. Growing up in China, the young Owen was educated at home, and then sent to boarding schools in Switzerland and England. Failing to win a scholarship to Oxford, he never attended university, instead returning to China to work in an import-export business. There he met another expatriate, Eleanor Holgate. After marrying in 1926, the two embarked on a rigorous, audacious honeymoon trip through Inner Asia during a period of civil unrest in China. Their personal romance was consummated in the midst of the centuries-long romance of exotic Mongolian lands, and recreated in a series of ethnographic adventure narratives that launched his career as popular travel writer and interpreter of Asia.[34]

Lattimore's was an unorthodox career from many points of view. In 1931, after achieving notoriety for his travel books on Mongolia, he belatedly added Mongolian to his command of Chinese (he would eventually also learn Russian). Despite not having a university degree, let alone a Ph.D., in 1934 he took over the editorship of the journal *Pacific Affairs*, a medium for examining U.S. policies in Asia.[35] In 1938 he became the director of the Walter Hines Page School of International Affairs at Johns Hopkins. During the war, on the recommendation of President Franklin Roosevelt, Lattimore served as a top advisor to the Chinese nationalist leader Chiang Kai-shek (Jiang Jieshi), and as a traveling companion in Northeast Asia to Vice President Henry Wallace. An itinerant autodidact could scarcely have enjoyed a higher profile, mostly on the basis of firsthand knowledge of "secret" Mongolia.

Lattimore's biography took an unexpected turn, however, when he and other so-called China hands were blamed for the "loss" of China to Communism in 1949.[36] Joseph McCarthy falsely accused Lattimore of being a secret communist and the top Soviet espionage agent in the United States, primarily because Lattimore's writings had been favorable to Communist achievements in Mongolia and the Soviet Union, and because of his insistence that it was not possible to solve world problems by excluding the USSR. After being suspended from teaching in 1950 (with pay), Lattimore was finally cleared and reinstated in 1955, but the Page School of International Affairs was liquidated and he continued to live under a cloud.

In 1962, the community of China specialists supported an offer for Lattimore to relocate to the University of Leeds to direct England's largest program in China studies. He took it, returning to the United States only upon the death of his wife in 1970, having retired from Leeds and become, the year before, the first Westerner elected to the Mongolian Academy of Sciences.[37] Lattimore remains better known for his "ordeal by slander," as he called it, than his many writings. But in his travel books and a number of speculative essays from the 1930s to the 1950s, he put forth an intriguing vision of Inner Asia, especially the Sino-Soviet borderlands, that was grounded in geopolitics.

Relying mostly upon personal observation, as well as upon scattered reading, Lattimore wrote metahistory, often covering the period from the Neolithic age to the present era in a single essay or book.[38] In a characteristic example, he began a 1938 essay on the "geographical factor in Mongol history" with a nod to Arnold Toynbee, and proceeded to outline a Toynbee-like meta-interpretation of the steppe society and culture. Acknowledging the periodic encroachment on the steppe of sedentary peoples, Lattimore theorized that the steppe permitted no society other than that of the nomadic herdsman, and that steppe societies knew little internal evolution. Change, he suggested, came in the form of repetitive cycles, or on the margins. In a word, geography, at least in this case, set limits to human habitation.[39]

Lattimore was no geographical determinist, however. In a 1937 essay on migration in Asia, for instance, he pointed to economic and political factors, rather than climatic (or racial) ones, to explain the contrast between the Chinese—large numbers of whom moved north into Manchuria and Inner Mongolia, and south into Malaysia—and the Japanese, who "failed" to migrate in any considerable numbers to their colonial territories.[40] Throughout his work, Lattimore spotlighted environment, territory, and patterns of habitation as the foundations upon which politics rested. And politics for him ultimately meant the great power rivalries among empires or civilizations.

Typically, in a 1934 essay Lattimore interpreted the establishment by Japan of the Manchukuo puppet state in 1932 as a decisive shift in the trajectory of Asian history, marking a turn from the maritime regions back to the internal areas north of China's Great Wall where Japan and the Soviet Union confronted each other. Emphasizing strategic concerns and dramatizing his subject, Lattimore wrote that Mongolia, "of which the world knows less than it knows of China, Siberia, or Manchukuo"—but on which he was an expert—provided "the key to the destiny of the whole Far East." Using the popular language of the day, he suggested that Mongolia formed a kind of geo-strategic "pivot" whose control would supposedly serve as a basis for continental domination. For East Asia he predicted war, and less presciently for the Mongols, civil war.[41]

After World War II, Lattimore noted that Outer Mongolia had provided an effective buffer for the Siberian frontier and posed challenges for a Japanese army that might have tried to cross it.[42] Indeed, following Japan's defeat and its military disengagement from Inner Asia, Lattimore slightly shifted his gaze from Mongolia to Chinese Turkestan. Retaining his geohistorical approach, and his focus on long-term migration and settlement patterns beneath imperial rule, he now called Xinjiang, or Chinese Turkestan, "the pivot of Asia" and argued that it constituted a "new center of gravity . . . in the world," accessible to Soviet Russia but not to America. The long, yet remote, frontier between Russia and China remained "the key" to world Politics.[43]

In sum, the Inner Asian frontier, "though divided between Chinese, Soviet, and other sovereignties," retained "a character of its own," as Lattimore wrote in the introduction to his collected papers in 1962.[44] That character consisted in its way of life, which supposedly provided no basis for a stable polity.[45] Despite its distinctive identity, therefore, Inner Asia was destined to be dominated from without. Such was the sober, geopolitical message of Lattimore's romance with Mongolia.

Developed Satellite or Dominated Colony?

Under Lattimore's direction, a seminar on Inner Asia was established at the Page School at Johns Hopkins.[46] Lattimore also sponsored a number of publications, the most important of which for our purposes was Gerard Friters' book, *Outer Mongolia and its International Position* (1949). Completed in 1939 but withheld for a decade following the outbreak of war, the book explored Mongol relations with Russia/USSR, China, and Japan, using published Russian sources (but no Chinese or Japanese ones). Field work in the "closed" country of Mongolia was then impossible.[47]

Friters argued that Soviet interest in Mongolia was not a response to the failure of revolution in Europe but to the security threat posed by retreating White or counterrevolutionary armies during the Russian civil war. He contrasted

China's failed attempt to take advantage of Russian distraction and disarray from 1914 to 1921 with the USSR's ability beginning in 1921 to deepen the close ties forged by the tsarist regime and become the *de facto* arbiter of Mongolian affairs. Meanwhile, Japan's foray into Inner Asia was blunted by the Soviet victory at Nomonhan in 1939, turning the Japanese southward, while Nazi Germany's war strategy did not in time envision a coordinated attack with the Japanese against the eastern Soviet Union. In short, Soviet hegemony in Mongolia seemed to arise for *bona fide* reasons, and so remained unchallenged.[48]

In a preface, Lattimore sought to elaborate some of Friters' themes. He highlighted the importance of Russia as a counterweight to Chinese pressures, especially settlement, in Mongol lands. For a time, some Mongols in Inner Mongolia saw Japan as a counterweight to the Chinese, but in his view the legacies of Russian and Japanese influence were strikingly different. Whereas the USSR "developed" Outer Mongolia, giving it institutions and helping build a modern nation, the Japanese reinforced the "non-modern" or "feudal elements" of Inner Mongolia, namely the princes and the church. The Japanese presence supposedly carried little long-term positive import. For these reasons Lattimore concluded that the Soviet position in Mongolia was not really imperialist.[49]

Soviet "developmentalism" constituted a favorite theme of Lattimore's. Writing of a visit to the Mongolian People's Republic in 1962, with memories of the despair he had witnessed in the Inner Mongolia of the 1930s, Lattimore asserted that the former Outer Mongolia represented "an outstanding example of the successful economic development of one country by a planned program of aid from another country," and that "today the Mongols are better fed and better clothed than any other people in Asia," while their housing, education, and employment levels, and distribution of income were also highly praiseworthy. He claimed to have seen not just an economic boom, but a truly popular government whose "alliance" with Russia was "regarded by the people as their alliance, not just a deal between politicians."[50]

To be sure, Lattimore noted that "things were not always so smooth" and that the unfolding of a Marxist, urban, proletarian revolution in a nomadic society seemed paradoxical. But with or without Marx, he argued that there would have been a showdown with the Lamaist church, for "the Mongols of the twentieth century had either to modernize their society and state or perish as a people." The close association with Russia, a reversal of the Mongols' historic relationship with China, accelerated that confrontation and propelled Outer Mongolia into the modern world. And far from annexing Mongolia—except for the region of Uriankhai which became Tannu Tuva and which Lattimore overlooked[51]—the Russians had created a state that supposedly served Mongol interests as much as Russia's. The clincher in the argument for Lattimore was Mongolia's escape from "wartime occupation."[52]

To many, Lattimore's version of *Realpolitik* constituted an apology for the USSR. One of Lattimore's most impassioned critics was Nicholas Poppe, who was particularly provoked by Lattimore's introduction to the 1955 English translation of the official biography of the Mongol revolutionary Sükhebaatur, whom Lattimore called a political leader on par with Vladimir Lenin or Sun Yat-sen (Sun Zhongshan), as if the Mongols had not been utterly dependent on their Soviet "advisers."[53] Poppe, who felt that nothing short of complete independence for Mongolia was acceptable, had little trouble adducing evidence of Soviet domination, from the bloody purges to the close parallels between Mongolian and Stalinist cultural manifestations.[54]

Citing published works that Lattimore had not consulted and that made for a far less benevolent picture of Mongolian subordination to the USSR, Poppe viewed Mongolia not as an example of Soviet developmentalism but as a "springboard" for Soviet penetration of Asia. Furthermore, Poppe interpreted the subordination of Mongolia by the USSR as a harbinger of the fate of eastern Europe after 1945: "Had the Western world known the way that Mongolia had been turned into a Soviet satellite, the Western world would have behaved significantly more carefully" in its dealings with Stalin at Yalta and after.[55]

On the defensive, Lattimore wrote that not all instances of state-to-state subordination were identical. He argued that the term satellite was usually equated with colony or puppet, but ought not to be. Rather, a satellite was formed when a minority in the subordinate state willed such status as a lesser evil. Lattimore further contended that Poppe ignored Chinese encroachment upon Mongol territories and its accompanying Sinification, as well as the 1930s Japanese thrust, which buttressed the backward-looking Mongol princes and lamas in Inner Mongolia. In short, Poppe wrote of Soviet "domination" without reference to the full picture of external events. "National emergency may or may not be a moral justification," Lattimore wrote, "but in politics it is a reality," adding that "it was only because Mongolia lay under the shelter of Soviet protection that it was not overrun by Japan."[56]

Regarding internal developments, Lattimore rebuked Poppe for the idea that the Mongols were mere pawns in the Soviet embrace. Even if they were ordered to act by the Soviet authorities, Lattimore contended that the Mongols who collectivized agriculture were "driven by real convictions of their own, *wanting* to do what they did, and engaged in real controversies with other Mongols." In conclusion, Lattimore hinted that the postwar Japanese political and economic relationship to the United States might similarly fall under the rubric of satellite—an occupation, for the most part accepted by Japan's ruling elite, and aimed not at exploiting but at developing Japan.[57]

From today's vantage point, it is not difficult to see that Outer Mongolia was both a developed satellite and a dominated colony; that the views of Poppe and Lattimore are complementary rather than diametrically opposed. To put the matter another way, the experience of twentieth century Mongolia has been contradictory. Poppe offers a corrective to Lattimore's apologia; Lattimore provides a dose of realism to soften Poppe's visceral anti-Communism. Lattimore comes at the issues with a sense of constrained possibilities; Poppe, with an uncompromising spirit. But each in their own way remained Mongolophiles.

During the dark days of McCarthyism, Poppe was summoned to testify against Lattimore. He noted that some of Lattimore's works were superficial, but he did not accuse Lattimore of being a secret communist or a spy. According to Poppe, Lattimore expressed his gratitude in a letter. But Lattimore later accused Poppe in print of having been an SS "officer" during the war—a charge that Poppe felt compelled to refute with exonerating documents obtained from German archives. The irony of Lattimore, who was slandered as a Communist, later smearing Poppe as a Nazi, is a poignant reminder of the bruising battles fought by the generation born in the twentieth century.[58]

A Developing Historiography

Dating back to the *Secret History of the Mongols*, written in 1228 or 1240, the Mongols have had a rich tradition of chronicles and epics centered on the supposed words and deeds of Chinggis Khan and his successors. Although no writings survive from the period after the Mongols' expulsion from China in 1368 until the large-scale conversions to Buddhism in the late sixteenth century, writings from the seventeenth century onward exist in abundance. These voluminous sources have served as a basis for imagining a historical community of considerable antiquity, rooted in clan and church.[59]

After the 1911 revolution, when Outer Mongolia declared its independence (Inner Mongolia remained a part of China), participants' reminiscences and biographies helped establish a new nationalist historiography that also drew on the ancient texts, many of which were soon rediscovered. With the Soviet-supported revolution of 1921, the Mongolian People's Republic encouraged historical research, emphasizing the former world empire and the new national community. Strongly anti-aristocratic, though not fully Marxist, this historiography competed with the glorifications of Chinggis Khan coming out of Chinese-controlled Inner Mongolia that also served to mobilize youth with nationalism.

By around 1950, however, independent Mongolia had abandoned the traditional Mongolian script for Cyrillic and turned the focus of history writing away from nationalist adulations of Chinggis to socioeconomic themes. In 1954, Mongolian scholars, teaming up with their Soviet counterparts, published *The History of the Mongolia People's Republic*, the first comprehensive effort that covered prehistory to the present, in both Russian and Mongolian.[60] Its heavy-handedness and falsifications notwithstanding, this overview, together with monographic studies on the prerevolution, opened up a range of heretofore unexamined issues as counterpoints to the emphasis on heroes and war. Similar comprehensive histories of Inner Mongolia, in Chinese as well as Mongolian, appeared not long thereafter.

In short, as one moves deeper into the postwar period, one begins to see, particularly by the 1960s, a developing historiography on Mongols and Mongolia in the twentieth century written by the Mongols themselves. Writings on the Mongols by outsiders increased as well. In the USSR, a barrage of publications emerged in the 1960s and 1970s, many supervised by Il'ia Zlatkin.[61] Even in China, at Beijing's Central Nationalities Institute (founded in 1951) and the

Inner Mongolian University in Höhhot (opened in 1957), Mongol studies became more or less well-established following the 1949 revolution.[62] (China also regained a presence in Outer Mongolia, posting an ambassador, reviving trade relations, and exporting contract laborers.)

In the Anglophone world, Britain achieved a certain prominence in the 1960s with Owen Lattimore at Leeds, and Charles R. Bawden (b. 1924) at the School of Oriental and African Studies in London, who wrote a readable and comprehensive history.[63] Bawden took as his subject the twentieth-century state formed in Outer Mongolia, noting that its borders were rather arbitrary, excluding more Mongols than were included. Yet he argued that states were nothing to sneer at in Inner Asia, as the case of Tibet demonstrated. Even though much was lost as well as preserved, Bawden hailed the recovery of a national state—at least for some Mongols—as a major achievement.[64]

In the United States, Denis Sinor, a Hungarian émigré, founded a Mongolian studies society at Columbia University in 1961, and moved it with him to Indiana University in 1963. A medievalist, Sinor set out to develop a syllabus and course outline for what he variously called Central Eurasian and Inner Asian history.[65] He also trained a number of specialists in Mongol languages and history, including some on the twentieth century, and helped make Indiana one of the centers for Mongol studies in America, alongside the University of Washington under Nicholas Poppe.[66]

Poppe's most celebrated student was Robert Rupen (b. 1922), who turned his 1954 dissertation into a masterly study published by the Indiana University Press a decade later. Even though the Mongol state formed the basic unit of analysis, Rupen cast his net broadly. He began with, and developed at length, the role played in Mongol history by Buriat intellectuals, whom he called "the most progressive indigenous leadership in Central Asia in the early twentieth century." He also gave attention to pan-Mongolism, and its religious variant, pan-Buddhism, both of which he called "the most powerful indigenous idea in Central Asia in the twentieth century." The pan-Mongolist aspiration, he showed, was meticulously frustrated by Russian policies. In fact, the Russians and Mongols often disagreed, yet they were united in their opposition to the Chinese. Herein lay the key to Rupen's approach.[67]

In contrast to prevailing views, Rupen contended that "the Russians assumed a position in Mongolia with some reluctance," and that they were encouraged to do so by the Buriats as well as by what became pressing strategic concerns. In a way, Rupen's book can be said to have traced the gradual displacement in Outer Mongolia of Chinese by Russian influence, a turn of events that appears inevitable only in hindsight. He restored a sense of contingency, and also sought to characterize the evolving nature of Soviet influence in Mongolia.[68]

Rupen argued that "purges, secret police, and other apparatuses of totalitarian control do not tell the whole Mongolian story. Literacy and education, health and sanitation, science and modernization, were and are an important part of the Communist program." In his treatment, the 1930s became not solely a story of internal Stalinist convulsion. "Japanese aggression on the Asian mainland," he insisted, "explains more than any other single factor the Mongolian developments of the 1930s." In sum, Rupen's Mongolia was neither an unmitigated tragedy nor an overwhelming victory, but the "bittersweet tale of a small people that survived in a hot corner of Asia."[69]

Supplementing Rupen's treatment of the Mongol experience as a problem of Russian/Soviet history, another prominent American scholar, Henry Schwarz, analyzed the Mongols in their relation to China. Schwarz lamented the general lack of serious attention among Americans to minorities in China, yet he was able to fashion an impressive program of Mongol studies in the United States around the subject of Chinese minority policies and the experience of minority communities. Adding political weight to the project, a good number of the scholars on Inner Mongolia inside China were by this time Mongols, a striking development of the post-1949 environment.[70]

Schwarz, who taught briefly at the University of Washington before transferring to Western Washington University in Bellingham, never wrote a study of Mongols *per se*, but he provided Mongol studies with renewed impetus and an institutional home. After Poppe's retirement and the discontinuation of Mongol studies in Seattle, Schwarz in effect inherited Poppe's mantle, as well as his friendship, patronage, and private book collection.[71] It was Schwarz (and Western Washington) who published and edited Poppe's memoirs, and it was Schwarz (and Western Washington) who, with Poppe's assistance, among that of others, held the first North American conference on Mongolia in 1978.[72] The participants resolved to make such a conference an annual event, a goal that proved ambitious.

Conferences in the U.S. on Mongolia or Mongol studies have become less—not more—frequent. In the introduction to a 1994 *Festschrift* for Schwarz, the editors pointed to their initial acquaintance with him in the late 1960s as the high watermark for Mongol studies in America.[73] This claim may prove to be unduly pessimistic, however. One is tempted to conclude that the attention across the twentieth century devoted to Mongols and Mongol affairs will endure, if only because of the strategic location of the Mongols amid the Russians, Chinese, and Japanese, and the experience Mongols have acquired as a kind of landlocked cosmopolitan.

Mongolia as Touchstone

Mongol history, for better or worse, is Russian history and it is Chinese history. What of Japan? As we have seen, precisely the absence of a strong Japanese link to the Mongols has been cited as an allegedly happy result of Soviet involvement in Mongolia.[74] Outer Mongolia can be listed among a limited number of nations in Asia where Japanese war guilt is a nonissue. Today, perhaps not coincidentally, Japanese involvement in Mongolian affairs, through investment and training, is extensive, and welcomed. Japanese study of Mongols and Mongolia has long flourished, as two major bibliographies published in the 1970s demonstrate.[75]

Covering works issued since 1900, these compendiums reveal the vastness of Japanese-language materials on Mongolia, including intelligence reports and more scholarly studies that were produced in great quantity during the interwar period, largely as a consequence of Japan's political and military ambitions on the Asian mainland. Of course, Japan's role in Asia has changed over time, and so has the impetus for Japanese study of Asia, including Mongolia. Indeed, Japan's postwar refashioning of a new role for itself in Asia can be read in its Mongol studies. It is surely no coincidence, therefore, that Mongolia could be seen by one prominent Japanese scholar, Hidehiro Okada, as the starting point of world history—a world history that commences in Asia.

In sum, twentieth-century Mongol studies in Japan—as in Russia, China, Germany, Hungary, Britain, America, or anywhere else—provide a revealing window onto the trajectories traversed by these various countries. In writing about the Mongols, foreign scholars have often been writing about themselves and their own countries, as Mongols from their own experiences know only too well. The search for Mongols and Mongolia in the twentieth century has turned out to be a multinational odyssey.

This is no mere academic matter, for with the imperial retreat and then dissolution of the Soviet Union, the Mongolian state found itself charged with the task of reinventing its institutions and its modern identity. That identity cannot be limited to a recuperation of the exploits of Chinggis Khan, the Buddhist Church, and other elements with which to forge a national community, but must take account of Mongolia's struggles to achieve modernity within a geopolitical triangle not of its own making. That triangle, moreover, has opened up to include a fourth member, the United States. Mongolia's population of 2.3 million—75 percent under the age of 35, more than 50 percent under 21—is being buffeted by the epoch of "globalization."

The inescapable international character of Mongolian history seems destined to continue. But if, as Robert Rupen wrote in 1964 (and his opinion is even more true today), the cliché of "Unknown Mongolian" has become a relic of the past, the historical connections across political divides in Northeast Asia are only now beginning to be rediscovered following the demise of Communism.[76] With the reestablishment of transnational ties in Northeast Asia may come a renewed appreciation of the exceptional experience of the Mongols, a renewal we hope this volume of conference papers strengthens. Truth be told, even in the darkest depths of cold-war imposed isolation, Mongols never lost their transnational identities, whose formation and transformations in the crucible of geopolitical rivalries are explored in the essays that follow.

Notes

1. Hidehiro Okada, *Sekaishi no tanjō* (Tokyo, Japan: Chikuma shobo, 1992).

2. General overviews of Russian study of the Orient are provided by Richard Frye, "Oriental Studies in Russia" and Wayne Vucinich, "The Structure of Soviet Orientology:

Fifty Years of Change and Accomplishment," in Wayne Vucinich, ed., *Russia and Asia* (Stanford: Hoover Institution Press, 1972), pp. 30-51, and 52-134, respectively.

3. For a detailed history of oriental studies in Russia, see Vasilii V. Bartol'd, *Istoriia izucheniia Vostoka v Evrope i Rossii* (St. Petersburg, 1911; 2nd ed. Leningrad, 1925); also contained in volume nine of the author's collected works: *Sochineniia* 9 vols. (Moscow, 1963-1977). Born in St. Petersburg into a family of Baltic Germans, Bartol'd (1869-1930) is often seen as Russia's premier Orientalist. See N.M. Akramov, *Vydaiushchiisia russkii vostokoved V.V. Bartol'd: Nauchno-biograficheskii ocherk* (Dushanbe, 1963); and Bartol'd, *Sochinenia*, vol. 1, pp. 14-21.

4. Translations of accounts by early Russian travelers to the Mongols can be found in John F. Baddeley, ed., *Russia, Mongolia, China; being some record of the relations between them from the beginning of the XVIIth Century to the Death of the Tsar Alexei Mikhailovich A.D. 1602-1676* 2 vols, (London: Macmillan, 1919).

5. The information and assessment of Chinese Mongol Studies in the text were provided by Christopher P. Atwood. See also Christopher P. Atwood, "Chen Yuan [Ch'en Yüan]," in D. R. Woolf, gen. ed. *A Global Encyclopedia of Historical Writing* (New York: Garland Publishing, 1998), vol. 1, pp. 156-57. For a harsher evaluation, see Robert A. Rupen, *Mongols of the Twentieth Century* vol. 1 (Bloomington: Indiana University Press, 1964), p. 111.

6. Francis Woodman Cleaves, *The Secret History of the Mongols: for the first time done into English out of the original tongue and provided with exegetical commentary* (Cambridge, MA: Harvard University Press, 1982). *The Secret History*, which recounts the genealogy of Chinggis Khan, his life and campaigns, and the positions awarded to his successors, is the only Mongolian historical work that survives from the thirteenth century.

7. Zhang Mu in Arthur Hummel, ed. *Eminent Chinese of the Ch'ing Period (1644-1912)*, (Washington, D.C.: U.S. Government Printing Office, 1943-44); Ye Dehui and Wang Guowei in Howard L. Boorman, *Biographical Dictionary of Republican China*, (New York: Columbia University Press, 1967-79).

8. In the nationalist era one of the few scholars who continued the rich Qing tradition of Inner Asian research was Chen Yuan (1880-1971), a historian of the Yuan dynasty and Chinese religion. From 1929 he headed Beijing's Furen University (a Catholic institution). During World War II he remained at Furen, under Japanese occupation. After the Communist victory he participated in the land reform of 1951, and in 1952 became president of Beijing Normal University (Furen's successor). But he did little active research after 1949. Zhou Kangxie, ed., *Chen Yuan xiansheng jinniannien shixue lunji*, (Hong Kong: Ch'ungwen, 1971); cited in Atwood, "Chen Yuan [Ch'en Yüan]," pp. 156-57.

9. Aleksei M. Pozdneev, *Mongoliia i mongoly* 2 vols. (St. Petersburg, 1896-98), and *Mongolia and the Mongols* (Bloomington: Indiana, 1975). This was the basis for a book published in emigration by the former Russian imperial minister to Peking and Urga (1907-12). Iwan J. Korotsovetz, *Von Cinggis Khan zur Sowjetrepublik: eine kurze Geschichte der Mongolei unter besonderer Berucksichtigung der neuesten Zeit* (Berlin and Leipzig: Walter de Gruyter, 1926). A 1943 translation appeared in Japan, *Moko kinseishi.*

10. Douglas Carruthers, *Unknown Mongolia: A Record of Travel and Exploration in Northwest Mongolia and Dzungaria* 2 vols. (London: Hutchinson, 1914), with a foreword by Lord Curzon; H.G.C. Perry-Ayscough and R.B. Otter-Barry, *With the Russians in Mongolia* (London: John Lane, 1914). Both these accounts were preoccupied with the effect of Russian successes on British imperial interests.

11. S.C.M. Paine, *Imperial Rivals: China, Russia, and Their Disputed Frontier* (Armonk, NY: M.E. Sharpe, 1996), pp. 29, 115.

12. Ivan Maiskii, *Sovremennaia Mongoliia* (Irkutsk, 1921), reissued in abridged form as *Mongoliia nakanune revoliutsii* (Moscow, 1960). In the new edition Maiskii retrospectively described his work as the first "Marxist" study of Mongolia, but his original chapter on political history was severely truncated in the new edition, reflecting the struggle to bring scholarship into line with what was understood as Marxist ideology.

13. Maiskii's book included much valuable statistical material, such as the results of the first Mongol census, conducted under tsarist auspices. Mention might also be made of the monumental works of G.E. Grum-Grzhimailo (1860-1936): *Zaepadnaia mongoliia i Uriankhaiskii krai* vol. 1 (St. Petersburg, 1914), vol. 2 (Leningrad, 1926), whose comprehensive footnotes contain a veritable encyclopedia of publications. (The author's discussion of Chinggis Khan, to whom vast feats of historical transformation are attributed, predates Stalin's revolution from above by a mere three years.) Anatolii D. Kallinikov (1899-1940), a member of Maiskii's expedition, wrote a number of works about agrarian relations and the Mongol "revolution," including "Agrarnye otnosheniia i antifeodal'naia agrarnaia revoliutsiia v Mongolii," in A. Mineev, ed., *Agrarnyi vopros na Vostoke* (Moscow, 1933), pp. 96-142.

14. As Robert Rupen wrote, "the common struggle against Russification, and the long common experience of Russian administrative control, in fact led to identification as 'Buriats' rather than as members of this or that clan and tribe. Clan and tribal differences became less important, and something approaching a common national consciousness developed." Rupen, *Mongols of the Twentieth Century* vol. 1 (Bloomington: Indiana University Press. 1964), p. 32.

15. Biographical information is taken from Nicholas Poppe, *Reminiscences* (Bellingham: Western Washington University Center for East Asian Studies, 1983). The Asian Museum was founded in 1818 as a division of the Kunstkammer.

16. Ibid., p. 86. Poppe returned to Mongolia the following year and in 1929, in between traveling among the Buriats. After 1929 Poppe was not granted a Soviet exit visa to travel to Mongolia, but he continued to make numerous trips to Russian Buriatiia up to 1941.

17. Born in Wilna and a student of St. Petersburg University, Kotwicz followed other Russian-empire Poles who were orientalists, including Józef Kowaleski (1800-78) and Antoni Michulanski (1808-77). Marian Lewicki, "Wladyslaw Kotwicz," in Lewicki et al., *Szkice z dziejów Polskiej orientalistyki* (Warsaw, 1957), pp. 7-30.

18. Vladimirtsov wrote a biography of Chinggis Khan (1922), which was translated into English and French. His major work was published posthumously: *Obshchestvennyi stroi mongolov: Mongol'skii kochevoi feodalizm* (Leningrad, 1934), which has been translated into French. For a review of his publications, see G.N. Rumiantsev, "Trudy B.Ia. Vladimiretsova po istorii Mongolov," in *Filologiia i istoriia mongol'skikh narodov* (Moscow, 1958).

19. Leningrad's Institute of Oriental Studies (*vostokovedenie*), formerly the Asian Museum, should not be confused with the Institute of Living Oriental Languages, where Poppe also worked and which was founded in 1920 (it was closed in 1938). For further details of the early years of Soviet Mongol studies, see the posthumously published memoirs of another Vladimirtsov student, Aleksei V. Burdukov (1883-1943), *V staroi i novoi Mongolii: Vospominaniia, pis'ma* (Moscow, 1967).

20. Poppe wrote the first full grammar of Khalkha Mongolian (1951), a complete

grammar of the Buriat language (1938), plus various works on many other languages, including an up-dated Yakut grammar and glossaries for Medieval Mongolian. He prepared a number of translations of folklore and epics. Poppe, *Reminiscences*, pp. 261-79. See also Arista Maria Circautas, *Nicholas Poppe: Bibliography of Publications from 1924 to 1977* (Seattle: University of Washington Press, 1977).

21. Poppe, *Reminiscences*, pp. 148-49.

22. A sense of Poppe's wartime work can be found in a later publication: Nicholas Poppe, "The Economic and Cultural Development of Siberia," in Erwin Oberländer et al., eds., *Russia Enters the Twentieth Century, 1894-1917* (London: Temple Smith, 1971), pp. 138-51. During the war Poppe also taught Altaic languages at Berlin University, evidently at the invitation of Eric Haenisch (1880-1966), the German Mongolist and Sinologist whom Poppe had first met in Leningrad during the 1920s (a brief description of Haenisch's career can be found in *Studia Sino-Altaica: Festschrift für Erich Haenisch zum 80 Gebursttag*, ed. by Herbert Franke [Wiesbaden: Franz Stiener, 1961]).

23. This author failed to take note of Washington's Far Eastern and Russian Institute in a review of the study of Russia in Asia. Kotkin, "Introduction: Rediscovering Russia in Asia," in Kotkin and David Wolff, eds., *Rediscovering Russia in Asia: Siberia and the Russian Far East* (Armonk, N.Y.: M.E. Sharpe, 1995), pp. 3-15.

24. Poppe was not the only Mongolist to emigrate from the USSR. Valentin A. Riasanovskii, a specialist on Mongol law who taught at Moscow University, became head of Harbin University before coming to the United States and teaching at the University of Oregon, Eugene. His son, Nicholas V. Riasanovsky, taught Russian history to the editors of this volume at the University of California, Berkeley.

25. A brief description of Central Asian studies at Bonn under Heissig can be found in Hans-Rainer Kaempfe, "Central Asian Studies at Bonn," *The Mongolia Society Newsletter*, no. 1, December 1985, pp. 5-6.

26. With the important exception of the *Secret History*, no Mongolian texts have survived from before the late sixteenth century. Seventeenth-century texts exist in abundance. Walther Heissig, *Ein Volk sucht eine Geschichte: die Mongolen und die verlorene Dokumente ihrer grossen Zeit* (Dusseldorf: Econ Verlag, 1964), translated as *A Lost Civilization: The Mongols rediscovered* (London: Thames and Hudson, 1966). His two-volume magnum opus covered not just Mongol literature but religion, art, stone inscriptions, script, and more—eloquent testimony on the culture of steppe peoples. Heissig, *Geschichte der Mongolishcher Literatur* 2 vols. (Wiesbaden: Harrassowitz, 1972).

27. Heissig recruited "natives," such as Mathew Haltod and Rashidondug—who were refugee officials from Japanese-held Inner Mongolia, opposed the Communists, and did not want to stay on Taiwan—to study in Bonn. Parallels could be drawn to the Scandanavian scholars Sven Hedi (1865-1952) and Christensen Henning Haslund (b. 1896), who like Heissig were conservative.

28. See, for example, Heissig, ed., *Collectanea Mongolica: Festschrift für Professor Dr. Rintchen zum 60. Geburtstag* (Wiesbaden: Harrassowtiz, 1966), part of his series called Asiatische Forschungen. This particular volume had contributions from Germany, England, the United States, Czechoslovakia, Hungary, Japan, India, and Mongolia, in various languages.

29. Nikolai Poppe, "Mongolovedenie v SSSR," *Institut zur Erforschung der Geschichte und Kultur der UdSSR*, 1 (14), 1955, pp. 25-43.

30. E.N. Iakovlena, *Bibliografiia Mongol'skoi narodnoi respubliki* (Moscow, 1935).

31. Partial lists of victimized Mongol scholars were published in *Narody Azii i Afriki,*

1990, no. 4, pp. 113-25, and no. 5, pp. 96-106; and in *Vestnik Akademii Nauk SSSR*, 1990, no. 12, pp. 110-21.

32. For example, N.P. Shastina, "Mongolic Studies," one of the pamphlets in the English-language collection *Fifty Years of Soviet Oriental Studies (Brief Reviews)* (Moscow, 1967). Shastina singled out Boris Vladimirtsov as the last representative of "the Russian classical school of Orientalism" in which Mongol studies formed "an integrated complex of various fields," including history, linguistics, literature, and ethnography, all handled by a single researcher. Following Vladimirtsov, she argued, that each subfield evolved into a separate field of inquiry, with research often inspired by his writings and hypotheses. In her summary Buriat and Kalmyk studies were not treated, evidently to avoid any hint of pan-Mongolism.

33. Poppe wrote that Britain's Charles Bawden and the Heissig student Klaus Sagaster of Berlin turned down solicitations to relocate to America, and that Hidehiro Okada of Japan accepted such an invitation but left after two years because of homesickness. In any case, Poppe explained that the university was compelled to find ways to reduce its budget. Poppe, *Reminiscences*, p. 241. Later, Far Eastern and Slavic languages were separated into two departments (Washington's Slavic department was almost abolished in 1995).

34. Owen and Eleanor each wrote a book describing their separate routes from Beijing to Chinese Turkestan—she across Siberia on the Transsiberian, he across Mongolia on the camel caravan route—and then collaborated on a description of their joint travel from Chinese Turkestan on to Kashmir. Owen Lattimore, *The Desert Road to Turkestan* (Boston: Little Brown, 1929); Eleanor Holgate Lattimore, *Turkestan Reunion* (New York: John Day, 1934); and Owen Lattimore, *High Tatary* (Boston: Little Brown, 1930). In a self-critical preface to the 1972 reissue of *The Desert Road*, Lattimore wrote that he was attracted to interwar Asia by the rise of Japan and the stirrings of nationalism in India and China (xii), rather than by romance.

35. The journal was founded in 1928 by the Institute of Pacific Relations in Honolulu.

36. Robert P. Newman, *Owen Lattimore and the "Loss" of China* (Berkeley: University of California, 1992).

37. John G. Hangin and Urgunge Onon, *Analecta Mongolica: Dedicated to the Seventieth Birthday of Professor Owen Lattimore* (Bloomington: The Mongolia Society, 1972), pp. 10-18; *Ordeal by Slander* (vii). John T. Flynn argued that the accusations of espionage were true, and that their ill effects were made possible by the thin ranks of U.S. Asia specialists as compared with those on Europe. Largely concentrated, according to Flynn, in the Institute of Pacific Affairs, this small group of supposedly inventive Asia specialists aimed to defeat Chiang Kai-shek and deliver China, as well as Korea, to the communists by public propaganda and backstage consulting work for the State Department. Behind it all Flynn saw Stalin. Flynn, *The Lattimore Story* (New York: Devin-Adair, 1953).

38. Lattimore, *Inner Asian Frontiers of China* (New York: American Geographical Society, 1940).

39. Lattimore, "The Geographical Factor in Mongolian History" (1938), *Studies in Frontier History*, pp. 241-58.

40. Lattimore, *Studies in Frontier History*, pp. 85-96. For further discussion of Chinese settlement among Mongols see George Cressey, "Chinese Colonization in Mongolia: A General Survey," and Lattimore, "Chinese Colonization in Inner Mongolia: Its History and Present Development," in W.L.G. Jones, ed., *Pioneer Settlements* (Worcester, MA: Commonwealth Press, 1932), pp. 273-87 and 288-312, respectively.

41. Owen Lattimore, "Mongolia Enters World Affairs," *Pacific Affairs,* 7 (1), 1934, pp. 15-28.

42. Owen Lattimore, "Inner Asia: Sino-Soviet Bridge" (1952), *Studies in Frontier History*, pp. 160-64.

43. Owen Lattimore, *Pivot of Asia: Sinkiang and the Inner Asian Frontiers of China and Russia* (Boston: Little, Brown, 1950).

44. Owen Lattimore, *Studies in Frontier History: Collected Papers 1928-1958* (New York: Oxford, 1962), p. 29. Over the years Lattimore alternated names for the strategic area that occupied his studies, from High Tartary to Inner Asia. See the definition he elaborated in Lattimore, "The New Political Geography of Inner Asia" (1953), *Studies in Frontier History*, pp. 165-79. Lattimore's fascination with the Sino-Soviet borderlands and rivalry was evident in his first travel book, *High Tartary*, published in 1930, when he called the Sino-Russian clash "a play of primal forces, far more significant than superficial considerations of politics." Then he put forth the thesis that not just Mongolia but Xinjiang was moving into the Soviet orbit, a fear that Lattimore had picked up from Chinese officials during his travels and later repudiated in the preface to the 1975 edition. His Russophilia on full view, he speculated in 1975 that the Russians had not been motivated by "villainous designs" in their forward policy, even if such a policy was at variance with the USSR's pronouncements against imperialism! Lattimore, *High Tartary*, pp. 226-27, 74, 78. See also Lattimore, "The Inland Crossroads of Asia" (1944), *Studies in Frontier History*, pp. 119-33.

45. Owen Lattimore, "Origins of the Great Wall: A Frontier Concept in Theory and Practice," *Studies in Frontier History*, pp. 97-118.

46. Like Heissig, Lattimore recruited several refugee "native" scholars from Inner Mongolia, including Urgunge Onon and Gombojab "John" Hangin, who later became president of the Mongolia Society in America. In a tribute on the occasion of Lattimore's return to the United States and seventieth birthday, they lauded their mentor as "the pioneer in initiating Mongolian studies as a coherent discipline in the 1940s" in the United States. John G. Hangin and Urgunge Onon, eds., *Analecta Mongolica: Dedicated to the Seventieth Birthday of Professor Owen Lattimore* (Bloomington: The Mongolian Society, 1972), p. 7, with a bibliography of Lattimore's publications on pp. 123-42.

47. As Robert Rupen has written, "essentially, no 'outsider' saw any part of Outer Mongolia for even one week's visit in the whole thirty years between 1926 and 1956 (excepting Japanese POWs in Ulaanbaatar 1945-47)." Rupen, *Mongols*, p. 271.

48. Friters, *Outer Mongolia and its International Position*. Compare Friters to the much inferior G.D.R. Phillips, *Russia, Japan, and Mongolia* (London: Frederick Mueller, 1942), a work of vapid generalization and speculation without scholarly notes.

49. Lattimore, in Friters, pp. ix-xlv.

50. Owen Lattimore, *Nomads and Commissars: Mongolia Revisited* (New York: Oxford, 1962), pp. 170-73. The book was based upon a two-month trip undertaken at the invitation of the Mongolian Academy of Sciences. Lattimore's emphasis on Soviet developmentalism vis-a-vis the Mongols as a model for other countries could have been lifted directly out of Soviet publications. It was echoed by many other writers in English.

51. On Tuva, see Rafael M. Kabo, *Ocherki istorii i ekonomiki Tuvy. Chast' pervaia: dorevoliutsionnaia Tuva* (Moscow-Leningrad, 1934), and Otto Mänchen-Helfen, *Reise ins Asiatische Tuva* (Berlin: Der Bückerkreis, 1931). Kabo noted that tsarist Russia had designs on Tuva as early as the 1880s, and that aided by the Transsiberian railway, Russian settlement in Tuva picked up decisively after 1905 (especially after 1911), forming

an important element in advancing Russian policies. In English, there is William Ballis, "Soviet Russia's Asiatic Frontier Technique: Tana Tuva," *Pacific Affairs,* 14, March 1941, pp. 91-96, published under Owen Lattimore's editorial direction and largely a reiteration of Lattimore's position on Soviet developmentalism.

52. In an earlier essay, he had written that "Mongolia came through the years of the rise of Hitler and Japanese militarism with less suffering, bloodshed, and economic loss than any other country in Asia," thanks to its association with the USSR. The bloody 1930s, however, were not mentioned. Lattimore, "Mongolia's Place in the World" (1949), *Studies in Frontier History,* pp. 270-95; the preface to Friters book.

53. Owen Lattimore, *Nationalism and Revolution in Mongolia* (Leiden: E.J. Brill, 1954).

54. N.N. Poppe, "Mongol'skaia narodnaia respublika," *Vestnik Instituta po Izucheniiu Istorii i Kul'tura SSSR* [Munich], No. 4 (11), July-August 1954, pp. 7-24.

55. Ibid.

56. Lattimore, "Satellite Politics: The Mongolian Prototype" (1956), *Studies in Frontier History,* pp. 296-303.

57. Lattimore, "Satellite Politics," pp. 301-03. Poppe and Lattimore clashed in print again, when Poppe reviewed Gerard Fritters, *Outer Mongolia and its International Position* (Baltimore: Johns Hopkins, 1949), for which Lattimore wrote a preface. See *Yale Review,* 39, 1949-50, p. 57.

58. Owen Lattimore, *Nomads and Commissars* (New York, 1962), p. 125; Poppe, *Reminiscences,* pp. 214-18. Poppe had submitted a request for help in finding an American academic post to Lattimore following the defeat of Germany in World War II, but Lattimore rejected the plea, citing Poppe's wartime work for the Germans.

59. Christopher P. Atwood, "Mongolian Historiography and Historical Writing," in D. R. Woolf, gen. ed., *A Global Encyclopedia of Historical Writing* (New York: Garland Publishing, 1998), vol. 2, pp. 629-31.

60. The *History* went through two further editions: 1966 and 1983. There exists an English translation of part of a three-volume history in Mongolian: *History of the Mongolian People's Republic,* translated and annotated by William A. Brown and Urgunge Onon (Cambridge, MA: Harvard University Press, 1976), with a review of historiography, including that in the Mongol language, pp. 5-44.

61. Russian-language publications on Mongolian history written by Soviet and Mongol authors, sometimes in collaboration, are reviewed from a Soviet "Marxist" point of view by Mark I. Gol'man, "Problemy novoi istorii," in Il'ia Zlatkin, ed., *Obshchestvennye nauki v MNR* (Moscow, 1977), pp. 65-106. See also Gol'man, *Problemy noveishei istorii Mongol'skoi narodnoi respubliki v burzhuaznoi istoriografii SSHA* (Moscow, 1970). Gol'man's book was notable for revealing to a Soviet audience that many non-Soviet authors considered Mongolia to be a Soviet satellite or colony, and that there had been a major uprising in Mongolia in 1932 against Soviet-enforced policies. See also Il'ia Zlatkin's *Mongol'skaia narodnaia respublika--strana novoi demokratii* (Moscow, 1950), which was translated into German and Chinese, and later revised as *Ocherki novoi i noveishei istorii Mongolii* (Moscow, 1957).

62. True, non-Han peoples comprise a minority among students and faculty in Höhhot, and many themes are forbidden and publications are restricted for interal use, but the existence of a community of scholars dedicated to matters Mongol is undeniable. See the dated remarks of Henry Schwarz, "Mongolian Studies in China," *Zentralasiatische Studien,* 14, 1980, pp. 211-16, based on a visit in 1979 to Beijing and Hohot.

63. Charles Bawden, *The Modern History of Mongolia* 2nd ed. (London: Kegan Paul International, 1989; first issued 1968).

64. His book remains the best one-volume historical overview available in English, while his legacy has been continued by Alan Sanders, who brought out an updated edition of the text, and by Caroline Humphrey of the Mongol Studies Unit at Cambridge University. A.J.K. Sanders, *The People's Republic of Mongolia: A General Reference Guide* (London: Oxford University Press, 1968); Ibid., *Mongolia: Politics, Economics, Society* (London: Francis Pinter, 1987); Caroline Humphrey, *Karl Marx Collective: Siberian Collective Farm* (Cambridge: Cambridge University Press, 1983). For basic information on the Mongolian Studies Unit at the University of Cambridge, directed by Caroline Humphrey, see *The Mongolia Society Newsletter*, no. 3, February 1987, p. 22.

65. Sinor expounded on the premise that "the greatest achievements of humanity, the main centers of civilization, lie on [Eurasia's] edges," and concluded that the primary role of the "barbarian" nomadic peoples of the interior has been that of "an intermediary" between these "great sedentary civilizations." Sinor, "Central Eurasian" in *Orientalism in History* (Cambridge: Cambridge University Press, 1954), pp. 82-103. See also idem., *Inner Asia: A Syllabus* (Bloomington: Indiana University Press, 1969); and idem., "Introduction: The Concept of Inner Asia," in *The Cambridge History of Early Inner Asia* (Cambridge: Cambridge University Press, 1990).

66. John Krueger, "The Activities and Publications of the Mongolia Society (1978) and Mongolistic Activities at Indiana University," in Henry G. Schwarz, ed., *Studies on Mongolia: Proceedings of the First North American Conference on Mongolian Studies* (Bellingham: Western Washington University Center for Asian Studies, 1979), pp. 130-31. The Society's newsletter, begun in 1963, eventually became a bulletin, and then in 1974 a journal, which continues to be published.

67. Robert A. Rupen, *Mongols of the Twentieth Century* 2 vols. (Bloomington: Indiana, 1964). The second volume was a bibliography. Rupen wrote several other works, including *How Mongolia is Really Governed: A Political History of the Mongol's People's Republic 1900-1978* (Stanford: Hoover Institution Press, 1979), originally published in 1966 with a different title.

68. Rupen, *Mongols,* pp. 67-75, 203, 211, 363.

69. Ibid.

70. Schwarz, *China's Policies towards Minorities* (Bellingham: Western Washington University, 1971); idem., *The Minorities of China: A Survey* (Bellingham: Western Washington University Center for Asian Studies, 1984). Mention should also be made of Joseph Fletcher (1934-1984), who taught at Harvard and whose *Studies on Chinese and Islamic Inner Asia* (Brookfield, VT: Varorium, 1995) was published posthumously.

71. Schwarz, ed., *Mongolian Publications at Western Washinaton University* (Bellingham: Western Washington University Center for Asian Studies, 1984).

72. Henry G. Schwarz, ed., *Studies on Mongolia: Proceedings of the First North American Conference on Mongolian Studies* (Bellingham: Western Washington University Center for Asian Studies, 1979).

73. Edward H. Kaplan and Donald W. Whisenhunt, eds., *Opuscula Altaica: Essays Presented in Honor of Henry Schwarz* (Bellingham: Western Washington University Center for Asian Studies, 1994).

74. An excellent example, available in abridged English translation, is Yasuo Mishima and Tomio Goto, *A Japanese View of Outer Mongolia* (1942), originally published as *Gaimo jinmin kyō wakoku -- soren no kyokutō no zenei* (1940).

75.   *Mongoru kenkyū bunken mokuroku* (Tokyo, 1973); and Yamane Yukio, ed., *Gendaishi kenkyū bunken morkuroku* (Tokyo, 1971). For discussion see Man-Kam Leung, in Schwarz, *Studies on Mongolia,* pp. 133-35. For earlier bibliographies of Japanese works see *Moku kenkyū bunken mokuroku, 1900-1950* (Kyoto University, 1952), and *Récherches sur les bibliographies de Mandchourie et de Mongolie* (Dairen, 1933).

76.   Rupen, *Mongols,* p. 304.

Part I

Sino-Russian
Competition over Outer Mongolia

Tsarist Russia lost the Crimean War (1854-55) in the Near East but not long thereafter, in the Far East, Russia gained control of the Amur Basin. In 1862, the Amur Committee of the Russian Ministry of Foreign Affairs concluded that if the Manchu Empire in China were to ever collapse, then Russia's goal should be to form "an independent domain . . . in Mongolia and Manchuria."[1] For Russia, Outer Mongolia had enormous geostrategical and historical importance, and the Russian government supported a long-range expansionist policy intended to one day strip control of Mongolia away from China.[2]

During the nineteenth century, Sino-Russian trade crossed through Mongolia, but very few products emanated from Mongolia itself. At the same time, British and American, not Russian goods, dominated the small Mongolian market by the 1890s, while Chinese traders dominated Mongolia's commercial affairs. Diplomatically, Russian expansion into Mongolia ran up against first, British, and later, Japanese, resistance. This international resistance had to be neutralized before Russia could challenge Chinese control directly. Russia's success in displacing the Chinese in Outer Mongolia was remarkable.

* * *

Tsarist Russia's gradual expansion into Mongolia was made possible by the Manchu dynasty's weakness. The Manchus initially took control of Inner Mongolia in 1636, prior to the conquest of Beijing in 1644. Between 1655 and 1691, they gradually absorbed Outer Mongolia, and in the 1750s, they conquered the Oirats, the Western Mongols who inhabited Jungaria. Until the early 1900s, however, China treated Outer Mongolia as a militarized buffer area largely cut off from Han colonization. Outer Mongolia's geographical isolation north of the Gobi desert gave it a certain amount of administrative autonomy; Inner Mongolia, located to the south of the Gobi desert, became closely tied to the Qing administrative system.[3]

Until the beginning of the twentieth century, China directed Outer Mongolia's military affairs from Urga (K'u-lun in Chinese, Ulaanbaatar under the Mongolian People's Republic).[4] China had long had a policy of maintaining control over the Mongols by keeping them divided not only administratively, but also by religion. To prevent the "Yellow Hat" Buddhist church from becoming too strong, Beijing supported rival incarnate Lamas in the church's Tibetan, Inner Mongolian, and Outer Mongolian branches. The Chinese also tried to weaken the nobility by superimposing a banner system which did not strictly conform to the former tribal divisions: tribes were divided into multiple banners, each under the control of Beijing. Until the late Qing period, Chinese rule was greatly facilitated by the fact that the Mongol nobility tended to identify with the dynasty.[5]

But, as Mei-hua Lan discusses in her essay on the "New Administration" reforms in Outer Mongolia, China's traditional *laissez-faire* attitude toward Mongol internal administration changed in the early 1900s, when the Chinese government adopted a two-fold policy of centralizing the Mongol administration under that of China proper, while at the same time encouraging Han colonization of Mongol lands. In 1909, the Russian minister in Beijing, I.Y. Korostovets, warned that China's goal was to end Mongolia's special status and to transform it into a Chinese province.[6] Indeed, in July of 1911, on the eve of the collapse of the Qing dynasty, the Chinese government decided that Inner and Outer Mongolia should be formally incorporated into China.[7] Although Beijing intended these measures to strengthen and modernize Outer Mongolia, the Mongols bitterly resented enforced modernization under Han tutelage, an attitude that helped open the door for Russian economic and political expansion into Outer Mongolia.

* * *

Growing Mongol hostility to Han rule provided an opportunity for Russia to proffer its services as mediator and gradually increase its economic influence. Russia pursued a low-profile policy designed to avoid attracting the attention of the other powers, and slowly yet methodically worked to pry Outer Mongolia out of the Chinese sphere of influence. This policy came to fruition immediately after the collapse of the Qing dynasty in 1911-12.

Economic developments under the Qing helped pave the way for the Russians. Particularly important was the fact that the number of monasteries and monks in Outer Mongolia increased, with as many as 45 percent of the adult male population in Outer Mongolia (and 35 to 65 percent in Inner Mongolia) in the priesthood.[8] The monasteries were used as trade depots, so that the expansion of monasteries throughout Mongolia allowed Han Chinese traders to penetrate the region. Railway construction soon connected Mongolia's markets to Russia and China.

Mongol prohibitions prevented the development of a native trading class, so most of the trade among Mongols ended up in the hands of Han middlemen. The Han merchants took advantage of the seasonal nature of Mongol produce to buy Mongol animal products at low prices, while selling Chinese merchandise on credit throughout the year. This soon led to the accumulation of enormous debts, thus impoverishing Mongols, who had little choice but to take on more debt.

By 1911 the total debt in Outer Mongolia to Han traders amounted to 15 million tael or about 500 tael per household. The growing Mongol indebtedness to Han moneylenders fed ethnic tensions and hostility to Qing rule.[9] Qing administrators, for their part, became more partisan, favoring Han merchants over Mongol consumers. This meant that the Mongols directed their hostility not only at Han merchants, but more broadly at the entire Qing administration of Mongolia.

As Elizabeth Endicott discusses in her essay, the Russian government took advantage of China's problems to support increased Russian trade in Outer Mongolia and to reduce the Chinese commercial presence. Such, for example, were the aims behind the government-organized trade expedition to Outer Mongolia in 1910. When the Qing dynasty collapsed in 1912, therefore, Russian merchants were prepared to fill the space formerly occupied by their Chinese competitors.

* * *

Diplomatically, Russian expansion into Mongolia was made feasible when St. Petersburg came to terms with Great Britain and later Japan. In the summer of 1891, Russia and Britain disputed the demarcation line between Afghanistan and Xinjiang.[10] On March 11, 1895 Russia and Britain came to an agreement, without consulting China, that settled the Pamirs issue.[11] Thereafter, on April 28, 1899 Russia and Britain exchanged identical notes delimiting their respective spheres of interest in China. Russia agreed to abstain from any involvement in new railway construction in the Yangtze Basin in return for a British promise to do the same for Chinese territories north of the Great Wall. The Anglo-Russian delimitation of spheres of interest was completed on August 31, 1907, when each recognized Tibet as part of China; this treaty brought the so-called "Great Game" in Central Asia between the British and Russian empires to a lull.[12]

After the the Russo-Japanese War, Russia also came to similar diplomatic understandings with Japan: for example, in 1907 the Russian foreign minister, Aleksandr Izvol'skii, and the Japanese ambassador to Russia, Motono Ichiro, signed a secret treaty which divided Manchuria and Mongolia into two spheres of interest, with Russia in the north and Japan in the south; Outer Mongolia formally became a part of the Russian sphere.[13] Later, Russia and Japan reconfirmed these spheres of influence in another pair of treaties, one public and one secret, on July 4, 1910.[14] Beijing, which suspected that Russia and Japan were dividing up northern and northeastern China, denounced this treaty on July 21, 1910. However, the harsh policies that Beijing adopted in Outer Mongolia to fend off Russia ironically so frightened the Mongols that the latter turned to Russia for protection.

As Tatsuo Nakami shows in his essay, the Mongols first sought to force China to reassert the *status quo ante*, and only when this failed, to assert independence. These events opened the door for further Russian expansion, and on July 8, 1912, Foreign Minister Sergei Sazonov and Motono signed a third secret agreement extending the line delimiting their respective spheres so that Russia now gained all of Outer Mongolia as well as the western portion of Inner Mongolia.[15] Russia later confirmed its position in 1915 by signing a tripartite treaty with China and Outer Mongolia supporting Mongolia's autonomy, while simultaneously acknowledging that China still held suzerainty over Outer Mongolia.

While World War I would intervene to prevent Imperial Russia from realizing this plan, on July 3, 1916, Sazonov and Motono did sign another pair of treaties in St. Petersburg: in the public one, their countries agreed not to join any alliance against the other; in the secret one, Japan and Russia agreed to try to prevent China from falling into the hands of a third country and to cooperate in the event of war. The Chinese did not learn of the 1916 secret treaty until the Bolsheviks published it at the end of 1917 as part of their general campaign to discredit the secret diplomacy of the Tsarist government. The cumulative effect of these agreements, however, was to give Soviet Russia a free hand in Outer Mongolia.[16]

* * *

Faced with Russian expansion on its border, the Chinese government belatedly realized that Russia would find it difficult to absorb territories if they had a significant Han population. Thus, between 1901 and 1910, the Chinese government abolished prohibitions against intermarriage among Chinese, Mongols, and Manchus; the speaking of Chinese by Mongols; Chinese officials bringing their families to Mongolia, and Han settlement. To facilitate Han colonization, in 1907 the Chinese government opened a Department of Colonization within the Ministry of Dependencies. In 1910, it abrogated all statutes preventing Han reclamation of Mongol lands, and in 1911 opened a colonization bureau in Urga to promote Han colonization directly.[17]

Chinese colonization of Inner Mongolia proceeded rapidly, with Han merchants also speeding the process by accepting payments in land and then renting these lands to Han farmers. The Chinese government simultaneously tried to force peoples friendly to the Russians, such as the Buriats and the Kazakhs, to move away from the strategic border areas. Ironically the very railway system built by the Russians, to which the Chinese had so strenuously objected, facilitated Han migration to Inner Mongolia. This sudden influx of Han migrants, in turn, exacerbated tensions in Mongolia, and galvanized Mongols.[18]

As Yeshen-Khorlo Dugarova-Montgomery and Robert Montgomery write in their essay, frustrated pan-Mongol sentiments in both Russia and Chinese led to attempts by Mongol intellectuals, such as the Buriat scholar Agvan Dorzhiev, to link the divided Mongol groups by developing new alphabets and writing systems. Although Dorzhiev's 1905 alphabet was repressed by the Tsarist government, and Dorzhiev himself later died in a Soviet prison, his efforts were not in vain. They spurred other Mongolian nationalists into attempting to bridge the geographical and cultural gaps between the diverse Mongol tribes.

Notes

1. Thomas Ewing, *Between the Hammer and the Anvil? Chinese and Russian Policies in Outer Mongolia 1911-1921* (Bloomington: Research Institute for Inner Asian Studies, 1980), p. 19.

2. A.L. Popov, "Tsarskaia Rossiia i Mongoliia v 1913-1914 gg." (Tsarist Russia and Mongolia from 1913 to 1914), *Krasnyi arkhiv*, 37 (1929): pp. 10-11.

3. According to Salomon: "While the Manchu policy in both Inner and Outer Mongolia tended to avoid disrupting already existing Mongol institutions, this policy was more pronounced in Outer Mongolia. The Ch'ing rulers treated Outer Mongolia with much more caution than they did Inner Mongolia. The Manchus had expanded into Outer Mongolia later, and moreover, if the Kalkhas were sufficiently aroused they might appeal to the Dzungars or Russians for support." Hilel Benami Salomon, "China's Policy toward Outer Mongolia, 1912-1920," Ph.D. diss. Columbia University, 1969, p. 14.

4. Owen Lattimore, *The Desert Road to Turkestan* (1929; reprint, New York: AMS Press, Inc., 1972), p. 361; John K. Fairbank, ed. *The Late Ch'ing, 1800-1911*, Part I, vol. 10 of *The Cambridge History of China* (Cambridge: Cambridge University Press, 1978), p. xii; G. V. Glinka, ed., *Atlas Aziatskoi Rossii* (Atlas of Asiatic Russia) (St. Petersburg: Izdanie Pereselencheskogo upravleniia glavnogo upravleniia Zemleustroistva i zemledeleniia, 1914), no. 58.

5. Owen Lattimore, *Nationalism and Revolution in Mongolia* (New York: Oxford University Press, 1955), pp. 48-49.

6. Korostovets to Izvol'skii, 28 January 1909 (10 February 1909) ARFP, f. *Kitaiskii stol* (China Desk), d. 130, 92-93.

7. Sharap Bodievich Chimitdorzhiev, *Rossiia i Mongoliia* (Russia and Mongolia) (Moscow: Glavnaia redaktsiia vostochnoi literatury, 1987), p. 133.

8. Joseph Fletcher, "Ch'ing Inner Asia c. 1800," in Fairbank, ed. *The Late Ch'ing*, p. 54.

9. Popov (p. 11) puts the figure at 12 million rubles.

10. *Otchet po Aziiatskomu Departamentu za 1891* (Report on the Asiatic Department for 1891) ARFP, f. otchet MID op. 475 za 1891, pp. 134-46.

11. *Otchet po Aziiatskomu Departamentu za 1893* (Report on the Asiatic Department for 1893) ARFP, f. otchet MID op. 475 za 1893, pp. 153-66.

12. "Anglo-russkoe soglashenie o sferakh zheleznodorozhnykh interesov" (Anglo-Russian agreement on spheres of interest for railways), in E.D. Grimm, *Sbornik dogovorov i drugikh dokumentov po istorii mezhdunarodnykh otnoshenii na Dal'nem Vostoke [1842-1925]* (Collection of Treaties and Other Documents on the History of International Relations in the Far East [1842-1925]), (Moscow, 1927), pp. 137-38. For the Anglo-Russian delimitation of spheres of interest on August 31, 1907, see Alastair Lamb, *British India and Tibet 1766-1910*, 2nd ed. (London: Routledge & Kegan Paul, 1986), p. 283.

13. Edward Batson Price, *The Russo-Japanese Treaties of 1907-1916 Concerning Manchuria and Mongolia* (1933; reprint, New York: AMS Press, 1971), appendix: "Russo-Japanese Political Convention of July 17/30th 1907," pp. 107-12. Also see Price, pp. 26-38 for an analysis of the 1907 agreements.

14. Ibid., appendix: "Russo-Japanese Secret Convention of 1910," pp. 113-16.

15. Ibid., appendix: "Secret Convention between Russia and Japan in Regard to Mongolia," pp. 117-20.

16. Ibid., appendix: "Russo-Japanese Convention of July 3, 1916," and appendix: "The Secret Convention between Russia and Japan of July 3rd, June 20th, 1916," pp.

121-23. Price speculates that this defensive alliance was aimed either at a victorious Germany, or more likely, against the United States. Ibid., pp. 86-90, 95.

17. Col. Adabash of the General Staff, "O sovremennom nastroenii Kitaia k Rossii" (On the contemporary mood in China toward Russia), 31 March 1905 (13 April 1905) Central State Military History Archive of the USSR, Moscow, f. 447, ed. khr. no. 85, pp. 1-2. For two centuries the Qing Dynasty had not permitted the colonization of Mongolia as part of its buffer state policy. Peter S.H. Tang, *Russian and Soviet Policy in Manchuria and Outer Mongolia 1911-1930*, (Durham, N.C.: Duke University Press, 1959), p. 289.

18. Owen Lattimore, *Inner Asian Frontiers of China* (New York: American Geographical Society, 1940), p. 99; Tang, pp. 294-95.

1. The Living Buddha in his Seventeenth Year, c. 1900. *Source*: Frans August Larson, *Larson, Duke of Mongolia* (Boston: Little, Brown, and Company, 1930).

2. The Wooden Frame of a Yurt, c. 1900. *Source*: Frans August Larson, *Larson, Duke of Mongolia* (Boston: Little, Brown, and Company, 1930).

3. Interior of a Mongolian Temple, c. 1900. *Source*: Frans August Larson, *Larson, Duke of Mongolia* (Boston: Little, Brown, and Company, 1930).

4. Mongolian Women, c. 1900. *Source*: Frans August Larson, *Larson, Duke of Mongolia* (Boston: Little, Brown, and Company, 1930).

5. Mongolian Herdsmen, c. 1900. *Source*: Frans August Larson, *Larson, Duke of Mongolia* (Boston: Little, Brown, and Company, 1930).

6. Mongolian Wrestlers, Tsagan Nor, 1922. *Source*: Roy Chapman Andrews, *On the Trail of Ancient Man* (New York: G. P. Putnam's Sons, 1926).

7. Preparing Felt for a Yurt, 1922. *Source*: Roy Chapman Andrews, *On the Trail of Ancient Man* (New York: G. P. Putnam's Sons, 1926).

8. Mongol Collecting Salt Near the Altay Mountains, 1922. *Source*: Roy Chapman Andrews, *On the Trail of Ancient Man* (New York: G. P. Putnam's Sons, 1926).

9. Camel Caravan South of Tsagan Nor, 1925. *Source*: Roy Chapman Andrews, *On the Trail of Ancient Man* (New York: G. P. Putnam's Sons, 1926).

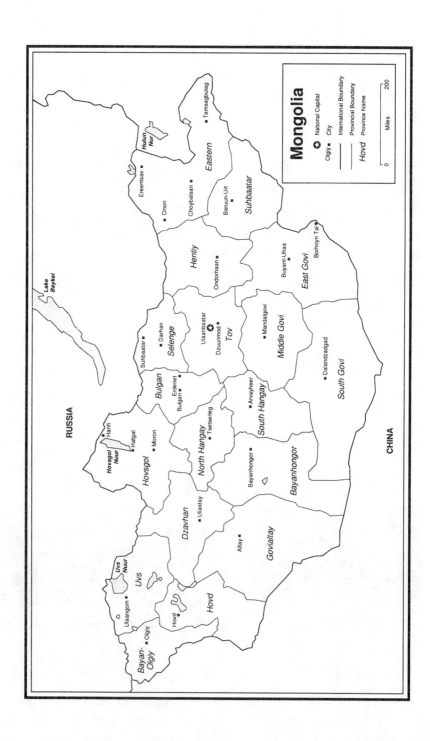

China's "New Administration" in Mongolia

Mei-hua Lan

The reasons for Mongolia's twentieth-century independence movement were multiple and multi-layered. Mongols participated in this movement for personal interests or the common good, for political liberation or socioeconomic relief, for the restoration of historical glory or the creation of future happiness. Nevertheless, they all had one thing in common: they were not satisfied with the *status quo*. Changes, possibly even revolution, seemed justified.

The drastic change of the Manchu policy toward Mongolia from a conservative-protective one to an aggressive-colonial one, particularly the initiation of the "New Administration" (*Xinzheng*), has long been considered the factor most responsible for the onset of the Mongolian independence movement. However, few scholars have described in detail what comprised the New Administration, how the Manchu officials carried it out in Mongolia, to what extent they achieved success, and in what manner the Mongols responded to this program. This essay will address these questions through the investigation of primary materials, both published and unpublished.

Origin of the New Administration

When the Manchus established political and military dominance in Mongolia during the seventeenth and eighteenth centuries, they developed a complicated system to deal with the Mongols. The Manchu policy evolved according to different needs, but its primary purpose remained the same: to use the Mongols as a mobile military reserve in order to defend the Manchu empire, especially its northern region. As part of this effort, the Manchus exploited the banner system to restrict the Mongols' possible migration among banners as well as to prevent the conflicts between banners that competed for pasture land. This system was considered largely responsible for the failure of the emergence of a political leader who could unify all the Mongols.[1]

The Manchus used a well-designed system of reward and coercion to keep Mongolia under their control. They reconfirmed and elaborated the Mongolian feudal system, and respected Mongolian religious beliefs and traditional law. Additionally, the Manchus tried very hard to preserve the pastoral nomadism of the Mongols as well as to protect them from Han Chinese influence. They did not want the Mongols to form some sort of liaison with the Chinese that might ruin the Manchu policy of "divide and rule."

From the Manchu point of view, their policy in Mongolia was basically successful. They took appropriate measures according to local conditions, and won the support of the Mongolian secular and religious leaders. The land beyond the Great Wall was relatively peaceful, compared to the continuous turmoil it had suffered during other Chinese dynasties.

Manchu policy in Mongolia succeeded partly because the Manchus and the Mongols had similar traditions, and so the former knew which policy would work best. However, after the Qing dynasty gradually evolved into a Chinese-style regime and was dragged into the international maritime entanglements, the Mongols' role became increasingly less important and the relations between the Manchus and the Mongols became less close. Nevertheless, Mongolia remained under the Manchus' control until the very end of their dynasty in 1912.

With the exception of the early Qing period, the Manchu government set up strict rules against Han immigration to Mongolia. Although the number of Chinese immigrants continued to grow, and cultivation of Mongolian land continued to develop, the official Manchu policy of prohibition remained intact until 1902, when it was changed to a policy supporting colonization. The Manchu government changed its policy due to its fear of aggressive penetration by Russia and Japan into Manchuria and Mongolia; from the mid-nineteenth century, China suffered increasingly from imperialistic expansion within its territory. By the end of that century, China became a semi-colony of the imperialist powers.

Faced with such a threat, it is not surprising that the Manchu government changed its policies to enforce greater control over Mongolia, especially since the prevailing practice of illegal cultivation demonstrated that prohibition was no longer practical. Financial difficulties were also responsible for this change: the Manchu government needed financial resources to pay for the indemnity it owed the great powers as part of the terms of settlement after the Boxer Rebellion, as well as to pay for the expenses required to enforce the New Administration, a reform program through which the Manchu government tried to save itself from destruction.

From the mid-nineteenth century on, the attempts at reform—namely, the restoration during the Tongzhi reign and the self-strengthening movement—had been adopted to strengthen China in order to counter imperialist ambition. However, they were considered a failure after China was defeated in the Sino-Japanese war of 1894-95. The subsequent reform effort of 1898 ended with the *coup d'état* of the Empress Dowager Cixi and her supporters.

After China suffered humiliation with the foreign intervention of the eight powers during the Boxer Rebellion in 1900, the Qing government made its last effort to survive. The Guangxu Emperor announced the initiation of new reforms on January 29, 1901. In April, the Supervisory Bureau of Political Affairs (*duban zhengwu chu*) headed by Prince Qing Yikuang was established to take charge of the new reforms.[2] This marked the beginning of the New Administration that continued until the end of the Manchu rule.

The New Administration included reforms in almost every aspect of governmental affairs. In the sphere of education, the Qing government abolished the eight-legged essays in the civil-service examinations in 1902, established a Ministry of Education in 1905, and eventually abolished the civil-service examinations in 1906. It also converted traditional academies into western-style schools, encouraged people to study abroad, and recognized the necessity for women to receive a modern education.

In the realm of the military, the Qing government clearly recognized the necessity of having well-trained troops with western-style equipment, and so reorganized the provincial army system, abolished traditional military examinations, created military academies in each province, and reorganized central military organs by creating a new bureaucracy. Finally, they reduced the Green Standard forces and later converted them into patrol battalions.

With regard to political reforms, the Qing government considered constitutionalism vital to the wealth and strength of China. It finally announced in September 1906 that it would adopt constitutionalism after several years of preparation. According to this decree, before the Manchu court could adopt constitutionalism, there were several preliminary reforms that needed to be completed: the reorganization of government offices, the compilation of laws, the promotion of education, the rearrangement of finance, the creation of a modern military, and the establishment of a police force.[3]

In 1908 the government issued the Principles of the Constitution, modeled on the Japanese Meiji constitution. Assembly members of different administrative levels were elected, and local self-governments established. Nevertheless, these were merely advisory bodies without real power. Since centralization was vital for carrying out the reforms, however, the Qing government did standardize and centralize the currency, standardize weights and measures, and centralize its financial administration. Other reforms included revision of the legal codes, compilation of a new criminal code, prohibition against foot-binding and opium-smoking, and abolition of discrimination between Manchus and Han Chinese.[4] Official sponsorship of modern industry also continued during this period.

It was during this period of reform that the Qing government officially changed its policy toward Mongolia. Since Mongolia was different from China proper, both in terms of political and socioeconomic structures, the primary focus of the New Administration was different in this region. While in China proper the Qing government hoped to use the New Administration to prevent the growth of anti-Manchu forces and to secure support of the Chinese provincial governors and foreigners, in Mongolia it sought to prevent any further foreign penetration and to convert this region into a regular Chinese province. Therefore, the colonization of Mongolia by Han Chinese was emphasized.

In 1897 Hu Pinzhi, Governor of Shanxi Province, sent a memorial to the Qing court that it should open up Mongolian land near the provincial borders both to increase the population and to protect the border.[5] In 1902, the Guangxu Emperor approved the proposal of Hu's successor, Cen Chunxuan, to open up Mongolia for cultivation. He appointed Yigu,[6] one of the vice-ministers of the Board of War, as commissioner to take charge of matters concerning cultivation of the Chakhar region and the Ulaanchab and Yekhe Juu leagues.[7] Yigu's appointment marked the onset of the new Manchu policy toward Mongolia.

The New Administration in Inner Mongolia

In his proclamation of April 26, 1902, to the Mongols and Chinese within his jurisdiction, Yigu clarified the purposes of the opening-up of Inner Mongolia: to exploit land productivity, to relieve the Mongols' poor economy, to secure the border internationally, and to eliminate hidden dangers domestically. He urged the Mongols to cooperate, so that they too could derive benefits from this reform by preventing corrupt conduct caused by illegal private renting-out.[8] Yigu set up his headquarters, the General Bureau of Cultivation Affairs (*kenwu zongju*), in Höhhot. The region where he first took charge of cultivation affairs was divided into two parts: eastern and western. The eastern part included the Chakhar banners, and the western part the two leagues of Ulaanchab and Yekhe Juu.

Yigu's work in Chakhar went smoothly, primarily because the Chakhar banners were *zongguan* banners governed not by local Mongolian princes, but by appointed officials. One of Yigu's objectives in Chakhar was to eliminate the influence of land-merchants (*dishang*) who occupied huge amounts of land by paying the banners a low rent, and then sold or rented out this land to newly arrived Chinese immigrants at a higher price. Many land merchants used force and bullied local officials, thus extending the illegal cultivation while refusing to pay taxes.[9] A cultivation corporation (*kenwu gongsi*) was established in Kalgan (Zhangjiakou), with capital equally provided by government and private sectors, to replace the land-merchants. Another similar corporation was set up in Baotou to take care of the leasing of land in the Ulaanchab and Yekhe Juu leagues.[10]

The opening-up of Inner Mongolia brought in two kinds of revenue: land-contract fees (*yahuang yin, huangjia yin*) and annual land taxes (*shengke yin*). Yigu promised that half of the contract fees and all the land taxes would be given to the banners.[11] As for the tenant farmers, there was not a large difference since they now paid rent to the cultivation corporations instead of to the land-merchants. However, this reform did make a huge difference to the Manchu government because it could now bring the cultivation affairs under its direct supervision, and by so doing receive greater revenues. Due to the cooperative nature of the Chakhar banners, the task of opening-up in the Chakhar region was completed within two years.

Unlike what he had encountered in Chakhar, however, Yigu's task did not go so well in the Ulaanchab and Yekhe Juu leagues. From the very beginning these two leagues did not cooperate. Their leaders not only refused to go to Höhhot to discuss matters concerning cultivation, but also sent letters to the General-in-Chief at Suiyuan (*Suiyuancheng jiangjun*) to express their opposition. The letter from the Ulaanchab League argued that there would be no place for the Mongols to live if pasture land was opened up for cultivation, and that there had never been any benefit for the Mongols to live together with Chinese cultivators.[12] These two leagues also sent the *Lifan Yuan* (the Court of Colonial Affairs) letters requesting that they be excluded from the official opening-up.[13]

The Mongolian nobles of the Ulaanchab and Yekhe Juu leagues did not really oppose cultivation, because it had long been practiced in those regions. What they in fact opposed was the official large-scale opening-up of Mongolian land. They considered this a threat that would hinder the practice of nomadism and reduce the income they could draw from renting out the land themselves. The administrative power of the Mongolian jasags (a ruling prince of a banner) was also weakened because Chinese-style administrative units were created whenever many Chinese peasants settled permanently in Mongolia. The existing cultivators were also suspicious that their land might be taken away and given to others.[14]

While facing such opposition, Yigu asked the *Lifan Yuan* to put pressure on the two league heads.[15] His request was met. On September 21, the Guangxu Emperor further granted Yigu the title of Board President (*shangshu*) of the *Lifan Yuan* to ease his work among the Mongols.[16] As for the Yekhe Juu League, not until late April 1903 did two of its seven banners, namely Khanggin and Dalad, finally send their representatives to Höhhot, and reach agreements with Yigu. Only after hearing that Arbinbayar, the league head and jasag of the Khanggin Banner, had agreed to open up his banner for cultivation, did the jasags of other banners follow suit.[17]

Nevertheless, Arbinbayar and the Mongols of his banner disapproved of what their representative had done. Arbinbayar dismissed the representative from office, and accused other banners of compromising too much.[18] Arbinbayar's continuous opposition angered Yigu and caused him to be removed from the post of league head in December 1903.[19] Shocked by Yigu's tough action, Arbinbayar soon backed down, and agreed to open up some land for cultivation.

In addition to the Khanggin Banner, other banners also demonstrated resistance against the opening-up even after they had agreed to make available some pieces of land for cultivation. For example, the Mongols of the Üüsin Banner organized twelve opposition groups in the form of *duguilang*. Therefore, nothing was actually accomplished there during Yigu's tenure.[20]

In early 1905, when Yigu sent his subordinates to create a branch office in the Jegüngar (Jungar) Banner, the Mongols and Chinese of that area rebelled under the leadership of Dampil. The rebellion soon spread. Government troops were sent in to repress the rebels. Dampil was captured, and executed in early 1906.[21]

It was even more difficult for Yigu to conduct his work in the Ulaanchab League. Unlike the ruling nobles of the Yekhe Juu League who could not unite against the opening-up, the higher and lower nobles in the Ulaanchab League were united in defending their league's interests. Therefore, their opposition was stronger and lasted longer.

Although the Manchu court tried again to ease Yigu's work by appointing him General-in-Chief at Suiyuan in early October 1903,[22] the princes of the Ulaanchab league soon sent the *Lifan Yuan* a letter accusing Yigu of misconduct and demanding that he be removed from office.[23] They did not change their attitude until April 1906, when they were strongly criticized by Prince Su (*Su Qinwang*). The league head Lhawangnorbu realized that if he continued his opposition, he might face the same fate as Arbinbayar. Therefore, he and other nobles decided to open up some of their land, although it was a relatively small amount in comparison to the land that the Yekhe Juu had already agreed to open up.[24]

With great efforts, Yigu eventually started the official opening-up in western Inner Mongolia. His goal was partly achieved. More Chinese immigrants settled and began cultivating there; several administrative units were created; revenue was drawn from the opening-up; and land-merchants were replaced by the cultivation corporations.

However, Yigu was dismissed from office in May 1908 due to his impeachment by Wenzhehun, one of his former colleagues. Yigu was impeached for "fooling the Mongols, [and] making private profits."[25] Because of Yigu's dismissal, the opening-up in western Inner Mongolia was suspended. Still, during Yigu's six-year tenure of managing the opening-up affairs, more than 100,000 *qing* (i.e., 1,513,000 acres) of land were opened up for cultivation.[26]

Since the leagues of Josotu and Juu Uda were located in the most southern region of Inner Mongolia, close to China proper, they were already familiar with agriculture and the land in these two leagues was good for farming. Long before the official opening-up started in the late Qing period, the land of Josotu and Juu Uda was already largely cultivated. Many Mongols of these two leagues had left herding behind and become peasants. The opening-up in the late Qing period was the last stage in the transition of the economy of Josotu and Juu Uda from nomadism to agriculture. Nevertheless, the Mongols of these two leagues still did not welcome the official opening-up because it might cause the banners to lose their ownership of the land, and to receive less money than before.[27]

In the Jirim League, the official opening-up became even more necessary after the Russians completed the construction of the Chinese Eastern Railway in Manchuria. The official opening-up of the Jirim League began in 1902, starting with the Jalaid Banner and from 1903 to 1911, more than 4,540,000 *shang*[28] of land were opened up in the Jirim League. In comparison with other leagues mentioned above, more unused land was opened up in the Jirim League than in the other leagues, since most of the land they agreed to open had already been undergoing cultivation.[29] This amount was also about 2.4 times the land opened up in the previous ninety years. Finally, during the Qing period, this accounted for about 20 percent of the banner land being opened up and later brought under the jurisdiction of the Three Eastern Provinces.[30]

Although nobody knows exactly how many Chinese immigrants moved into Inner Mongolia during the official opening-up, the number was definitely substantial. For example, according to a statistic published in 1919, there were altogether 697,164 Mongols (11.6 percent) and 5,297,844 immigrants (88.4 percent) living in the four leagues of Jirim, Josotu, Juu Uda, and Shili-yin Gool. The immigrants were all Han Chinese with the exception of approximately 29,000 Manchus who moved into the Jirim League. With the notable exception of Shili-yin Gool, where few Han Chinese lived, the other three leagues were crowded with Chinese immigrants.[31]

Following the opening-up, many new administrative units were established. Additional land was brought under the provincial jurisdiction, and the Mongolian banners lost many of their rights of land-control to the provincial governments. Other projects such as the creation of military establishments, exploitation of natural resources, railway construction, postal and telegram services, schools, police, banks, and others were also meant to be carried out or created from scratch under the name of the New Administration.[32]

Regulations designed to prevent Mongols from encountering and being influenced by Chinese culture were also abolished. In September 1910, the Manchu court announced that Chinese people were now allowed to enter Mongolia to farm, to mortgage Mongolian land, and to contract Mongolian land and pasture for farming in banners that were already opened up. They were also allowed to marry Mongolian women. In addition, Mongols were now allowed to hire Chinese teachers, to write official documents in Chinese, and to use Chinese names.[33] As a result, the preservation of traditional Mongolian social, political, and economic structures was no longer a high priority of the Manchu government, especially since the latter had itself already been transformed into something resembling a Chinese government.

The New Administration in Outer Mongolia

The New Administration in Outer Mongolia began several years later than in Inner Mongolia. After the new policy was adopted, it faced immediate opposition from the Mongols. In particular, when the Manchu authorities asked the aimags (i.e., tribes) to report land suitable for cultivation, the aimags replied that there was no land available for such a purpose.

In his letter of June 28, 1906, the head of the Setsen Khan aimag replied to Yanzhi, the Manchu amban (i.e., imperial agent) at Urga, that there was no land in his aimag available for agriculture because of geological and climatic unsuitability, and because the limited suitable land was already being used to breed their herds. He continued by stating that the Mongolian tradition was to use good pasture land to breed animals, not to cultivate land and build villages; that the pasture land available for animal husbandry would decrease if Chinese people came to cultivate and build houses and shops, and; that the opening-up would inevitably cause trouble and conflict because Chinese people did not understand the Mongolian language and customs. He concluded by requesting that the Manchu amban exclude their land from cultivation.[34]

Thereafter, in August, the nobles of the Tüshiyetü Khan aimag sent a similar letter to the Manchu amban.[35] Yanzhi sent a memorial to the Manchu court that Outer Mongolia was not suitable for agriculture, and suggested that it would be more useful to build railways and to open gold and coal mines in this region.[36] In 1907, he sent officials and functionaries to the Tüshiyetü Khan and Setsen Khan aimags to measure the cultivated land.[37]

As for the exploitation of natural resources in Outer Mongolia, only gold mines were worth mentioning. Earlier in 1900, a Russian-Belgian joint stock company ("Mongolor") was created to mine gold in the Tüshiyetü Khan and Setsen Khan aimags, but it was faced with the threat of bankruptcy only a year later.[38] From the very beginning, the Mongols opposed gold-mining. In May 1900, they sent a letter to the *Lifan Yuan* to express their opposition. In this letter they said that gold-mining was harmful both to their way of living and to their land.[39] In October 1903, the Military Governor of Uliastai (*Wuliyasutai jiangjun*) Lianshun[40] asked for imperial approval to mine gold in the two aimags with Baron Victor von Grot, who had participated in the operation of Mongolor, as the manager, but he did not receive approval.

Nevertheless, in 1906, von Grot started to mine gold without permission. When Yanzhi told Beijing about it and asked for instructions, the Qing government granted approval for von Grot to mine gold for twenty-five years after he submitted the statute of the company.[41] This gold mining company was nominally a Sino-Russian joint company. However, since the Russian side provided all the capital and took charge of the management, the Chinese side had no power over it except taxation. In 1910, the Chinese side received a tax of 200,000 taels (i.e., 10 percent of the company's total revenue).[42]

Railway construction was considered crucial to the success of the new reforms. The Manchu officials strongly believed that when a line from Beijing to Kalgan, then under construction, was completed, that the railway should be extended to Urga. This would benefit military operations, favor commercial expansion, and counter-balance the Russian government's territorial ambitions.[43] In January 1911, the National Assembly (*cizheng yuan*) approved three railway lines (Kalgan to Kiakhta, Kalgan to Jinzhou, and Urga to Ili).[44] However, none of these were put under construction by the end of the Manchu rule.

Although the Manchu officials in Mongolia were often accused of incompetence, they were not blind to the local situation, and sometimes made honest reports to the Manchu court. In 1903, when the Manchu officials in Outer Mongolia replied to the proposal of turning Mongolia into regular provinces, both the Military Governor of Uliastai and the Hewei-Amban of Kobdo (*Kebuduo canzan dachen*, Assistant Military Governor of Kobdo) reported that such a proposal was unfeasible and harmful, and the Amban of Urga considered it difficult for Outer Mongolia to follow the example of China proper because the situation was different in Outer Mongolia. The Amban of Urga argued that there was still plenty of fertile land in the Three Eastern Provinces where villages and towns existed before officials were appointed by the Manchu court to those regions; therefore, it was natural to create administrative units in those provinces. By contrast, he continued, since the Chinese in Outer Mongolia were not permanent settlers, it would simply frighten the Mongols and cause trouble to promote cultivation in Outer Mongolia and to turn the region into provinces.[45]

When Yanzhi carried out the reforms, he did so in a very deliberate way. Sando (Sandowa),[46] a sinicized Mongol with a Chinese-style courtesy name (*zi*) as Liuqiao, succeeded Yanzhi as Amban of Urga on November 26, 1909. He soon changed the moderate tempo of his predecessor to a more aggressive one. Sando arrived in Urga in March 1910.[47]

In August 1909, when Sando served as Deputy Lieutenant-General in Höhhot, he proposed that the whole of Mongolia be reorganized into four aimags, with one minister and twelve subordinate bureaus in each aimag to take charge of the administration, and that the expenses be financed by the Mongols themselves after five years.[48] Although his plan was not approved by the Manchu court, it clearly shows his goal of promoting extensive reform in Mongolia. Due to his sinicized character and aggressive attitude, Sando, though a Mongol, was not welcomed by the Khalkhas.

After arriving in Urga, Sando aggressively carried out the New Administration. Such aggressiveness was not only a personal decision of Sando, but also a policy of Beijing. Offices of the Central Government, the Cabinet and the General Staff Council (*junzi fu*) in particular, repeatedly urged Sando to carry out various projects immediately. Additionally, the fact that Russia's policies in Outer Mongolia became more rapacious certainly contributed to the change to an aggressive policy.[49]

A Mongolian delegation went to St. Petersburg in 1911 to seek Russian assistance for Mongolian independence. The delegates presented the Russian government a letter in which the Mongols complained that the Chinese authorities had allowed Chinese to settle and cultivate land in some northern banners of Outer Mongolia.[50] Apparently, the intention of the Chinese authorities was to protect the northern part of Outer Mongolia from Russian penetration.

The first step Sando took was to recruit 100 patrolmen and an additional 44 policemen, and to set up the Bureau of Military Matters (*yingwu chu*).[51] In May 1910, he requested a salary raise for the officials in Urga in order to lighten the Mongols' burden by allowing them to pay lower customary fees. He reorganized the Office of Vaccination into the Office of Sanitation to expand its business, including helping people quit opium-smoking. He also chose several Mongolian children to begin to learn Russian at the school set up by the Russian Consulate.[52]

In July 1910, Sando sent a memorial stating that the post-service was already in operation, and asked to set up a branch office in Beijing to take care of the post with Urga.[53] By that time, according to Sando's telegram to Beijing, he had already set up two half-day schools, and two newspaper-reading areas in Urga and Kiakhta. He also sent out people to investigate natural resources and collect information about railway construction and cultivation.[54]

In January 1911, an Army-Training Office (*bingbei chu*) was created under the leadership of newly arrived Tang Zaili[55] to train a modern army. The Bureau of Military Matters was abolished. All the *Xuanhua* soldiers (first stationed in Urga in 1888), patrol battalions, officials and soldiers of the relay stations and watch-posts, and military matters in the two eastern aimags were put under Tang's supervision. The tax drawn from gold-mining was used to fund army training.[56] During that summer, Sando and Tang began to organize the New

Army, recruiting Mongols into the cavalry, as well as local Chinese people and banner soldiers from Suiyuan into the machine-gun battalion.[57]

In February 1911, Sando established an office to take charge of negotiations with Russia regarding Outer Mongolia, and asked the Chinese Foreign Ministry to send its representative to Urga.[58] Later, he suggested that since, in terms of frontier defense, garrisoning worked only temporarily while colonization worked permanently, all available veterans in China proper should be transferred to Outer Mongolia to cultivate land around the watch-posts.[59]

In May 1911, Sando reported that local taxes on timber, carriages, and camels were collected in order to subsidize the future law courts in Urga and Kiakhta. Local taxes were also levied to replace customary fees as well as to subsidize the New Administration.[60] The Bureau of Cultivation Affairs was established in August 1911 to open up the land of the Tüshiyetü Khan aimag for cultivation.[61]

As for the preparation for constitutional rule, Sando's predecessor had reported that no qualified Mongols were available to form an assembly or self-governing body. Therefore, in addition to schools and police, Sando set up an office to take charge of relevant preparation for self-government. He also investigated and made annual reports on population and household statistics, revenues and expenses, and the administrative budget.[62]

The New Administration was carried out elsewhere in Outer Mongolia. In February 1910, the Military Governor of Uliastai, Kunxiu, reported that he planned to build a primary normal school in Uliastai, to increase policemen, to set up a bureau to help people quit opium-smoking, to organize a chamber of commerce, and to create an office to take charge of the New Administration. He requested 20,000 taels as an annual subsidy.[63]

In his report of September 15, 1910, Zhongrui, Amban of Kobdo (*Kebuduo banshi dachen*),[64] indicated that the new reforms in the Altai region included school-founding, garrison-cultivation, financial restructuring, budgeting, and census. The schools would begin after receiving funds. Zhongrui urged the necessity for the exploitation of abundant metals, which had long been ignored due to financial and personnel shortage, in order to bring in revenue and to counter-balance Russian eagerness for these precious metals. But, owing to financial difficulties and his fear that the army might become too powerful to be controlled, Zhongrui suggested that the army-training in the banners be postponed.[65] In January 1911, the acting Amban of Kobdo Yannian stated that he had already invited experts to investigate the mines, and planned to organize a fur and leather company.[66]

When the Manchu government accelerated the speed of the New Administration, the Khalkha Mongols soon realized that the deteriorating Qing regime was ready to impose an aggressive policy of colonization of their homeland. The Khalkhas had been watching the developments in Inner Mongolia closely. In the letter which the Mongolian delegation presented to the Russian government in 1911, the Khalkhas listed various unbearable changes made by the Chinese authorities in Inner Mongolia: colonizing, creating Chinese administrative units, reducing the power of banner jasags, and replacing Mongolian garrisons with Chinese troops along the Russo-Bargu frontier. The letter also mentioned the Chinese uprising of 1891 against the Mongols in Josotu and Juu Uda leagues.[67]

Since the Khalkhas were familiar with the developments in Inner Mongolia, they knew perfectly well what the Chinese colonial policy entailed. They hoped to avoid facing the unbearable situation of their kinsmen in Inner Mongolia. Therefore, they decided to separate Outer Mongolia permanently from the Manchu state in order to save their homeland from the Manchu-Chinese colonization. A movement for Mongolian independence was the result.

Mongolian Response to the New Administration

In Inner Mongolia, the New Administration included changes in various domains. The most controversial change was the official opening-up of land for cultivation. Since it greatly hindered existing political, economic, and social structures, the Mongols certainly did not support it. Initially, they tried to stop the opening-up by signing petitions. When their requests were ignored, they impeded land surveys, refused to pay contract fees, and stopped paying land taxes. The most resolute opponents took up weapons to defend their interests. They opposed not only the officials who were in charge of the opening-up, but also their own Mongolian princes who agreed to open up land for cultivation.

Vast revolts against the opening-up occurred in every Inner Mongolian league. In addition to the opposition activities in the leagues of Yekhe Juu and Ulaanchab mentioned above, there were also activities led by renowned rebellious leaders such as Chogdalai and Togtakhu Taiji of the Jirim League, and Bayandalai of the Josotu League. All of them were supported by angry Mongols, who obstructed land surveys, murdered officials involved in the opening-up, and plundered Chinese local governments. The rebels were generally called "Mongolian bandits" (*mengfei*) by the Manchu authorities, but they saw themselves as impoverished and grieved Mongols who were forced to take up weapons to fight for their survival.[68]

Owing to various opposition activities, the official opening-up was carried out under military coercion. Wherever land was measured, troops followed to reinforce a smooth carrying-out of the work.[69] There were a number of incidents between the Mongolian opposition and the authorities, including direct confrontation with the Chinese immigrants. However, there was a lack of cohesion among these activities. Although hatred existed against the Chinese, Mongolian nationalism had not yet entered the scene. Most incidents were related to economic and social discontent. Mongols of different regions and different classes were not ready to unite in order to work together for a higher political goal.

After the New Administration began in Outer Mongolia, anti-Manchu feeling deepened, and opposition activities increased. In September 1908, the Tüshiyetü Khan aimag, the Setsen Khan aimag, and the *Shabi Yamen* jointly sent a letter to Yanzhi. They requested that the regiment of *Xuanhua* troops in Urga since 1888 be withdrawn from Outer Mongolia, because the troops had failed to accomplish their mission of suppressing the bandits led by Togtakhu Taiji, but instead were simply another burden to the Mongols. They added that Mongolian troops could be mobilized whenever necessary. Nevertheless, their request was not granted. The Manchu amban considered their request improper as long as Russian troops were allowed to stay in Urga and Kiakhta.[70]

The Mongols demonstrated their opposition openly and repeatedly against the New Administration. They considered the idea of assembly and election unsuitable for Mongolian society, since most Mongols were nomadic and had not settled in defined places.[71] They especially opposed the opening-up of pasture lands. In March 1911, the two eastern aimags promised the Manchu amban that each of them would offer 2,000 taels annually to the Manchu authorities if the latter agreed to stop opening up Mongolian land for cultivation.[72]

Among all the new agencies created in Mongolia, the Army-Training Office led by Tang Zaili was particularly hated by the Mongols because of Tang's aggressiveness. Tang's firm attitude resulted from his belief that Russia would try its best to take control of Mongolia in a few years if China did not act immediately to consolidate its position in this region.[73] Tang himself admitted that opposition arose immediately after he began his work in January 1911.[74]

The creation of the Army-Training Office and the organization of the New Army further burdened the Mongols. Considering Tang and his followers undisciplined and haughty, the Mongolian leaders and the Russian Minister at Beijing requested that the Office be abolished, and that the army-training officers be recalled. Eventually, Tang was forced to leave Outer Mongolia. The Manchu court soon approved of the abolition of the Army-Training Office in late November 1911.[75]

The Mongols did not like Sando either. Soon after his arrival in Urga, a conflict between Chinese and Mongols occurred on April 6, 1910, when a couple of lamas got into a quarrel over prices with the clerks at a Chinese carpenter's shop called Deyiyong. The so-called Deyiyong Incident soon developed into a riot against the Manchu-Chinese authorities in Urga. When Sando and his people went to investigate, they were stoned by the gathered Mongols. Sando handled this incident harshly. In May 1910, the two eastern aimags and the *Shabi Yamen* wrote the *Lifan Yuan*, complaining about Sando's oppression, and requested his discharge. They accused Sando of turning lamas into soldiers and policemen and of twisting the facts of the Deyiyong incident by listening to only one-side of the story.[76]

Sando's harsh handling of the incident made him unpopular among the Mongols, and the New Administration under his charge was consequently hated by them as well. After Mongolian independence activities quickened, the Qing government had to abandon the New Administration. Nevertheless, it was too late for it to regain Mongolian support. With the fall of the Manchu dynasty in early 1912, independence became a natural choice for the Mongols.

The New Administration and the Mongolian Independence Movement

With the 1911 Revolution in China, and the fall of the Manchu empire in 1912, Outer Mongolia and the Bargu region declared their independence in December 1911 and January 1912, respectively. The direct causes of these independence attempts varied in different regions, but they were all related to the new Manchu policy of colonization.

Some banners in Inner Mongolia also tried to seek independence, but only those under Udai's leadership took up weapons to fight for it. The independence attempts of the Inner Mongolian banners were soon suppressed by the newly established Republican government. But not until 1915 was the independence of Outer Mongolia and the Bargu region abolished after the conclusion of the Tripartite Treaty of Kiakhta and the Sino-Russian Agreement Concerning Khölön Buir (i.e., Bargu).

The blame that many authors have accorded to the New Administration for creating the independence movement in Outer Mongolia has probably been overestimated. Although the Manchu authorities indeed intended to carry out the New Administration in Outer Mongolia, relatively little was accomplished due to the desperate financial condition, time limitations, and the Mongols' opposition. As a result, the most important parts of the new Manchu policy in Inner Mongolia—the large-scale Chinese immigration, the opening-up of land for cultivation, and the creation of Chinese-style administrative units—did not take place in Outer Mongolia.[77] The Han Chinese people in Outer Mongolia were traders, workers, cultivators, and bureaucrats.[78] In addition to the small number of cultivators, most of them were not permanent settlers.

The Manchu officials understood Outer Mongolia's desire to retain its traditions. Even Chinese officials as aggressive as Tang Zaili had such an understanding. In his description of the military situation in Outer Mongolia, Tang wrote, "It is needless to say that it is an urgent danger to frontier defense to have aged useless soldiers fight with young energetic enemies, and to defend vast land of ten thousand *li* with several hundred people. Beginning from the first month of this year [i.e., February 1911], the old army began to learn modern military skill. However, it is inadequate, and will not better the situation."[79]

In a memorial to the emperor from September 15, 1910, Zhongrui stated, "Inner Mongolia can be considered plentiful and populous; therefore, the task there is to educate (*jiao*). However, Outer Mongolia is extremely exhausted, and its nation weakened. The task there should be to nurture (*yang*). Since they are different, how can the policies toward them be the same?" He continued, "If someone wants to carry out a general program by praising only its positiveness and benefit without seeing widely enough and without considering the frontier situation, what he says are simply empty words."[80] In short, the Manchu officials tried their best to ensure Manchu control in Outer Mongolia without disregarding the local situation.

But if the New Administration reforms had barely started in Outer Mongolia, why did the Mongols decide to seek independence? Certainly, the very brevity of the reforms meant that the Mongols failed to benefit from them. It is also a reasonable assumption to suggest that even though little was done, the Mongols could predict their fate by watching the developments in Inner Mongolia. However, the main reason underlying the Mongolian independence movement was certainly the decline of the Manchu dynasty. Even before the New Administration began in Outer Mongolia, the Mongols had already tried to obtain Russian assistance in their separation from the Manchu empire. If the memory of Diluwa Khutugtu is reliable, the Jebtsundamba Khutugtu dispatched Badamdorji to St. Petersburg in 1894 to seek Russian support for Mongolian independence. It was during this year that China entered into a disastrous war with Japan.[81] It happened again in 1900, the year in which the Qing government suffered humiliation during the Boxer Rebellion.

According to custom in the steppe, clans gathered around a capable leader in times of success and deserted him if he failed or when he died; a nomadic state was a confederation under a charismatic leader for common interest, and it was to be dissolved when the reasons for their early alliance ceased to exist. The Mongols considered their relations with the Manchus one of alliance. Therefore, if the Manchu state appeared incompetent or its actions failed to benefit them, the Mongols certainly were not reluctant to break relations with the Manchus.

In the Mongolian proclamation of independence, the first words were: "At present we often hear that in the southern land the Manchus and the Chinese are creating disturbances and are about to precipitate the fall of the Manchu dynasty. Because our Mongolia was originally an independent country, we have now discussed and decided to establish a new independent state, based on our old tradition, without the interference of others in our own rights."[82] This declaration clearly indicated that the collapse of the Manchu dynasty was the main reason for the Mongols to seek independence.

During the post-1911 period of Outer Mongolian independence, many princes of Inner Mongolia sent letters to Urga expressing their willingness to join the new Mongolian state,[83] but most of them were in fact fence-sitters who turned subsequently to support the Chinese republican government. This leads to another important question: why did most of the Inner Mongolian banners never proclaim independence, or soon gave up such attempts even though they suffered more from the new Manchu policy than the banners of Outer Mongolia did?

Owen Lattimore has provided part of the answer. He has argued that: 1) the Inner Mongolian princes believed that independence under the initiation of Outer Mongolia would lead to their being over-shadowed by the princes of Outer Mongolia; 2) the Inner Mongolian princes had greater economic dependence on China than the Outer Mongolian princes; 3) the Inner Mongols felt that a republican China would be a weak state with which they could manage their relations as they pleased; 4) the Inner Mongols feared the spread of Russian influence in Outer Mongolia, and believed they would have more real freedom in nominal association with China than under a nominal independence controlled in reality from Russia.[84] Additionally, the great number of permanent Chinese settlers in Inner Mongolia, the extensive administrative control, the modern arms and railways that provided the possibility for China to suppress troubles rapidly, all made it difficult and risky for the Inner Mongols to seek independence or to unite with Outer Mongolia.

Since the Inner Mongols suffered more under the New Administration than their kinsmen in Outer Mongolia, armed opposition against the Manchu-Chinese colonization happened more extensively in Inner Mongolia than in Outer Mongolia. Nevertheless, the Inner Mongolians lacked secular or ecclesiastic leaders who could unify them for a higher political goal. This was because most of their ruling princes were already partly sinicized and some of the Inner Mongolian princes approved of the New Administration.

For instance, in his report to the emperor of March 13, 1911, Amurlinggui proposed that, in order to save Mongolia from imperialist control, loans from foreign powers other than Russia should be secured to develop industry and business, and Chinese-style administrative units should be created in that region.[85] The interests of the Inner Mongolian princes were not in accordance with those of the commoners. They were inclined to compromise and to offer support to the Chinese government.

From the development of the New Administration in both Inner Mongolia and Outer Mongolia, and the response of the Mongols to it, several conclusions can be drawn. First, while the Manchu authorities in Inner Mongolia were successful in carrying out reforms, Chinese officials in Outer Mongolia accomplished little during the period of the New Administration. Second, although some of the Manchu officials in Outer Mongolia tried to carry out the new reforms in an aggressive manner, they were not blind to the local situation, and so generally tempered their efforts. Third, the fact that the Manchu empire was in the process of collapsing proved to be as important a factor underlying the Mongolian decision to seek independence as the New Administration itself.

Although the New Administration reforms have been widely blamed for creating the Mongolian independence movement, a comparison of Inner and Outer Mongolia undermines this argument. In fact, the Inner Mongolian banners decided not to declare their political independence or to join the new Mongolian state mainly because Inner Mongolia and Outer Mongolia had gradually changed during the Manchu rule, and thus their political and economic priorities were no longer the same. Such cultural and political separation of peoples who speak essentially the same language and reside inside a single state perhaps should lead us to be more cautious when looking at the viability of separatist movements to unite peoples who are divided by international boundaries.

Notes

1. Sechin Jagchid, *Essays in Mongolian Studies* (Provo, Utah: David M. Kennedy Center for International Studies, Brigham Young University, 1988), p. 176.

2. *Daqing Dezong Jing (Guangxu) huangdi shilu* [Veritable records of Dezong, the Great Qing Emperor Jing] (hereafter *Guangxu shilu*) (reprint, Taipei: Hualian chubanshe, 1964), 476/8a-10b, 481/4b. Although Yikuang was nominally the head of the Bureau, Ronglu was indeed the leader of the new reforms until his death in April 1903.

3. *Guangxu shilu,* 562/8a-9b.

4. For a general introduction to the reforms, see Chuzo Ichiko, "Political and Institutional Reforms, 1901-11," in John K. Fairbank and Kwang-ching Liu, eds., *The Cambridge History of China,* vol. 2, *Late Ch'ing 1800-1911* (New York: Cambridge University Press, 1980), pp. 375-415. For a more detailed study of the reforms, see Merideth E. Cameron, *The Reform Movement in China* (Stanford: Stanford University Press, 1931). In the process of reform, many institutions had been entirely abolished, others had been re-organized, and some had been called into existence. Regarding institutional change, see H.S. Brunnert and V.V. Hagelstrom, *Present Day Political Organization of China* (Shanghai: Kelly and Walsh, Limited, 1912).

5. Mao Peizhi, comp., *Bianfa zhiqiang zouyi huibian* [A collection of memorials on reforms and the self-strengthening movement] (1901; reprint, Taipei: Wenhai chubanshe, n.d.), vol. 2, pp. 179-83; *Guangxu shilu,* 406/10.

6. Yigu was a Manchu of the Bordered Yellow Banner. He achieved a *jinshi* degree in 1892. When the Empress Dowager Cixi fled to Xian after the allies of eight powers entered Beijing in August 1900, Yigu followed her and was then appointed as vice-minister of the Board of War. Yigu's career came to an end in 1908. He died in 1926.

7. *Guangxu shilu,* 490/14b-15a.

8. Baoyu, comp., "Mengqi kenwu dang'an shiliao xuanbian [Selected historical archival documents on the cultivation affairs in leagues and banners] (I)," *Lishi dang'an,* no. 4 (1985), pp. 34-35.

9. Yigu, *Kenwu zouyi* [Memorials on cultivation affairs] (reprint, Taipei: Wenhai chubanshe, 1974), pp. 34-35; Anzai Kuraji, "Shinmatsu ni okeru suien no kaikon [Cultivation of Suiyuan in the late Qing period] (1)," *Mantetsu chōsa geppō* 18, no. 12 (December 1938), p. 25.

10. Yigu, *Kenwu zouyi,* p. 49.

11. Ibid., pp. 19-20.

12. Baoyu, pp. 37-39.

13. Sodubilig (Sude), "Ulaganchab. Yeke Juu-yin chigulgan-u wang güng ijagurtad-acha Igü-yin atar khagalburilakhu-yi esergüchegsen temechel-ü tukhai tursin ügülekhü ni [On the struggle of the princes and nobles of the Yekhe Juu League against Yigu's cultivation of virgin land]," (M.A. Thesis, University of Inner Mongolia, 1991), pp. 40-41, 99-101.

14. Yigu, *Kenwu zouyi,* p. 20; Anzai, "Shinmatsu ni okeru suien no kaikon (2)," *Mantetsu chōsa geppō* 19, no. 1 (January 1939): 23-24.

15. Yigu, *Kenwu zouyi,* pp. 41-43.

16. Ibid., p. 55.

17. Ibid., pp. 90, 109-10.

18. Sodubilig, "Ulaganchab. Yeke Juu-yin...," pp. 55-57; Liang Bing, *Yikezhao meng*

de tudi kaiken [Land cultivation in the Yekhe Juu League] (Höhhot: Neimenggu daxue chubanshe, 1991), pp. 63-64, Anzai; "Shinmatsu ni okeru suien no kaikon (2)," p. 29.

19. Yigu, *Kenwu zouyi*, pp. 156-60.

20. Yigu, *Kenwu zouyi*, pp. 114, 259; Yigu, *Mengken xugong* [Subsequent memorials on cultivation affairs of Mongolia] (reprint, Taipei: Wenhai chubanshe, 1974), p. 2; Anzai, "Shinmatsu ni okeru suien no kaikon (2)," pp. 38-40; Li Keren, "Qingdai wulanchabu meng kenwu chutan," [A preliminary study of the cultivation affairs in the Ula'anchab League in the Qing period], Liu Haiyuan, ed., *Neimenggu kenwu yanjiu* [Studies of the cultural affairs of Inner Mongolia], vol. 1 (Höhhot: Neimenggu renmin chubanshe, 1990), pp. 113-114. *Duguilang* literally means "circle." It was a "secret society" type of group, the members of which signed their name in a circle in order to cover who the leader was. It was a commoners' organization.

21. Sodubilig, "Ulaganchab. Yeke Juu-yin...," pp. 71-90; Anzai, "Shinmatsu ni okeru suien no kaikon (2)," pp. 40-44.

22. Yigu, *Suiyuan zouyi* [Memorials from Suiyuan] (reprint, Taipei: Wenhai chubanshe, 1974), p. 11.

23. Sodubilig, "Ulaganchab. Yeke Juu-yin...," pp. 102-104, 114-16.

24. Ibid., pp. 109-11.

25. Yigu, *Kenwu zouyi*, pp. 114, 259; *Mengken xugong*, p. 2.

26. Zhao Erxun, ed., *Qingshi gao* [Draft history of the Qing] (Beijing: Qingshi guan, 1928), 459/10b.

27. Xue Zhiping, "Shilun Qingdai Zhuosuotu meng, Zhaowuda meng de fangken [On the opening-up of land for cultivation in the Josotu and Juu Uda leagues]," Liu Haiyuan, ed., *Neimenggu kenwu yanjiu*, vol. 1, pp. 315-16.

28. Du Xinkuan, "Qingdai Zhelimu meng kenwu jiqi tudi guanxi [The cultivation affairs and land relationship of the Jirim League in the Qing period]," Liu Haiyuan, ed., *Neimenggu kenwu yanjiu*, vol. 1 (Höhhot: Neimenggu renmin chubanshe, 1990), pp. 276, 280-81.

29. A measure in Manchuria, said to be an area of land a farmer can sow in a day.

30. Tian Zhihe and Feng Xuezhong, *Minguo chunian mengqi "duli" shijian yanjiu* [A study of the independence events of the Mongolian banners in the early years of the Republican period] (Höhhot: Neimenggu renmin chubanshe, 1991), p. 107.

31. Kashiwabara Takahisa and Hamada Jun'ichi, *Mokō chishi* [A topography of Mongolia] (Tokyo: Tomiyama Bō, 1919), 1: 739-57.

32. Zhu Qiqian, ed., *Dongsansheng mengwu gongdu huibian* [A collection of official documents on the cultivation affairs of the Three Eastern Provinces] (reprint, Taipei: Wenhai chubanshe, 1985), 1/12a- 16a.

33. *Daqing Xuantong zhengji shilu* [Political records of Xuantong of the Great Qing] (hereafter *Xuantong zhengji*) (reprint, Taipei: Hualian chubanshe, 1964), 41/2a-3b.

34. *Mongolyn ard tümnii 1911 ony ündesnii erkh chölöö, tusgaar togtnolyn tölöö temtsel, barimt bichgiin emkhtgel (1900-1914)* [Mongolian people's struggle of 1911 for national freedom and independence, a collection of documents (1900-1914)] (hereafter *Barimt bichgiin emkhtgel*) (Ulaanbaatar: Ulsyn Khewleliin Gazar, 1982), pp. 32-37.

35. *Barimt bichgiin emkhtgel*, pp. 38-41.

36. *Guangxu shilu*, 568/6a.

37. L. Jamsran, *Mongolyn sergen mandaltyn ekhen (1911-1913)* [The awakening of Mongolia, the beginning of restoration, 1911-1913] (Ulaanbaatar: Soyombo Khewleliin Gazar, 1992), p. 24.

38. Robert A. Rupen, *Mongols of the Twentieth Century* (Bloomington: Indiana University, 1964), vol. 1, p. 58; Gerard M. Friters, *Outer Mongolia and its International Position* (Baltimore: The Johns Hopkins Press, 1949), pp. 49-50. The Mongolor was a project under a broader plan of S. Yu. Witte, Russian Minister of Finance, who had tried to mobilize under the Russian autocracy's aegis a considerable amount of capital of extremely varied national origin, giving its monopolistic tendencies a promising organizational unity, and interesting it in the successes of the autocracy's foreign policy in the Far East. One of Russia's major concerns in the Far East after 1895 was to prevent Japan from entering Manchuria before Russia completed the construction of the Siberian railway. See B.A. Romanov, *Russia in Manchuria,* trans. Susan Wilbur Jones (Ann Arbor, Mich.: American Council of Learned Societies, 1952; reprint, New York: Octagon Books, 1974), pp. 332-34.

39. *Barimt bichgiin emkhtgel,* p. 10.

40. Lianshun was a Manchu of the Bordered Blue Banner. He followed his elder brother, Jinshun, to many military battles in Mongolia and Xinjiang.

41. *Guangxu shilu,* 521/4b, 567/7b-8a, 572/3a, 585/6b-7a; The First Historical Archives of China (referred to below as FHAC), Junjichu lufu zouzhe [Memorial pocket copy of palace memorials of the Grand Council], minzu lei, document 2490, LTX32/7/1 (the 1st day of the 7th month of the 32nd year of the Guangxu reign).

42. Tang Zaili, "Kulun bianqing diaocha ji [Investigation of the situation in Urga]," compiled by Wu Fengpei, in *Zhonge guanxi wenti,* 1982, no.4, p. 19.

43. FHAC, Junjichu lufu zouzhe, minzu lei, document 2490, LTX32/7/1; FHAC, 1523-315, XT2/2/19; Li Tingyu, *Youmeng riji* [Diary of a journey in Mongolia], in Wu Fengpei comp., *Qingmo menggu shidi ziliao huicui* [A collection of historical and geographic material on Mongolia] (Beijing: Quanguo tushuguan wenxian suowei fuzhi zhongxin, 1990), pp. 576-77.

44. *Xuantong zhengji,* 21a-22a.

45. *Guangxu shilu,* 514/12a, 517/2b, 518/16a; FHAC, 1523-195, LTX29/4/23, LTX29/leap 5/2.

46. Sando, born in 1875 in Hangzhou of Zhejiang Province, was a Mongol of the Plain White Banner. He received good training in both military and literary skills and received the *juren* degree at the age of seventeen. Before he was appointed Amban of Urga, he held several civil and military offices in Zhejiang, Beijing, and Höhhot. After the collapse of the Qing dynasty, he continued to serve the Republican government. He died after 1940.

47. *Xuantong zhengji,* 23/54a; Sanduo (Sando), *Sanduo Kulun zougao* (Memorials of Sando from Urga], in Wu Fengpei, comp., *Qingmo menggu . . . ,* p. 259.

48. *Xuantong zhengji,* 16/14b-15b.

49. Chen Lu, *Zhishi biji* [Notes taken in the study called *Zhishi*] (1917; reprint, Taipei: Wenhai chubanshe, 1971), pp. 7, 179.

50. L. Dindub (Dendew), *Monggol-un tobchi teükhe* [A brief history of Mongolia], originally printed in Ulaanbaatar, 1934, reprinted with a title as *A Brief History of Mongolia in the Autonomous Period* as well as an introduction and index in English by Gombojab Hangin, The Mongolia Society Special Papers, Issue 6 (Bloomington, 1977), p. 9: *Barimt bichgiin emkhtgel,* p. 165.

51. *Sanduo Kulun zougao,* pp. 268-69.

52. Ibid., pp. 285-97.

53. Ibid., pp. 303-304.

54. FHAC, 1523-160, XT2/6/29. We do not know exactly what newspapers were available. Nevertheless, at that time, a Mongolian-language weekly named *Monggol-un Sonin Bichig* (Mongolian Newspaper) published in Harbin by the Russian administration of the Chinese Eastern Railroad was quite popular with readers in Outer Mongolia. See *Information Mongolia*, comp. and ed. Academy of Sciences MPR (New York: Pergamon Press, 1990), p. 393. Chinese newspapers and official announcements might have also been available in these reading places.

55. Tang Zaili (1880-1964) was born in Shanghai. At the age of twenty-one, he studied artillery in Japan. After returning to China, Tang held a military office in Zhili Province, and was then appointed to train the new army in Urga. He later held several offices in the Republican government.

56. *Sanduo Kulun zougao*, pp. 373-376; *Xuantong zhengji*, 48/24.

57. *Xuantong zhengji*, 56/17.

58. Ibid., 48/26a.

59. FHAC, 7-46 (2), XT3/4/27.

60. Ibid., 1523-183, XT2/6/29; *Sanduo Kulun zougao*, pp. 397-400.

61. *Xuantong zhengji*, 58/2b.

62. FHAC, 1523-183, XT3/l/24; *Sanduo Kulun zougao*, pp. 349-50, 365-69.

63. *Xuantong zhengji*, 29/6a-8b.

64. On May 26, 1904, the office of the Assistant Amban of Kobdo (*Kebuduo bangban dachen*) was ordered to move to Sira Süme (*Chenghua Si*) to take charge of the affairs of the Altai region, and was retitled as Amban of Kobdo, even though the office was no longer located in the city of Kobdo. See *Guangxu shilu*, 529/9b.

65. FHAC, 1509-155, XT2/8/12.

66. Ibid., 1523-181, XT2/12/3.

67. Dindub, *Monggol-un tobchi teükhe*, pp. 9-10; *Barimt bichgiin emkhtgel*, pp. 165-66.

68. Jagchid, *Essays in Mongolian Studies*, p. 191. For more details on the activities of these rebellious leaders, see G. Navaangnamjil, "A Brief Biography of the Determined Hero Togtokh," in Urgunge Onon, ed. and trans., *Mongolian Heroes of the Twentieth Century* (New York: AMS press, 1976), pp. 43-76; Michael Underdown, "Banditry and Revolutionary Movements in Late 19th and Early 20th Century Mongolia," *Mongolian Studies*, vol. 6 (1980), pp. 111-112; *Menggu zu tongshi* [Complete history of the Mongolian nation] (Beijing: Minzu chubanshe, 1991), 2: 1072-82.

69. Yigu, *Kenwu zouyi*, p. 173; Zhu Qiqian, *Dongsansheng mengwu gongdu huibian*, 1/16a.

70. *Barimt bichgiin emkhtgel*, pp. 63-66.

71. Ibid., p. 71.

72. Ibid., p. 95.

73. Tang Zaili, "Kulun bianqing diaocha ji," p. 18.

74. Tang Zaili and Tang Zaizhang, *Menggu fengyun lu* [Record of the drastic change in Mongolia] (Nanchang, 1912), p. 2a; Chen Lu, *Zhishi biji*, p. 179.

75. Chen Lu, *Zhishi biji*, pp. 179-180, 182-183; *Xuantong zhengji*, 65/10a.

76. *Barimt bichgiin emkhtgel*, pp. 87-89.

77. According to a statistic published in 1919, there were roughly 1,500 *qing* (i.e., 22,695 acres) of land under cultivation by about 150 Chinese households (including 47 households engaged in trade) in the Setsen and Tüshiyetü Khan aimags. See *Mengzang*

Yuan diaocha waimeng tongji biao [Statistical tables of investigations in Outer Mongolia compiled by the Board of Mongolian and Tibetan Affairs], Beijing, 1919, pp. 5-7.

78. According to the data Maiskii collected during his expedition of 1918, there were about 100,000 Chinese in Outer Mongolia. They were traders (75 percent), artisans and workers (15 percent), farmers (5 percent), and then bureaucrats and professionals (5 percent). See I.M. Maiskii, *Sovremennaia Mongoliia* [Contemporary Mongolia] (Irkutsk, 1921), pp. 70-72; I.M. Maiskii, *Mongoliia nakanune revoliutsii* [Mongolia on the eve of the revolution] (Moscow: Izdatel'stvo Vostochnoi Literatury, 1959), pp. 84-86.

79. Tang Zaili, "Kulun bianqing diaocha ji," p. 17.

80. FHAC, 1509-155, XT2/8/12.

81. Owen Lattimore and Fujiko Isono, *The Diluv Khutagt: Memoirs and Autobiography of a Mongol Buddhist Reincarnation in Religion and Revolution* (Wiesbaden: Otto Harrassowitz, 1982), pp. 67-68.

82. For the Mongolian document in Uighur script, see Urgunge Onon and Derrick Pritchatt, *Asia's First Modern Revolution: Mongolia Proclaims its Independence in 1911* (New York: E.J. Brill, 1989), pp. 127-30. This document is also collected in *Barimt bichgiin emkhtgel*, pp. 110-11.

83. It was said that among the forty-nine banners of the six Inner Mongolian leagues, thirty-five banners had sent letters to express their submission to the new Mongolian state. For a list of the banners see *Bügd nairamdakh Mongol ard ulsyn tüükh* [History of the Mongolian People's Republic] (Ulaanbaatar: Ulsyn Khewleliin Khereg Erkhlekh Khoroo, 1968), 2: 450. Additionally, the banners of Bargu, Chakhar and western Tümed, the banners of Köke Nuur and Chinese Turkestan had also done so. See Onon and Pritchett, *Asia's First Modern Revolution: Mongolia Proclaims its Independence in 1911*, p. 23.

84. Owen Lattimore, *The Mongols of Manchuria* (New York: The John Day Company, 1934), p. 18.

85. FHAC, Junjichu lufu zouzhe, minzu lei, document 2526, XT3/2/13.

Russian Merchants in Mongolia:
The 1910 Moscow Trade Expedition

Elizabeth Endicott

In the summer of 1910, six Russian merchants from Moscow, accompanied by twelve Cossacks, a few interpreters, and six other individuals with various scholarly or practical backgrounds in Mongolian affairs, travelled throughout Mongolia investigating the then current state of Russo-Mongolian trade and its future prospects. This merchant delegation, representing seventy-three Moscow firms that had underwritten the expedition's costs, was clearly expansionist-minded. The Russian merchants were in search of new markets to which they might export their textiles and other manufactured products, and they were evaluating Mongolia as a source of unprocessed raw materials (woolens, hides, furs) which were being imported back to Russia.

In 1912, the printing house of the main sponsor and organizer of the expedition, P.P. Riabushinskii, published a volume entitled *The Moscow Trade Expedition to Mongolia*,[1] a collection of essays written by six of the expedition's participants. This volume provides a wealth of information on trade routes, trading centers, the daily lives of the Mongols themselves, and the perceived threat to Russian interests posed by Chinese mercantile competition.

The Moscow Trade Expedition (MTE) report gives the reader a vivid, anecdote-filled account of Mongolia in its final years before autonomy (1911-19) and revolution (1921) reordered its social, political, and economic landscapes; the MTE report combines aspects of a straightforward business report with colorful flashes of narrative prose more akin to the Reverend James Gilmour's classic *Among the Mongols* (composed in the 1870s) and George N. Roerich's *Trails to Inmost Asia* (1931).[2] As a historical source, therefore, this largely untapped document deserves inclusion in the corpus of Western travel literature on Mongolia in the nineteenth and twentieth centuries.

Several chapters provide statistics on Mongolian imports and exports. Although these statistics should be treated with caution, especially given the immense distances between frontier customs posts on the Russian-Mongolian border and the ease with which traders could evade detection, they do provide compelling evidence, however rough, that Russian commerce with Mongolia was in decline, the victim of more aggressive Chinese mercantile practices.

The MTE report raises many historical questions. Perhaps the most important question is whether, had the Qing Dynasty not abdicated in 1912, and had the steady trend toward Chinese domination of trade in Outer Mongolia continued, would Outer Mongolia have fallen into the Russian sphere of influence? This essay will suggest that the removal of the Qing administrative-military presence, as personified in the Manchu amban in Urga and the Manchu garrison forces, gave Russian merchants an unprecedented opportunity to expand their influence in Outer Mongolia.

The flowering of Russian merchant trade, as we now know, was short-lived. The Mongolian Revolution of 1921 and subsequent events shut Outer Mongolia off from free trade, foreign investment, and other market forces. Mongolia would have to wait another seventy years for private enterprise to displace the Soviet-installed planned economy. Thus, the MTE report at times suggests linkages between the pre-revolutionary decades and the immediate post-socialist decade of the 1990s, as a new wave of foreign investors now explores possibilities for profit in Mongolia.

The Russo-Chinese Commercial Rivalry in Mongolia

The impetus behind organizing a trade expedition to Outer Mongolia in 1910 was fear of the growing Chinese commercial influence in Mongolia. In 1908 a memorandum written by a long-time Mongolia "hand," Colonel V.L. Popov, was circulated among Moscow's merchants.[3] In the memorandum, Popov outlined the displacement of Russian traders in Mongolia by the Chinese, and he urged an on-site investigation into the situation.

In April of 1910, P.P. Riabushinskii, a prominent Old Believer and Moscow merchant, convened a conference of representatives from seventy-three of Moscow's industrial-commercial firms and banks. The conference resolved to dispatch an expedition to Mongolia that same summer to survey travel routes, trade centers, the nature of imports and exports between Mongolia and Russia, the way of life and needs of the Mongolian population, and, in particular, the situation in the northern and northwestern Mongolian towns of Urga, Uliastai, and Kobdo. Special focus was to be put on the inroads allegedly being made by Chinese merchants in the northwest. On June 1, the expedition set out from Kiakhta for Mongolia.

The report resulting from the expedition's three-month-long trip expresses great concern over the decline in Russian trade with Mongolia and the concurrent successes of Chinese merchants. To the dismay of the expedition observers, the area of northern and western Mongolia, defined roughly as the region from Chuguchak[4] to Urga, a region previously considered safely within the Russian zone of mercantile influence, was being overrun by Chinese competitors:

> Hundreds of Chinese merchants have surged into this area. Well organized and united, making use of the support of the local authorities and relying on firmly established credit, the Chinese little by little have managed to concentrate in their hands all trade of the region, gradually shoving the Russians into the background.[5]

Chinese merchants are depicted as selling (in addition to Chinese goods) English, American, and German wares to the Mongols, while Russian traders, disorganized and dispersed, were reduced to buying up Mongolian raw materials and shipping them back to Russia. Citing statistics from customs stations and from foreign trade records, the report outlines a fairly steady decline in Russian exports to Mongolia between 1899 and 1909.

Different customs-house districts along Mongolia's western and northern border with Russia were compared, and the most precipitous decline in Russian exports to Mongolia was noted in the Kiakhta district. Other districts showing decline included Bakhta, Zaisan, and Kosh-Agach. The one area relatively safe from Chinese intrusion was Chuguchak and the Black Irtysh River region, undoubtedly owing to its immense distance from China.

Among the major Russian exports to Mongolia in the early twentieth century, cotton textiles were first and foremost. Yet, between 1899 and 1909, the volume of such exports declined dramatically; in the Kiakhta customs district, for instance, export of cotton textiles declined by more than 50 percent. The MTE report blamed this decline upon "[t]he inundation of the Urga region by foreign cotton textiles brought by Chinese traders."[6]

After cotton textiles, the major Russian exports to Mongolia consisted of iron and steel, followed by processed hides, lumber, and wood products. Each of these export categories experienced decline in the first decade of the twentieth century. Only exports of sugar, flour, and grains experienced various degrees of increase during this period.

Meanwhile, imports from Mongolia into Russia were on the increase. Chinese goods—mainly tea, cotton, and silk fabrics—vastly outnumbered purely Mongolian goods imported into Russia across the Russo-Mongolian border. Yet, even excluding Chinese items, the value of imported Mongolian raw and semi-processed materials and livestock more than doubled between 1903 and 1909. These imports into Russia consisted largely of unprocessed hides, undyed wool and furs, horsehair, unprocessed lumber, felt, cattle, horses, sheep, and goats. (Remarkably, the nature of Mongolian exports abroad today is much the same, consisting mostly of animal-origin raw materials. The only major difference between 1910 and 1993 is that copper in 1993 headed the list of exports.[7])

It disturbed the Moscow Trade Expedition that Russian traders in Urga were focusing more and more on the purchase of Mongolian raw materials, while cutting back on the distribution of Russian goods. Some Russian traders had even liquidated their businesses and departed Mongolia. In the eyes of the Moscow merchants, the rapid increase in the flow of Mongolian raw materials through Kalgan to China and to other foreign markets also posed a threat to Russia's overall trading position with Mongolia. While Russia's trade relations with western Mongolia (Chuguchak and the Black Irtysh region) remained stable, the MTE report stressed that the northern Mongolian market "is slipping out of our hands."[8]

Many of the 1912 report's conclusions were summarized earlier in Riabushinskii's newspaper, *Utro Rossii.* For example, an October 14, 1910 article in *Utro Rossii* reported the conclusions drawn by the returned expedition: that the Russian-Mongolian border city of Kiakhta was dying, that the caravan sheds there were empty, that homes were boarded up, and that there was little traffic in the streets. In Urga, the article continues, the branch of the Russo-Chinese bank had already been closed, since there was evidently little for it to do there. Urga itself was described in this news report as having turned almost overnight from a Russian-Mongolian city into a Chinese city.

A December 15, 1910 article in the same newspaper reported that a large meeting of industrialists, bankers, professors, and a representative from the Russian Ministry of Finance met at Riabushinskii's Moscow apartment to discuss how to reverse this trend. The expedition members present complained that for every Russian firm in Mongolia, there were ten Chinese firms. The main problems to be surmounted were summarized as follows: the lack of support from local (i.e., Qing) officials in Mongolia, problems of establishing credit, and disorganization.

The 1910 trade expedition report gives ample evidence of this last problem (i.e., the widespread disorganization seen in Russian companies). For example, upon their arrival in Urga in June 1910, the expedition members were appalled to find that they were not even greeted in a formal reception at the Russian consulate. To quote the report's sarcastic words: "The consul was afraid to ruin his dignity as an excellency by a personal meeting with the expedition."[9] The resident Russian merchant community also "remained aloof from the expedition."[10]

When, finally, a social gathering was arranged, the resident Russian merchants "spoke at length, but mostly complained about the government, the consulate, and industry. The expedition did not hear any broad opinions or generalized conclusions on the history and nature of trade."[11] The expedition members were clearly disgusted by the pettiness and limited hospitality of the Russian merchants whom they encountered in Urga.

By contrast, according to the MTE report: "The Chinese merchants, at the first hint of a desire to have a joint talk, organized the matter brilliantly."[12] Invited over to the Maimaicheng (lit. "trade city"), the expedition members were cordially entertained over lunch, and hosts and guests exchanged opinions on trade-related matters. The Chinese invited the expedition to view their warehouses and shops and were apparently very open in their discussion of how Chinese firms operated in Mongolia. The Chinese merchants were clearly well organized and very well-informed, a poignant contrast to the Russian merchants in Urga.

The expedition's assessment of the overall Russian position in Urga was devastating:

> After forty years of the Russian consulate's existence, under strikingly favorable circumstances, so little has been accomplished by us that we have to be astounded by our inertia and by the neglect that the Russian consulate impresses upon a newcomer. [The] permanent Russian inhabitants of Urga number 600. Such a large Russian colony has claimed nothing for itself. Scattered, uncoordinated, competing among themselves for inconsequential gains, devoid of civic ideals and missions, the Russian colony lives a miserable life, not having established during its multi-year

existence a predominant, influential position, nor even any sort of noticeable, distinctive character.[13]

This indictment applied to all Russians in Urga, not only to the resident Russian merchant community.

Tuva and Geo-Political Considerations

While Uriankhai (later called Tuva) was not an area of primary focus for the Moscow Trade Expedition, the report nonetheless devoted a chapter to the question of navigation along the upper reaches of the Yenisei River, and it called for future dredging of the river channel so that a portion of Mongolian cargo could proceed from Kobdo and Uliastai by the Yenisei up to Minusinsk and Krasnoyarsk. The region of Uriankhai seemed fairly protected from Chinese mercantile expansion in 1910, with both exports from Russia and imports from the region to Russia increasing in the early twentieth century.

The MTE report expressed some rather singular ideas, however, concerning Uriankhai's ethnic composition and political identity; these ideas were destined to bear fruit only during the Soviet period of Russian expansion:[14]

> The Uriyangkhai region . . . is no longer Mongolia. The Uriyangkhai do not belong to the Mongolian tribes. Side-by-side with the indigenous population there are several Russian settlements and individual holdings. The Uriyangkhai region represents disputed territory, and its position remains uncertain. The head of the Moscow Trade Expedition, Colonel V.L. Popov, verified that the Chinese frontier goes along the Tannu-Ola range, where Chinese boundary markers also extend. Nonetheless, the Chinese collect taxes from the Uriyangkhai, and the latter believe that they are subject to China. Russian boundary markers go along the Sayan range. There are many grounds for considering the Uriyangkhai region as rightfully belonging to Russia, which only on account of some strange misunderstanding has not up to now established its actual dominion here. Little by little the region is being colonized by Russian settlers, and it must be expected that Russia finally will claim its rights to it.[15]

This statement was a harbinger of Uriankhai's disappearance as an independent entity in 1944, when the Soviet Union annexed outright the Tuvan People's Republic, which had existed as a supposedly independent polity from 1924-44. It reflects striking, and perhaps deliberate, ignorance of the fact that the Tuvinian or Uriankhai people were at least part Mongolian in ethnic composition, and socially and culturally very much a part of a greater Mongolia.

In 1929, the German scholar Otto Mänchen-Helfen formed a different opinion of Uriankhai's place in the Mongol world. After travelling there he wrote:

For centuries Tuva was Mongolian territory; the Tuvans never had the thought of separating from Mongolia. The two countries have the same economic systems and the same religion. The administrative language of Tuva was and is Mongolian. It is understandable, therefore, that the Tuvans, after the collapse of foreign rule—Chinese and later Czarist—viewed themselves as belonging to Mongolia, and the Mongols regarded Tuva as a Mongolian province.[16]

Mänchen-Helfen also wrote that with the retreat of Tsarist troops from Uriankhai after the onset of the 1917 Revolution, the people burned down Russian settlers' homes, emptied the merchants' warehouses, and murdered Russian citizens.

The MTE report, while arguing in favor of Russia's right to Uriankhai, nonetheless provides evidence that Uriankhai's territory constituted an unclaimed pocket of land north of Chinese boundary-markers (in the Tannu Ola mountains) and south of Russian boundary markers (in the Sayan range). The British geographer, Douglas Carruthers, who travelled extensively in Uriankhai in 1910-11, also viewed the region as a sort of no-man's land, and noted its incongruous political identity: "I realized that this region, although within the limits of the Chinese Empire, is essentially Siberian in character. . . . Physically, politically, and economically the [Upper Yenisei] basin should belong to Russia, and not to Mongolia. . . ."[17] Nominally, however, Uriankhai had been under the Qing administration, which was based in Uliastai, since the mid-eighteenth century.[18]

Clearly, the Moscow Trade Expedition had geopolitical goals in addition to economic ones. This is evidenced not only by the discussion of Uriankhai as rightfully belonging to Russia, but also by the report's statements about the importance of trade in Mongolia itself:

> Mongolia has significance not only as a market for the products of Russian industry and as a supplier to us of its raw materials; we also have political tasks here. The reinforcement of our trade position in Mongolia undoubtedly will also promote the strengthening of our political influence in this region.[19]

The report calls for "serious support" from the Tsarist government and a strong initiative from Russia's commercial-industrial class to expand trade and political influence in Mongolia. The December 15, 1910 issue of *Utro Rossii* stresses that the dramatic decline in Russian trade in Mongolia was not just an economic problem, but also a problem of national concern. Foreign (i.e., Chinese) "penetration" of Mongolia, it was argued, could lead to "penetration" of Siberia, which would have grave consequences.

Clearly, the Moscow industrialists were attempting to push the Tsarist government into a more activist role in supporting Russian trade interests in Mongolia, by pointing out the geopolitical ramifications to the northward expansion of Chinese commerce. The Moscow merchants were aware of the political turmoil in China and predicted with some accuracy and great optimism the effects of that turmoil on Mongolia's future:

> It is difficult, of course, to foresee the results of the civil strife occurring in China, but one result it is sure to have is the principle of autonomy [for Mongolia] within the future [Chinese] imperial system. The autonomy of Mongolia would without question be in the interests of Russia. Autonomy would weaken the ties of Mongolia to central China. The Mongolian princes, having received great freedom of action, undoubtedly would direct their efforts toward liberating themselves and their country from economic bondage to the Chinese. Obstacles to the intrusion of the Chinese would be set up; the privileged position of Chinese traders would be weakened; and, of course, through this, more favorable conditions for the strengthening of Russian trade in Mongolia would arise. We simply have to take advantage of this favorable state of affairs. . . .[20]

But, instead of China maintaining its "imperial system," a Chinese republic was declared. While Mongolia did enjoy autonomy briefly (1911-19), one type of "economic bondage" to Chinese merchants was replaced by a different form of dependency—in the name of revolution and obedience to Soviet authority—from the 1921 Soviet-sponsored Mongolian revolution until very recently.

Mongolian Attitudes Towards Trade

Mongolian cultural attitudes toward foreign trade have taken form over many centuries. Previous to Qing dynasty political control of Mongolia, the Mongols had shown great talent at exploiting other peoples' resources, most notably through foreign conquest, but also through money-lending practices and long-distance trade partnerships (a Mongolian institution known as *ortogh*) of the Mongolian empire period (thirteenth and fourteenth centuries).[21] In the two centuries following the Dolonnuur Convention of 1691, which signaled Khalkha Mongolian submission to Qing rule, wave after wave of Chinese merchants reached Mongolia, some operating legally, others evading Qing restrictions on the numbers and locations of merchants in Mongolia. For a vivid description of the excesses of Chinese merchants and money-lenders in Mongolia, one need only skim through M. Sanjdorj's well-documented *Manchu Chinese Colonial Rule in Northern Mongolia*: there are abundant examples of shoddy goods from China sold at inflated prices to the Mongols, of Chinese traders taking back to China huge herds of livestock confiscated from the Mongols for unpaid debts, and so on.[22]

Given this historical context, it is not surprising to find the MTE report portraying the Mongols as "pathetic herdsmen, exploited by Chinese merchants and officials."[23] Chinese merchants, however, were not the only group to direct exploitative practices at the Mongols. The MTE report suggests that Russian merchants, while not being able to rely upon a governmental strong arm to press their claims, were nonetheless adept at taking advantage of the Mongols.

For example, the MTE report provides an interesting anecdote concerning the Mongols' perception of Urga's resident Russian merchants. Soon after arriving in Urga in June 1910, members of the expedition received an invitation to visit the palace of the Bogda Gegen, the patriarch of the Northern Mongolian Buddhist establishment. With two wagonloads of goods, some intended to be sold and some intended as gifts, the expedition merchants arrived at the palace. It was a pleasant visit, and the Russian merchants spent an afternoon giving an impromptu concert of Russian folk and religious music, as well as displaying their wares.

When the Bogda Gegen selected the items that he desired to purchase, the expedition members, after a brief conference, decided to offer those items to the Bogda Gegen as a gift "from Moscow." Then, the Bogda Gegen, not desiring to be in their debt, placed an order for various goods from Moscow, and paid over 1,000 roubles in advance. In the words of the MTE report: "[W]e had the opportunity to observe personally that our Urga merchants skillfully and unceremoniously exploited the Bogda Gegen, selling him all sorts of rubbish at prices more than ten times its value."[24]

A few days after their visit, the expedition was called upon by the Bogda Gegen's attendants, requesting that several more orders be placed for goods from Moscow. The attendants quoted the Bogda Gegen as saying: "These are genuine Russian merchants, not exploiters. We can buy from these."[25]

It occurred to some members of the expedition that, using the patronage of the Bogda Gegen, they could open a special avenue of trade with Urga's monastic and princely population, and even expand this special relationship throughout Mongolia. "But we came not to do business, but to do research," the report quickly adds.[26] In any case, the Moscow Trade Expedition had already met with the open hostility of the resident Russian merchants of Urga, who apparently feared just such an intrusion upon their turf.

Noticeable by its absence in the MTE report is virtually any mention of Mongolian traders. In the report's discussion of nineteenth-century trade agreements between Russia and China, references to "unregulated and duty-free trade for traders of both nations" apply only to Chinese and Russian traders.[27] There were indeed very few Mongolian traders, since Qing registration laws, pinning Mongol households down to their home banner territory and forbidding long-distance travel, made commerce on an international scale a virtual impossibility for Mongols.[28] The exception was a small-scale, illegal trade carried on by some Khalkhas with Uriankhai. There were also Mongols who carried on trade in the employ of Chinese shops, rather than on independent terms.[29]

Comparisons: 1910 and the 1990s

"The trade and economic relations between Mongolia and Russia are experiencing hardships. Every passing year witnesses a decrease in the volume of bilateral trade turnover, the credit cooperation has shrunk to its minimum, and it is becoming increasingly difficult to maintain regular economic contacts."[30] This is not a statement from the 1910 Moscow Trade Expedition, although it would have fit neatly into the MTE report. Rather, it is a statement by Mongolia's then Vice Minister of Trade and Industry, Ts. Yondon, as reported in the October 14, 1994 issue of *The Mongol Messenger.*

Whereas in 1994 decreasing trade between Mongolia and Russia was viewed within the larger perspective of difficulties both countries face in the transition to a market economy, in 1910 the decreasing volume of Russo-Mongolian trade was viewed—from the Russian perspective at least—as a symptom of Chinese mercantile predominance throughout Mongolia. Today, China plays a significant role in the Mongolian economy as exporter of cheap goods to Mongolia and as controller of Mongolia's access to foreign markets, but clearly that role is not comparable to China's predominant status in Mongolia in 1910.

As the evidence in this essay strongly suggests, without the collapse of the Qing Dynasty and the withdrawal of the Qing protective military-administrative presence in Outer Mongolia, Chinese merchants would certainly have continued to dominate the Mongolian market at the expense of the Russians. One result of this economic domination would have been a stronger political barrier to Russian, and later Soviet, political expansion into Mongolia. As it turned out, after 1912 the Russians received a windfall opportunity that the MTE report could not have possibly predicted or foreseen.

Notes

1. *Moskovskaia Torgovaia Ekspeditsiia v Mongoliiu* (Moscow: Publishing House of P.P. Riabushinskii, 1912). Hereafter, to be cited as MTE. On the history of Russian expeditions to Mongolia in the nineteenth and early twentieth centuries, see E.V. Boikova, "Rossiiskie puteshestvenniki o Russkikh v Mongolii v nachale XX veka," in E. V. Boikova, ed., *Vladimirtsovskie chteniia* (Moscow: Institut vostokovedeniia RAN, 1995), pp. 34-40; and E. V. Boikova, "Creation of Database on Russian Expeditions to Mongolia at the End of the XIX—in the Beginning of the XX Century," unpublished paper presented at the Seventh International Congress of Mongolists, Ulaanbaatar, August, 1997.

2. *Among the Mongols* (London: The Religious Tract Society, n.d.); *Trails to Inmost Asia* (New Haven: Yale University Press, 1931). One of the best known nineteenth-century Russian travellers to Mongolia was Aleksei M. Pozdneev. In English translation, see *Religion and Ritual in Society: Lamaist Buddhism in Late 19th-Century Mongolia*, ed. by John R. Krueger, trans. from the Russian by Alo Raun and Linda Raun (Bloomington: The Mongolia Society, 1978); and *Mongolia and the Mongols*, ed. by John R. Krueger and Fred Adelman, trans. from the Russian by John Roger Shaw and Dale Plank (Bloomington: Indiana University, Uralic and Altaic Series Vol. 61, 1971).

3. MTE, p. 21.

4. Chuguchak, or Tacheng, is a border city in Xinjiang, China.

5. MTE, p. 2.

6. Ibid., p. 7.

7. All data on Mongolian-Russian trade is from MTE, chapter one, unless otherwise

noted. For a discussion of 1993 exports from Mongolia abroad, see *The Mongol Messenger* 1:131 (Jan. 4, 1994), p.2.

8. MTE, p. 17.

9. Ibid., p. 42.

10. Ibid.

11. Ibid., p. 43.

12. Ibid.

13. Ibid., p. 41.

14. Ibid., pp. 17-18.

15. Ibid.

16. Otto Mänchen-Helfen, *Journey to Tuva. An Eye-Witness Account of Tannu-Tuva in 1929*, trans. from the German by Alan Leighton (Los Angeles: University of Southern California, Ethnographics Press, 1992; originally published in German in 1931), p. 22.

17. Douglas Carruthers, *Unknown Mongolia. A Record of Travel and Exploration in North-West Mongolia and Dzungaria* (New Delhi: Asian Educational Services, 1994 reprint of the 1913 London ed.), vol. 1, p. 97.

18. For historical background on Tuva, see "Tuva" by Michael Underdown, in John R. Krueger, ed., *Tuvan Manual. Area Handbook, Grammar, Reader, Glossary, Bibliography* (Bloomington: Indiana University, Uralic and Altaic series Vol. 126, 1977), pp. 3-5; on the ethnic origins of the Tuvinian people, see Sevyan Vainshtein, *Nomads of South Siberia. The Pastoral Economies of Tuva*, trans. from the Russian by Michael Colenso (New York: Cambridge University Press, 1980), p.43.

19. MTE, p. 23.

20. Ibid., p. 24.

21. The most comprehensive English-language treatments of the *ortogh* are: Thomas T. Allsen, "Mongolian Princes and Their Merchant Partners, 1200-1260," *Asia Major*, 3rd series, 2:2 (1989), pp. 83-126; and Elizabeth Endicott-West, "Merchant Associations in Yüan China: The Ortoɣ," *Asia Major*, 3rd series, 2:2 (1989), pp. 127-54.

22. M. Sanjdorj, *Manchu Chinese Colonial Rule in Northern Mongolia*, trans. from the Mongolian by Urgunge Onon (New York: St. Martin's Press, 1980). See also G.S. Gorokhova, *Ocherki po istorii Mongolii v epokhu man'chzhurskogo gospodstva* (Moscow: "Nauka," 1980), pp. 81-88.

23. MTE, p. 1.

24. Ibid., p. 45.

25. Ibid., p. 46.

26. Ibid.

27. Ibid., p. 20.

28. The legacy of Chinese and Russian abuses in this period can still be seen today. Dr. Alicia Campi, when discussing the obstacles to foreign-imposed "cures" for the ailing economy, concluded that "trade over the centuries has come to be viewed by Mongols as not a valid way to build wealth, but as the instrument for exploitation." The large foreign debt, a legacy of Soviet economic assistance, coupled with the Mongols' apprehensions over China's intentions (i.e., fear that increased trade might promote new forms of Chinese political domination over Mongolia) preclude a rapid change in the Mongols' long-standing negative attitudes toward trade. *The Mongol Messenger* 42:172 (Oct. 21, 1994), p. 3.

29. See Sanjdorj, *Manchu Chinese Colonial Rule*, pp. 101-2.

30. *The Mongol Messenger* 41:171 (Oct. 14, 1994), p. 2.

Russian Diplomats and Mongol Independence, 1911-1915

Nakami Tatsuo

In the early twentieth century, land empires such as Ottoman Turkey, Romanov Russia, Habsburg Austria, and Qing China dominated much of the earth. After the collapse of these empires, however, several new nation-states were born within the former borders of each empire. Many of today's ethnic conflicts and border disputes originate from the dissolution of these empires. In this respect, Qing China does not follow the pattern set by the other empires. The successors to the Qing, including the Republic of China and the People's Republic of China, largely succeeded in their attempts to retake control over Qing China's ethnic groups and border areas. The major exception were the Mongols in Outer Mongolia. Why was it that only the Mongols could break away from the "Middle Kingdom"? The beginning point for this investigation will be the events surrounding the 1911 Mongol declaration of independence.[1]

European and American scholars have traditionally maintained that the 1911 Mongol declaration of independence was initiated and sponsored by Imperial Russia.[2] Some accounts have even suggested that the Russians forced the Mongols to declare their independence; this view is still held by scholars from the PRC and Taiwan.[3] In the Mongolian People's Republic (MPR), the communist regime traditionally deemphasized the importance of the 1911 declaration, pointing instead to Mongolia's "Socialist Revolution" of 1921.[4] However, since the beginning of Mongolia's era of "democratization" in the early 1990s, Mongolian scholars have begun to reevaluate this period and have initiated new studies on the 1911 declaration of independence and the formation of the Bogda Khagan regime.[5]

Formerly, students of Mongolia were restricted to a limited number of sources. For example, many American, European, and Russian scholars based their accounts of Mongolia on Russian secondary materials, and in so doing overlooked important first-hand literature in the Mongolian, Chinese, and Japanese languages. Meanwhile, the preconceptions of PRC and Taiwanese researchers that Mongol independence was merely a Russian plot, led them to overlook important documentary evidence to the contrary. Finally, even Mongolian scholars were hampered by the fact that archival documents were difficult to obtain.

This situation began to change during the mid-1980s, as new archival sources became available. This essay attempts to take advantage of this new era of openness, and will present recently released documentary evidence from archives in Taiwan, the PRC, Mongolia, and Russia. The National Central Historical Archives in Ulaanbaatar, in particular, have provided a wealth of formerly unavailable information on the 1911 declaration of independence.[6]

A Secret Letter, a Russian Consul, and the Mongol Delegation

The Manchu-Qing dynasty established political and military dominance over the Mongols during the seventeenth and eighteenth centuries. This relationship conformed to the typical tributary system: the relationship of the lord—the Qing emperor—to his vassals—the Mongols. This tributary policy allowed the Mongols to retain an independent social structure, so long as they respected the Qing Emperor and the authority of the central government.

During the centuries that followed the founding of the Qing dynasty, the traditional Mongolian nomadic society declined. This was less the result of the Qing government, than the Han Chinese merchants, who gradually established intricate commercial networks that covered most of the Mongolian plateau.[7] As a result of this development, Mongol nobles and commoners became ever more subordinate to the Han merchants. In addition, the number of Han immigrants cultivating Mongol land was also increasing; this trend was most noticeable in the eastern regions of Inner Mongolia.

Since the mid-nineteenth century, the Qing dynasty had been threatened by two new developments: the first was external—the foreign encroachment by imperialist powers—while the second was internal—the increasing threat of Han Chinese movements against the Manchu dynasty. In 1906, the Qing government adopted bureaucratic reforms—the so-called New Admini-stration reforms discussed at length in an earlier essay—aimed at countering these two trends: in addition to increasing central control over Mongolia to oppose foreign imperialism, increased immigration to Mongol lands was intended to solve the Han Chinese overpopulation.

The enforcement of these new policies was given to a new Qing Resident Minister (*Kulun banshi dachen* or Amban), named Sandowa, who arrived in Urga on March 11, 1910. Before Sandowa's arrival, the political leaders of Khalkha Mongolia had hoped they would be able to convince the Qing government not to adopt these reforms in Mongolia, but with Sandowa's appearance all such negotiations proved to be fruitless.

In fact, one of Sandowa's actions was to demand that the Jebtsundamba Khutugtu, one of the so-called Living Buddhas and therefore an important spiritual symbol to the Mongols in Khalkha, dismiss an anti-reform official—named Badmadorji—from his Secretariat General. This event helped to solidify Mongol resentment against the reforms, and Badmadorji evidently decided at this juncture to flee Mongolia and complain of China's mistreatment to the more sympathetic Russian government.[8]

The Chinese reforms directly threatened Mongolia, and prompted the Mongols to reconsider their long-time relationship with the Qing dynasty. Mongol leaders began to search for alternatives to protect the traditional Mongol social structure, and in July 1911 the political leaders of Khalkha Mongolia decided to send a secret delegation to Russia to ask for support. Later, on December 1, 1911, these Mongol leaders—in the midst of the chaos of the Chinese revolution—declared independence. They quickly organized an independent government, which was called the Bogda Khagan's government. Thus, the Mongols attempted to separate from the "Middle Kingdom."[9]

By far the most difficult aspect of studying the political process leading to Mongolian independence is to trace the ideas and activities of the small group of Khalkha Mongol princes and Buddhist priests who authorized the Mongol delegation to Russia. Since their anti-Qing activities were dangerous, especially if they came to the attention of Qing officials in Urga, this group was secretly organized and did not keep records of its meetings. Although the Central Historical Archives in Ulaanbaatar are rich in materials on the Mongol "nationalist" movement, they offer little information about this group. About the only document still available that reflects on this group's actions was a secret letter addressed to the Russian Tsar, which was carried to St. Petersburg by the Mongol delegates.

Mongol secondary sources include some valuable information on this period of Mongol history. For example, Magsurjab's *Monggol ulus-un sin-e teüke* [A New History of Mongolia] quotes many official documents of that time period that were relevant to the Bogda Khagan.[10] Even Magsurjab was forced to simplify his description of the origins of the Mongol declaration of independence, however, because of limited primary sources. Finally, there are a couple of Mongol reminiscences that provide useful background information to these events.[11]

While the Mongol sources describing the 1911 delegation are scarce, they vastly outnumber the Chinese sources; it is clear that word of the Mongolian mission's appearance in St. Petersburg caught the Qing officials in Urga completely by surprise. Although Qing documents housed in both Beijing and Taipei confirm that Mongol leaders had presented petitions opposing the Qing government's "new policy," and there are even reports of outbreaks of Mongol-Han violence such as the Gandan Temple incident, the Qing officials in Urga simply could not imagine a Mongol secret plot to send a delegation to St. Petersburg to ask for Russian assistance.[12]

In fact, news of the Mongols' arrival in Russia first appeared in Russian newspapers, and the Chinese Legation in St. Petersburg then relayed this information through official channels to Beijing. The unexpected announcement of this news from Beijing understandably angered Sandowa, still the main Qing official in Urga, and his staff. Their immediate reaction was to put the Jebtsundamba Khutugtu under official observation.

In sharp contrast to Mongol and Chinese sources, the Russian archives show that the Russian consul in Urga knew about the Mongol delegation well in advance. When the secret meeting was convened in July 1911, the most influential princes and priests in Mongolia attended. As soon as they decided to send a delegation to Russia they informed V.N. Lavdovskii, the Russian consul, and he reported this fact in a telegram to St. Petersburg on July 28, 1911.

Although Lavdovskii advised the Mongols to wait, perhaps until he received a response from Russia, the delegation left Urga on the very next day. The very rapidity of these events perhaps led to a basic misunderstanding between the

Mongols and Russians. While the participants at the July 1911 meeting agreed to send a delegation to Russia, the delegation's goals were less clear; the most radical of the Mongol leaders advocated declaring independence from China, others hoped that Russia would agree to intervene on Mongolia's behalf, but there were still many more who argued in favor of compromising with Beijing. Therefore, what it was decided the Mongol delegation should ask of Russia was its "khamagalakhu," a word in Mongolian that can mean "to take care of," "to guard," or "to protect." In his haste to report the Mongols' intentions, however, Lavdovskii translated this word in its strongest possible sense as "protection" and further stated that "in St. Petersburg, the [Mongol] delegation will officially offer to the Russian Government a request of accepting Khalkha under her protectorate."[13]

This apparent, perhaps deliberate, misunderstanding over terminology was to have serious repercussions. For the Mongols, what they wanted from Russia was help in stopping the Qing government's reforms in Mongolia. However, Lavdovskii had only recently replaced the former Russian Consul General in Urga, Y.P. Shishmarev, who had had many years of experience in Mongolia. The new consul clearly did not understand the underlying complexities of the political situation in Mongolia, and so perhaps exaggerated the Mongols' desire for closer ties to Russia. Either way, relations between Lavdovskii and the Bogda Khagan government formed later in 1911 were to become so strained that he was soon replaced by another new Consul General, V.F. Liuba.

The Mongol Delegation in St. Petersburg

When the Mongol delegation arrived in St. Petersburg, the Russian government vaguely expected the Mongol delegates to request that Outer Mongolia be made a protectorate, as Lavdovskii had reported. Instead, the official letter the delegation carried from the Jebtsundamba and the four khans of Khalkha pointedly asked Russia only for "assistance" and "protection" in foiling the Qing reforms. But, to make matters worse, the Mongol representatives in the delegation issued their own memorandum to the Russian government which claimed that their goal was to make Mongolia an independent nation. Since all of these views in one way or another contradicted each other, the Russian officials were initially at a loss as to which policy to follow.

When the Russian government received a copy of the Jebtsundamba's letter entrusted to the Mongolian delegation, they were most likely surprised to discover that there was no mention of Mongolia becoming a Russian protectorate. On the contrary, according to the Mongolian text of this letter, the Mongol people, voluntarily "submitting to the Manchu Emperor," had "dwelt in peace" with China for more than 200 years. Therefore, it was only the on-going Qing reforms that had caused division, as "recently the Han Chinese bureaucrats have grabbed the political power [of the Qing] and have brought confusion and discord to the affairs of the state."[14]

Rather than request that Russia take over Mongolia, this letter appeared to oppose any changes: "We followed the Manchu Emperor because he was a believer in Buddhism and a man of great compassion, but this turned out to be all talk and no substance, with the result that our suffering has only increased over the years." Specifically, the letter pointed out, "we cannot bear" the new policy of the government, which was designed to "search out ways to turn Mongol land into farmland, which, if accomplished, will inevitably destroy our traditional way of life."[15]

Finally, after detailing the crisis that threatened the Mongolian way of life, the letter stated: "If we follow the example of small nations who have depended on large nations and you cooperate with us, then we will not have to suffer the loss of our traditional way of life. Buddhism will continue to exist and prosper, and we will be able to dwell in peace and tranquility." In conclusion, the letter stated: "We have now related all these matters to you [Russia] openly and freely and ask for your assistance and protection."[16]

Clearly, this letter would not have satisfied the expansionist-minded Russian, who were expecting a Mongolian invitation to take them away from China. Instead, the letter emphasized that the traditional Qing-Mongol relationship, which was being undermined by the new Qing policy, should be restored if the Mongolian social order and society hoped to remain stable. Rather than a concrete petition for Russian intervention, therefore, this letter vaguely sought Russian assistance in opposing the "New Administration" reforms; this request was particularly ironic since China had been forced to adopt these reforms largely in response to territorial encroachment by foreign powers, chief among them being Imperial Russia.

Much more to the Russians' liking was a separate memorandum issued by the individual members of the Mongol delegation. Composed of Khanddorji, Tserengchimed, Khaisan, and five assistants including a medical doctor, the delegation represented some of Mongolia's most radical reformers; Khanddorji, Tserengchimed, and Khaisan had been involved in the anti-Qing movement for some time and supported Mongolian independence.[17] This memorandum, which the Mongolian delegates submitted directly to the Russian government, stated: "Mongols aimed to make the Jebtsundamba their emperor and build a Mongol state."[18]

The three different versions of the Mongolian delegation's mission—Lavdovskii's telegram, the Jebtsundamba's letter, and then the delegates' own memorandum—help explain why there has continued to be so much confusion among historians concerning Mongolia's goal in declaring independence in 1911. Although historians have argued persuasively for each of the three above-stated goals—protectorate, *status quo*, and independence—the evidence presented here suggests that the goal of the majority of Mongolia's leaders during the summer of 1911 was neither for protectorate, nor for independence, but merely to return to the *status quo ante*.

Russian Policy in Mongolia, 1911

How did the Russian government respond when the Mongol delegation arrived in St. Petersburg? According to Donald Treadgold, immediately following Russia's 1905 defeat in the Russo-Japanese War, Russian foreign policy in the Far East could be characterized as "a tune played in a lower key than before. The gains to be expected from expansion here or there were more or less rationally estimated by the Russian cabinet from an economic, political, and military standpoint."[19] St. Petersburg may have been cautious in implementing its Far Eastern policies, but this changed somewhat following the 1907 Russo-Japanese Entente, in which Japan recognized that Russia had special interests in Outer Mongolia.

After receiving the Jebtsundamba's letter and the Mongol delegation's memorandum, the Russian government was uncertain whether Outer Mongolia really intended to seek independence from China. However, St. Petersburg was indeed very concerned about the effect of the ongoing Qing reforms in Outer Mongolia, since the reforms might shift the traditional pro-Russian balance-of-power along the Russo-Chinese border in China's favor.

Therefore, during a special meeting of Ministers on August 17, 1911, it was decided that "from the standpoint of a mediator between the Qing empire and Mongolia, Russia supports the desire of the Mongols to maintain their autonomy through diplomatic channels without severing their relations to their lord, the Great Qing Emperor."[20]

Soon afterward, on August 28, the Russian Minister in Beijing, I.Y. Korostovets, formally requested that the Qing government abandon its reforms in Outer Mongolia.[21] Although the Qing government had previously refused similar Russian requests, on the grounds that Russia had no right to intervene in Mongolian questions because they were a domestic issue wholly under the control of the Qing empire, this time Beijing blinked, and on September 3, it ordered Sandowa to halt enforcement of the new policy.[22]

Russo-Chinese negotiations continued on this important issue, but were interrupted by the Wuchang Uprising of October 10, 1911. With the Qing dynasty tottering on the verge of collapse, the pro-independence faction in Mongolia gained ground. In November 1911, Qing officials in Urga were driven out. On December 1, 1911, the nobles and priests of Khalkha Mongolia declared their political independence. The new government was officially founded on December 29, 1911, when the Jebtsundamba Khutagtu was declared emperor, or *Bogda Khagan*.

Although the Bogda Khagan government was founded in Khalkha Mongolia, it soon spread throughout all of Outer Mongolia. Many important Inner Mongolian leaders also flocked to Urga to join the new government, and the Bogda Khagan government hoped to unify Outer Mongolia and Inner Mongolia into a single country, the so-called Great Mongolia State or *Yeke Monggol ulus*. To accomplish this goal, however, would first require Russia's agreement and support.

Russian Policy in Mongolia, 1912-1915

The evolution of Russian policy in Mongolia during 1912-15 has already been examined in great detail elsewhere.[23] In brief, the Russian government did not immediately recognize Mongolian independence, but continued to try to work as a mediator between China and Mongolia. Only after Beijing refused to agree to St. Petersburg's offer, did Imperial Russia decide to negotiate separately with, first, Outer Mongolia, and, second, China.

Through early 1912 the Russian government continued to offer its services in mediating the dispute between Mongolia and China. When the new Republican government in Beijing refused to negotiate, however, the Russian Minister proposed during May 1912 that Russia adopt a more aggressive policy. Thereafter, on May 6, 14, and 18, the Ministry of Foreign Affairs hosted an "Inter-Ministry Meeting on the Mongol Problem." Chairing this meeting was A. Neratov, the Vice Minister of Foreign Affairs, plus two representatives from his Ministry—Korostovets and G.A. Kozakov. The other officials invited to this meeting included two representatives from the Ministry of Internal Affairs, two from the Central Office of Land-Development and Agriculture, two from the Ministry of Transportation, two from the Ministry of Commerce and Industry, two from the Ministry of Finance, and one from the Ministry of War.[24]

Neratov, Korostovets, and Kozakov played the most important role at this meeting in discerning and adjusting the disparate goals of these various government departments vis-a-vis Outer Mongolia. By the end of the meetings, three main principles were decided: 1) Russia would support the Bogda Khagan government's goals by sponsoring the formation of an autonomous Outer Mongolia under the suzerainty of China; 2) China would be pressured to guarantee Outer Mongolia's autonomy by agreeing not to deploy troops, colonize, or establish administrative organs in Outer Mongolia; and 3) Russia would seek to obtain special economic rights and interests in Outer Mongolia.[25]

On August 15, 1912, the Council of Ministers in St. Petersburg convened a special council meeting to discuss the decisions of the "Inter-Ministry Meeting on the Mongol Problem." The Council quickly decided that St. Petersburg would negotiate directly with the Bogda Khagan government, and would acknowledge Outer Mongolia's autonomy in return for special economic concessions in Outer Mongolia that would guarantee Russian predominance there.

Instead of trying to resolve the Mongolian question in a simultaneous agreement with both Outer Mongolia and China, the Russian government opted for a two-stage solution, in which it would first come to agreement with the Bogda Khagan government, and then deal with Beijing. The first stage of this plan was achieved on November 3, 1912, when Russia and Outer Mongolia signed the Russo-Mongolian agreement. Later, on June 7, 1915, China was persuaded to sign a tripartite agreement with both Russia and Outer Mongolia that embodied these same points. By 1915, therefore, the Russian government had succeeded in separating Outer Mongolia from China's sphere of influence.

Mongolian Independence

In Mongolian studies, it has not been uncommon for European and American scholars to conclude that the 1911 Mongol declaration of independence was initiated and sponsored by Imperial Russia, while many PRC and Taiwanese scholars have insisted that Russia forced Outer Mongolia to declare its independence. As the archival information presented above shows, however, these views largely ignore the real situation in Mongolia. In fact, as early as July 1911, factions within Mongolia were advocating independence, and these factions came to the fore in November 1911, following China's 1911 revolution.

Archival sources also allow for a reexamination of Russia's response to the Mongol declaration of independence. In spite of Lavdovskii's misunderstanding in July 1911, once the Mongols' true intentions were known the Russian government adopted a "wait-and-see" attitude. During most of this period, day-to-day responsibility for Mongolian affairs rested with Kozakov, Director of the Far Eastern Department at the Ministry of Foreign Affairs. All pertinent information on Mongolia was collected and judged by him.

For assistance in decision-making, Kozakov kept in close contact with the diplomats serving at the Russian Legation in Beijing, such as Korostovets and M.S. Shchekin. Through 1911, Korostovets's position as Minister to China allowed him to decide several important issues, in addition to feeding ideas to Kozakov. Following Korostovets's resignation due to scandal, Shchekin became *chargé d'affaires* in Beijing, continuing the task of sending information and ideas to St. Petersburg. However, following the May 1912 "Inter-Ministry Meeting on the Mongol Problem," Korostovets once again became a major figure; in particular, he was sent to Mongolia as a diplomatic agent to negotiate and sign the Russo-Mongolian Agreement.

The decision-making process toward Mongolia during the 1911-15 period was conducted among a very small bureaucratic group, with Kozakov at the center. This was because of the fact that following the Russo-Japanese War the focus of Russian foreign policy shifted to Europe. For most Russian officials, European affairs were of greater interest than Asia, and Mongolia—in particular—was considered "off the beaten track."[26] Thus, professional diplomats exercised responsibility over decision-making, without outside interference. This narrowly based decision-making process was equally evident in the rest of Russia's Far Eastern diplomacy.

Instead of showing any great foresight or planning on the part of the government, Russia's policy toward Outer Mongolia during the 1911-15 period was highly realistic and prudent. Rather than foment Mongolian independence, Russia merely reacted to it. Cautious not to upset the other great powers—such as Japan—if it moved too quickly, the Russian government opted for Mongolian autonomy rather than outright independence. In effect, Imperial Russia hoped to achieve maximum gains for a minimum of effort.

Notes

1. Nakami Tatsuo, "Mongoru-no dokuritsu to kokusai-kankei" [The Mongol Independence and its International Relations], *Ajia-kara kangaeru (3): Shuuen-karano rekishi* (Tokyo: Tokyo daigaku shuppankai, 1994), pp. 79-106.

2. For two standard scholarly views representing American and European views on this period of Mongolian history, see Robert A. Rupen, *Mongols of the Twentieth Century* (Bloomington: Indiana University Press, 1964), and Charles R. Bawden, *The Modern History of Mongolia* (London: Weidenfeld and Nicolson, 1968).

3. For typical examples of this viewpoint, see Yu Shengwu, "Sha'e yu Xinhai geming" [Tsarist Russia and the Xinhai Revolution], *Jindaishi yanjiu* No. 3 (1981); Zhaqisiqin [Jagchid Sechin], "Waimenggu duli, zizhi he sazhi" [Independence, Autonomy, and its Abolition in Outer Mongolia], *Zhongguo xiandaishi congkan*, Vol. 4 (1954); Li Yushu, *Mengshi luncong* [Collection of Articles on Mongolia], (Taipei: Liwen shuju, 1990).

4. For Mongolian scholarship on the 1910s, see Ts. Puntsagnorow, *Mongolyn awtonomit üyeiin tüükh* [A History of the Mongolian Era of Autonomy], (Ulaanbaatar: Ulsyn khewlel, 1955); Sh. Sandag, *Mongol ulsyn töriin gadaad khariltsaa, 1850-1919* [Foreign Relations of Mongolia, 1850-1919], Vol. 1 (Ulaanbaatar: Shinjlekh ukhaany akademiin khewlel, 1971).

5. L. Jamsran, *Mongolchuudyn sergen mandaltyn ekhen* [The Beginning of the Restoration of the Mongols], (Ulaanbaatar: Soyombo khewleliyn gazar, 1992).

6. For a general survey of the historical sources at the National Central Historical Archives in Ulaanbaatar, see Nakami Tatsuo, "Mongoru bunsho-shiryō to arufifu" [On Archival Sources and Archives in Mongolia], *Gengo bunka sesshoku* Vol. 6 (1993), pp. 249-74.

7. For Mongolia under the Qing, see Joseph Fletcher's excellent chapters in *The Cambridge History of China*, Vol. 18, Part 1, John K. Fairbank, ed., (Cambridge, MA: Harvard Univesity Press, 1978), pp. 48-57, 352-59; Nakami Tatsuo, *Nairiku Ajia: Chiiki-karano sekaishi 6* [Inner Asia], (Tokyo: Asahi shinbun-sha, 1992), pp. 135-56.

8. Archives of the Russian Ministry of Foreign Affairs, Moscow (hereafter referred to as AVPR), f. 143 [*Kitaiskii stol*], op. 491, d. 644, I.

9. For the Mongols' attitude to the 1911 Revolution in China, see Nakami Tatsuo, "A Protest Against the Concept of the 'Middle Kingdom': The Mongols and the 1911 Revolution," in Eto Shinkich and Harold Z. Schiffrin, eds., *The 1911 Revolution in China: Interpretive Essays*, (Tokyo: University of Tokyo Press, 1984), pp. 129-49.

10. Magsurjab's original manuscript of "Monggol ulus-un sin-e teüke" is preserved at the State Central Library of Mongolia. Recently, a Cyrillic version was published as N. Magsarjaw, *Mongol ulsyn shine tüükh* [A New History of Mongolia], (Ulaanbaatar: Instituti Historiae Academiae Scientiarum Mongolici, 1994).

11. For example, see Nawaannamjil G., *Öwgön bicheechiin ügüülel* [Reminiscence of an Old Clerk], (Ulaanbaatar, Ulsyn khewleliyn gazar, 1956); Ts. Damdinsüren, ed., *Öwgön Jambalyn yaria* [Reminisense of Old Jambal], (Ulaanbaatar: Shinjlekh ukhaan, deed bolowsrolyn khüreelengiin erdem shinjilgeenii khewleliin gazar, 1959).

12. The First Historical Archives of China, Beijing, or *Junjichu dang'an*, Memorial packet copy of the Palace Memorial from Sandowa and Pungcugcering, Xuantong 2. III. 9.

13. AVPR, f. 143, op. 491, d. 644, 1.103, telegram No. 691, from Lavdovskiy to St. Petersburg, 28 (15) July 1911.

14. The original letter addressed to the Russian Tsar, written in Mongolian, has not been found at the AVPR in Moscow or at the Central State Historical Archives in St. Petersburg. However, a copy of this letter is at the Central State Historical Archives in Ulaanbaatar, A-4-1-22, while a Russian translation of the letter is in Moscow, AVPR, f. 143, op. 491, d. 644, II.130-131.

15. Ibid.

16. Ibid.

17. AVPR, f. 143, op. 491, d. 644, I.161, report of the General Staff Office No. 4015, 18 (5) August 1911.

18. AVPR, f. 143, op. 491, d. 644, I.158.

19. Donald W. Treadgold, "Russia and the Far East," in Ivo J. Lederer, ed., *Russian Foreign Policy: Essays in Historical Perspective* (New Haven and London: Yale University Press, 1962), p. 547.

20. AVPR, f. 143, op. 491, d. 644, II.133-135, *Journals of special conference on the Far Eastern Problem*, 17 (4) August 1911.

21. The First Historical Archives of China, Beijing, or *Waiwubu dang'an*, Interview with the Russian Minister in Peking, I.Y. Korostovets, Xuantong 3. VII, 5.

22. The National Palace Museum in Taipei, Record of Telegraphed Edicts to Ministers and Generals in Outer Mongolia, Xuantong 3. VII. 11.

23. Nakami Tatsuo, "1913 nen no Ro-chū sengen: Chū ka-minkoku no seititsu to Mongoru mondai" [On the Russo-Chinese Declaration of November 5, 1913: The Emergence of the Republic of China and the Mongol Problem], *Kokusai seiji*, No. 66 (1980), pp. 109-27; also see Nakami Tatsuo, "A Protest. . . "

24. AVPR, f. 143, op. 491, d. 646, II.238-264, *Journals of Inter-Ministry Conference on the Mongol Problem, Organized at the Ministry of Foreign Affairs*, 6, 14, and 18 May (23 April, 1 and 5 May) 1912.

25. Ibid.

26. A. Popov, "Tsarskaia Rossiia i Mongoliia v 1913-1914gg." [Imperial Russia and Mongolia in 1913-1914], *Krasnyi arkhiv*, Vol. 6/37/ (1929), p. 9.

The Buriat Alphabet of Agvan Dorzhiev

Yeshen-Khorlo Dugarova-Montgomery
and Robert Montgomery

Language and writing have long been intimately connected with questions of cultural unity and shared identity among the Buriat Mongols of southeastern Siberia. The Eastern and Southern (Transbaikal) Buriats' adoption of the traditional Mongolian writing system along with Buddhism in the seventeenth century strengthened cultural bonds both among these Buriat groups and between them and the rest of the Mongol world. Most Buriats west of Baikal, however, were largely cut off from Mongolian writing by the Russian autocracy's anti-Buddhist policies and were thus culturally isolated from the larger Mongol milieu.

The Buriat Buddhist leader Agvan Dorzhiev's creation of a new Buriat writing system at the beginning of the twentieth century represented the first attempt to bridge this cultural gap. But Dorzhiev's alphabetic creation was immediately perceived as a threat by Imperial Russia, since increased pan-Mongol sentiments might lead to nationalist demands that the Buriats be allowed to unify with the rest of Mongolia, which was at that point an administrative unit of China. Therefore, the Tsarist government opposed Dorzhiev and his alphabet.

Although Dorzhiev's alphabet was repressed, and its proponents were uprooted and even exiled by the Russian government, it did serve as an early example of a pan-Mongol alphabet intended to unify all Mongols. Later, during the early Soviet period, the Bolshevik government sponsored the creation of a new system, based on the Latin alphabet, to help draw the Mongol people together; the propaganda value of using the easier-to-typeset and read Latin script, especially in Mongolian areas not directly under the Soviet government's control, should not be overlooked.

Finally, with Japan's 1931-32 creation of Manchukuo, which included parts of Inner Mongolia, pan-Mongolism was once again seen by the Russians as a threat, since Japanese-sponsored propaganda called on the Mongol people to break with the USSR. In 1938, the Latin Buriat alphabet was replaced with a Cyrillic alphabet. As a result, the pan-Mongol movement was all but destroyed in Buriatia.

Although Dorzhiev's alphabet was created for the Buriats, many other Mongols were forced to go through similar linguistic turmoil. For example, in 1924 the Kalmyks adopted a Cyrillic alphabet, changed to a Latin alphabet later during the 1920s, and then went back to Cyrillic in the 1930s. Likewise, on the Chinese side of the border in Inner Mongolia, worsening Sino-Soviet relations in the 1950s discredited the use of the new Cyrillic alphabet and a Latin alphabet was briefly promoted. Thus, it can be seen that the twentieth-century linguistic battles over the various Mongol scripts closely paralleled the political ones.

The Buriats and Their Linguistic Heritage

By the beginning of the twentieth century, the Buriat lands were divided administratively by the boundary between Transbaikal Oblast' and Irkutsk Guberniia. According to the 1897 census, the Irkutsk, or Western Buriats numbered 110,000 (out of 515,070 persons in Irkutsk Guberniia as a whole); the Transbaikal (Eastern and Southern)Buriats numbered 170,000 (out of 672,072 persons in Transbaikal Oblast' as a whole).[1] The Transbaikal Buriats' main economic activity was cattle-breeding; most Irkutsk Buriats had turned to farming, abandoning nomadic pastoralism
    Religion separated the Irkutsk and Transbaikal Buriats as well. The Transbaikal Buriats were overwhelmingly Buddhist, whereas most of the Irkutsk Buriats either retained their ancient shamanist beliefs or had converted—at least nominally—to Orthodoxy by 1900. The Buriats were first introduced to Tibetan Buddhism by Mongolian and Tibetan missionaries during the mid-seventeenth century, and Buddhism claimed many adherents in the easily accessible steppes east and south of Baikal. Buriat Buddhism centered around monasteries, or datsans, which served as institutions of literacy and learning. For many Buriats the datsans were "the only cultural centers . . . where [they could] lead a settled life, share their ideas and feelings, learn to read and write, and attain various levels of intellectual achievement . . . Laymen of all ages [came] there . . . to learn literacy in their native language along with the tenets of religion."[2]
    The datsans provided instruction in Buddhist theology and philosophy, as well as secular disciplines such as astronomy, Tibetan medicine, Sanskrit and Tibetan languages, and mathematics; the largest datsans contained sizable libraries of Tibetan and Mongolian works on these subjects. Datsan schools also instructed their pupils in Classical, or Written Mongolian—the literary language of educated Buddhist Buriats. By printing Mongolian and Tibetan works by using the xylographic (wood-block) method and by graduating a steady supply of former monks who served as tutors, the datsans helped to spread Mongol literacy far beyond their walls.[3]
    By the early 1850s, the Buriats possessed thirty-four datsans that held 4,546 lamas and served nearly 125,000 believers. Tsar Nicholas I opposed the expansion of this alien faith on nationalistic grounds; urged on by East Siberian Governor-General Nikolai Murav'ev-Amurskii, in 1853 he restricted the number of lamas to 285 and forbade the construction of new datsans. The extensive Buddhist presence east and south of Baikal made infractions difficult to detect in the Transbaikal, but it was another matter in Irkutsk province, where Buddhism had made fewer inroads.[4] There, violations were severely punished: during the Church's campaign of forced conversion in the 1860s-1890s, Buddhists were flogged and their datsans destroyed. Only after the 1905 Revolution did the autocracy relax its enforcement of Nicholas I's ban. By that time, however, the 1853 decree had effectively severed most Western Buriats from their Buddhist brethren, and so cut them off from the common Mongolian cultural environment.[5]

It is important to keep in mind that the Buriats do not speak in a uniform language but in a number of dialects that often differ significantly from each other. These dialects can be roughly divided into three main groups: Western, Eastern, and Southern.[6] The Western dialects (sometimes called "Northern") are distributed to the west of Baikal in Irkutsk Oblast and in the Sayan area of the Buriat Republic; their speakers belong to the Ekhirit, Bulagat, and Khongodor tribes. The Eastern dialects are spoken east of Baikal in the central and southeastern areas of the Buriat Republic and in Chita Oblast by members of the eleven Khori clans.

Whereas the Eastern and Western dialects share linguistic features that distinguish Buriat from all other Mongolian languages, the Southern dialects stand on the border between the Buriat and Khalkha-Mongol languages. Their speakers, the Tsongols and Sartuls, are not Buriats proper, but rather the descendants of Khalkha clans (Khatagins and Tabanguts, etc.) from Mongolia, who settled in the Selenga River basin in the seventeenth century. These Selenga Buriats, as they are sometimes called, live south of Baikal in the Selenga and Dzhida Raions of the Buriat Republic.

The Buriat dialects differ from each other to varying extents and in different ways: phonetically, morphologically, and lexically. Lexical differences are rooted both in vocabulary (i.e., the use of different words to refer to an identical concept) and in semantics (i.e., the use of the same word to express different meanings), and abound not only in specialized terminology, but in the most common everyday words as well. As a result, although the various Buriat dialects hold a considerable amount of linguistic material in common, the contrasts between them are at times so striking that Buriats without frequent exposure to dialects other than their own consider them to be somewhat alien.

Buddhism had brought to the Transbaikal Buriats a writing system that had been common to the majority of Mongol peoples since the thirteenth century and had provided them with a high degree of cultural unity in spite of their dispersal over vast territories divided by the Russo-Chinese border. Classical Mongolian's usefulness as a literary language stemmed from its close grammatical and lexical proximity to the spoken tongues of the Buriats and other Mongol peoples. The phonetic and morphological differences between Classical Mongolian and the Mongolian vernacular languages (including Buriat) were on the whole highly regular and predictable for a literate native speaker. Classical Mongolian thus represented a "superdialectical" language for the Buriats and other Mongols, since it was not tied to any one local form of speech.[7]

The Eastern and Southern Buriats used Mongolian for manuscript chronicles, genealogies, personal and business correspondence, and to record legends, customary law, and documents. The chronicles of the Khori, Selenga, and Barguzin Buriats are especially notable for their "brilliant style and exemplary language."[8] At least two Russian-Mongol bilingual newspapers were in Chita by 1917: *Zhizn' na vostochnoi okraine* [Life on the Eastern Frontier] (1895-1897) and *Kooperativnoe slovo* [The Cooperative Word] (1916-1918).[9]

Besides providing a common literary language, Buddhism had also helped break down linguistic provincialism. Since the practice of Buddhism often exposed Buriats to a variety of Buriat and Mongolian dialects, they became accustomed to hearing and accepting—and ultimately understanding—different forms of speech. For instance, datsan students came from a variety of linguistic backgrounds, and they had to communicate orally with each other and with their teachers (some of whom were Khalkhas or other non-Buriats). Lay Buddhists often made pilgrimages to distant Buriat and Mongolian datsans to worship and consult with lamas, and they too had no choice but to attune their ears to each other's speech and mentally reconcile differences in pronunciation and vocabulary.

West of Baikal, however, the spread of Classical Mongol was hampered by the scarcity of Buddhist institutions and the autocracy's use of education as a tool of Russification, particularly in the latter half of the nineteenth century. Customs officials and censors even blocked the importation of Mongol books into Western Buriat territory. Petitions by Buriat teachers and the Baikal region's State Duma delegates to make Buriat and Mongol the means of instruction in native schools after 1905 fell on deaf ears.[10] Furthermore, since shamanism and Orthodoxy did not require travel or formal study in a multi-dialect setting, Western Buriats were deprived of the "cosmopolitan" experience of their Eastern compatriots and experienced much greater difficulty in understanding dialects other than their own.

Buriat Nationalism and Agvan Dorzhiev

The rise of the Buriat nationalist movement in the first decade of the twentieth century occasioned the first specific attempts to overcome the pre-existing cultural bifurcation. The most direct impetus to the development of Buriat nationalism was Tsarist legislation that reduced their landholdings, increased the number of Russian settlers in their native region, and abolished their quasi-autonomous administrative organs. In addition, a May 23, 1896 decree transferred Buriat land holdings in excess of 15 desiatins[11] to a colonization fund for Russian settlers in Irkutsk province; similar legislation affecting the Transbaikal Buriats was passed on June 5, 1900. Besides causing significant economic loss, this threatened Buriat cultural survival by paving the way for a flood of Russian colonists whose settlements divided previously contiguous groups of Buriats.

Another decree from April 23, 1901, replaced the "steppe dumas" and other native-language organs of local self-government, originally created by Governor-General Mikhail Speranskii's 1822 Siberian reforms, with Russian-style institutions that used the Russian language in recordkeeping and official business. The Buriats' reaction was public outcry. Some Buriats sent petitions and delegations to the local and central administrations demanding the rescinding of the new laws. Others took over the confiscated lands, closed the new Russian administrative organs, and reopened the steppe dumas. Forcibly baptized Buriats renounced Russian Orthodoxy; at the same time, Buddhism began to expand west of Baikal.

Emboldened, perhaps, by the 1905 Revolution, Buriats held native congresses and formed political groups for the first time. The All-Regional Congress of Transbaikal Buriats—during April 1905 in Chita—and the All-Province Congress of Irkutsk Buriats—during August 1905 in Irkutsk—discussed issues vital to the Buriats' well-being and survival as a people: administrative organs and divisions, courts, land use, and universal and compulsory public education for both sexes in Buriat and Russian. In 1906, the Mongolist and educator Tsyben Zhamtsarano (1880-1938) founded the "Banner of the Buriat People" [*Buriyaad zonoi tug*], an illegal nationalist union consisting of about sixty Buriat teachers, mainly from Irkutsk Province, that agitated for the use of Buriat and Mongol in local schools.[12]

In this context of heightened national awareness, the Buriat Buddhist leader Tsanid-Khambo Agvan Dorzhiev began to consider using a new written language to enhance cultural unity between the Buriats and the rest of the Mongol world. Dorzhiev was arguably the most prominent figure in the history of Buriat Buddhism. Born in 1853 in the village of Khara-shibir' in the present-day Zaigraevo region of southeastern Buriatia, he attended Buddhist institutions in Buriatia, Mongolia, and Tibet before receiving the high monastic rank of lharamba in Lhasa in 1888. He became the tutor and political advisor of the XIII Dalai Lama (1876-1933) and served as a diplomatic liaison between Lhasa and St. Petersburg in the 1890s and early 1900s.

Dorzhiev was one of the most widely travelled Buriats of his day. India, China, Japan, Germany, France, and England number among the countries he visited. He was active in promoting Buddhism, and played a central role in the construction of a Buddhist temple in St. Petersburg between 1908 and 1915. During the 1910s and 1920s, he led a reform movement directed toward eliminating monastic venality, luxury, and dissipation and recreating the austerity and asceticism of an idealized early Buddhism.

Dorzhiev also later served as a defender of Buddhism before the Soviet government, stressing the clergy's loyalty and asserting the compatibility of Buddhism and Communism. As a result of the Stalinist war against religion, however, Dorzhiev was exiled to Leningrad in 1931 and spent most of the decade there. He was arrested in November 1937 on charges of treason, counterrevolutionary terrorism, and plotting to separate Buriatia from the USSR; he died in prison in Ulan-Ude in January of the following year.[13]

In the opinion of the group of Buriat intellectuals headed by Dorhziev, what was indispensable for Buriatia was a writing system that would incorporate the Western Buriats into the common Mongolian culture. Due to Buddhism's role as the "shelter of the national spirit" among the Mongols and Transbaikal Buriats,[14] this culture was naturally understood to be a Buddhist one. As Zhamtsarano noted, many Buriats, even west of Baikal, shared the view that Buddhism was central to Mongolian culture:

> The more strenuously the government and missionaries pursued their policy of Russification and religious conversion, and the more widely

they subjected the Buriats to persecution and violence, the stronger and more unanimous became the movement toward Buddhism and towards those of their brethren [i.e., Transbaikal Buriats and Mongols] who had conserved their writing and national integrity and solidarity thanks to Buddhism.[15]

Bringing the Western Buriats, who were literate in Russian, when literate at all, directly to literacy in Classical Mongolian seemed an insurmountable task, since they did not have the cultural habit of using a written language whose orthography and pronunciation diverged so radically. But, writing Buriat in Cyrillic was absolutely unacceptable to Dorzhiev and his followers, since it was associated with Russification and colonization.[16] A compromise was eventually found: to offer the Western Buriats a form of writing that would be based on the Uighur-Mongol script, but refined in order to reflect their living conversational language. This approach was not without precedent in the history of the Mongols: such an alphabet had been created for the Oirats in the seventeenth century.[17]

Agvan Dorzhiev and the New Buriat Writing System

Agvan Dorzhiev, or Vagindra,[18] as he is known through his writings, first introduced the new Buriat writing system in a pamphlet written in Classical Mongolian and published in St. Petersburg, most likely in 1905. It bore the innocuous title *A Manual Explaining the Differences between the Old and the New letters, Etc.*[19] Zhamtsarano was almost certainly a co-author of the project and Dorzhiev also consulted with the Buriat philologist Bazar Baradin (1878-1937).[20]

Perhaps to hide his true intentions, nowhere in the pamphlet did Dorzhiev specifically indicate toward which Mongol people the reform was to be oriented. The fact that he presented his project in terms of the Mongolian, not European, tradition of grammar-writing—for instance, he began with a semi-legendary history of writing among the Mongols[21]—could indicate that he considered the alphabet of ultimate significance to all Buriats and Mongols.

Still, it is clear that Dorzhiev's main target was the Western Buriat population. He noted the disparity between the vernacular and the written language, which in his view reflected an ancient tongue not spoken by any modern Mongol and presented special difficulties for those who must concentrate their efforts on learning "other language(s)," that is Russian:

If one were to study primarily this (Classical Mongolian) alphabet, one could succeed in learning it well. However, because nowadays there is an urgent necessity to study diligently other language(s); (and because as a result) we are unable to understand writing in our own language, and even if we do understand it, we are not able to write in it, we are (therefore) at the point of losing our own language. The books and treatises translated and published and written with the tremendous pains of our holy ancestors are about to become no more than objects of worship (i.e., venerated but not read). Therefore, if correspondences between the old and new alphabets' letters are created, not only will our language develop (literally, "our language will not be held back") through (our) learning an easy-to understand new alphabet and through reading quickly [sic], we will also eventually understand the old (script).[22]

Like Classical Mongol, the new alphabet was written vertically and consisted of seven vowel and twenty-one consonant letters, each of which had the same form in all positions and always represented the same sound. The only exception was the letter 'a,' which was represented as in the Uighur-Mongolian script—with a combined "crown" [*titim*] and "tooth" [*shidün*] in initial position, and with one "tooth" in the medial and final positions. Some of the new alphabet letters were based on the graphemes and diacritical marks of the existing Mongolian writing systems (Uighur-Mongolian, Galik, and Oirat), while new letters and diacritical signs were devised for others. Therefore, the language was a somewhat artificial construct combining different Buriat dialects and Classical Mongolian.

The 1906 *New Mongol-Buryat Alphabet*[23]—a pamphlet including a printed chart of the new alphabet that indicated its letters' pronunciation by means of modified Cyrillic characters—introduced several changes in orthography. In the same year, *The Brief Biography of Buddha and the Biography of the Prince Boyanto* was published in the new alphabet using a typeset font.[24] The first section briefly narrated the life of Buddha, while the second presented the story of one of the rebirths of Buddha from the famous Indo-Mongolian collection *Üliger-ün Dalai* (*Ocean of Tales*).

The next collection of works in the new script, 1907s *The Buriat Word*, Volume 1[25]—contained three short tales of Mongolian-style didactic teachings, and examples of the minor genres of Ekhirit and Bulagat aphoristical poetry—sayings, ritual felicitations, and riddles recorded by Zhamtsarano in 1902. At the end of the collection, the author listed the letters of the new alphabet with their Russian and Mongolian equivalents and described their usage.

The collection was notable for the variety of approaches it took to the issue of dialect diversity. In the tales and the minor genres of Western Buriat aphoristic poetry, the vernacular speech of the Irkutsk Province Buriats was reproduced as faithfully as possible. The vocabulary of the tales and minor genres consisted of words of specifically Western Buriat origin, and common Buriat and All-Mongolian words were used according to Western Buriat semantic principles.

Four more pamphlets followed in 1908.[26] The language of these materials was made to approximate the Western dialects as closely as possible, with the exception of Classical Mongolian words without Western Buriat equivalents: these were given in their original phonetic form and explained in brackets in either Russian or (Western) Buriat in the letters of the new alphabet. Dorzhiev and Vampilay noted that "when we translated these teachings for improving the thoughts into the language of the Buriats of the northern shore of the Ocean [Baikal], it turned out that there were no words for some concepts in it. For the enrichment of this language, we introduced word-concepts from the written language."[27]

The next publication was *The Fairy Tale "The Golden Fish" Written by the Russian Pushkin*—issued in 1910.[28] This book consisted of a translation of Pushkin by the Irkutsk Buriat teacher Nikolai Amagaev (1868-1932) and a two-page address to Buriat youth by Agvan Dorzhiev consisting of maxims on literacy, diligence, and right behavior. The language of this brochure was notable in that the Common Mongolian *s was used throughout in place of the pharyngeal 'h.'

The 1910 *Novyi mongolo-buriatskii alfavit*[29] written by Nikolai Amagaev and "Alamzhi-Mergen" (the pseudonym of the Buriat nationalist El'bek-Dorzhi Rinchino [1885-1938]) summed up activity on the introduction of the new alphabet among the Western Buriats (see Chart 1). It also settled the orthography and norms of the new literary language in parallel Buriat and Russian texts.[30] This book was also noteworthy, because for the first time in the entire history of the new Buriat alphabet it explained the project in Russian as well as Buriat and employed the terminology and methods of the European linguistic tradition. For example, Amagaev and Rinchino elucidated the laws of vowel harmony and vowel assimilation (the latter is strictly observed in the Western dialects), which had not been addressed in the earlier pamphlets.

Although this was most likely an attempt to maximize the work's accessibility to Russian-literate Western Buriats, who would have found an explanation in the style of the Mongolian grammatical tradition vague and incomprehensible, the 1910 publication of *Chano batur*,[31] Nikolai Amagaev's transcription of a Western Buriat song about the legendary Oirat hero Shono Baatar, proved to be the last work written in the Dorzhiev writing system.[32] In the spring of 1917, there was some talk among Western Buriat teachers of reviving it for use in native schools, but it was rejected in favor of Classical Mongolian, which was thought to offer a more direct route to cultural union with the Eastern Buriats and the Mongolian world as a whole.[33]

The Failure of Agvan Dorzhiev's New Buriat Writing System

The reasons for Dorzhiev's failure are not entirely clear. It is tempting to lay the blame on the way the project dealt with questions of orthography and dialect choice. Since the new Buriat writing system was phonetic, its proponents had to either choose one dialect or a group of closely related dialects as the standard to allow speakers of each dialect to write as they spoke, or combine traits from different dialects into an artificial hybrid language. The latter course was eventually chosen in order to make the new alphabet serve the widest possible audience and break the Western Buriats out of their linguistic and cultural isolation. One could argue that such a hybrid literary language would be difficult for speakers of any dialect or language of the Mongolian group to master.

Yet as was noted above, Buddhist Buriats who were frequently exposed to other forms of Buriat and even Mongolian proper had managed to accept and

Начертания букв	Принятая в научных работах транскрипция	Новый латинский алфавит	Произношение в передаче знаками русского алфавита
a	*a*	а	а
o	*o*	о	о
u	*u*	u	у
e	*e*	e	э
y	*y*	у	в русск. академич. транскр. ӯ
θ	*θ*	θ	» » » » ö
i	*i*	ı	я
g	*g*	g	г
x	*x*	k	х
m	*m*	m	м
n	*n*	n	н
ŋ	*ŋ*	ng	в русск. академич. транскр. ң
ž	*ž*	ē	ж
ç	*ç*	ç	ч
š	*š*	š	ш
z	*z*	z	з
c	*c*	c	ц
s	*s*	s	с
d	*d*	d	д
t	*t*	t	т
b	*b*	b	б
p	*p*	p	п
l	*l*	l	л
r	*r*	r	р
j	*j*	j	в русск. академич. транскр. j
v	*v*	v	» » » » w

Chart 1: The Amagaev-Rinchino Alphabet.

Source: N.N. Poppe, *Buriat-mongol'skoe iazykoznanie* (Leningrad: Akademiia nauk SSSR i Institut kul'tury BMASSR, 1933), p. 89.

understand them without extraordinary difficulty. Moreover, the enthusiasm with which the new writing system was received suggests that learning it was not an unusually arduous task. Zhamtsarano's "Banner of the Buriat People"—whose members were teachers and thus would certainly have been able to detect any shortcomings in the new alphabet—advocated teaching the Dorzhiev alphabet in Buriat schools—first of all, in Irkutsk province—as early as 1906. According to Amagaev and Rinchino, the alphabet was taking hold among Mongol-illiterate Western Buriats, and it even enjoyed some popularity east of Baikal.[34] So, nothing in the nature of the new writing system appears to have been responsible for its demise.

The Buriat intelligentsia's lack of unity on the question of writing for the Buriats could conceivably have hindered the spread of the new alphabet, but if so, only to a small degree. The publicist and historian Mikhail Bogdanov (1878-1920)[35] strenuously opposed the new Buriat alphabet on the grounds that "the development of capitalism on the Buriat territories inevitably will lead to assimilation. Therefore, the Buriats should adopt Western European culture and science and the Russian language. Attempts at the further development of the Buriat linguistic culture through the Dorzhiev writing are completely pointless, since Buriat literature can consist only of pitiful translations at best."[36]

Moreover, at the same time as Dorzhiev and his supporters were promoting their new script, Baradin was experimenting with another, Latin-based Buriat writing system. But Bogdanov's national nihilism was not a significant competitor to the nationalistic and pan-Mongolist philosophy of the Dorzhiev script's proponents; and Baradin's project, which resulted in only one small publication,[37] does not seem to have received significant support.

Even Dorzhiev himself seems to have abandoned his creation for one reason or another. It is conceivable that his attention was distracted from the alphabet by his involvement with the construction of a Buddhist temple in St. Petersburg, which provoked hostility and threats from Orthodox Church leaders, the city administration, and conservative Russian opinion.[38] At any rate, he obviously lost interest in the alphabet project: his rhymed autobiography, written in 1921 in Classical Mongolian, does not even mention this remarkable page of his life.[39]

The most likely cause of the new script's disappearance, however, was hostility from the Tsarist administration, which had little reason to support the spread of a writing system specifically created to serve nationalistic and pan-Mongolist ends. According to Amagaev and Rinchino, "contemporary conditions, in which civic activities—even of a narrowly educational character—were exceptionally difficult, were completely unfavorable to the realization of the alphabet and cultural measures that were connected to it. Not a few of its supporters, and intellectual workers in general, were put out of action."[40]

As Nicholas Poppe further testified: "The [Tsarist] government even took measures toward the uprooting of the new alphabet, going so far . . . as to exile those involved [in spreading its use]."[41] In particular, Zhamtsarano was exiled to Mongolia, depriving the project of one of its most talented proponents.[42] The failure of the Dorzhiev alphabet would appear to be a classic example of the close links in Russia between linguistics and politics.

Dorzhiev's Alphabet and Pan-Mongolism

Following Dorzhiev's failure, subsequent Buriat attempts to forge cultural unity on the basis of writing took place in the context of Classical Mongolian. These efforts were facilitated by the Bolsheviks' unification of the Buriat lands in 1923 into the Buriat-Mongolian ASSR. During the initial years of Soviet rule in Buriatia, linguistic pan-Mongolism was the order of the day. Classical Mongolian was used to print hundreds of books, newspapers, journals, and pedagogical materials; even west of Baikal, it was slowly but steadily gaining ground. The early Bolshevik policy of *korenizatsiia* ("rooting," or nativization) promoted the use of Buriat dialects and Classical Mongolian in public institutions.

Influenced by latinization in the Caucasus and Central Asia, and convinced that written Mongolian was too archaic and awkward to serve as a tool of Buriat and Mongol cultural development, Bazar Baradin brought forth in September 1926 a project for a latinized common Mongolian literary language that would employ Khalkha phonetics and grammar and incorporate vocabulary from all of the languages and dialects of the Mongolian group. He found few supporters: most Buriats—including the cultural and political leadership—considered his hybrid tongue artificial and unwieldy and were loathe to abandon the traditional writing system while the other Mongols still used it.

Official support for latinization came only at the very end of the 1920s, when Communist ideologues launched attacks on pan-Mongolism and Buriat nationalism. Unlike the Dorzhiev script, the Latin alphabet was unquestionably promulgated under pressure "from above": a modified version of the 1926 Baradin project was approved in 1929 by the All-Union Central Committee of the New Turkic Alphabet and the Central Executive Committee of the Buriat-Mongolian ASSR, and in 1930 by the Buriat Regional Organization (*obkom*) of the Communist Party, with virtually no public input.

The government's aim of using a written language to draw the Mongol peoples closer together was evident throughout the 1920s. The new writing system's proponents intended that it be used by all Mongol peoples—although only the Buriats and Kalmyks actually adopted it—and they retained the 1926 project's emphasis on Khalkha until 1931. In the early 1930s, however, the Khalkha grammar and phonetics were suddenly replaced by those of Southern Buriat; the choice of Tsongol-Sartul may have represented a compromise between opponents and supporters of pan-Mongolism, since the Southern dialects combine characteristics of both Khalkha and Buriat proper. The timing of this change with Japan's successful invasion of Manchuria and Eastern Inner Mongolia was probably not coincidental, and showed a new Soviet awareness of the possible dangers inherent in pan-Mongolism.

A much more serious blow at linguistic pan-Mongolism was struck in 1936, as Japan was making further inroads into Inner Mongolia, when Khori was made the official Buriat literary dialect. Not only did choosing Khori put the speakers of other dialects—Western and s-speaking Tsongol and Sartul—in a subordinate position culturally and linguistically, it also isolated the Buriats from other Mongols. The mass purging of the Buriat intelligentsia and the cyrillicization of Buriat in July 1938—again, without public input—completed this separation.[43]

The Buriats are not the only Mongol people who have undergone drastic transformations in their written language in the twentieth century: the rest of the Mongolian-speaking world has experienced similar changes. The Kalmyks—the Oirats of Russia—were first among the Mongol peoples to adopt a new alphabet, switching voluntarily to Cyrillic in 1924. Changes to Latin and then back to Cyrillic in the 1930s, however, reflected the same political pressures that were present in the Buriats' alphabet changes.

Although under strong Soviet domination, the Khalkha Mongols of the Mongolian People's Republic possessed their own, at least nominally independent state, so they were able to preserve their traditional writing system longer than the Buriats. But in the 1940s, with the Soviet-backed incorporation of Tannu Tuva into the USSR, they too were induced to adopt Cyrillic; the Khalkhas only began to move back to their traditional writing system at the end of the 1980s, as a result of weakening Soviet influence.

Among the Mongols of Inner Mongolia, the use of the traditional writing system was unquestioned until the mid-1950s, when the government of the Inner Mongolian Autonomous Region (IMAR) proposed a new Cyrillicized literary language based on Khalkha, but augmented with elements of Inner Mongolia's central Shili-yin Gool, Chakhar, and Ordos dialects. This would have significantly advanced linguistic unity between the Mongols of the MPR and those of the IMAR. But, preparatory work on the new literary language was cut short by the general movement towards latinization of non-Han scripts after 1957. Without a doubt, the worsening of Sino-Soviet diplomatic relations during this period also served to discredit the Cyrillic system.

Although the Latin alphabet failed to take root in the IMAR, official pressure in favor of Sinicization increased. Between 1966 and 1975, the Mongol script was banned: Mongol-language schools and publishing houses were closed, Mongol educators and scholars were purged, and the use of spoken Mongol in public life was forbidden. Only in the late 1970s were these prohibitions lifted.[44]

The issues of language and identity that engaged the Buriats at the beginning of the twentieth century retain their immediacy at the century's close. For decades, Soviet nationality policies deemphasized the Buriats' cultural and linguistic ties with the rest of the Mongol world—the word "Mongolian" was dropped from the title of the Buriat-Mongolian ASSR in 1957—and Classical Mongolian was long excluded from the curriculum of Buriat schools.

Pan-Mongol consciousness is thus weak among many modern Buriats: a 1990 campaign by native intellectuals to return the word "Mongolian" to the Buriat

ASSR's title floundered due to lack of public interest. Language loss presents, therefore, a significant threat to Buriat identity. For example, in the 1970s, Russian was made the language of instruction in almost all native schools, with Buriat remaining only as an elective, if at all. Finally, Buriat-language publishing was sharply curtailed.

As a result of these governmental changes, the level of native-language maintenance is now officially 86 percent, but is probably 10 or so percentage points less. The actual situation is much worse than these figures would imply, however, since the removal of sizable Western and Eastern Buriat territories from the administrative control of the Buriat-Mongolian ASSR in 1937 severed tens of thousands of Buriats from their compatriots. This was an especially heavy blow to Western Buriat cultural survival and national identity, since it intensified their previous isolation. This isolation was increased further by Western Buriats' resentment at the choice of Khori as the official dialect, which has led many of them to reject the modern literary language.

In the Gorbachev era, the Buriats struggled to ameliorate the consequences of earlier policies of denationalization and de-Mongolization. The Buriat language was reemphasized in Buriatia's schools and in local television and radio programming, and a 1991 language law gave Buriat a legal status equal to that of Russian. The end of official restrictions on cultural pan-Mongolism allowed the appearance of a Buriat/Russian parallel edition of *The Secret History of the Mongols*,[45] which presents a nationalistic account of Chinggis Khan's rise to power and is usually considered to be the most prominent work in the Mongolian literary heritage. Finally, at long last, these reforms, continued since 1991, have allowed the return of Classical Mongolian to Buriat classrooms.[46]

Notes

1. B.V. Bazarov, L.V. Kuras, Iu.P. Shagdurov, I.N. Shagdurova, *Istoriia Buriatii, konets XIX v.-1941 g. Chast' 1* (Ulan-Ude: Ministerstvo obrazovaniia Respubliki Buriatiia. Obshchestvenno-nauchnyi tsentr "Sibir'," 1993), p. 9.

2. Bazar Baradin, quoted in Bogdanov, "Ocherki istorii buriat-mongol'skogo naroda," p. 151. Also see Poppe, "The Buddhists," p. 184 and N. Koz'min, "Mikhail Nikolaevich Bogdanov. Iz lichnykh vospominanii" *Zhizn' Buriatii* (1925) 3-4: 18-26, p. 19.

3. G.R. Galdanova, K.M. Gerasimova, D.B. Dashiev, G.Ts. Mitupov, *Lamaizm v Buriatii XVII-nachala XX veka, Struktura i sotsial'naia rol' kul'tovoi sistemy* (Novosibirsk: Nauka, 1983), pp. 12-13, 17-18, 27, 62-63, 74-78; M.N. Bogdanov, *Ocherki istorii buriat-mongol'skogo naroda* (Verkhneudinsk: Buriat-Mongol'skoe gosudarstvennoe izdatel'stvo, 1926), pp. 122-23 and (with B. B. Baradin) pp. 135-46; Nicholas Poppe, "The Buddhists," in *Genocide in the USSR: Studies in Group Destruction* (New York: Scarecrow Press, 1958), pp. 182, 185-86; Aleksei Matveevich Pozdneev, *Religion and Ritual in Society: Lamaist Buddhism in Late 19th Century Mongolia* trans. Alo and Linda Raun, ed. John R. Krueger (Bloomington, IN: The Mongolia Society, 1978), 195ff, Robert Rupen, *Mongols of the Twentieth Century* 2 vols. (Bloomington, IN: Indiana University Press, 1964), vol.

1, p. 35; and György Kara, *Knigi mongol'skikh kochevnikov* (Moscow: Glavnaia redaktsiia vostochnoi literatury, 1972), pp. 104-52. Particularly gifted graduates of Buriat datsans, for instance the Buddhist leader Agvan Dorzhiev, continued their studies in the great seminaries of Tibet.

4. Buddhism was not unknown among the Western Buriats. It had gained a notable following among the Tunka, Oka, Zakamensk, and Alar Buriats, who had built at least four datsans by 1853. Even after the ban on Buddhist expansion, the "Yellow Faith" continued to slowly gather adherents among the Western Buriats, over 14,000 of whom professed Buddhism by the end of the century. Galdanova et al., *Lamaizm v Buriatii*, pp. 41, 44; James Forsyth, *A History of the Peoples of Siberia: Russia's North Asian Colony, 1581-1990* (Cambridge, UK: Cambridge University Press, 1992), p. 171.

5. Galdanova et al., *Lamaizm v Buriatii*, pp. 29-30; *Ocherki istorii kul'tury Buriatii I*, ed. D.D. Lubsanov (Ulan-Ude: Buriatskoe knizhnoe izdatel'stvo, 1972), p. 284; Bogdanov, *Ocherki istorii buriat-mongol'skogo naroda*, p. 155; V. Vashkevich, *Lamaity v Vostochnoi Sibiri* (St. Petersburg: Tipografiia Ministerstva vnutrennikh del, 1885), pp. 127-37; Forsyth, *History of the Peoples of Siberia*, pp. 170-71; Carolyn Humphrey, *Karl Marx Collective: Economy, Society and Religion in a Siberian Collective Farm* (Cambridge, UK: Cambridge University Press, 1983), p. 419.

6. There is still no general agreement among linguists on the classification of Buriat dialects and subdialects. Nicholas Poppe, the most renowned investigator of Buriat linguistics, lists the main dialects as Ekhirit, Bulagat, Bokhan, Alar, Tunka, Nizhneudinsk, Barguzin, Khori, Tsongol, Sartul and (in Manchuria) Bargu-Buriat. Nicholas Poppe, *Buriat Grammar* (Bloomington, IN: Indiana University Press, 1960), p. 1. Other linguists have settled upon different classifications; these have been discussed most recently in V.I. Rassadin, "Zvukovoi sostav prisaianskoi gruppy buriatskikh govorov" in *Segmentnye i prosodicheskie edinitsy iazykoy baikal'skogo regiona*, ed. L.D. Shagdarov (Ulan-Ude: Buriatskii institut obshchestvennykh nauk, 1991), pp. 3-6.

7. L.D. Shagdarov, *Stanovlenie edinykh norm buriatskogo literaturnogo iazyka v sovetskuiu epokhu* (Ulan-Ude: Buriatskoe knizhnoe izdatel'stvo, 1967), pp. 6-8; Kara, *Knigi mongol'skikh kochevnikov*, pp. 35, 47; Galdanova et al, *Lamaizm v Buriatii*, p. 78.

8. G.N. Rumiantsev, "Buriatskie letopisi kak istoricheskii istochnik" *Trudy Buriatskogo kompleksnogo nauchno-issledovatel'skogo instituta, Seriia vostokovedeniia* vyp. 3 (1960): 3-15, p. 3. See also Ts. B. Tsydendambaev, *Buriatskie istoricheskie khroniki i rodoslovnye* (Ulan-Ude: Buriatskoe knizhnoe izdatel'stvo, 1972).

9. *Ocherki istorii kul'tury Buriatii I*, pp. 373-74; B. Ts. Dondokov, *Vozniknovenie i razvitie partiino-sovetskoi pechati v Buriatii (1918-1937 gg.)* (Ulan-Ude: Buriatskoe knizhnoe izdatel'stvo, 1960), pp. 10-11, 19, 124, 126.

10. Robert Montgomery, "Buriat Language Policy, 19thc-1928: A Case Study in Tsarist and Soviet Nationality Practices" (Ph.D. dissertation: Indiana University, 1994), pp. 99-130; Ts. Zhamtsarano, "Narodnicheskoe dvizhenie buriat i ego kritik" *Sibirskie voprosy* (1907) 21: pp. 16-21, (1907) 23: pp. 17-20, (1907) 25: pp. 15-21; "Buriatskie uchitelia na uchitel'skom s"ezde" *Sibirskie voprosy* (1907) 18: pp. 22-26, (1907) 19: pp. 24-28; (1907) 19, p. 2; A.F. Efirov, "Dorevoliutsionnye russifikatorskie nerusskie shkoly Sibiri" *Uchenye zapiski nauchno-issledovatel'skogo instituta NKP RSFSR* 3 (1940): 45-78, p. 47. Under Alexander III, some local officials (e.g., Zabaikal'skaia oblast's school inspector Baron Maidel') blocked the teaching of Classical Mongolian even in schools east of Baikal. V.I. Andreev, *Istoriia buriatskoi shkoly (1804-1962 gg.)* (Ulan-Ude: Buriatskoe knizhnoe izdatel'stvo, 1964), p. 144.

11. 1 desiatina = 2.7 U.S. acres.

12. *Istoriia Buriatii, konets XIX v.-1941 g.*, pp. 12-15; Montgomery, "Buriat Language Policy," pp. 149-50; T.M. Mikhailov, "K voprosu o dukhovnoi zhizni i ideologii u buriat v kontse XIX-nach. XX vv.," in *Natsional'no-osvoboditel'noe dvizhenie buriatskogo naroda* ed. N.V. Kim, T.M. Mikhailov, and G.L. Sanzhiev (Ulan-Ude: Buriatskoe knizhnoe izdatel'stvo, 1989), pp. 26-30.

13. R.E. Pubaev, "Agvan Dorzhiev," in *Natsional'no-osvoboditel'noe dvizhenie buriatskogo naroda*, pp. 94-98; Rupen, *Mongols of the Twentieth Century*, vol. 1, pp. 106-11; and Agvan Dorzhiev, *Dorjiev: Memoirs of a Tibetan Diplomat* trans. and ed. by Thubten J. Norbu and Dan Martin (Tokyo: Hokke Bunka Kenkyu, 1991) and John Snelling, *Buddhism in Russia: The Story of Agvan Dorzhiev, Lhasa's Emissary to the Tsar* (Shaftesbury, Dorset: Element Books, 1993), passim.

14. Zhamtsarano, "Narodnicheskoe dvizhenie buriat i ego kritik" *Sibirskie voprosy.* (1907) 21, p. 21.

15. Zhamtsarano, loc. cit.

16. Several attempts had already been made to create writing systems for the Western Buriat dialects based on the Cyrillic alphabet. Two Western Buriat teachers, Iakov Boldonov (1808-1849) and his nephew N.S. Boldonov (1835-1899), used such a modified Russian alphabet to translate Russian primers and religious materials into Western dialects between the 1840s and 1860s. Orthodox missionaries also published over a dozen cyrillicized-Buriat religious tracts between 1886 and 1913. Some Russian-literate Western Buriats used Cyrillic to carry out correspondence and other everyday tasks in their native dialects, but the extent of this practice is unknown. "Popytka prosveshcheniia buriat" *Zapiski Imperatorskago Russkago Geograficheskago Obshchestva* (1863) 2: 39-42; Andreev, *Istoriia buriatskoi shkoly*, pp. 156, 159-60, 181-84; I. Shpitsberg, "Tserkov' i russifikatsiia buriato-mongol pri tsarizme" *Krasnyi arkhiv* 53 (1932): 100-24, pp. 121-22; Poppe, *Buriat-mongol'skoe iazykoznanie* (Leningrad: Akademiia nauk SSSR i Institut kul'tury BMASSR, 1933), pp. 41-44, 94-97; F. Kudriavtsev, "Rol' russkoi kul'tury v razvitii buriat-mongol'skogo naroda v XVIII-XX vekakh" *Voprosy istorii* (1946) 10: 85-94, p. 90; *Ocherki istorii kul'tury Buriatii I*, pp. 213, 375-76.

17. Zaya Pandita (1599-1662), an Oirat lama, had created a special alphabet on the basis of the Uighur Mongolian vertical script. Descriptions of this Oirat *todo bicig* ("clear script") and sources for its investigation are to be found in Ts. Shagdarsüren, *Mongol üzeg züi. Tergüün dewter (ert üyees 1921 on khürtel)* [The Mongolian Script, Part 1: from Antiquity to 1921] (Ulaanbaatar: BNMAU shinjlekh ukhaany Akademi khel zokhiolyn khüreelen, 1981) and Kara, *Knigi mongol'skikh kochevnikov.*

18. B. Rinchen, *Mongol bichgiin khelnii züi. Udirtgal*, (Ulaanbaatar: Shinjlekh ukhaany akademiin khewlel, 1964), pp. 172-75; Kara, *Knigi mongol'sikkh kochevnikov*, p. 97; Shagdarsüren, *Mongol üzeg züi. Tergüün dewter*, pp. 113-17.

19. Vagindra, *Sine qaucin üsüg-üd-ün ilgal terigüten-i bicigsen debter orosibai* [A Manual (Explaining) the Differences between the Old and the New Letters, Etc.] (St. Petersburg: n.p., n.d), 16 pp.

20. Baradin's participation is mentioned in passing in Vagindra, *Bur'ad şine uzugtu tarūlhaŋ Zurxeŋ Tolto geži exilegdehen anxaŋ debter oroşibay* [The First Volume of Artery of the Heart, Accomodated to the New Buriat Alphabet] (St. Petersburg: Tipo-Litografiia V. Avidona, 1908), p. 27. There is evidence suggesting that Zhamtsarano played a considerable role in the creation and propagation of the new alphabet. György

Kara (*Knigi mongol'skikh kochevnikov*, p. 167) notes that the Zhamtsarano fond of the Leningradskoe otdelenie institute vostokovedeniia Akademii nauk (LOIVAN)'s collection of Mongolian manuscripts contains a manuscript project of the new Buriat alphabet bearing the notation "at the end of Fall 1905, on October 31 ... we [Agvan Dorzhiev and I] created this [alphabet] (*enēni biçibe bide*)." Mikhail Bogdanov, a Buriat opponent of the alphabet project, named Dorzhiev and Zhamtsarano as its chief proponents. M. N. Bogdanov, "Buriatskoe <<vozrozhdenie>>" *Sibirskie voprosy* (1907) 3: 38-49, pp. 39-40. It may be more than a coincidence that after around 1910—the time of Zhamtsarano's exile—there is no more evidence of activity related to the new alphabet.

21. Compare *Sine qaucin üsüg*... with, for example, Dandzan-Dagba's *Jirüken-ü tolta-yin tayilburi* [Commentary on the "Artery of the Heart"], a grammatical treatise of the eighteenth century.

22. Vagindra, *Sine qaucin üsüg*.... pp. 6-7.

23. [Anonymous]. *Moŋgol bor'ād şine uzug oroşiba* [The New Mongol-Buriat Alphabet] (St. Petersburg: Tipo-litografiia N. Evstif'eva, 1906), 8 pp.

24. Vagindra, *Borxan bagsīŋ gegēni xor'aŋgoy namtar boloŋ Boyanto xaŋ xūbūni namtar oroişbay* [The Brief Biography of Buddha and the Biography of Boyanto] (Pitirbūrgedū, n.p., 1906), 19 pp.

25. [Anonymous], *Bur'ād xur. Turūsiŋ debter* [The Buriat Word. Volume I] (P'et'erburge: Naraŋ gedeg moŋgol bur'ād nom bişig gargaxo oroŋ, 1908), 31 pp.

26. These were 1) A grammatical composition, *The First Volume of "Artery of the Heart" Accommodated to the New Buriat Alphabet.* Vagindra, *Bur'ād şine uzūgtū tārūlhaŋ Zūrxeŋ Tolto geži exilegdeheŋ anxaŋ debter oroşibay* [The First Volume of "Artery of the Heart," Accomodated to the New Buriat Alphabet] (St. Petersburg: Tipo-Litografiia V. Avidona, 1908), 27 pp. The title "Zūrxeŋ Tolto" [Artery of the Heart] was taken from a grammatical treatise, *Jirüken-ü tolta*, that was written in the fourteenth century by the famous translator Choskyi Odzer but has not survived to our day. Only grammatical compositions written by Mongols as a commentary on Choskyi Odzer's work have come down to us. See P. B. Baldanzhapov, *Jirüken-ü tolta-yin tayilburi, Mongol'skoe grammaticheskoe sochinenie XVIII veka* (Ulan-Ude: Buriatskoe knizhnoe izdatel'stvo, 1962). 2) Tales from the *Üliger-ün dalai* rendered into the new script by Dorzhiev and the teacher Bayarto Vampilay, *Tales of the Prince Boyanto and the Prince Saran Gereltu.* Agvaŋ Bayarto xoyor, *Boyanto xaŋ xūbūŋ Saraŋ Gereltu xaŋ xūbūŋ xoyari üliger* [Tales of the Prince Boyanto and the Prince Saran Gereltu] (St. Petersburg: Tipografiia Busselia, 1908), 48 pp. 3) Excerpts of didactic Mongol literature in two parts: *1. Tales for Instructing the Mind and Improving the Thoughts.* Lharamba ŋagvaŋ Dorziŋ sorgūliŋ bagşi Bayarto Vaŋpilay xoyor, *1. Uxān hurgaži sedxel hayžirūlxo üligernūd oroşiba* [1.Tales for Instructing the Mind and Improving the Thoughts](Pit'erbūrge xotodo: "Naraŋ" Moŋgol-Bor' ād nom biçig garaxo oroŋ, 1908), 33 pp., and 4) *2. Teachings for Instructing the Mind and Improving the Thoughts.* Cannid Xambo Agvaŋ hurgālīŋ bagşi Bayarta xoyor, *2. Uxāŋ hurgaži sedxel hayžirūlxo hurgalnūd oroşiba* [2 Teachings for Instructing the Mind and Improving the Thoughts](Pit'erbūrge xotodo: "Naraŋ" Moŋgol-Bor' ād nom

biçig garaxo oroŋ, 1908), 23 pp.

27. 2. *Uxāŋ hurgaži sedxel hayžirūlxo hurgalnūd oroşiba*, 22.

28. Nikuulay Amagayyib, Agvaŋ, Orod Pùşkeni zurasaŋ Altaŋ Zagasuŋ ontoxo oroşiba [The Fairy Tale "The Golden Fish" Written by the Russian Pushkin] (N.p.: n.p., 1910), 12 pp.

29. N. Amagaev and Alamzhi-Mergen, *Novyi mongolo-buriatskii alfavit* (St. Petersburg: Tipografiia Imperatorskoi akademii nauk, 1910), 51 pp.

30. Ibid., p. 9.

31. *Chano batur, Geroicheskaia poema irkutskikh buriat-oiratov* zapis' N. Amagaeva; posleslovie Agvana (Pitirburgede: Tipo-Litografiia B. Avidona, 1910), 12 pp.

32. We have seen only one brief reference to another work that may have existed: a "Collection of Mongol-Buriat Folk Songs" allegedly compiled by Amagaev, Alamzhi-Mergen, Zhamtsarano, the ethnographer Mikhail Khangalov, and the bard P.P. Batorov at about the same time as *Chano-Batur* and printed by the Academy of Sciences. G.M. Amagaev, "Zhizn' i deiatel'nost' N. I. Amagaeva (1868-1932)," in *Tsybikovskie chteniia 6: Problemy istorii i kul'tury mongol'skikh narodov. Tezisy dokladov* ed. Sh. B. Chimitdorzhiev, D.D. Nimaev, and G.A. Dyrkheeva, p. 25.

33. P. Sibirskii, "K istorii obshchestvenno-revoliutsionnogo dvizheniia uchitel'stva v Buriatii" *Zhizn' Buriatii* (1927) 4-6: pp. 68-72, (1927) 7-9: pp. 5-56, (1927) 10-12: pp. 70-74; (1927) 4-6, pp. 70-72.

34. Montgomery, "Buriat Language Policy," p. 159; Amagaev and Alamzhi-Mergen, *Novyi mongolo-buriatskii alfavit*, p. 3. Amagaev and Alamzhi-Mergen do note (loc. cit.) that some conservative Transbaikal lamas disliked the idea of replacing the traditional Mongol script.

35. During the course of his life, Bodganov's views evolved from advocacy of assimilation and rejection of the Buriat and Mongolian heritage to promotion of Buriat nationalism and autonomy. At the time of the Dorzhiev alphabet project, Bogdanov considered that the cultural homogenization attendant to the development of capitalism would inevitably lead to the Buriats' assimilation into the Russian majority; since Russification was the sole means of Buriat economic and cultural advancement, attempts to preserve and develop Buriat culture and language were not only futile but counterproductive. But the autocracy's continuing oppression of non-Russian nationalities and the racism Bogdanov encountered among many ordinary Russians gradually led him to reject his identification with Russian culture and defensively adopt Buriat nationalism. N.N. Koz'min, "Mikhail Nikolaevich Bogdanov. Iz lichnykh vospominanii" *Zhizn' Buriatii* (1925) 34: pp. 18-26, and "Mikhail Nikolaevich Bogdanov," in *Ocherki istorii buriat-mongol'skogo naroda*, pp. 173-83; Rupen, *Mongols of the Twentieth Century*, vol. 1, pp. 18-19.

36. M.N. Bogdanov, "Buriatskoe 'vozrozhdenie'" *Sibirskie voprosy* (1907) 3: pp. 38-49. Bogdanov's article was vigorously attacked by Zhamtsarano and the Russian ethnographer Dmitrii Aleksandrovich Klements (1848-1914) in two subsequent articles in *Sibirskie voprosy*: Zhamtsarano, "Narodnicheskoe dvizhenie buriat i ego kritik" (cited above) and D. Klements, "Pessimizm na buriatskoi pochve" (1907) 10: pp. 7-23. Zhamtsarano and Klements pointed out that the alphabet was still too new for anyone to judge its usefulness and cited the multinational Austro-Hungarian empire as proof that the assimilation of small nationalities was not inevitable in the modern age.

37. Badzar Baradin, *Otryvki iz buriatskoi narodnoi literatury, Teksty/Buriaad zonoi uran ugiin deeji* (St. Petersburg: Tipografia Imperatorskoi akademii nauk, 1910).

38. Snelling, *Buddhism in Russia*, pp. 129-41, 144-46, 157-62; Dorzhiev, *Dorjiev: Memoirs of a Tibetan Diplomat*, pp. 35-36; A. I. Andreev, *Buddiiskaia sviatynia Petrograda / The Buddhist Shrine in Petrograd* (Ulan-Ude: Agentstvo Eko-Art, 1992), passim.

39. Vagindra, *Dalai-yi ergijü bitügsen domog sonirqal-un bicig tedüi kemeküi orosiba* [A Curious Story (about) Travels around the Ocean] (1921), LOIVAN, Mong. S 531.

40. Amagaev and Alamzhi-Mergen, *Novyi mongolo-buriatskii alfavit*, p. 3.

41. Poppe, *Buriat-mongol'skoe iazykoznanie*, p. 97.

42. Nicholas Poppe, *Introduction to Altaic Linguistics* (Wiesbaden: Otto Harrassowitz, 1965), p. 87. Poppe asserts elsewhere that Zhamtsarano was simultaneously stripped of his Russian citizenship. Nicholas Poppe, *Reminiscences*. ed. Henry G. Schwarz (Bellingham, WA: Western Washington University Press, 1983), p. 43. This claim is highly doubtful, however, since Zhamtsarano worked for the Russian embassy while in Mongolia and was allowed to return to Russia for brief visits, primarily as a translator for Mongolian delegations. Sh. B. Chimitdorzhiev, "Russko-mongol'skie sviazi v oblasti kul'tury i prosveshcheniia (nach. XX v.)," in *Olon ulsyn mongolch erdemtnii V ikh khural* [Fifth International Congress of Mongolists] 3 vols. ed. Sh. Bira (Ulaanbaatar: Olon ulsyn mongol sudlalyn kholboo, 1992), vol. 1, pp. 186-87; D. Tsend, "Mongold elegtei khün," in *Tsyben Zhamtsarano: Zhizn'i deiatel'nost. Doklady i tezisy nauchnoi konferentsii, posviashchennoi 111-letiiu vydaiushchegosia uchenogo, obshchestvennogo i nauchnogo deiatelia buriat-mongol'skogo i khalkha-mongol'skogo narodov Tsybena Zhamtsaranovicha Zhamtsarano* chief ed. V. Ts. Naidakov (Ulan-Ude: Buriatskii institut obshchestvennykh nauk, 1991), pp. 29-30; V. E. Radnaev, "Ts. Zh. Zhamtsarano kak perevodchik i populizator znanii," in *ibid*, p. 45.

43. Montgomery, "Buriat Language Policy," pp. 224ff; Ts. B. Tsydendambaev, "Itogi i nasushchnye problemy iazykovogo stroitel'stva v Buriatii," in *Filologicheskie zapiski* ed. Ts. B. Tsydendambaev, L. E. Eliasov, R. P. Matveeva (Ulan-Ude: Buriatskii institut obshchestvennykh nauk, 1973), pp. 65-78; I. Dampilon. *Itogi iazykovogo stroitel'stva Buriat-Mongolii. Doklad i zakliuchitel'noe slovo na lingvisticheskoi konferentsii BMASSR 1-8 iiulia 1936 g.* (Ulan-Ude: Institut iazyka, literatury istorii pri TsIK BMSSR, 1936), pp. 43-48; Sh. B. Chimitdorzhiev, *Kto my--buriat-mongoly?* (Ulan-Ude: Assotsiiatsiia literatorov Buriatii, 1991), pp. 50-54. Adherence to pan-Mongolism was one of the most common charges brought against Buriats during the Great Purges. Iu. P. Shagdurov, "Statisticheskie dannye o massovykh repressiakh v 1937-1938 godakh v Buriat-Mongolii," in *Tsybikovskie chteniia 6: Problemy istorii i kul'tury mongol'skikh narodov*, pp. 65-66.

44. Arash Bormanshinov, *Kalmyk Manual* (Washington, D.C.: American Council of Learned Societies, 1963; Research and Studies in Uratic and Altaic Languages, Project No. 26), pp. 42-43; D. A. Pavlov, "Formirovanie i razvitie kalmytskogo natsional'nogo iazyka," in *Problemy mongol'skogo iazykoznaniia: sbornik nauchnykh trudov* ed. L. D. Shagdarov (Novosibirsk: Nauka, 1988), pp. 98-100; Kara, *Knigi mongol'skikh kochevnikov*, pp. 102-103; Rupen, *Mongols of the Twentieth Century*, vol. 1, p. 243; C. R. Bawden, *The Modern History of Mongolia* 2nd ed. (London: Kegan Paul International, 1989), p. 377; B. Kh. Todaeva, *Iazyk mongolov Vnutrennei Mongolii: Ocherk dialektov* (Moskva: Nauka, 1985), pp. 4-9; A. A. Moskalev, *Politika KNR v natsional'no-iazykovom voprose* (Moskva: Nauka, 1981), pp. 71, 98-99, 110, 130-31, 151.

45. *Mongoloi niuusa tobsho / Sokrovennoe skazanie mongolov* trans. Ch. R. Namzhilov and S. A. Kozin (Ulaan-Üde: Buriaadai nomoi kheblel, 1990).

46. Montgomery, "Buriat Language Policy," pp. 311-15.

Part II

International Diplomacy Concerning Outer Mongolia

International diplomacy has played a decisive role in Outer Mongolia's post-World War I history. In 1921, the Red Army invaded Outer Mongolia, ostensibly to oust the last anti-Bolshevik White forces.[1] Even though Moscow had renounced in its 1919 Karakhan Manifesto all former Tsarist "unequal treaties" with China, on November 5, 1921, the Bolsheviks signed a treaty recognizing the legitimacy of the new Soviet-backed Mongolian government.[2]

On May 31, 1924, China and the USSR formally opened diplomatic relations. In the public treaty, the Soviet government acknowledged that Outer Mongolia was an integral part of China and promised to revise all unequal treaties.[3] A secret protocol attached to this agreement, however, stated that pending the future negotiation of these new treaties, the USSR and China agreed that all former treaties "will not be enforced."[4] Moscow interpreted this protocol to mean that so long as a new treaty was not signed, the terms of the former Tsarist treaties continued to apply; simply by postponing negotiations on a new treaty, therefore, the Bolsheviks were able to reinstate Tsarist Russia's former rights and privileges in Outer Mongolia.[5]

This Soviet diplomatic maneuver soon led to the establishment, on November 25, 1924, of the Mongolian People's Republic (MPR), the first communist country to be formed outside of the official borders of the Soviet Union.[6] China was powerless to resist the USSR's imperial domination of lands that even Moscow had publicly acknowledged were Chinese territory. But following the unification of China under the Nationalists in 1928, tensions over the Chinese Eastern Railway in Manchuria led to a 1929 border war between the USSR and China; Japanese accounts suggested that the treaty ending this conflict favored Moscow.[7]

As Elena Boikova discusses in her essay on Soviet-Mongolian relations, the USSR signed a series of diplomatic agreements with the MPR between 1929-39.[8] These included the June 27, 1929 "Agreement on the Main Principles of Mutual Relations Between the USSR and Mongolia," and the March 12, 1936 "Protocol on the Mutual Assistance Between the USSR and the MPR." As a result, the Red Army was granted direct access to the Mongolian border with China, effectively making the Sino-Mongolian border the USSR's first line of defense against China and, later, against Japan. The MPR was turned into a Soviet buffer state, and in this capacity protected one of the most vulnerable parts of the Soviet frontier from the mid-1930s until the 1991 dissolution of the USSR.

* * *

Moscow's success in asserting its "colonial" rule over Outer Mongolia formed part of the Russo-Japanese struggle to define their mutual spheres of interest in Northeast Asia. Arguably the first stage in this struggle began in 1860, when Russia acquired hundreds-of-thousands of square miles of formerly Chinese territory in Siberia by means of the Treaty of Peking and then founded, during the same year, the Pacific Coast city of Vladivostok, which translates as "Ruler of the East." Japan, which had its own imperial ambitions, was alarmed. Russo-Japanese tensions over Korea in the early 1890s led to the 1894-95 Sino-Japanese War, which Japan won. Although China ceded the Manchurian Liaodong peninsula to Japan in 1895, the so-called triple intervention of Russia, Germany, and France forced Tokyo to give it back. When Russia later took this same territory, Japan went to war and became the first Asian power to defeat a European one.[9]

As a result of the 1904-05 Russo-Japanese War, China's northeastern provinces in Manchuria were divided into competing Russian and Japanese spheres of influence. The Russo-Japanese struggle to divide Northeast Asia was carried on behind the scenes. The two governments signed a series of secret agreements in 1907, 1910, 1912, and 1916, that granted the Russian government Outer Mongolia and Northern Manchuria in return for Japan retaining Korea, Southern Manchuria, and parts of Inner Mongolia.

Although it was long assumed that these secret agreements were terminated by the Bolsheviks' 1917 revolution, in 1925 the Soviet and Japanese governments once again formally recognized these agreements by publicly agreeing to revise all former treaties, but then never actually doing so.[10] This diplomatic strategy closely parallelled the USSR's negotiating technique with China, since so long as new treaties were never signed all of the former Russo-Japanese terms continued to be valid. Faced with the Soviet Union's 1929 consolidation of power over Outer Mongolia, and the prospect of its expansion into Manchuria, Japan's aggressive military forced the creation of the puppet state of Manchukuo in 1931-32.

As Bruce Elleman argues in his essay, the final stage in the division of Northeast Asia was achieved soon after the 1939 conflict at Nomonhan, with the April 13, 1941 signing of the Soviet-Japanese non-aggression pact. In a joint declaration attached to this pact, Tokyo recognized the territorial integrity and inviolability of the Mongolian People's Republic in exchange for Moscow's recognition of Japan's puppet state in Manchukuo, thereby completely delimiting the Soviet and Japanese spheres of interest in Northeast Asia. Later, the Soviet government promised Chiang Kai-shek's Nationalist government that it would not support the Chinese Communists in return for China's agreement to recognize the independence of Outer Mongolia; after the 1949 creation of the People's Republic of China, Mao Zedong openly criticized Moscow for dominating Outer Mongolia, but he was powerless to reverse this circumstance.

* * *

Mongol aspirations to create a so-called Greater Mongolia have existed ever since the initial partitioning of Mongolia in 1911-1915. During the 1920s, for example, the newly created Mongolian People's Republic strove to regain Uriankhai, Inner Mongolia, and Bargu, but these aspirations were "successfully checked" by international events and by the Soviet government.[11]

At the end of World War II the Mongol people in Inner and Outer Mongolia had high hopes, if only for a short time, that they might be able to reunify the two divided areas into one country, which they commonly referred to as "Greater Mongolia." During 1945-46, however, these hopes were dashed, as the so-called second partition of Mongolia granted Inner Mongolia to China, while the MPR remained in the Soviet orbit.

In his essay on the second partition, Christopher Atwood discusses the goals and activities of the Inner Mongolian separatists, who were at first actively supported by the Soviet leader Stalin and the MPR leader Choibalsang, but later abandoned to the Chinese as the price for the MPR's independence. New archival sources are used to relate the history of the Mongolian question, the Sino-Soviet negotiations concerning Inner and Outer Mongolia, and the MPR's forced repudiation of its nationalistic goal of uniting with Inner Mongolia. Moscow's opportunistic policy of supporting "autonomous" governments, but then sacrificing them to further its own long-range diplomatic goals, has left a legacy of anger and mistrust among the Mongol people.

* * *

In the final essay of this section, we return to the question of Mongolia's diplomatic relations with Japan. Tsedendambyn Batbayar picks up the story of Mongolia's relations with Tokyo in the period after 1945. Following the opening of unofficial trade between Mongolia and Japan in 1959, extensive efforts to normalize relations were undertaken throughout the 1960s; these actions led to formal recognition in 1972. Economic cooperation soon followed, and during the 1980s the two countries experienced an enormous expansion of trade as a result of Mongolia's "open door" policy. The deepening of Japanese-Mongolian relations was followed by increased U.S.-Mongol ties, as the two countries opened relations in 1987.[12]

This almost thirty-year period of Japanese-Mongolian cooperation deepened after 1991, when Mongolia acheived true independence. As Batbayar shows, Japan has arguably played the leading role in promoting trade, in granting developmental aid, and in providing technical training and scientific assistance to Mongolia. In some ways, Japan's recent strengthening of relations with Mongolia may seem reminiscent of the 1930s (there have even been half-hearted suggestions that Japan form a political confederation with Mongolia). But, today's Japanese-Mongolian diplomatic relations continue to be based on economic cooperation, as the Japanese people assist the Mongols in this difficult period of transition from a socialist to a capitalist economy.

Notes

1. George G.S. Murphy, *Soviet Mongolia, A Study of the Oldest Political Satellite* (Berkeley, CA: University of California Press, 1966), pp. 1-28.

2. C. Martin Wilbur and Julie Lien-ying How, *Missionaries of Revolution, Soviet Advisers and Nationalist China, 1920-1927* (Cambridge, MA: Harvard University Press, 1989), p. 22; According to Wilbur: "Russia's unwillingness to permit China to control this buffer area was the stumbling block that prevented three Russian missions from effecting formal intergovernmental relations with Peking." Ibid., p. 5.

3. Allen S. Whiting, *Soviet Policies in China, 1917-1924* (Stanford, CA: Stanford University Press, 1968), pp. 208-35.

4. Sow-Theng Leong, *Sino-Soviet Diplomatic Relations, 1917-1926* (Taipei, Taiwan: Rainbow-Bridge Book Co., 1976), pp. 260-72.

5. Bruce A. Elleman, "Secret Sino-Soviet Negotiations On Outer Mongolia, 1918-1925," *Pacific Affairs* Vol. 66, No. 4 (Winter 1993): pp. 539-63.

6. Jeanne Nickell Knutson, *Outer Mongolia, A Study in Soviet Colonialism* (Kowloon, Hong Kong : Union Research Institute, 1959), pp. 74-77.

7. "Russo-Chinese Agreement," *The Japan Advertiser*, 23 December 1929.

8. *Sovetsko-Mongol'ski otnosheniia, 1921-1947. Dokumenty i materialy* (The Soviet-Mongolian Relations. 1921-1947. Documents and Materials), V. I. (Moscow, 1975).

9. John J. Stephan, *The Russian Far East, A History* (Stanford, CA: Stanford Univesity Press, 1994), pp. 53-61, 79-80.

10. Bruce A. Elleman, "The 1907-1916 Russo-Japanese Secret Treaties: A Reconsideration," *Asian Cultural Studies* Vol. 25 (March 30, 1999): pp. 29-44.

11. Gerard M. Friters, *Outer Mongolia And Its International Position* (London: George Allen & Unwin LTD, 1951), p. 133.

12. Alan J. K. Sanders, *Historical Dictionary of Mongolia* (London: The Scarecrow Press, 1996), pp. xxxviii-xli.

10. Religious Procession, Urga, 1922. *Source*: Roy Chapman Andrews, *On the Trail of Ancient Man* (New York: G. P. Putnam's Sons, 1926).

11. Choibalsang Frees the Captured Lamas, August 20, 1945. *Source*: Mongolian Central Party Archives, BX.01.208.

12. Marshal Choibalsang and Soviet Ambassador I.A. Ivanov Interview Local Inner Mongols, 1945. *Source*: Mongolian Central Party Archives, BX.01.199.

13. Marshal Choibalsang Visits the Poverty-stricken Chinese with Ambassador Ivanov. *Source*: Mongolian Central Party Archives, BX.01.200.

14. Marshal Choibalsang with the Soviet Commanders Reviews the Troops at the Victory Parade in Rehe, 1945. *Source*: Mongolian Central Party Archives, BX.01.179.

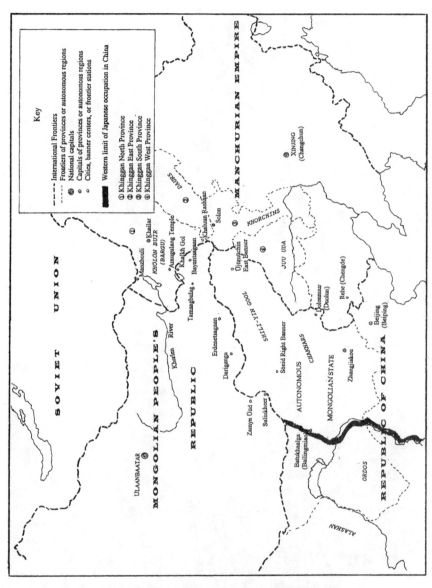

Map: Mongolia and Inner Mongolia, 1945
Source: Map courtesy of Christopher P. Atwood

Aspects of Soviet-Mongolian Relations, 1929-1939

Elena Boikova

By the end of the 1920s the principle of cooperation with the USSR to build "socialism through non-capitalist development" was proclaimed as the official state policy of the Mongolian People's Republic (MPR). An "Agreement on the Main Principles of Mutual Relations Between the USSR and Mongolia" was concluded on June 27, 1929, in Ulaanbaatar. Although top secret and not published at that time, this agreement in many respects defined the form and orientation of Soviet-Mongolian relations in the 1930s, as well as the general character of the Soviet presence in the MPR through 1936, when the USSR and the MPR signed a protocol closely linking their military forces; Outer Mongolian troops later fought and died side-by-side with the Red Army in the 1939 battle at Khalkhingol (Nomonhan), in the name of opposing Japanese expansion.[1]

For a long time, the contents of the 1929 agreement and the 1936 Protocol were unknown even to specialists. In hindsight, it is fairly clear that the classification of these documents sought to hide an underlying duplicity in the USSR's foreign policy toward China and Mongolia: although admitting publicly that Outer Mongolia was an integral part of China, the Soviet government's policies in fact treated the MPR almost as if it were a part of the USSR.

The Soviet Union's apparently contradictory policies with regard to China and Outer Mongolia sought to achieve several important strategic goals. The first was to use the MPR as a buffer state to demilitarize and protect the USSR's lengthy border with China. The second was to link the Soviet and Mongolian military forces to oppose Japanese expansion in Manchuria and Inner Mongolia. Finally, an important third goal was to support the Comintern's long-range policy of promoting additional Far Eastern revolutions—most importantly, in China—that would lead to the inevitable "world revolution."

This essay will use recently declassified Soviet archives to examine Soviet-Mongolian relations from 1929-39. Although the Soviet government's relations with the MPR were publicly characterized as fraternal—with the USSR the 'elder brother' and Outer Mongolia the 'younger brother'—the MPR was clearly a junior partner at best. In fact, although the USSR's diplomatic relations with China guaranteed Outer Mongolia's autonomy, it denied the Mongolian people the true independence they desired. Faced with the threat of Japanese expansion into Outer Mongolia, the Soviet authorities ordered the MPR army to fight Japan, while simultaneously repressing pan-Mongolian tendencies among the Outer Mongolian people. The legal character of Soviet-Mongolian relations—with Outer Mongolia obtaining *de facto* independence from China at the same time as its government and military were under tight Soviet control—was arguably a phenomenon unique in the history of international law.

The Soviet-Mongolian Agreement of June 27, 1929

The Sino-Soviet Agreement of 1924 recognized Outer Mongolia as a part of China, but this agreement did not hinder the subsequent development of bilateral relations between the USSR and Mongolia. The Soviet-Mongolian Agreement of 1929 was drawn up in accordance with the USSR's political and ideological aims: to promote class struggle and the non-capitalist development of the MPR, to exclude foreign and private capital from the Mongolian economy, and to further agricultural cooperation through collectivization.

The opening of Sino-Soviet diplomatic relations in 1924 raised many complicated issues for the foreign policies of both the Soviet Union and Mongolia. In accordance with "The Agreement on the General Settlement of Principles for Soviet Russia and the Chinese Republic of May 31, 1924," the Soviet Union acknowledged Mongolia as an integral part of China.[2] But even though the USSR claimed in 1925 that all Red Army troops had left Outer Mongolia, close military links were secretly retained. Increased Sino-Soviet friction along the Chinese Eastern Railway in Manchuria during May 1929 made it imperative that the USSR and the MPR clarify their diplomatic relations.

With the signing of the June 27, 1929 Agreement, the Soviet Union once again appeared to recognize the People's Government of Mongolia as the only legitimate government on the territory of Outer Mongolia. This decision contradicted its 1924 treaty with China, and once again confirmed the USSR's recognition of Outer Mongolia as originally stated in "The Agreement Between the Government of the Russian Federation and the People's Government of Mongolia on Establishing Friendly Relations Between Russia and Mongolia of November 5, 1921."[3]

But it is important to note that the 1929 Agreement regulating relations between the USSR and Mongolia was careful not to address the fundamental question of mutual recognition of sovereignty and independence of both parties. This omission later allowed the Soviet government to insist to China that it continued to abide by the 1924 Sino-Soviet treaty, even though the Soviet government's actions clearly showed that Outer Mongolia was not a part of China.

Faced with possible anti-Soviet aggression by the Chinese government in Manchuria, both the USSR and Mongolia considered that they had many mutual interests in common, and that the development and strengthening of their economic and political cooperation would achieve these aims. The official Mongolian view was expressed in the preamble to the 1929 Agreement, which stated that the working people of Mongolia had made a decision on the non-capitalist development of their country by promoting their own industry, enlarging and further developing their own cattle-breeding and agriculture, collectivizing agriculture, developing cooperative and state trade, and having the government regulate the economy.[4]

The contents of the 1929 Agreement were narrower than its title, however, since it regulated mainly trade and economic relations between the two countries.

To achieve these goals, the document outlined the main principles of trade cooperation, including the activity of such Soviet economic organizations in Mongolia and the USSR as the mutual Soviet-Mongolian Trade-Industrial Bank and transport organizations. The USSR also agreed to cooperate with Mongolia in health service and in veterinary medicine, to help train Mongolian students in the Soviet Union, and to send Soviet specialists to Mongolia.

In addition, by means of the 1929 Agreement the USSR obtained most-favored-nation status in the MPR. This meant that the Soviet Union officially became the first—and practically the only—trading partner of Mongolia. The 1929 Agreement further stated that the exceptional privileges which the USSR and Mongolia granted to each other should not be applied to other countries, since that "would not correspond with the aims and tasks of both contracting parties."[5]

This clause helped buttress the legal position of the Soviet government as it sought to monopolize almost all economic relations with the MPR. In fact, as a result of these close economic links, Soviet-Mongolian relations inevitably became stronger, first in political and ideological matters, and then later in the military arena.

Although the Chinese authorities soon learned that the USSR and the MPR had signed an agreement, its "top secret" contents were never published and so the Chinese government was not in a position to denounce its contents. Clearly, the Soviet Union and Mongolia signed the agreement as a warning to China not to interfere in Outer Mongolia. The agreement was also intended to show China that Outer Mongolia could conduct its international affairs without first gaining permission from the Chinese government.

The 1929 Soviet-Mongolian Agreement not only reoriented the foreign contacts of Mongolia mainly toward the USSR, but it also created the legal foundation for the establishment of a Soviet monopoly in trade and economic relations with Mongolia. This agreement confirmed the economic orientation of Mongolia toward the Soviet Union for the next sixty-odd years. It was eventually denounced in 1990, by the opposition Mongolian Social Democratic Party, as having prohibited Mongolia from establishing "economic relations with other countries, [and thereby] isolating it."[6]

Although the signing of the 1929 Soviet-Mongolian Agreement was a direct response to increasing Sino-Soviet tensions and was intended to warn China not to interfere in Outer Mongolia, it also proved to China that the USSR would continue to deal with the Mongolian government directly, irrespective of its legal status and the degree of its dependence on China. However, Mongolia's legal standing according to international law was that it remained an integral part of China, which meant that other countries remained unwilling to establish official diplomatic relations with the MPR. As a result, Outer Mongolia's diplomatic isolation gave the Soviet Union an unhampered opportunity to consolidate its own political and economic position in Mongolia, and the Agreement of 1929 soon became the foundation of a Soviet-Mongolian *entente*.

Soviet-Mongolian Interaction and Cooperation

The Agreement of 1929 became the basic treaty underlying Soviet-Mongolian relations. According to the treaty, there were principal disagreements or major differences in opinion between Soviet and Mongolian leaders over political and strategic questions, such as transport, industry, trade, banking, and joint Soviet-Mongolian organizations in Mongolia.[7] Mongolia was interested in promoting interaction and cooperation with Soviet organizations primarily in order to achieve greater economic development. The Soviet Union, for its part, following its ideological principles and geopolitical interests, concluded the treaty to further pull the Mongols within the sphere of Soviet influence. Controversially perhaps, it can be argued, taking into consideration the complicated nature of international politics in the 1930s, that the 1929 agreement served the interests of both the USSR and the MPR.

Soviet policy regarding the "Mongolian question" at the end of the 1920s revolved around ways to draw the MPR further from China and closer to the USSR. This policy was consistent with Moscow's long-range aims in the Far East, as Moscow sought to strengthen its political position in Mongolia by first strengthening its economic sphere. For example, in the second half of the 1920s the Soviet Union—with the assistance of the Mongolian authorities—began to force China out of the Mongolian economy. The foreign trade figures show that the USSR was largely successful in this endeavor: in 1927, Mongolian exports to the USSR were 16,900 thousand tugriks and to China—12,800 thousand tugriks; in 1928—21,000 thousand tugriks and 10,780 thousand tugriks, respectively; in 1929—21,500 thousand tugriks and 8,500 thousand tugriks, respectively; in 1930—21,500 and 6,040 thousand tugriks, respectively. Meanwhile, imports from the USSR to Mongolia (in thousands of tugriks) increased rapidly: in 1927—4,000, in 1928—7,100, in 1929—11,300. By contrast, imports from China to Mongolia (in thousand tugriks) fell: in 1927—27,600, in 1928—25,400, in 1929—8,700.[8]

One of the most important factors that influenced the sharp lowering of the Mongolian-Chinese commodity circulation was the closing of the border in the Kalgan district, in connection with the conflict on the Chinese Eastern Railway. Spurred on by this political dispute, the Soviet Union assumed first place in Mongolia's foreign trade by the beginning of the 1930s. Even more importantly, Soviet representatives and advisers in Mongolian foreign trade organizations took control not only over the quantity of Chinese goods, but also over the growth of trade with the USSR. In the opinion of the Soviet plenipotentiary in Mongolia, the resumption of Mongolian-Chinese trade in anything resembling the previous volume was impermissible.[9]

In the 1930s, the Mongolian leadership cooperated in the Soviet efforts to carry out measures to weaken Chinese influence in the country. Many Chinese merchants occupied in private trade were deported from Mongolia; other Chinese merchants were severely limited in their commercial activities.[10] Throughout this period, the Mongolian secret police also continued its policy of identifying Chinese "counter-revolutionary elements" in Mongolia and deporting them to Inner Mongolia.[11] In addition, Mongolia supported its own intelligence network in China: on October 10, 1935, the Mongolian State Internal Guard reported to the Executive Committee of the Comintern and the People's Commissariat for Foreign Affairs of the Russian Federation that an agent named Zhu Shifu, supported by twenty-seven Mongols and Chinese, had been sent from Ulaanbaatar to China to carry out intelligence activities there.[12]

In the beginning of the 1930s, the Mongolian government accepted the inevitable and agreed that the main trading partner and companion in its internal development would be the Soviet Union. Bilateral trade cooperation proceeded in accordance with prior agreements, while military cooperation between the USSR and the MPR was strengthened and a legal framework was constructed by the middle of the 1930s. The Soviet Union and Mongolia signed a series of special agreements in the military sphere, including one on the installation of a radio network in Mongolia in 1933, and one on a military loan from the USSR in 1934.

Under the constant threat of the heightening of international tension in the Far East, just one of the results of Japan's aggression in Manchuria, the problem of Mongolian security and proper Soviet guarantees of the MPR became more urgent. On April 4, 1934 the Council of the Ministers of the MPR adopted a resolution declaring that the Mongolian Army was ready to repulse the Japanese in case of their aggression against Mongolia. Under these circumstances it became necessary to strengthen the Mongolian Military Forces.[13]

Working on its own, the Mongolian government paid special attention to its military preparedness problem and passed concrete reforms to resolve the problem. For example, in 1933 the government mandated compulsory military service; in 1934, the government authorized the additional mobilization of 21-25 year-old men to active service; in 1936, the State Internal Guard Forces were reorganized within the Ministry of Interior Affairs. But the Mongolian government did not have enough financial and human resources to carry through on their official declaration. Under the threat of a Japanese armed attack on Mongolia via the territory of Manchukuo, near the end of 1934 the Chairman of the Council of Ministers of Mongolia, P. Gendün, officially applied to the Soviet government to assist Mongolia in case of any military attack by a third country.

Gendün's request opened the door for the USSR and the MPR to initiate diplomatic negotiations to conclude a mutual defense treaty. Clearly, it was in the interest of the Soviet Union and the Mongolian People's Republic to carry out bilateral military cooperation in the early 1930s, but by the mid-1930s this was seen by the USSR to be insufficient. Moscow exerted pressure on Ulaanbaatar to extend joint military cooperation into an enlarged treaty framework. The resulting negotiations eventually led to the Soviet goal of completing a Protocol on Mutual Assistance between the USSR and the MPR, signed on March 12, 1936. This protocol outlined the general principles of future Soviet-Mongolian cooperation in the military sphere.

Mongolian Opposition to the Soviet-Mongolian Protocol

After the Russian-Mongolian treaty of 1921, the Protocol of 1936 became the first official state treaty to include military cooperation between the USSR and the MPR. Both sides could take this step because they had formerly concluded other bilateral treaties and agreements—such as the 1929 agreement—to test the character of China's official reaction to them. Though China's reaction to the 1936 Protocol was negative, Chinese authorities had little choice but to submit to its conditions. Most importantly, the Protocol gave Soviet troops the option, interacting with the Mongolian Army, to create a covering detachment to counter the Japanese-Manchurian troops already on the Manchurian-Mongolian border. Since this almost assured that any Soviet-Japanese conflict would be fought on Mongolian territory, this protocol was initially opposed by top officials in the MPR government.

The background of the 1936 Soviet-Mongolian protocol can be traced back to the note of the Mongolian government of February 27, 1925, discussing the withdrawal of the Soviet Military troops from Mongolia. This document stated: ". . . the people and the Government of our Republic firmly believe in the help of the Soviet Union and the Red Army if, beyond expectation, the circumstances similar to those which were in 1921 come again."[14] By the early 1930s, the Mongolian authorities did not exclude the possibility of appealing once more to the Soviet government to render military assistance and support. However, during the middle of the 1930s the internal situation in Mongolia was complicated by a sharp struggle for power within the leadership. During 1934, a cooling in diplomatic relations occurred between Stalin and the Chairman of the Mongolian Council of Ministers, Gendün.

The reason for this cooling was Gendün's open disagreement on the need for a political alliance between the USSR and the MPR. With regard to such an alliance, Gendün vocally opposed the "interference with the internal affairs of the Mongols from outside."[15] In particular, Gendün spoke out against the planned annihilation of more than 100,000 Mongolian lamas, which the Soviet representatives in Mongolia warned were the primary supporters of the Japanese.[16]

Gendün's political independence from Moscow was confirmed in confidential reports by the Soviet Embassy in Mongolia. In the midst of talks with Soviet diplomats, Gendün stated: "We lean on the Soviet Union not for its sake and in the same way not for the international revolution, but in the interests of the constant strengthening of our national independence."[17] The Minister of Defence of the MPR, G. Demid, also spoke of broadening economic relations not with only the USSR, but also with other countries; he considered that a one-sided orientation on the Soviet Union could make Mongolia a Soviet colony.[18]

In the mid-1930s, the Mongolian authorities made a last-ditch effort to contain the process of growing Soviet influence in Mongolia. The leaders of Mongolia explained that their measures were necessary to teach the Mongols to work independently. In January 1934, Gendün issued an order to reduce the number of

Soviet instructors and specialists employed in jobs in Mongolia who could be replaced by Mongol specialists.[19] Clearly, Gendün hoped to oust the Soviet specialists from the state's central and local administration agencies. A special commission was created whose task was to curtail the number of foreign instructors and specialists, as well as to check the correspondence of the remaining instructors and specialists with the goal of replacing them with Mongolian specialists. Thus, there was an attempt made to "mongolize" almost all middle and top management.

That attempt, however, was not successful because of the simple fact that though the overall number of Soviet instructors and specialists was reduced, they continued to dominate the key posts and positions; for example, in the education and culture division, political section, and military spheres there were still many Soviet instructors, advisers, and specialists.[20] In addition, the Mongolian leadership soon realized that the Mongols who were trained in the Soviet Union could not replace Soviet specialists overnight.

Faced with a serious dearth of Mongolian specialists, the Mongolian authorities realized the necessity of taking into consideration the wishes, and even demands, of the Soviet Union and the necessity of making concessions. Later, this led to the full rejection of the MPR's own national interests. Gendün and Demid, who had attempted to retain the MPR's independence in Soviet-Mongolian relations, were accused in 1934 of trying to create a counter-revolutionary organization to weaken the MPR's cooperation with the Soviet Union.[21] Gendün was subsequently executed in the Soviet Union in 1937, while Demid suffered a violent death that same year. The loss of two of the MPR's most respected leaders indicated to the Mongolians that any effort to obtain greater independence would be punished by the Soviet secret services.[22]

Following the political defeat of Gendün and Demid, a 1934 visit of a Mongolian governmental delegation to the USSR led to the conclusion of a so-called Gentleman's Agreement on November 27, 1934. This agreement appeared to answer the interests of both countries by providing for "mutual support by all means to prevent the threat of military attack and render assistance and support in case of the aggression of any third country against the USSR and the MPR."[23] Yet, in accordance with this agreement, in times of need Mongolia gave the USSR the right to carry out military actions against Japan on Mongolian territory, in order to stop Japanese troops from penetrating Soviet territory.

The conclusion of just such a military-political agreement between the Soviet Union and the Mongolian People's Republic clearly contradicted Article V of the Sino-Soviet Agreement of 1924, which stated that the Soviet government recognized Outer Mongolia (the MPR) as part of the Chinese Republic and respected the sovereignty of China therein. It also violated the 1924 provision that the Soviet Union would not conclude any treaties or agreements with Outer Mongolia without special concordance with "the center" (e.g., with Beijing).[24] Finally, the conclusion of the Gentleman's Agreement showed that Moscow was prepared to use Mongolian territory to fight Japanese expansion, whatever the implications for the MPR's interests.

The Soviet-Mongolian Protocol of March 12, 1936

In the middle of the 1930s the Soviet leaders began to put more pressure on the Mongolian authorities to sign a formal military agreement. The result of this pressure was the loss of what little was left of the former balance in the Soviet-Mongolian relations in favor of the ever-strengthening of the Soviet influence in Mongolia. The rational for signing this military agreement was that Japan, after it could not carry out its plans to destabilize the domestic affairs of the MPR, was now preparing for direct military aggression against Mongolia.

Beginning in 1935, there were frequent border conflicts between the Mongolian Frontier Guards and Japanese troops along the lengthy Mongolian border with Manchukuo; for example, on January 24, 1935, the Japanese troops attacked the Mongolian frontier post in Buir Nuur. A powerful drive was organized in Mongolia to oppose the Japanese-Manchurian troops. Mongolian youth were mobilized to study military science and the MPR also transferred lower lamas from religious into secular positions, with the goal of drawing them into the defense of their country since only a small part of the male population of Mongolia were in secular positions. The small pool of available men was seen as one of the main reasons for the weakness of the MPR Army, a situation which often led Mongolian troops to retreat before Japanese-Manchurian troops.

Appearing at a meeting of the workers of state, economic, military, and social organizations, Gendün claimed that Soviet troops were not necessary. All of the cases of retreat were temporary and could be ascribed to political motives, and sooner or later the government and army would be able to fight to defend the border and territory of Mongolia. But the Mongolian authorities must have known that their country would not be able to struggle against the powerful troops of the enemy only by their own means. Since it was impossible even to hope for Chinese military assistance, the Mongolian leaders realized that they could get real help only from the Soviet Union, especially since the latter was interested in halting any Japanese aggression into the Far Eastern sections of the Soviet Union.

In January 1936, a Mongolian delegation arrived in Moscow and handed the Soviet government an official request by the MPR to register in written form the 1934 Gentleman's Agreement. On January 25, 1936, this request was repeated by the Presidium of the Small People's Khural and the Council of Ministers of the MPR in an appeal signed by the Chairman of the Small Khural, A. Amur, and the Chairman of the Council of Ministers, Gendün. This appeal was addressed to the Chairman of the Central Executive Committee of the USSR, M. Kalinin, and the Chairman of the Soviet Government, V.M. Molotov.

As a result of negotiations that followed these appeals, a "Protocol on the Mutual Assistance Between the USSR and the MPR" was signed on March 12, 1936. Its primary concern was the military defence of the Mongolian border, and the preamble of the Protocol noted that both countries were motivated by the goal of retaining peace in the Far East. To achieve peace, the governments of the

Soviet Union and of Mongolia pledged to render each other all necessary assistance—including military aid—in case of military aggression against one of the participants of the treaty.[25]

The Protocol between the USSR and the MPR specified the following commitments: 1) the Soviet government gave the Mongolian government a loan of 10 million gold rubles to open an Ulaanbaatar-Chita airline; 2) both countries were to build a railway between Ulaanbaatar and Chita; 3) the USSR was to render assistance in strengthening Mongolia's military forces; 4) in case of necessity, the Mongolian government was to provide the USSR favorable conditions for moving Soviet Army troops through the territory of Mongolia.[26]

Soon after this Protocol was signed, the former leaders of the MPR were removed, and new leaders took power. Not surprisingly, these new leaders better conformed to the interests of the USSR; for example, the practice of using Soviet instructors and specialists in Mongolian organizations was renewed. Unlike before, this new crop of Soviet specialists was intent on changing the Mongols' traditional lifestyle, as the MPR expressed interest in 1939 in receiving veterinary doctors, livestock experts, printing workers, and workers in culture and arts.[27]

In October 1939, Kh. Choibalsang, the new Mongolian Prime Minister, also forwarded a letter to the Soviet leaders to send instructors to the Central Committee of the Mongolian People's Revolutionary Party and the Mongolian Revolutionary Youth League, to teach agitation, propaganda, and mass media, and to send three teachers of social sciences for Party schools, special courses, and secondary schools. According to Choibalsang, "in its present state the Party is not able to be at the head of the leadership of the country to educate young generation in the correct way and to lead people." [28] He went on to state, "the Party remains a weak part . . . [hampering] the revolutionary development of the people."[29]

Choibalsang further admitted the Mongols' low level of development in Leninist and Stalinist studies, the absence of political science textbooks for the Army, the members of the MRYL, and the *arads*, as well as the lack of a clear Party Statute. Choibalsang requested a team of consultants who would help to write textbooks, to elaborate a Party Statute, and a Constitution. He also asked for an extra forty doctors, forty doctor's assistants, and ten pharmacologists.[30] In reply, the USSR decided to send the following specialists: 1) one instructor to the Central Committee of the MPRP; 2) a total of ninety-three medical workers instead of ninety; 3) an economic adviser for the Mongolian Government; and 4) two history teachers.[31]

As for sending consultants to work out the new Party Statute, the Soviet leaders decided that there was no point in rushing this question as the Mongols themselves had formed a Commission to work out a draft, with the goal of sending the draft for consideration to the Central Committee of the Russian Communist Party. Besides that, Stalin's "Short Course of the History of the Russian Communist Party" had been translated into Mongolian; by that time 12,000 copies of that book had been published and were ready to be sent to Mongolia.[32] The Sovietization of the MPR was nearing completion.

The International Reaction to the Soviet-Mongolian Protocol

The international reaction to the 1936 Soviet-Mongolian protocol was immediate and harsh. In particular, Japan called the mutual measures of the two countries for strengthening the defense potential of Mongolia the "militarization" of Outer Mongolia. The sharp deterioration in the Far East after 1936 can be linked with the signing of this treaty. Undoubtedly, by concluding the 1936 Protocol the Soviet leaders intended not only to render assistance to Mongolia in defence of its border, but also to further their own interests. The Soviet authorities understood quite well that in case of the Japanese-Manchurian troops' successful aggression against Mongolia, the MPR would not be able to defend itself and so could not avert the advance of the aggressor's troops to the USSR border.

During the mid-1930s, as a result of the 1936 Protocol, a Japanese-supported propaganda campaign on the creation of an "independent Mongolia" became more active. The central idea behind this campaign was to liberate Mongolian territory from the Soviet presence. The realization of this plan, according to the Japanese press, would allow Japanese troops to move up to the Ural Mountains. Trying to attract the Mongols to its side in the mid-1930s, Japan aimed to show its peaceful intentions toward the Mongols by "helping" the latter to obtain independence and by becoming the guarantor of the Mongolian state security. There were many publications in the Japanese mass media in which it was explained that the Mongols and the Japanese were the representatives of the same race deeply rooted in the Ural-Altaic group.

As Yoshimura Chuzo wrote in his article "The Importance of the Mongolian Question" in *Gakan* magazine, in spite of the differences in history and culture between the Mongolian and the Japanese nations, they had many common national characteristics; for example, he wrote that the Mongols were braver than the Chinese. The author then proposed to begin the migration of the Japanese to Mongolia to enlarge the population of the latter and by that to strengthen the power of the Mongolian state as it was at the times of Chinggis Khan. One of his arguments was that the movement of Japanese to Mongolia could not constitute the oppression of one nation by another nation, since both belonged to the same yellow race.[33]

No doubt such propaganda filled both the Soviet and the Mongolian authorities with apprehension, especially since there were many Mongols who preferred being a Japanese protectorate rather than a Soviet one. In one article published in *Pravda*, it was written that the Japanese plans of creating the state "Mongo-Kuo" in Mongolia were even more important for Japan than the creation of Manchukuo, since that would untie its hands for realization of its policy on the continent and for carrying out its ultimate plan of dominating all of Asia.[34] Therefore, faced with possible aggression, the USSR and the MPR sought to demonstrate their readiness, if necessary, to resist.

Japan was not the only country to pay heed to the 1936 Protocol. The Protocol provoked a sharp negative reaction among some European countries, but even more so, in China. The Nationalist government quickly denied Mongolia's right for self-independence when signing such a treaty. Japanese officials, including the military authorities, backed up the Chinese government and the Foreign Ministry of Japan called the Protocol nothing less than a proposed military union of two countries. Clearly indignant at the Soviet Union and Mongolia, the Japanese authorities declared that they protected the interests of China, which were infringed as a result of the conclusion of the Protocol. Japan urgently demanded that the Nanjing government make an official protest against the conclusion of the Protocol, which in fact violated the Beijing Agreement of 1924.

Japan, backed by several Western countries, also insisted that China make a complaint against the USSR's actions in Mongolia to the League of Nations so as to reestablish its sovereignty over Mongolia. The Ministry of Foreign Affairs of the Chinese Republic appealed twice—on April 7 and April 12, 1936—to the People's Commissariat for Foreign Affairs of the USSR and protested the conclusion of the Protocol. In the note of April 7, the Chinese protested that the conclusion of the Protocol violated the sovereign right of China and contradicted the Chinese-Soviet Agreement of 1924.[35]

Officially, even after the 1936 Protocol, Outer Mongolia remained part of China. In an April 8, 1936 note by the People's Commissar for Foreign Affairs addressed to the charge d'affaires of the Chinese Republic in the USSR, M. Litvinov wrote that "the Soviet Government hereby confirms again that the aforesaid Agreement [1924] as it concerns the USSR, keeps its strength of law,"[36] and denied that "either the fact of the conclusion of the Protocol, or its separate articles . . . violate China's sovereignty and do not permit and contain whatever territory claims of the USSR toward China or the MPR."[37]

The governments of some European countries, including Germany, France, Great Britain, and others, considered the exchange of notes between the Soviet Union and China to be a diplomatic trick. They concluded that China's composed attitude toward both the fact of the conclusion of the Soviet-Mongolian Protocol and its further realization in practice could be explained only by a "secret agreement" between the USSR and China on the matter. But the Japanese Foreign Ministry took the Chinese protest at face value. The Chinese government on its part seemed to be satisfied since the Soviet government officially denied its intention to violate Chinese sovereignty, and claimed that it did not intend to influence the formal character of the relations between Mongolia and China.

The Soviet Union's relations with Mongolia in the 1930s clearly took into consideration the internal political situation in China, where certain political forces were interested in finding a counterbalance to the strengthening of Japanese influence in China. For example, during the 1930s, the Mongolian leaders had contacts with the Chinese Communist Party and as early as November 1931, the Congress of the Soviets of China announced the official recognition of independence of Mongolia by the Central Soviet Government of China.[38] That position completely differed from the Chiang Kai-shek government in Nanjing.

Soviet-Japanese Military Tensions over Mongolia

By concluding the Protocol of 1936, the Soviet Union finally consolidated its position in Mongolia and in fact ejected China once and for all from that country, not only economically but politically. The Soviet government's primary goal was to use the MPR as a buffer state to demilitarize and protect the USSR's lengthy border with China. A second important goal was to oppose Japanese expansion in Manchuria and Inner Mongolia. A third goal may have been to promote future Soviet expansion into China on behalf of the "world revolution."

The most important immediate impact of the 1936 Protocol was that it gave the USSR the opportunity to move its defensive network to the Sino-Mongolian border. While, on the one hand, the 1936 Protocol permitted Mongolian troops to better oppose the Japanese and the Mongolian authorities felt more confident of Soviet support in case of rising tensions on the Mongolian-Manchukuo border, on the other hand, the 1936 Protocol allowed the Red Army easy access to the border areas, and cases of reconnaissance work by Mongolian and Soviet cavalrymen and airplanes deep into Chinese territory became more common. In a February 1937 statement to the Soviet Ministry of Foreign Affairs, the Manchukuo Foreign Minister accused the MPR troops of crossing their mutual border at least five times during late 1936.[39] Instead of insuring peace, therefore, the 1936 Protocol may have intensified tensions in this sensitive area.

In conformity with the 1936 Protocol, Japanese expansion was countered by mixed Soviet-Mongolian troops. During 1937, for example, the Soviet Union sent its own troops into Mongolia. These troops were distributed in Dornogowi, Töw, Dornod, Khentii, and Sükhbaatar aimaks (i.e., in all strategically important areas coterminous with China). Thereafter, the joint armies of the Soviet Union and Mongolia held military operations against the Kwantung Army during May, July, and August 1939 in Khalkhingol (Nomonhan).

Soviet-Mongolian military cooperation allowed both countries to successfully prepare for military action against Japanese troops. Evidence from the Mongolian archives, and from the Mongolian press, have estimated that Mongolia's losses during the Khalkingol operation were more than 700 killed and wounded; the Soviet losses were 24,800 men, including 8,900 killed and 15,900 wounded. In sharp contrast to these numbers, the losses of Japan were reported to be 48,600 men, including 18,100 killed and 30,500 wounded.[40]

These numbers show that while Soviet troops primarily held off the Japanese, Mongolian troops participated in numbers out of proportion to the population of Mongolia. In addition, the MPR was forced to mobilize all its economic and military potential in order to retain its territorial integrity. Later, during August 1945, when the USSR declared war on Japan, the MPR followed suit and also cooperated in sending troops into Japanese-held territory. From the vantage point of the MPR, the USSR promoted the Comintern's long-range policy of instigating Far Eastern revolutions, specifically in China and other Northeast Asian countries, that would lead to the inevitable "world revolution."

The MPR as a Soviet Buffer State

The June 1929 "Agreement on the Main Principles of Mutual Relations Between the USSR and Mongolia," the 1934 Gentleman's Agreement, and then the 1936 Protocol, were all defensive in character, but they also promoted the strengthening of the USSR's geopolitical position throughout Northeast Asia. During World War II, the USSR clearly counted on further expansion into the Far East, and was especially interested in China and Korea. But even while acknowledging this fact, it would be wrong to suggest that the USSR's interest in strengthening its position in Mongolia was unilateral. The MPR, too, was interested in gaining support to separate even further from China, and sought Soviet guarantees of its territorial integrity and national security.

To ensure that it would have sufficient guarantees to safeguard its security, however, the Mongolian government had to concede to the USSR many questions, first among them political power. Therefore, the development of Soviet-Mongolian relations in the 1930s shows quite clearly that though it did not subordinate Mongolia legally in many domestic spheres, the USSR did become Mongolia's political and military patron. By the end of the 1930s, this model of Soviet-Mongolian relations was formulated as the difference between "the elder brother" and "the younger brother," and Choibalsang tactfully stated in one of his trips to Moscow that "he had come to the Soviet Union to receive political orientation in the main questions of the MPR development."[41]

Until the experience of postwar Eastern Europe, the Soviet Union's relationship with Mongolia was unique in many ways. Although the Soviet Union did not consider Mongolia as its vassal, treating it more as a junior partner, especially in the further advancement of the "world revolution" in the Far East, the Mongolian leaders did not have the option of breaking away from the USSR or of limiting Soviet political control. While appearing to be helping the Mongols to achieve their long-time aspiration of Mongolian sovereignty and independence, the USSR worked to repress pan-Mongolist sentiments among the Mongolian population.

The USSR gave Mongolia certain political and military guarantees of retaining its *de facto* national independence from China, but Soviet diplomacy with China continued to affirm that Outer Mongolia was an integral part of China. While Mongolia represented an outpost of Soviet expansion into the Far East, its most important role in Moscow's geopolitical strategy was as a barrier to defend against external aggression. According to the People's Commissar for Foreign Affairs, G. Chicherin, "our borders are quite safe for the huge length, covered by friendly Mongolia."[42] The primary advantage that Moscow could get from Mongolia, therefore, was that once the latter became a reliable satellite of the USSR it could almost single-handedly be used to protect the most vulnerable part of the Soviet frontier. The Soviet-Mongolian political alliance forged in the 1929-39 period remained virtually unchanged until the beginning of the 1990s.

Notes

1. The text of the Soviet-Mongolian Agreement of 1929 was published in Mongolia twice. The first appeared in *Mongol-Zöwlöltiin ard tümnii gan bat nairamdal, 1921-1940* (Ulaanbaatar, 1967) and the second in the journal *Ediin zasgiin asuudal*, (1990, 1, pp. 45-54). In the former Soviet Union the text of the agreement was never published in its entirety.

2. *Dokumenty vneshnei politiki SSSR* (The Documents of the Foreign Policy of the USSR). V. VII. (Moscow, 1963), pp. 331-35.

3. *Sovetsko-Mongol'ski otnosheniia, 1921-1947. Dokumenty i materialy* (The Soviet-Mongolian Relations. 1921-1947. Documents and Materials). V. I. (Moscow, 1975), pp. 58-61.

4. *Arkhiva vneshnei politiki MID RF* (Foreign Policy Archives of the Russian Federation), folio 0111, file 04, p. 1. Hereafter referred to as AVPRF.

5. Ibid., p. 2.

6. *Mongolyn sotsialist-demokrat namyn ankhdugar ikh khural.* (Ulaanbaatar, 1990), p. 10.

7. *Ünen,* November 29, 1989.

8. *Rossiiskii tsentr khraneniia i izucheniia dokumentov noveishei istorii* (Russian Center for the Storage and Study of Modern History Documents), folio 495 (The Oriental Secretariat of the Comintern), list 152, file 143, pp. 62-64. Hereafter referred to as RTsKhIDNI.

9. AVPRF, folio The Secretariat of L. Karakhan, list 12, folder 81, file 021-Mo, pp. 120-21.

10. Ibid., folio 495, list 152, file 156, p. 111.

11. Ibid., folio 495, list 152, file 155, p. 4.

12. Ibid., p. 5.

13. *Ardyn erkh,* 29 (152), April 9, 1934.

14. *Sovetsko-Mongol'ski otnosheniia,* p. 106.

15. *Ünen,* October 4, 1990.

16. Kh. Choibalsang in his speech at the 3rd Plenary Session of the Central Committee of the MPRP (October 22-26, 1937) said that the Japanese in their activity in Mongolia rested first of all on the lamasery, expecting to raise the Mongols for the struggle against the Party and the Government under the banners of Religion. AVPRF, folio 0111, list 20, file 1, folder 20, p. 48.

17. AVPRF, folio II, Oriental Department, list 18, folder 15, p. 10.

18. Ibid., folio 111, list 20, file 1, folder 20, p. 109.

19. Ibid., folio 111, list 15, file 4, folder 147a, p. 76.

20. According to the information ultimately derived from the Chinese mass media, for instance, in the Ministry of Social Security in 1936 there were 250 employees including 20 Mongols and 3 Chinese (Communists from Moscow). The others were Russians. AVPRF, folio 111, list 19, folder 18, file 19, p. 216.

21. Ibid., folio 111, list 18, file 15, folder 159, p. 6.

22. An article of the Mongolian journalist S. Ichinnorov, published in the *Ünen* newspaper on October 4, 1990, was dedicated to this matter. The author was very critical of the USSR's development of Mongolia. In particular, he condemned Soviet meddling into the internal affairs of Mongolia in the 1930s.

23. *Sovetsko-Mongol'ski otnosheniia,* p. 548.

24. The withdrawal of the Soviet troops from Mongolia in 1925 was carried out without any agreement with the Chinese Government, though the fifth Article of the Soviet-Chinese Agreement provided for the fact that the Soviet Union would withdraw its troops from Mongolia after all the questions concerning the deadline of the withdrawal of the Soviet troops and the measures on the safety of the Mongolian-Chinese border were coordinated between the Soviet and the Chinese sides at the special conference. Thus the Chinese Government in the middle of the 1920s appears to have admitted that the USSR could take certain measures concerning Mongolia without mutual discussion of the problem. For a different view of this situation, see Bruce A. Elleman, *Diplomacy and Deception: The Secret History of Sino-Soviet Diplomatic Relations, 1917-1927* (Armonk, NY: M.E. Sharpe, 1997), pp. 107-8.

25. *Sovetsko-Mongol'ski otnosheniia,* p. 339.

26. AVPRF, folio 111, list 20, folder 79, file 13, p. 2.

27. Ibid., folio 111, list 20, file 5, folder 164, p. 28.

28. Ibid., folio 111, list 20, file 2, folder 164, p. 4.

29. Ibid., p. 3.

30. Ibid., p. 5.

31. Ibid., pp. 7-9.

32. Ibid., p. 11.

33. *Gakan,* November 1935.

34. *Pravda,* February 10, 1936.

35. *Sovetsko-Mongol'ski otnosheniia,* p. 342.

36. Ibid., p. 344.

37. Ibid., p. 343.

38. Yu. Tsedenbal. *Izbrannyi stat'i i rechi* (Selected Articles and Speeches). V. 2. (Moscow, 1962), p. 87.

39. AVPRF, folio 111, list 20, file 8, folder 20, p. 13.

40. *Mongolia News,* August 24, 1994.

41. From the conversation of Choibalsang with the Deputy People's Commissar for Foreign Affairs of the USSR V. G. Dekanozov.-AVPRF, folio 111, list 20, file 5, folder 164, p. 106.

42. A letter of G.V. Chicherin to V.I. Lenin (October 18, 1921). RTsKhIDNI, folio 495, list 152, file 9, p. 40. *Sovetsko-Mongol'ski otnosheniia,* pp. 58-61.

The Final Consolidation of the USSR's Sphere of Interest in Outer Mongolia

Bruce A. Elleman

From the 1890s through the 1940s, Russia's and Japan's struggles to carve out spheres of interest in Northeast Asia were focused on Mongolia and Manchuria. This half century of conflict was finally resolved by the April 13, 1941 Soviet-Japanese non-aggression pact, in which Tokyo publicly recognized the territorial integrity and inviolability of the Mongolian People's Republic (MPR), in exchange for Moscow's recognition of the Japanese puppet state of Manchukuo. The USSR's sphere of interest in Northeast Asia was subsequently accepted by China in 1945, when the MPR gained *de jure* independence from China.

This essay will first set the historical stage through 1939 by briefly discussing the origins of the Russo-Japanese conflict in Northeast Asia, the division of Mongolia and Manchuria into Russian and Japanese spheres of interest, the impact of World War I on Russian and Japanese imperialism, and the resurgence of Soviet imperialism in Northeast Asia after the 1917 October Revolution. Particular emphasis will be put on the key role played by secret diplomacy.

A second section discusses the 1939 battle of Nomonhan, fought exclusively on Mongolian and Manchurian territory, when Soviet and Japanese troops struggled to extend their respective spheres of interest. The resulting military stalemate forced diplomatic negotiations which not only determined the bilateral relations between the MPR and Manchukuo, but also led to the delimitation of new boundaries between the Soviet and Japanese spheres of interest.

A third section examines the secret negotiations that led to the signing of the April 13, 1941 Soviet-Japanese non-aggression pact. In a joint declaration the USSR recognized Manchukuo in return for Japan's recognition of the MPR and, thereby, fixed the Soviet and Japanese spheres of interest in Northeast Asia. Subsequent negotiations defined these spheres' political and economic relations.

A fourth section shows how secret Sino-Soviet talks in June-August 1945 led to China's recognition of the USSR's sphere of interest. In the process, Chinese diplomats not only acknowledged that the MPR was an integral part of the USSR, but they let the MPR retain control over Chinese land ceded to it earlier by Manchukuo. Once China accepted the Soviet division of Northeast Asia in 1945, it remained largely in effect until the USSR's collapse in 1991.

Documents from archival sources in Taiwan, Japan, and the United States provide a new level of understanding about formerly secret Soviet-Japanese and Sino-Soviet diplomatic negotiations during the 1940s.[1] Most importantly, these negotiations allowed the USSR to complete the process of consolidating its sphere of interest in Outer Mongolia. Soviet foreign policy in Northeast Asia represented the culmination of Russia's long-term expansionist aims, therefore, and these events remain at the heart of contemporary Russo-Chinese tensions.

The Origins of the Soviet-Japanese Conflict Over Northeast Asia

Following Imperial Russia's defeat in the Crimean War and the resulting restrictions put on Russian expansion to the South and West, East Asia became the focus of its quest for territorial and economic expansion.[2] Between 1858 and 1860, Russian diplomats signed a series of treaties with China which ceded to Russia the northern bank of the Amur, the Maritime Province, and territories in Xinjiang. During the early 1860s, the Russian government decided to expand its influence even further, by including in its expansionist goals Mongolia and Manchuria.[3]

Russia's expansion put enormous pressure on Japan, and after China's defeat in the 1894-95 Sino-Japanese War, Japan claimed concessions in Manchuria's Liaodong peninsula. But Russia, Germany, and France forced Japan to give up these concessions. In 1896, Russian diplomats then bribed Chinese officials to permit the construction of the Chinese Eastern Railway.[4] This railway cut through northern Manchuria and occupied more than 250,000 acres of land, making it the largest foreign concession in China.[5] Thereafter, in 1898, Russia took the same concessions in Liaodong for itself. This infuriated Japan and helped lead to the 1904-05 Russo-Japanese War. Following Russia's defeat, the 1905 Portsmouth Peace Treaty transferred to Japan all Russian concessions in southern Manchuria, including the South Manchurian Railway, that segment of the Chinese Eastern Railway south of Harbin.[6]

These general spheres of interest were further demarcated during 1907-12, when Russia and Japan signed a series of secret treaties.[7] On July 30, 1907, Russia agreed not to "interfere with nor to place any obstacle in the way of the further development" of Japan's interests in Korea, in exchange for Japan's promise: "The Imperial Government of Japan, recognizing the special interests of Russia in Outer Mongolia, undertakes to refrain from any interference which might prejudice those interests."[8] A special exchange of confidential notes on Outer Mongolia further reconfirmed that Outer Mongolia would be completely within the Russian sphere of interest.[9]

As a result of further secret negotiations, on July 4, 1910, the Russian and Japanese governments agreed to safeguard and defend these "interests."[10] Finally, on July 8, 1912, these spheres of interest were expanded into Inner Mongolia, with Japan acquiring the east and Russia the west. In addition, they agreed to "recognize and respect" the others' "special interests."[11]

Taking advantage of World War I, Russia and Japan continued to consolidate their spheres of interest. For example, Russia signed agreements with Outer Mongolia in 1913, and with Outer Mongolia and China during 1915, in which Outer Mongolia recognized the suzerainty of China in exchange for Chinese recognition of Outer Mongolia's autonomy.[12] In January 1915, Japan presented China with the so-called Twenty-one Demands, which ceded to Japan territorial and economic rights in Southern Manchuria and Inner Mongolia.

Although the Bolsheviks' July 25, 1919 "Karakhan Manifesto" renounced all of Russia's territorial concessions in China, the Red Army's 1921 invasion of

Outer Mongolia restored it to Russia's sphere of interest; during fall 1924, Moscow then formed the MPR under its aegis.[13] Thereafter, by signing a series of secret protocols with China, the USSR also retook control of the Chinese Eastern Railway, returning northern Manchuria to the Russian sphere of interest.[14] When Tokyo protested that these Soviet actions interfered with Japan's legitimate interests, Moscow explained on October 21, 1924 that "there exist no such rights or interests of foreign powers or their nationals in regard to the Chinese Eastern Railway."[15]

Following intensive diplomatic negotiations in Beijing, Moscow and Tokyo signed the January 20, 1925 Soviet-Japanese Convention, which opened relations between the USSR and Japan. As a result of this agreement, the USSR and Japan renewed their former spheres of interest in Northeast Asia by, on the one hand, recognizing the 1905 Portsmouth Peace Treaty and, on the other, agreeing to recognize all former Russo-Japanese treaties—including those dividing China into Russian and Japanese spheres of interest—until they were renegotiated; since these treaties were never subsequently abolished, their terms remained valid through the 1930s until 1941.[16]

The USSR's influence in Manchuria continued to grow during the 1920s. In May 1929, China's newly unified government in Nanjing forcibly took control of the Chinese Eastern Railway, demanding that the USSR keep its 1924 promise to return the railway to China. The resulting undeclared war shifted in the USSR's favor by December 1929, however, when the Red Army occupied the Manchurian cities of Khailar and Manzhouli.[17] Faced with certain defeat, China signed the Khabarovsk agreement, which enhanced "Russian prestige and influence in Manchuria."[18]

But in June 1931, it was reported that the USSR had agreed that China could buy back the railway by allowing all Soviet goods into Manchuria duty-free, a major concession to the cash-strapped Nanjing government.[19] This agreement clearly threatened Japan's economic standing in Manchuria, and also appeared to violate the 1925 secret agreement renewing the former spheres of interest in Manchuria. One newspaper warned: "This agreement, if it is completed, will probably arouse protests from the principal trading nations, particularly Japan."[20]

Indeed, Japan was concerned that if this agreement went through, the USSR's duty free goods would flood Manchuria. During August 1931, Japan's Foreign Ministry protested to Moscow that Soviet-Japanese treaties would remain valid "only on the basis of the existing Sino-Russian agreements."[21] Tokyo's concern over continued Soviet expansion perhaps served as a pretext for the Japanese army, which was eager to assert its power abroad. Therefore, when Tokyo's warnings were ignored, Japan occupied Manchuria, an action commonly known as the "Manchurian Incident." On October 14, 1931, Japan demanded that China agree "to prevent ruinous railway competition and to carry into effect existing railway agreements in Manchuria."[22] But China was instead forced closer to the USSR, leading one newspaper to predict: "By her conquest of Manchuria, Japan has driven China into the arms of Russia."[23]

Although by the middle of the 1930s, the USSR and Japan had once again delimited their spheres of interest in Northeast Asia, underlying tensions remained. In 1932, Japan consolidated full control over Manchuria by forming the puppet state of Manchukuo. Thereafter, Moscow's 1935 decision to sell the Chinese Eastern Railway to Tokyo, over Nanjing's virulent protests, helped Japan consolidate power. But in response, the USSR tightened its own hold over the MPR; on March 12, 1936, it signed a ten-year "Protocol of Mutual Assistance" creating a military alliance against Japan. Soviet-Japanese tensions along the MPR-Manchukuo border continued to escalate. After hundreds of border clashes, these tensions culminated in the 1939 battle of Nomonhan.[24]

Soviet-Japanese Secret Negotiations After Nomonhan

The 1939 Nomonhan conflict took place exclusively on Mongolian and Manchurian territory, but this battle was fought by Soviet and Japanese forces in order to defend their respective spheres of interest.[25] For example, during May 1939, Soviet Foreign Commissar V.M. Molotov warned Japan that the USSR would defend the MPR's borders "as vigorously as we shall defend our own borders."[26] Similarly, Alvin Coox, the preeminent expert on Nomonhan, has concluded that Japan's primary goal was "to prevent a communization of Manchuria similar to that which befell adjoining Outer Mongolia."[27] Border negotiations began soon after this battle, but turned into a stalemate. However, a preliminary border agreement was reached by fall 1940.

Although the Red Army prevailed at Nomonhan only after sustaining heavy casualties, Tokyo apparently considered that any future Japanese aggression in Siberia would be futile. Therefore, on September 15, 1939, the Japanese Ambassador, Shigenori Togo, and the Soviet Foreign Commissar, Molotov, signed an armistice agreement in Moscow, which set up a joint commission composed of two USSR-MPR members and two Japan-Manchukuo members in order to "define the boundary between Manchukuo and Outer Mongolia in the districts where disputes occurred recently."[28]

The next day, Japan's foreign office announced that these talks would not only lead to a "thorough solution in due course of the conflict on the Manchukuo-Outer Mongolian border," but that this "would contribute toward the removal of general tension and the normalization of diplomatic relations between the two countries." Three days later, field negotiations resulted in an agreement that maps would be exchanged detailing the "present lines of both forces." The two sides were quick to announce "that the recognition of the stationary positions of the Japanese and Soviet Armies according to the field agreement did not include the question of Manchukuo-Outer Mongol border demarcation."[29] But so long as the border was not changed once again by renewed fighting, these maps showed what was soon to become the new MPR-Manchukuo border.

In November 1939, the USSR and Japan officially set up a joint commission to delimit the MPR-Manchukuo border. This commission was plagued by constant delays, but it eventually reached a preliminary decision and signed an agreement on July 18, 1940; on the same day, the MPR and Manchukuo reportedly signed an identical agreement.[30] Final border negotiations awaited a decision on whether the USSR and Japan would sign a non-aggression pact. In turn, signing a non-aggression pact rested on the Soviet government's willingness to recognize Manchukuo. During April 1941, Japan's Foreign Minister, Yosuke Matsuoka, explained in an internal document, marked "top secret," that it was Moscow's initial refusal to recognize Manchukuo that had stymied progress on the non-aggression pact.[31]

However, Japan also had to agree to pay a price for Stalin's recognition of Manchukuo: on October 3, 1940, Japanese diplomats recognized that the MPR was part of Russia's sphere of "traditional interests" (*dentōteki kanshin*). In addition, the Japanese diplomats agreed that the Soviet government would be given a free hand in the Chinese province of Xinjiang, if the USSR would let Japan do likewise in Inner Mongolia.[32] These agreements, therefore, generally conformed with maps, published by the Japanese press in 1937, that detailed the "red" sphere of interest in the Far East as including all of Outer Mongolia and much of Xinjiang.[33]

It is important to note that although Japanese negotiators agreed to refer to the MPR as if it were an independent country, they did not consider the MPR to be independent. In fact, a Japanese Foreign Ministry document from 1941 explained in some detail that since Japan made this pledge only to the USSR, but had refused to sign any agreement directly with the MPR, it did not consider that it had recognized the legitimacy of the MPR government. Thus, any pledge that Japan made to uphold the MPR's territorial integrity and inviolability was considered valid only so long as the MPR remained within the USSR's sphere of interest.[34]

Finally, Western press reports had warned all along that: "If a Russo-Japanese nonaggression treaty is signed . . . [it] would be implemented by a detailed understanding which would assure a preservation of the *status quo* in northern Asia and an extension of Russia's present sphere of influence in northwest and western China."[35] Other reports predicted that the non-aggression treaty would include provisions allowing "Japan and Russia to divide Central and Eastern Asia between them."[36]

In fact, Soviet and Japanese negotiators not only discussed the outright division of China, they also divided most of the rest of Asia into Soviet and Japanese spheres of interest. Negotiating records from the Japanese Foreign Ministry Archives, marked "top secret," reveal that the following Soviet-Japanese agreement delimiting Asia was also reached: "The USSR will recognize Japan's future expansion into Vietnam and Indonesia, in exchange for Japan recognizing the USSR's expansion into Afghanistan and toward Persia."[37] This agreement divided virtually all of the rest of Asia into Soviet and Japanese spheres of interest.

The 1941 Soviet-Japanese Non-aggression Pact

The Soviet Union and Japan concluded the process of dividing and redividing Northeast Asia on April 13, 1941, when Tokyo agreed, as part of the Soviet-Japanese non-aggression pact, to a Joint Declaration recognizing the territorial integrity and inviolability of the MPR, in exchange for Moscow's recognition of Japan's puppet state of Manchukuo. In addition, a series of confidential notes were exchanged discussing important questions—such as economic concessions, borders, and trade—that had a direct impact on the USSR's and Japan's respective spheres of interest in Asia. As a result, the Soviet-Japanese non-aggression pact fully justified Western fears that "Japanese plans apparently envisage Japan and Russia controlling or dominating the Far East in all fields."[38]

According to an account by Japan's Foreign Minister, Yosuke Matsuoka, concerning the final phase Soviet-Japanese negotiations, when he left Berlin for Moscow in early April 1941, he had no idea that the USSR would agree to sign the non-aggression pact. As outlined by Matsuoka to the Japanese Privy Council on April 24, 1941, in a document marked "top secret," after five days of talks with Molotov it seemed that the pact would never be accepted by Moscow. Therefore, Matsuoka reserved a berth on a Transsiberian train departing from Moscow at noon on April 13. But when paying a farewell visit to Stalin during the afternoon of April 12, Matsuoka recounted how Stalin stared intently in his eyes and suddenly exclaimed that Matsuoka could be trusted to keep his side of a bargain. Accordingly, final changes to the non-aggression pact were rushed through, and the pact was signed the very next day.[39]

Because of the rapidity of this final round of Soviet-Japanese negotiations, it came as somewhat of a shock to the world when the Japanese government announced on April 13, 1941, that it had "for some time been conducting negotiations with the Soviet government with a view to bringing about a fundamental adjustment of Japan's relations with the Soviet Union." Officially, the resulting Soviet-Japanese agreement was called a treaty of "neutrality," since it guaranteed the neutrality of each party in case of military action by "one or more third powers . . . throughout the entire period of such a conflict."[40] Although calling the agreement a neutrality pact looked better in the Japanese press, and fit better with the Soviet Union's propaganda, according to a confidential Japanese Foreign Ministry document the final pact was more accurately a non-aggression treaty, since it incorporated guarantees that neither party would attack the other.[41]

In addition to defending the USSR and Japan from outside attack, the Soviet-Japanese non-aggression pact's Joint Declaration promised to uphold the MPR's and Manchukuo's "territorial integrity and inviolability." As a result, the Soviet-Japanese non-aggression pact recognized the two countries respective spheres of interest in Northeast Asia. The Japanese government hoped that these two spheres could coexist without further conflict and publicly expressed its hope that this agreement would finally "bring tranquillity to the Manchukuo-Soviet and Manchukuo-Outer Mongolian borders."[42]

Tokyo also predicted that the pact would "serve as a basis for [the] rapid solution in a concrete manner of various pending questions between the two countries."[43] These outstanding questions were outlined in an exchange of "Strictly Confidential" English-language notes on April 13, 1941. These notes included discussion of a commercial agreement, a fishery convention, and the liquidation of Japan's oil concession in northern Sakhalin Island. More importantly, however, was that these notes agreed that "it is well for our two countries as well as Manchukuo and Outer Mongolia to find at the earliest date a way [of] instituting joint and/or mixed commissions of the countries concerned with the object of settling the boundary questions and of handling disputes and incidents along the border."[44]

In addition to settling the MPR-Manchukuo border, Moscow and Tokyo began to draft a second set of confidential notes regulating the trade between their respective spheres.[45] These notes determined that Japanese exports would be shipped through Vladivostok and Manchuria at the rate of "not less than 500,000 metric tons in the course of one year," while Japanese imports would be "not less than 300,000 metric tons in the course of the year."[46] Although it is not clear whether these agreements were ever ratified, trade between the two spheres did continue without interruption throughout most of World War II.

The Soviet-Japanese Joint Declaration and the confidential notes exchanged by Moscow and Tokyo completely delimited the Soviet and Japanese spheres of interest in Northeast Asia. With the ratification of these agreements by the USSR on April 25, 1941, and by Japan on May 6, 1941, they took effect for a period of five years. The border survey was never completed, however, since Japan suspended border talks as soon as Germany attacked the USSR in June 1941, adopting a wait and see attitude.[47] As a result, the MPR-Manchukuo border remained, for all practical purposes, as it had been left at the end of the Nomonhan conflict in the fall of 1939.

China's response to the Soviet-Japanese non-aggression pact was particularly negative. According to a "confidential" memorandum dated April 15, 1941, T.V. Soong, Chiang Kai-shek's brother-in-law and Chongqing's representative in Washington at that time, told President Roosevelt that "China was prepared for a Russo-Japanese Pack of Non-Aggression, but certainly not the recognition of Manchuria by Russia which is a very grievous blow to China." Soong further explained to Roosevelt that China's defense against Japan's invasion had been based on the "irreconcilability of Russia and Japan," and that the non-aggression pact was therefore not only a "blow to our morale," but had immediately led to "Russian material aid . . . [being] confined to a mere token trickle."[48]

On April 5, 1945, the USSR denounced the Soviet-Japanese non-aggression pact, one year before it was due to expire. At that time, Japan's defeat seemed inevitable. Meanwhile, China continued to press its claims for the return of the Manchurian territories that had been claimed by the MPR. Therefore, it became imperative for Moscow to open negotiations with the Chinese Nationalists so as once again to guarantee the USSR's sphere of interest in Mongolia.

Sino-Soviet Negotiations on Outer Mongolia

During June-August 1945, Soviet and Chinese negotiators secretly agreed that after a plebiscite, the Chinese Nationalists would recognize the MPR's full independence from China. In return, the USSR promised to respect Chinese sovereignty in Manchuria and Xinjiang, and to suspend support for the Chinese Communists.[49] Although the MPR was publicly portrayed as an independent country, it was privately treated as a Soviet satellite state. Stalin even explained to T.V. Soong, the head of the Chinese mission: "In our letter we will respect the independence and territorial integrity [of the MPR] so that you don't think that we will annex [it] (he laughs)." To this, Soong retorted: "You don't need to [annex], you are on such good terms."[50] In addition, the Chinese Nationalists eventually backed down and agreed that the MPR's borders would remain unchanged, thus ensuring that territory which the MPR had gained earlier from Manchukuo would remain a part of the Soviet sphere of interest.

After Stalin agreed not to support the Chinese Communists, Soong supported Chiang Kai-shek's proposal that a mock plebiscite be held in Outer Mongolia, promising that: "After the plebiscite Chinese Government will declare [the MPR's] independence."[51] During private discussions with Stalin, Soong emphasized that the plebiscite was: "Only a matter of form. The matter is settled."[52] Later, Soong explained why the form the agreement took was so important to China: "It is a question of form and I am sure the Soviet government will meet our views re form. Stalin said also Outer Mongolia will not join [the] Soviet Union either. For home consumption, it would be good if [the] Soviet Union say[s] that after independence [the] Soviet Union will respect its [Outer Mongolia's] territorial integrity." Bowing to China's wishes, Soviet officials agreed to hold the plebiscite, but only after Soong repeatedly promised: "I assure you there is no catch."[53]

Reaching an agreement on the Sino-Mongolian boundary proved to be more difficult, however, and on July 11, 1945, T.V. Soong suggested that the final Sino-Soviet treaty not mention the border at all, since many disagreements remained over its exact location. Stalin agreed, suggesting that they retain the "*status quo*," but Soong retorted: "There is [a] dispute about [the] *status quo*."[54]

In early August 1945, Soong tried once again to determine the exact boundary of the USSR's sphere of interest in Outer Mongolia by presenting Stalin with Russian and Chinese maps, stating: "We would like to come to agreement on Outer Mongolia before we recognize [its] independence—frontiers." Stalin refused to be pinned down on paper, however, and immediately disputed Soong's maps: "Re frontiers Chinese map is not well founded. Existing frontiers should be recognized."[55]

With Japan's surrender fast approaching, Soong wanted to conclude the Sino-Soviet treaty as soon as possible to ensure Chinese sovereignty in Manchuria and Xinjiang. But, the MPR's existing borders included extensive Manchurian and Inner Mongolian territories, as Stalin readily admitted:

Frontiers existing for twenty-six years [were] established without any disputes with China. Our topographers went there and drew on map a line which separated [the] Chinese and Mongolian guards. That's west and south. Re east there were disputes with [the] Japanese. Then there was an agreement concluded. If we re-examine [this agreement], it will take time, certain pieces will be taken, others given. Your Russian map is not valid.[56]

Stalin cunningly failed to note that the Soviet-Japanese border negotiations had never been completed, however, and that the agreement he mentioned was only a draft treaty. This was an important omission, since Stalin was in fact claiming on Outer Mongolia's behalf all Chinese territories taken in battle from Japan by the Red Army. Although it is difficult to know for sure, perhaps this Chinese territory was intended to compensate Outer Mongolia for the permanent loss of Tannu Tuva, a region in northwest Outer Mongolia that had been permanently annexed by the Soviet Union only months before during 1944.

On August 13, 1945, Japan's imminent surrender forced Soong to back down on the issue of borders. He resolved the border question in a haphazard fashion: "Chiang wanted [to] agree on boundaries first, but Stalin said it would take too much time. So Chiang accepts existing boundaries. That question is therefore excluded from [the] questions to be settled."[57] Thereafter, on August 14, 1945, China and the USSR exchanged notes which provided for a plebiscite in Outer Mongolia, after which China promised to recognize the MPR's independence, which it subsequently did in January 1946.[58]

By means of these Sino-Soviet negotiations, Stalin not only gained China's official recognition of the USSR's sphere of interest in Mongolia, but he also retained the MPR's expanded borders, which had been gained from Manchukuo as a result of the 1941 Soviet-Japanese non-aggression pact. Granting the MPR its independence meant much more to the Chinese Nationalists than simply losing control over Outer Mongolia; it also meant sanctioning the USSR's permanent hold over territory in Manchuria and Inner Mongolia that had traditionally been part of China. These territorial concessions later became a point of dispute between the Mongolian People's Republic and the People's Republic of China and exacerbated Sino-Soviet tensions along their own borders.[59]

After China's 1949 revolution, the PRC vehemently protested Outer Mongolia's inclusion in the Soviet sphere of interest, and denounced Soviet encroachments on Chinese territory. In fact, the Chinese Communists understood that the Soviet government had promised in 1922 to return the MPR to their control, so that China could reunite with Mongolia, Tibet, and Xinjiang.[60] The USSR's initial failure to allow negotiations on the Sino-Mongolian border to be reopened perhaps contributed to a series of Sino-Soviet border clashes during the 1950s and the 1960s.[61] Mao Zedong also openly criticized Moscow in 1964: "[T]he Soviet Union, under the pretext of assuring the independence of Mongolia, actually placed the country under its domination."[62]

Contemporary Russo-Chinese Border Negotiations

As a result of the secret negotiations leading to the April 13, 1941 Soviet-Japanese non-aggression pact, the USSR consolidated its sphere of interest vis-á-vis Japan. Thereafter, secret Sino-Soviet negotiations during 1945 resulted in China's recognition of the MPR's independence, thus confirming the USSR's sphere vis-á-vis China. Knowledge of the USSR's secret diplomacy with both Japan and China during the 1940s suggests, therefore, that the USSR's foreign policy in Northeast Asia was essentially the culmination of Imperial Russia's expansionist policies in Outer Mongolia.

The continuity between Imperial Russia's and the USSR's foreign policies in Outer Mongolia undermines former claims by Soviet and Western scholars that Tsarist and Soviet policies were radically different; one of the earliest historians to make this claim was Victor Yakhontoff, who in 1931 stated: "Russia actually renounced all special rights, privileges and concessions" in China.[63] Later Soviet scholars also supported this view, with Georgi Arbatov writing in 1983: "We changed our relations with Asian countries, too. Among other things, we renounced all the czarist governments' colonial claims in Asia."[64]

In fact, by means of its secret diplomacy with Japan and China during the 1920s, 1930s, and 1940s, the USSR not only consolidated its sphere of interest in Outer Mongolia, but it also expanded its sphere further into Manchuria and Inner Mongolia, thereby including territories that had long been considered an integral part of China. As a result of the USSR's expansion, fundamental disagreement over the location of the border has continued to hamper Russo-Chinese relations. In September 1994 the two sides announced the completion of a border treaty, but actual demarcation of the new Russo-Chinese border took much longer, with the 4,200-kilometer eastern section of the border being demarcated in November 1997, and the much smaller 50-kilometer western section being completed in November 1998.

However, ownership of the disputed Tarabanov and Bolshoi Islands in the Amur River near Khabarovsk, and one other island in the Argun River near Chita—islands that the USSR reportedly seized from Japan during the mid-1930s—have yet to be resolved.[65] The political dispute over these islands has been sharp: during February 1994, the Chinese grudgingly agreed to allow Russian farmers to continue cultivating the land until a final settlement was reached. In early September 1994, when Jiang Zemin, chairman of the People's Republic of China and general secretary of the Chinese Communist Party Central Committee, visited Russia, Moscow conceded that disputes still existed over these islands, but by adopting a policy known as a "border with holes," Russia hoped that these final disputes could be resolved gradually.[66] Thereafter, in October 1995, negotiators admitted that they were deadlocked over ownership of the three islands.

So long as ownership of these islands remain in dispute, all Russian and Chinese claims that their mutual borders are thoroughly settled is mere deception.

By March 1995, virtually all of the Far Eastern and Transbaikal members of the Russian Federation had joined the Maritime Province in denouncing the new borders, and the Far Eastern and Transbaikal military districts voiced their opposition to ceding the strategic islands. In addition, Anatoly Dolgolaptev, the deputy speaker of the Council of the Russian Federation, publicly stated that the border settlement with China was unfair to Russia.[67]

Faced with an almost united opposition, Boris Yeltsin apparently took Jiang Zemin by surprise in April 1996 when he announced that "Russia will not give China three of the disputed islands."[68] Although there is little evidence available as to why Yeltsin made this fateful decision, certainly the ongoing discussions with Japan on the status of the Southern Kurils played a significant role.[69] Therefore, Russia's border disagreements with China may remain active, and a full resolution may in fact be linked with Russia's efforts to resolve the Northern Territories dispute with Japan. For these reasons, Soviet secret diplomacy during the 1920s-1940s will probably continue to have a significant impact on Russia's Far Eastern diplomatic relations for some time to come.

Notes

1. This essay relies largely on documents from the Foreign Ministry Archives, Institute of Modern History, Academia Sinica, Taipei, Taiwan; the Japanese Foreign Ministry Archives in Tokyo, Japan; and from the Hoover Institution Archives, Stanford, CA. Although Mongolian archives have not been consulted, representatives of the MPR were not personally present either during the 1940-41 Soviet-Japanese diplomatic negotiations in Moscow or during the summer 1945 Sino-Soviet negotiations held in Moscow. The Soviet government appears to have made all major decisions largely on its own, which suggests that the MPR's influence was very limited, if not lacking altogether.

2. Dietrich Geyer, *Russian Imperialism, The Interaction of Domestic and Foreign Policy, 1860-1914* (New Haven: Yale University Press, 1987).

3. Thomas Ewing, *Between the Hammer and the Anvil? Chinese and Russian Policies in Outer Mongolia 1911-1921* (Bloomington: University of Indiana Press, 1980), p. 19.

4. Permission was obtained through the use of a 3,000,000 ruble fund to bribe Chinese officials. B.A. Romanov, "«Likhunchangskii fond» (Iz istorii russkoi imperialisticheskoi politiki na Dal'nem Vostoke" ("The Li Hung-chang file" (from the history of imperialistic Russian policies in the Far East)) Bor'ba klassov No. 1-2 (1924).

5. The concession was 105,661.98 "desiatins" (2.5 acres). "The Lands and Land Administration of the Chinese Eastern Railway Company, and the Incident of August 1, 1923." Taipei, Taiwan, Academia Sinica, Institute of Modern History, Foreign Ministry Archives, 03-32, 263, p. 4.

6. John V.A. MacMurray, *Treaties and Agreements with and concerning China,* (New York, 1921), pp. 522-25.

7. Ernest Batson Price, *The Russo-Japanese Treaties of 1907-1916 Concerning Manchuria and Mongolia* (Baltimore: The Johns Hopkins Press, 1933), p. 124.

8. Ibid., pp. 107-8; Appendix B: Russia-Japan, Secret Convention of July 17/30, 1907.

9. Ibid.

10. Japan, Ministry of Foreign Affairs, Archives of the Gaikō Shiryōkan, Tokyo (cited as Gaimushō below), Treaty Series Microfilm.

11. Price, *The Russo-Japanese Treaties* . . . , p. 117; Appendix D: Russia-Japan, Secret Convention of June 25/July 8, 1912.

12. MacMurray, 7 June 1915, "Tripartite agreement in regard to Outer Mongolia—Russia, Mongolia, and China," pp. 1240-45.

13. See Elleman, "Secret Sino-Soviet Negotiations On Outer Mongolia, 1918-1925," *Pacific Affairs* Vol. 66, No. 4 (Winter 1993): pp. 539-63.

14. See Elleman, "The Soviet Union's Secret Diplomacy Concerning the Chinese Eastern Railway, 1924-1925," *The Journal of Asian Studies* Vol. 53, No. 2 (May 1994): pp. 459-86.

15. Gaimushō, F 1925-117-19.

16. For more information on this important secret agreement, see Elleman, "The 1907-1916 Russo-Japanese Secret Treaties: A Reconsideration," *Asian Cultural Studies* Vol. 25 (March 30, 1999): pp. 29-44.

17. Gaimushō F 192 5-4-14.

18. "Victory of Russia Seen in Protocol," *The Japanese Advertiser*, December 21, 1929.

19. "China Revives Soviet Treaty Negotiations," *The New York Times*, February 20, 1931.

20. "Nanking May Buy Eastern Railway," *Shanghai Evening Post*, June 23, 1931.

21. Taipei, Taiwan, Academia Historical Archives, Microfilm No. 145, No. 1970.

22. "Promises and Statements of Policy Made privately to the United States Government by authorized representatives of the Japanese Government since September 18, 1931," Stanley Hornbeck Papers, Box 249, Hoover Institution Archives.

23. "Russia's Shadow Over China," *Morning Oregonian*, December 16, 1932.

24. On November 15, 1936, the Japanese press reported that during the previous five years there had been "roughly 330 disputes of varying sizes" on Manchukuo's borders with the USSR and the MPR. *Manchuria*, Vol. No. 10 (November 1936).

25. Alvin D. Coox, *Nomonhan: Japan against Russia, 1939* (Stanford, CA: Stanford University Press, 1990), p. 144.

26. William B. Ballis, ed. *Mongolian People's Republic* (New Haven, CT; Human Relations Area Files, Inc., 1956), Vol. II, p. 581.

27. Coox, p. 1078.

28. "Peace Restored On Manchu-Outer Mongol Border," *Manchuria*, Vol. 4, No. 18, September 15, 1939.

29. Ibid.

30. Robert Slusser and Jan Triska, eds., *A Calendar of Soviet Treaties 1917-1957* (Stanford, CA: Stanford University Press, 1959), pp. 136-37.

31. Gaimushō, B100-JR/1, p. 5.

32. Gaimushō, B100-JR/1, 2.1.00-23.

33. "The Present Situation of the Red Activities in China and Manchuria," *Contemporary Manchuria*, Volume 1, No. 1 (April 1937), pp. 73-96.

34. Gaimushō, B100-JR/1, 2.1.00-23, p. 319.

35. "Japan Hopeful of Signing Pact with Russia To Offset U.S. Political, Economic Pressure," *Washington Post*, October 16, 1940.

36. "Russian Fear Balks Pact With Japan," William Philip Simms, *Washington Daily News*, January 3, 1941.

37. Gaimushō, B100-JR/1, 2.1.00-23, p. 29.

38. "Russo-Japanese Agreement for Domination of Far East Reported Likely," Douglas Robertson, *Washington Post*, April 10, 1941.

39. Gaimushō, B100-JR/1, 2.1.0.0-23, p. 473.

40. Ibid., pp. 411-16.

41. Ibid., p. 473.

42. Ibid., p. 411.

43. Ibid., p. 411.

44. Ibid., p. 193.

45. Gaimushō, B200-JR/3, 2.2.0.0-21, pp. 94-96.

46. Ibid.

47. Gaimushō, B100-JR/1, 2.1.0.0-23, p. 143.

48. "Memorandum of Discussion" between T.V. Soong and President Franklin D. Roosevelt, "Confidential File," April 15, 1941, T. V. Soong Collection, Box A/32, Hoover Institution Archives, Stanford University.

49. Odd Arne Westad, *Cold War & Revolution* (New York: Columbia University Press, 1993), p. 41; also see Odd Arne Westad, ed. *Brothers in Arms: The Rise and Fall of the Sino-Soviet Alliance, 1945-1963* (Stanford, CA: Stanford University Press, 1998), pp. 7-8.

50. 2 July 1945 - 14 August 1945, "Notes taken at Sino-Soviet Conferences," pp. 18, 32; Victor Hoo papers, Hoover Institution Archives, Stanford University.

51. Ibid., pp. 17-19.

52. Ibid., pp. 19-20.

53. Ibid., p. 25.

54. Ibid., p. 31.

55. Ibid., pp. 47-49.

56. Ibid.

57. Ibid., p. 70.

58. These records help to explain why China did not protest when it was reported that 98.14 percent of Outer Mongolia's electorate voted in the hastily-arranged plebiscite, all of them for independence. Max Beloff, *Soviet Far Eastern Policy Since Yalta* (New York: Institute of Pacific Relations, 1950), p. 9.

59. Luke T. Chang, *China's Boundary Treaties and Frontier Disputes* (New York: Oceana Publications, Inc., 1982), p. 216.

60. See Elleman, "Soviet Policy on Outer Mongolia and the Chinese Communist Party," *The Journal of Asian History* Vol. 28 (1994): pp. 108-23.

61. Donald S. Zagoria, *The Sino-Soviet Conflict, 1956-1961* (York, PA: Princeton University Press, 1962), p. 344.

62. "Mao's Statement to the Japanese Socialist Delegation," August 11, 1964, Dennis J. Doolin, *Territorial Claims in the Sino-Soviet Conflict* (Stanford: Hoover Institution Studies, 7, 1965), p. 43.

63. Victor A. Yakhontoff, *Russia and the Soviet Union in the Far East* (New York: Coward-McCann, Inc., 1931), p. 137.

64. Georgi A. Arbatov, *The Soviet Viewpoint* (London: Zed Books, 1983), p. 49.

65. *OMRI Daily Digest,* Part 1, No. 44, March 2, 1995.

66. *The Current Digest of the Post-Soviet Press,* October, 1994.

67. Ibid., March, 1995.

68. Ibid., May, 1996.

69. Just as Russia occupied the three disputed Chinese islands during a period of war in the 1930s, it later occupied the Southern Kurils under exactly similar circumstances during the 1940s. If Moscow were to agree to return the three disputed islands to China, then Japan would certainly become even more insistent that Moscow adopt a parallel policy with regard to the Kurils. For more on the Soviet-Japanese dispute, see Bruce A. Elleman, Michael R. Nichols, and Matthew J. Ouimet, "A Historical Reevaluation of America's Role in the Kuril Islands Dispute," *Pacific Affairs* Vol. 71, No. 4 (Winter 1998/99): pp. 489-504.

Sino-Soviet Diplomacy
and the Second Partition of Mongolia, 1945-1946

Christopher P. Atwood

Since the early years of the twentieth century, the Mongols as an ethnic group
have been divided between the independent nation-state of Mongolia, with a
relatively homogenous population, and Inner Mongolia, under the control of the
huge multi-national state of China. Partition, in connection with the demands of
international politics, has defined the Mongols' modern existence.

The first modern partition of the Mongol people occurred from 1911 to 1915
when negotiations between Russia, China, and Japan determined that Outer
Mongolia or Mongolia proper would remain an autonomous state, while Inner
Mongolia would come under the rule of the new Chinese republic and Khölön
Buir would come under closer Russian control. The results of the turmoil of the
Russian revolution and the 1921 revolution in Mongolia only confirmed this
division between a *de facto* independent Outer Mongolia under the Soviet Union's
aegis and a Chinese-ruled Inner Mongolia. From this time on, the international
frontier between Mongolia and China remained constant and largely impassable
while the regimes on either side of it underwent revolutionary change.

For a brief period in the fall of 1945, however, the frontier appeared once
again to be fluid. Populations moved back and forth, delegations were exchanged,
and meetings held to hail the impending union of Inner Mongolia with their long
lost Khalkha brethren in Mongolia proper. But after a few months of uncertainty,
the border hardened again.

As the price for the Soviet Union's participation in the Asian-Pacific war,
China's national government formally recognized the independence of the
Mongolian People's Republic (MPR) in early 1946. The weeks of fluidity were
soon forgotten. The subsequent official histories of the Mongolian People's
Republic and the Inner Mongolian Autonomous Region had no room for the
ambiguities of independence and consigned them to the oblivion of historical
impossibilities, to a time when a few irresponsible politicians had struggled
vainly against the iron laws of history. Little significance was given to reviving
the tangled story of how Iosif Stalin and Mongolia's Khorloogiin Choibalsang
encouraged Inner Mongolian separatists, only to abandon them to Chinese enemies
a few months later. In the end, no change occurred in the frontier and the
partition of the Mongols was not undone.

Yet this obscure Soviet-Mongolian adventure in Inner Mongolia deserves to
be resurrected, both for the light it sheds on Stalin's diplomacy with his southern
neighbors and for the substantial influence it had on the eventual fate of Inner
Mongolia. The Inner Mongolian nationalists were not the only indigenous political
force on the southern extremity of the Soviet empire to be encouraged and then

discarded as instruments of Stalin's opportunistic expansionism. The Azeris and Kurds of northwest Iran and the Kazakhs of northern Xinjiang also endured similar experiences in the years following World War II.

Moreover, the status of Greater Mongolia, which includes both Inner Mongolia and the Mongolian People's Republic, was arguably the most important and most tangled issue in relations between China and Russia from 1911 to the Korean War. Any study of Sino-Soviet relations in the crucial years of 1945-46 which ignores the Mongolian question cannot fully capture the Soviet Union's relations either with the national government in Chongqing or the Chinese Communists in Yan'an. In addition, the brief period of Soviet-Mongolian patronage directly complicated Soviet relations with the Chinese Communists and so indirectly exercised a crucial influence on the subsequent relations of the Chinese Communists to the Inner Mongolian nationalist intelligentsia. As such, it was a vital factor in the history of Inner Mongolia and the development of the Chinese Communist Party's minority policy.

This essay relies primarily on archives, newspapers, and interviews collected in Ulaanbaatar, supplemented by published sources in Mongolian, Chinese, and English.[1] It will address three issues that are often ignored by students of Sino-Soviet foreign relations. First, it will argue that the "Mongolian Question," as one Inner Mongolian writer termed it in 1923, was at the center of Sino-Soviet relations, and tensions surrounding the Mongolian Question constantly disrupted the USSR's diplomatic relations with both the Chongqing and Yan'an governments.

Second, while the Mongols themselves were perhaps not the primary actors in the decisions taken concerning the Mongolian Question, they were considerably more important than has been formerly recognized; this essay will show that not only were the Mongols no mere puppets of Moscow or Yan'an, but the Inner and Outer Mongolians were far from unanimous in their interests and views.

Third, while the Mongols did not play the largest role in the decision-making process on the Mongolian Question, they were the most intimately concerned in the decisions made and have been forced to live with these decisions to the present. This fact alone would justify historians paying closer attention to their views and experiences.

The Diplomacy of the Mongolian Question

In the closing years of World War II, the ultimate disposition of sovereignty on the Mongolian plateau came down to decisions made by the governments in Moscow and Chongqing. Moscow effectively controlled the northern part of the plateau by its overwhelming influence on the Mongolian People's Republic, and its maximum leader, Marshal Choibalsang. While World War II still raged, Chongqing held only the sparsely populated far western part of Inner Mongolia. Meanwhile, the Japanese ruled the bulk of Inner Mongolia, and more than 80 percent of its population. Japan ruled Inner Mongolia through four Khinggan provinces, existing as culturally autonomous units within the Manchurian Empire, commonly called "Manchukuo," and an autonomous Mongolian state in China, ruled by the Mongolian aristocrat, De (De Wang or Demchugdongrub). Given the wide expectation of eventual defeat for Japan, from 1941 on, informed observers realized that Inner Mongolia would almost certainly revert to Chinese control. The course of military events, and more particularly the participation or non-participation of the Soviet Union in the final defeat of Japan, would determine precisely how this expected event would occur.

The legal claims, still nursed by the Republic of China, to sovereignty in Mongolia proper—Outer Mongolia—immensely complicated the whole issue of how to deal with the Mongolian plateau and its indigenous Mongol inhabitants. While the Republic of China had not actually held power on the territory of Mongolia since 1921, the dispute over Mongolian independence had repeatedly poisoned Sino-Soviet relations. While the Japanese invasion had forced China's national government to submerge its disagreements with the Soviet Union, it had also indirectly resulted in a substantially stronger central government presence in much of China's far western border regions of Xinjiang and Eastern Tibet.[2]

What is known about policy planning in Chongqing also indicates that China's national government believed an Allied victory in the war might well enable China to make good all its traditional claims of sovereignty in the border areas, even over Central Tibet under the Dalai Lama and over the Mongolian People's Republic.[3] Such expectations, however, only underlined the Chongqing regime's utter lack of preparedness to exploit such an opportunity when it arose. The Nationalists' intense pre-war concentration on securing control and development in the lower Yangtze area had resulted in an apparently deliberate decision to at least temporarily forgo the kinds of intelligence, propagandistic, educational, and networking activity that would have been necessary to turn emerging opportunities into lasting administrative strengthening in northern China, and increased influence and control in the border areas.

At the Yalta Conference in February 1945, Stalin secured from Roosevelt an American guarantee that the United States would recognize the "status quo" in Mongolia and prevail upon China to do the same.[4] Through the spring of 1945, information on the terms of the Yalta accords trickled down to the Chinese government. Knowing Chinese sensitivity on the subject, the U. S. government was most secretive about the provisions on Mongolia. But it would appear that to the extent that Chongqing knew of the stipulations about Mongolia, it interpreted "status quo" to mean a Chinese agreement not to interfere in the current *de facto* independence of Mongolia or to try to implement its claim to sovereignty. The Chinese government was fully prepared to agree since, as elsewhere among the United Nations, the war against fascism had given a markedly leftward thrust to at least the rhetoric of the combatant governments, particularly on ethnic and colonial issues.[5] China was no exception.

The Sixth Congress of the Nationalist Party, which met in May 1945, rejected the exclusive emphasis on national unity that had prevailed since 1929 in its explanation of nationalism. Instead it returned part of the way toward its 1924-27 program of self-determination and self-rule for the border peoples. The documents of Congress advocated assistance to the frontier racial groups in economic and cultural development and respect for their languages, religions, and customs. More explicitly, both the Manifesto and the Program of the Sixth Congress bound the party to grant "a high degree of autonomy" to Outer Mongolia and Tibet.[6] Given the expected post-war reality of victorious Soviet and British empires, these provisions could easily be interpreted as sanctioning non-interference with these empire's client regimes in Ulaanbaatar and Lhasa. The only stipulation would be that China's nominal sovereignty ought not to be impinged.

On June 12 the Soviet Union's new ambassador to China, Apollon Petrov, summarized the concessions China would have to make to conclude a Sino-Soviet friendship treaty. His preconditions closely followed the main points of Yalta, including the clause stating that the *status quo* of Outer Mongolia should be preserved. Still, Chiang did not give up hope that a more restricted interpretation of the phrase "status quo" would be adopted. On June 26, in meeting Petrov, Chiang Kai-shek even proposed "high level autonomy" as a compromise formula that would in effect embody a Chinese endorsement of the *status quo*. Chiang also allowed that a high degree of autonomy would include military and diplomatic autonomy and proposed that the Chinese claim in Mongolia would be to suzerainty, not sovereignty, thus amounting to a recognition of the *de facto* independence already existing in these areas. Chiang also pointed out that Chinese concessions on Mongolia would greatly weaken his position in Tibet, thus hinting that overly aggressive Soviet advances might likewise lead to aggressive British responses.[7]

On June 30, Chiang's brother-in-law and foreign minister T.V. Soong (Song Ziwen) landed in Moscow to begin negotiations for a Sino-Soviet friendship treaty. Since Soviet entry into the war was a certainty, Moscow and Chongqing would have to come to some agreement over how to dispose of their traditional territorial dispute in Mongolia, Inner Mongolia, and Northeast China. Without such an agreement, Stalin's gains at Yalta would remain legally in limbo while Chongqing might face either an outright Soviet occupation of Northeast China, or else Soviet aid to the Chinese Communists. By the evening of July 1, after the first official talks with Stalin, the status of the Mongolian People's Republic had emerged as the main outstanding issue.

The next night (as was Stalin's custom, all business was conducted in overnight sessions), Stalin bluntly told T.V. Soong that China's proposal on Mongolia (high-level autonomy with Chinese suzerainty) was unacceptable. The *status quo* in the Yalta agreement meant, stated Stalin, the MPR's full independence, and Chiang would have to formally recognize *that* if he wanted any treaty with the Soviet Union. Stalin made it clear he intended to put the independence of Mongolia beyond the power of any future Chinese government to revoke, warning the Chinese that only a firm agreement between China and the USSR could forestall a nationalist upsurge not only in the MPR but in Inner Mongolia as well. He claimed that such an upsurge would be harmful for China and the

Soviet Union. Shaken by the insistence of Stalin on full recognition, T.V. Soong said he would seek further instructions from Chiang Kai-shek.[8]

Apparently confident that the Chinese authorities would have no choice but to comply with his terms, Stalin had invited Choibalsang to Moscow to apprise him of these developments. Leaving Ulaanbaatar at 5 a.m. on July 3 (around midnight, July 2-3 Moscow time) on a military Douglas DC-3, and accompanied by the long-time Soviet ambassador to Mongolia, I.A. Ivanov, Choibalsang arrived the next day in Moscow. Greeted by the Soviet Union's Commissar for Foreign Affairs, V.M. Molotov, and others at the airport, Choibalsang had a meeting with Stalin on the night of July 5. While Ivanov had relayed to Choibalsang the substance of the relevant Yalta accords before, now Stalin and Molotov told Choibalsang of the deadlock that had occurred in the negotiations. Stalin told Choibalsang:

> China up till now still does not recognize your Mongolian state. This time, although our side has discussed China giving guarantees on Mongolia's independence and sovereignty, they still don't like it. In my opinion, the Chinese representatives will probably at the final point recognize it. When our negotiations conclude, I think the Republic of China will issue a communiqué on recognition of the independence of Mongolia. We should hear your opinion on this issue.[9]

Choibalsang thanked Stalin profusely for his concern for Mongolia, and the discussion turned to coordinating Mongolia's role on the coming attack on Japan.

Stalin and Molotov's confidence that the Chinese would come around was based on good information. By the morning of July 6, after futile efforts to secure U.S. support or a Soviet concession, Chiang had decided to give in and instructed T.V. Soong to make the necessary concessions. China would recognize Mongolian independence, but on two important conditions: 1) independence would be granted only within the frontiers of Outer Mongolia. This provision would prevent Mongolia or the Soviet Union from annexing neighboring regions of Inner Mongolia. 2) Mongolia would have to hold a plebiscite to demonstrate popular approval for independence before China would accord recognition. Such a plebiscite would give the Chinese authorities some excuse in Chinese public opinion for losing such a long-claimed area.[10]

Even before T.V. Soong officially presented this proposal, Stalin knew of Chiang's concession. Whether through intelligence in Chongqing, the Chinese embassy in Moscow, or through breaking Chinese codes, Stalin was able to inform Choibalsang of the important news that day. Stalin, Molotov, Choibalsang and Mongolia's ambassador in Moscow, Z. Sambuu met on the morning of July 7. Previous meetings had been without an interpreter, but now they planned a larger meeting and needed an official interpreter. B. Shirendew, rector of the Mongolian State University, was in Moscow with two other scholars to represent the Mongolian academic community at the celebrations of the 220th anniversary of the Soviet Academy of Sciences. Shirendew, although an academic, was also a member in good standing of Mongolia's ruling elite. Therefore, Sambuu went to the rector's rather luxurious room at the Metropol hotel to summon him to interpret at the upcoming meeting.

Shirendew dropped his plans, and after a late lunch at around 4:00 to 5:00 p.m., Sambuu escorted him to Choibalsang's special residence at Zarech'e. Choibalsang filled Shirendew in on the state of negotiations and told him that they would leave in a day or two, as the Chinese had already conceded Outer Mongolia. The two played billiards until the reception with Stalin was to begin, at around 6-7 p.m. The reception was held in the Kremlin's St. George's Hall, under the gaze of Russia's military heroes. Stalin was in a good mood. Before the reception he teased Choibalsang, asking, "What about inviting T.V. Soong and the Chinese representatives to this reception?" Choibalsang, not catching the joke, replied seriously, "No need, no need." The Soviet guests smiled and Stalin, laughing out loud, said, "Then let's go in ourselves and eat" and led Choibalsang into the reception room.

At the reception, Stalin sat at the head of the table with Choibalsang on his right and Molotov on his left; the other guests were arranged at the table below. Stalin told Choibalsang that matters had already been decided with the Chinese and explained the two conditions Chiang Kai-shek had mentioned. In his toast, Stalin expressed his wish that Mongolia's independence would prove to those in Mongolia who still supported the pro-Japan line that friendship with the Soviet Union had been the right path. Molotov raised his glass to Mongolian independence, to which Choibalsang responded with a toast to friendship. Music began and the principals discussed the imminent end of the war and the Mongolian situation.

Molotov and Stalin asked Choibalsang: "You have to organize a plebiscite. Do you have the experience?" Choibalsang noted that "Lots of people in Mongolia can't sign their names." Therefore, Stalin suggested that the voting registrars get their thumbprint instead. After this rather casual conversation, the reception broke up and the Mongolian prepared to fly home. Early in the morning of July 8, Choibalsang, I.A. Ivanov, and Shirendew flew back to Ulaanbaatar in the DC-3, accompanied by Ambassador Sambuu's wife and the two scholars who had accompaned Shirendew to the anniversary celebrations of the Soviet Academy of Sciences, J. Dügersüren and B. Rinchén. They arrived in Ulaanbaatar at 3:30 a.m. local time, and the next day Choibalsang convened the presidium of the State Small Khural to inform the members that the Soviet Union had successfully pressured the Chinese into recognizing Mongolian independence.[11]

Although Chiang Kai-shek had already instructed T.V. Soong to compromise on Mongolian independence in return for Soviet guarantees of Chinese sovereignty elsewhere, Soong attempted once more to avert the inevitable. Not knowing that Stalin had already celebrated China's surrender with Choibalsang only an hour or two before, Soong opened the July 7, 11:00 p.m. session, with a repetition of China's offers to agree to everything but formal recognition. Not surprisingly, given his knowledge of the real situation on the Chinese side, Stalin refused.

Only on the evening of July 9 did T.V. Soong finally formally concede recognition of Mongolian independence, asking in return for respect for Chinese sovereignty elsewhere, a plebiscite in Outer Mongolia, a Chinese unilateral declaration (thus implicitly recognizing China's legitimate sovereignty in Mongolia up until then), and the border to be drawn as on Chinese maps.[12] Given the major differences between Chinese maps and the actual line of control, this last condition would prove to be a major difficulty. Further negotiations deadlocked on these and other points and the talks were suspended when Stalin and Molotov left on July 13 to attend the Potsdam conference with Truman and Churchill.

War Plans and the Bid for Unification

At the same time as Stalin and Choibalsang had discussed the question of Mongolian independence, Choibalsang had also asked Stalin to allow the Mongolian People's Revolutionary Army to participate in the upcoming campaigns against Japan. Choibalsang had a long-standing desire to enhance Mongolia's international status by public participation in the U.N. coalition. During the war in Europe, he had asked Stalin to allow Mongolia to declare war on Germany, but Stalin told him that the battles against Germany were far too large for Mongolia's small force to make any difference. This time, however, Stalin agreed to allow Mongolia to declare war on Japan and join the Soviet offensive.[13]

As the Soviet build-up in the east intensified, the Mongolian government issued appeals and reminders to the people to tighten up discipline and strictly fulfill public duties, but Mongolia's promised participation in the conflict was still secret from the public.[14] Successful participation in the war would strengthen Mongolia's case not only to independence from China but also for membership in the United Nations. The need for such pressure became apparent at the second round of the Sino-Soviet negotiations.

T.V. Soong had resigned as Foreign Minister, not wanting to be associated with the concessions Chongqing was making to Moscow, and his successor Wang Shijie began the second round of talks on August 7. Desperate to get some agreement that would bind the Soviet Union to good behavior before its occupation of Northeast China began, Wang still tried his best to stall recognition of Mongolia.

When the Mongolian borders came up, Wang queried whether recognition would not depend upon prior border delimitation. Stalin merely stated that the Soviet government would be willing to consider any maps produced by China. Since Chiang Kai-shek had repeatedly and fruitlessly attempted to get U.S. support for a firmer position, Chongqing had little choice but to agree to Stalin's wishes.

From this point on, if not before, Stalin had decided that he would have to pressure China into recognizing Mongolia. To apply this pressure, the Soviet ruler allowed Mongolia to turn the war against Japan into a holy war for Mongolian unification. That way, if Chongqing reneged on its promise to recognize the

MPR, the Mongolian government would be in the position to secure its control over all or part of Inner Mongolia. This control could be used either to force concessions from China or, if Chongqing remained adamant, to strengthen Mongolia's strategic and economic position.

Of course this policy had risks. Even mere threats of further annexations would almost certainly mark Mongolia and its patron the Soviet Union as rogue nations in the eyes of the Allies, while successful use of Inner Mongolia as a bargaining chip would necessarily involve betrayal of Mongolian promises for unification. Choibalsang never reconciled himself to the cynical manipulation of Mongolian nationalist aspirations that such a policy entailed, and he continued to pester Stalin about Mongolian unification long after the recognition of Mongolian independence had been achieved.

As with the Soviet Union's 1939 annexations of Western Ukraine and Belarus', the possible annexation of Inner Mongolia would involve securing control and creating a ground-swell of public support for unification.[15] On August 8, the day before the projected attack on Japan, Choibalsang met with his Minister of interior, Lieutenant-General Bat-Ochiryn Shagdarjaw, and the Ministry's chief Soviet adviser, Gridnev. He ordered them to "organize mobile detachments immediately to work beyond the border in the rear of the Soviet-Mongolian Army." The detachments would: 1) secure the rear of the advancing armies and find and destroy armed groups of Japanese left in the rear; 2) arrest Japanese spies, "wreckers," as well as their supporters in Inner Mongolia. This included those Inner Mongolian nobility, officials, and intelligentsia who supported the Japanese in the autonomous Khinggan provinces of Manchuria and Prince De's autonomous Mongolian state in Inner Mongolia. It also meant the Mongolian citizens, who had fled the MPR during the abortive collectivization campaign of 1930-32, and the subsequent attacks on Buddhism. Finally, 3) keep the peace in the liberated areas and put in order the masses' daily life. This last item would certainly include reconstructing the political regime of Inner Mongolia and organizing for any possible unification with Inner Mongolia.

The head of the Border and Internal Military Affairs Office, Juramyn Namjil, with his Soviet adviser, A.A. Agzhanov, organized eight 250-men detachments by August 9, the day the war started. The distribution of tasks showed that none of the Mongolian troops would be sent east of the Khinggan range. Instead, they would occupy the whole of Prince De's Autonomous Mongolian State (traditional Chakhar, Shili-yin Gool, and the eastern part of Ulaanchab leagues), and of Khinggan North Province (the traditional Khölön Buir or Bargu area). Apart from these, the Solon and Khaluun Rashaan areas were only lightly inhabited districts in the midst of the Khinggan mountains, important more for the Japanese-built railway than for any native Mongolian population. Most importantly, the Mongolian troops would not occupy the major ethnic Mongol areas east of the Khinggan ranges. These areas, comprised of Khinggan East, South, and West provinces, included the heartland of the educational and nationalist renaissance that had occurred in Inner Mongolia under Japanese patronage:[16]

	Mongolian Staging Point	Direction in Inner Mongolia
Western Group:	Sulinkheer	Batukhaalga (Bailingmiao)
	Zamyn-Üüd	Dolonnuur (Duolun County)
	Dariganga	Zhangjiakou (Kalgan)
Eastern Group:	Erdenetsagaan	Üjümüchin East Banner
	Bayantsagaan	Solon (Suolun) County
	Khalkh Gol	Khaluun Rashaan (Arshan/Arxan)
	Tamsagbulag	Amugulang Temple (New Bargu Left Banner)
	Kherlen	Khailar City

As a result, the most active areas of the Inner Mongolian revolutionary nationalist movement came not under active Mongolian patronage, but under the more calculating Soviet one. While Choibalsang certainly hoped that his liberation of Inner Mongolia would be complete and even include those areas still under Chinese rule such as Ordos, Alashan, Qinghai (Kökenuur), and the Altay region of Xinjiang, as well as those east of the Khinggan Range, the immediate field of Soviet-supported secessionist activity was restricted to the Khölön Buir region on the one hand, and the Chakhar-Shili-yin Gool area on the other.

Separated from North and Northeast China by the Khinggan and the highlands of northern Hebei, these two areas formed a natural extension of the Mongolian plateau and had only a weak Chinese presence, Shili-yin Gool League in particular. Khölön Buir had long been an area of particular Russian and Soviet geopolitical interest due to the Chinese Eastern Railway, which crossed its territory. Since the Chinese government had already conceded a dominant Soviet role on this railway, some Soviet presence in Khölön Buir was unavoidable. Thus, while the Mongolian government would cast its larger expansionist ambitions in the language of ethno-national self-determination, its immediate goals during August, 1945, would include only those areas of Inner Mongolia most accessible to the MPR.

Propaganda distributed by the Soviet-Mongolian Army played an important role in prompting the Inner Mongols into appropriate action, especially in the crucial early days of invasion. This propaganda fell into two basic types, but all of the leaflets denounced the Japanese occupiers as part of a fascist world league against the peace and freedom of all nationalities. All denounced Prince De and the Manchurian emperor, Puyi, as collaborators. All promised liberation and a new regime of peace and free development of all nationalities. The leaflets differed, however, in their approach to the Mongol question in Inner Mongolia. Some ignored this aspect of liberation, while others, prepared literally on the eve of the attack, defined the war as a fight for the liberation of all Mongols.

D. Darjaa, a Mongolian journalist and author, was working on the staff of the party newspaper *Ünen*, with special responsibility for its satirical supplement

Matar ("Crocodile"), when Namtaishiryn Lhamsüren, the party's propaganda chief, called him in. Without giving any explanation, Lhamsüren commissioned Darjaa to write a "Benediction on Living in Unity" (*Negtgen suukhyn yörööl*) and asked that he do it quickly. Darjaa had no idea why the poem was needed so soon, but was happy to write it—he clearly thought liberating Inner Mongolia was a worthy goal. Two days later, Darjaa came back to Lhamsüren with a draft and asked him, "What do you think?" Lhamsüren said "It's fine" and took the draft, Darjaa's only copy. Later, Darjaa heard that thousands had been printed and dropped as a leaflet.[17]

Nor was this the only leaflet with irredentist content. D. Begdze, a Bargu Mongol who later emigrated to the MPR, told Mongolian officials how happy he was when the war began and he found a leaflet signed on August 8 by the Small Khural and government of the MPR. As he reported it, the message of the leaflet was: "All the Mongols shall become one country."[18]

Other leaflets gave no specific encouragement to Inner Mongolian secessionist plans. L. Jamsran, perhaps Mongolia's major scholar on Inner Mongolian history and Sino-Mongolian relations, recalls having seen a leaflet dropped from airplanes entitled "Letter of Attention" (*Ankhaarlyn bichig*). Written on durable brown paper, the letter did not mention any specifically ethno-national irredentist claims.

Jamsran also recounted a story which later circulated in Ulaanbaatar among those interested in Inner Mongolia: as an irredentist leaflet was being prepared for distribution in Inner Mongolia, it was halted right as it was coming off the presses. Choibalsang had been printing them himself and even signed them (presumably in his position as Prime Minister of Mongolia), but Stalin gave him an order to stop printing them, because any such advocacy ran contrary to the Crimean agreement.[19]

Despite some inaccuracy typical of an oral tradition (particularly the mention of Yalta, rather than the Sino-Soviet treaty, as precluding unification), the story may well be true. Two things should be noted: 1) at least some of these irredentist leaflets were printed and distributed in Inner Mongolia, as the testimony of D. Begdze indicates; and 2) as later evidence shows, Stalin had no categorical objection to encouraging irredentist sentiment. For example, in August Soviet military officers were to observe without objection Inner Mongolian assemblies called precisely to unify the long-sundered Mongol brethren.

If Stalin did have an objection to some of the Mongolian leaflets it was probably based on a fear that putting any such promise in writing, especially in a document to be distributed all over Inner Mongolian, might seriously damage relations with China and the United States. Inner Mongolian desire for unification had to be encouraged in a way that did not directly implicate Outer Mongolia and the Soviet Union and left them with an option to retreat. Still, these anecdotes, along with the known fact of Soviet opposition to irredentism outside of the Khölön Buir and Chakhar-Shili-yin Gool areas, indicated the degree to which Choibalsang and Stalin were, as the Chinese proverb says, "sleeping in the same bed, but dreaming different dreams."

The Sino-Soviet Friendship Treaty and the War on Japan

The Soviet Red Army crossed the frontiers into Prince De's Autonomous Mongolian State, as well as Puyi's Manchurian Empire, just after midnight on August 9, 1945. One of the two main offensives would jump off from Mongolia's Tamsagbulag salient, cross the Khinggan ranges, and strike toward Changchun. This force, and the one on its left flank which advanced from Transbaikal across Khölön Buir, consisted solely of Soviet troops. To the west, Colonel-General I.A. Pliev commanded a mixed Soviet-Mongolian force that would protect the right flank of the main force and pin down Japanese forces in North China (including central Inner Mongolia).

Molotov had read the Soviet Union's declaration of war to the Japanese ambassador in the late afternoon of August 8, but Mongolian troops followed their Soviet comrades into battle without any formal declaration. On the first day of the invasion, *Ünen* only apostrophized the populace: "Let us struggle unremittingly against indiscipline, shirking, and all leisurely attitudes." Even with Mongolian and Soviet troops already fighting in Inner Mongolia, the article only hinted: "Although the European war has finished, the war in Asia has not finished. While the Japanese imperialists, formerly friends of Hitlerite Germany, are still fanning the flames of war, how can we take a leisurely attitude?"[20]

Only on the next day, August 10, did Mongolia's standing legislature, the Small Khural, and the Mongolian government convene to issue a formal declaration of war against Japan, in accordance with the MPR's 1936 treaty of mutual defense with Moscow. That same day at 10:00 a.m., the commander of the internal and border troops, Namjil, returned from inspection at Tamsagbulag and reported to Choibalsang that all was ready for the mobile detachments to move into liberated Inner Mongolia.[21]

From its declaration of war through the next two weeks, Mongolia's political and media leaders portrayed the war to the people as a nationalist holy war for the liberation and unification of all Mongolian peoples. The declaration of war passed on August 10, and printed that day in *Ünen*, called on the all the various Mongol peoples—the Khalkha, Dariganga, Dörbed, Torgud, Oirat, and Buriats of the MPR, the Bargu, Chakhar, Ordos, Kharachin, and Alashan Mongols of Inner Mongolia, and even the High Mongol tribes of Qinghai and the Kazakhs and Uriankhai (Tuvans) of northern Xinjiang—to rise up against the Japanese, and defend their culture, language, customs, and religious beliefs.[22]

Not only did this summons give a specifically ethnic meaning to Mongolia's participation in the war, it also announced war aims that directly challenged the Republic of China: Ordos, Alashan, and the Qinghai Mongols were under Chinese rule, not Japanese, while the Kazakhs and Uriankhai of the Altay district were just then engaged in fighting the Xinjiang provincial government under the banner of the Soviet-supported East Turkestan Republic. In a radio address to the Mongolian people, Choibalsang made his war aims more specifically irredentist: "When we, together with the heroic Red Army and the United Nations, have destroyed the Japanese fascists and smashed the Japanese invaders, it will be the consummation of the unification of all the Mongols into a single fraternal country, free, independent, and sovereign."[23]

The party and government did all they could to generate popular support for this war of unification. Since mid-July 1945, *Ünen*, the main newspaper, had been printed in the still-unfamiliar Cyrillic-script Mongolian; but now, with the August 11 issue, the paper switched back to the traditional Mongolian script so as to reach more readers.

At the same time as Choibalsang was releasing long pent-up sentiments of nationalism, the Chinese in Moscow were still trying to avoid following through on their earlier concession to recognize Mongolia. On the evening of August 10, in a plenary session of the Sino-Soviet negotiations, Wang Shijie and T.V. Soong again demanded agreement on the border before China recognized Mongolia. Stalin stiffly insisted that the border had been known and accepted for the last twenty years and refused to even present maps. Totally unaware of the Mongolian aims in Inner Mongolia, the Chinese were especially worried about Mongolian claims in the Altay region. Stalin then decided to draw his interlocutors' attention to where the danger really lay. If a treaty was not signed soon, he warned, the Chinese Communists might well take the Northeast. Moreover if China did not drop its demand for delimitation of the border, the people of Inner Mongolia might demand to join Outer Mongolia.

When the Chinese negotiators referred back to Chongqing for instructions, Chiang at first refused to allow them to surrender on the delimitation issue. By August 13, however, Japan was clearly only a few days away from total surrender and Chiang conceded this issue too. The next day, negotiations were quickly concluded and a thirty-year Sino-Soviet Friendship Treaty signed in the Kremlin. Along with the treaty, which did not directly refer to Mongolia, Molotov and Wang Shijie exchanged notes on the status of Mongolia. Wang agreed, on behalf of the government of the Republic of China, that after receiving favorable results of a post-war plebiscite, China would recognize Outer Mongolia within its present frontiers. In return, Molotov promised that the government of the Soviet Union would recognize Mongolia's independence and territorial integrity.[24]

The signing of the Friendship Treaty, however, by no means relieved Stalin's suspicions of China. While the parties had announced the result of the negotiations to the press, the text of the treaty and associated notes were not to be published until ratification.[25] Apparently fearing that Chiang might let China's Legislative Yuan reject or amend the treaty and so wiggle out of its demands, the USSR continued to support Mongolian irredentist activities in Inner Mongolia.

Irredentist Assemblies and Petitions in Inner Mongolia

The large Shili-yin Gool League, which stretched along Mongolia's south-eastern border, fell easily into Soviet-Mongolian hands. The Japanese did not attempt to hold the area in force, instead fortifying the mountain passes in the Khinggan

Range to the east, and the hills sheltering Zhangjiakou to the south. Relatively untouched by Chinese colonization, Shili-yin Gool had also been only weakly influenced by the eight years of rule by Prince Demchugdongrub's Autonomous Mongolian State. Elsewhere in Inner Mongolia, Japanese rule stimulated a cultural revival based on a nationalist school-teaching intelligentsia. Some schools were based at Prince De's Sönid Right (West) Banner residence in Shili-yin Gool, but they remained alien grafts; few if any of the Shili-yin Gool commoners participated.

By August 10, the Mongolian government had received an official-sounding letter from the Budabal, the deputy chairman of Shili-yin Gool League and prince of the Abaga Left Banner. The message, delivered by several young Mongol officials and addressed to the Commander-in-Chief of the Mongolian Army, asked for unification with the MPR. It also appealed for Mongolia to send an official quickly to prevent chaos from breaking out and to reestablish regular government. At the same time as this appeal from the existing authorities, the educated Mongol youths (now stranded by the collapse of the Prince De regime) who had delivered Budabal's message, also delivered an appeal written by Sechin Jagchid (Jagchidsechen) in the name of Mongolian youth for unification and for the dispatch of a representative to lead youth work and reform the administration.[26]

These appeals, both printed in *Ünen* on August 22, gave the Mongolian government a legitimate governmental pretext and a revolutionary-sounding argument for its reorganization of the administration both in Shili-yin Gool and Chakhar to its south. On August 13, the MPR's Deputy Prime Minister, Badrakhyn Lamjaw, set out from Ulaanbaatar with a delegation to restore order in Shili-yin Gool. Crossing over into Inner Mongolia via the Dariganga frontier post on August 18, he travelled first through Chakhar, where he mostly reappointed the old banner heads or deputy heads to their positions. The only major change was designating Saichungga, a Japanese-schooled educator with progressive ideas, as head of Chakhar Mongolian affairs. The previous League Chairman, Jodbajab, had a strongly anti-Khalkha and anti-revolutionary past, and had not come to pay his respects to the new authorities, so he was not reappointed.

While this official activity took place, Inner Mongolians began to agitate against their reversion back to Chinese control. Already the Communist's Eighth Route Army was occupying seven of the counties of southern Chakhar, so Lamjaw felt no need to impose his own decisions on the areas. He did, however, consider himself to have the authority to appoint Ruyong, a Mongol official in the *ci-devant* General Affairs Department of Prince De's government, as head of Chinese county affairs for Chakhar.[27] As this story suggests, in the early days, while Soviet and Mongolian troops were still fighting in the direction of Zhangjiakou, many strange characters flourished in the political vacuum of the Chakhar steppes.

Right after the Soviet-Mongolian Army cleared the Japanese out of the area, the Narobanchin Lama, Danzangombo, formed his own "Revolutionary Party," and had the party members elect him as chairman. Originally a refugee from the

MPR in the 1930s, he now asserted that he had come to Inner Mongolia on secret assignment from the Mongolia's ruling People's Revolutionary Party (MPRP). Claiming to be an incarnate lama of the Narobanchin lineage, Danzangombo received his own territory in Minggan Banner's Boshoodai *sumu*, one heavily settled with his fellow refugees from the Dariganga area. Now recruiting largely among these refugees, he organized a 100-man armed bodyguard, which set up several big yurts with red flags. The party members also sewed red patches on their arms. The *bagshi lama* ("guru master") became the *bagshi uduridagchi* ("leader master").[28]

This new party did not have a fixed constitution or program, but the chairman Danzangombo sent representatives to Sönid Right to prepare a Party Congress. Sönid Right Banner had been Prince De's old palace with a small number of schools and offices serving the Shili-yin Gool League. For the next two months it would serve as a kind of *de facto* capital for Inner Mongolian nationalists in the Chakhar and Shili-yin Gool areas, now that the old official capital of Zhangjiakou had been occupied by the Chinese Communists.

Another nationalist group, the Young Men's Party (*Jaluus-un Nam*), was also gathering in conferences of five or ten and began to spread propaganda among the people. Like Danzangombo's party (and indeed the two may not have been strictly separate), the Young Men's Party did not have a program, a tight organization, or a mass following—it was composed of a handful of youths and college students. Although it had existed underground since about 1941, it only began public activity after the war.[29]

The young Mongols congregating in Sönid Right sent nine representatives to Ulaanbaatar in order to get Mongolian support for their secessionist aims. At the border town of Zamyn Üüd, they met General Shagdarjaw, Mongolia's Minister of the Interior, and his Soviet adviser, Gridnev. Shagdarjaw and Gridnev sent three of these representative—Dugarsürüng, Delgerchogtu, and Tsewangdamba—to Ulaanbaatar and sent the other six home. Dugarsürüng was Prince De's son and both he and Delgerchogtu had been educated in Tokyo, while Tsewangdamba was an aged lama—for the moment the Mongolian government was willing to deal with the widest variety of nationalists.[30]

The aim of these groups was primarily to avoid Chinese control. One of the self-appointed delegates from Chakhar Bordered Yellow Banner reported to the Mongolian authorities:

> In that banner's territory, soldiers of the Eighth Route Army of the Chinese revolutionary army have been able to enter. They said "The Mongols dwelling beyond China's Great Wall and brought under China's control, these Mongols will have the same banners and may establish a democratic free regime and party." Things being as they are, [we hope] there will be aid for us Mongols to escape from the hands of the Chinese. The banner people do not want to be under Chinese oppression. We hope we will certainly go with the Mongolian government of our own nation.[31]

Given these sentiments, the Mongolian authorities did not have to work hard to produce a convincing secessionist movement. For example, by October 9, 1945, when Lamjaw's Mongolian deputation left the Chakhar area, 117 officials had presented them with petitions asking for unity. Among these nationalist officials was Saichungga, the one appointed to head the Chakhar government in the interim.[32]

By around late August, Mongolian troops had begun organizing rural assemblies in which the Chakhar people would officially record their preferences. As one participant who lived in *sumu* No. 13 of Minggan Banner recalled, the new authorities called together all the household heads—no women or children participated—at the *sumu* center. Facing the 400-500 Chakhar Mongols was one MPRP representative and one from the Narobanchin Lama's party. These representatives said: "Now that the Japanese have been driven out, you must decide your future: Will you unite with China, be independent, or be united with Mongolia?" The people responded, "Well, we're Mongols, all one people, so let's be part of Mongolia." The representatives then asked them to sign their names to indicate their preference and the people then signed their names on a sheet of *muutuu* paper (a kind of low-quality brownish paper much used in Mongolia) next to the last of the three options, union with Mongolia. No one signed in the spaces next to the option to unite with China or to seek independence.[33]

In Khölön Buir, directly to the east of Mongolia, the situation was less complex than in the Chakhar area. Semi-autonomous for much of the Republican period, and united under the domination of a Daur Mongolian elite in Khailar city, Khölön Buir had a tradition of strong and relatively unified administration that did not desert it during the tumultuous Soviet invasion. Mongolian Interior Ministry troops had little work to do among the local population, only propagandizing the liberation thought (*chölöölökh bodlogo*) of the fraternal army. They were mainly concerned with disarming dispersed Japanese soldiers, arresting Khalkha refugees, and seizing the local Japanese intelligence files at Amugulang.[34] The old government system remained in effect and the new Mongolian authorities used the local officials to mobilize secessionist sentiment in Khölön Buir.

On August 28, N. Lhamsüren, the party propaganda chief and now the MPR's special representative to Khölön Buir, convened a congress at Yan Bulag. Representatives from the governments of all the Mongolian banners in Khinggan North Province (traditional Khölön Buir) attended. Shaariibuu, as the head of the Department of General Affairs of New Bargu Right Banner, attended and recalled that Lhamsüren announced a call for all Mongols to unite. With him on the podium were Erkhimbatu, the governor of Khinggan North Province before the Soviet invasion and a Bargu official with a long history of links with Ulaanbaatar. Also at the congress was a Soviet officer, Lieutenant-Colonel Setrov, who observed the proceedings but did not speak. The delegates unanimously called for unification of Khölön Buir's territory with that of Inner Mongolia. They also approved and signed a statement written by Erkhimbatu which congratulated the Soviet Union and Mongolia on its victory, reviewed Khölön

Buir's several hundred years of oppression, and called for its final liberation in union with the MPR.[35]

From this assembly, Lhamsüren went to Khailar, toured around, and returned to Mongolia with thirteen Khölön Buir Mongols in his train. The students, mostly young men in their twenties or thirties who had already entered political life, would receive retraining in Ulaanbaatar's party school. At the same time, two higher ranking Khölön Buir officials, Sanjimitub and Gonggorjab, also came to Ulaanbaatar, presumably to discuss in detail the future of their region.[36]

Ratification of the Sino-Soviet Treaty and the Retreat on Unification

By the time these assemblies were held in Inner Mongolia and representatives from Shili-yin Gool and Khölön Buir were able to gather, the ratification of the Sino-Soviet treaty had already ruled out the possibility of immediate unification. On August 24, Chiang Kai-shek presented the treaty to the Nationalist Party's Central Executive Committee. As might be expected, the Mongolian issue was the most controversial. Chiang argued that the desire of the national minorities for equality and independence could not be suppressed forever. Mongolia had in fact been independent for more that twenty years and China ought to recognize that fact and move on. With the support of Sun Ke (Fo) and the more centrist Political Science clique, Chiang was able to silence the objections of the conservative CC and Whampoa clique members.

Two days later, Sun Ke presented the treaty to the Chinese Legislative Yuan. The Legislative Yuan rarely opposed set party policy, but Sun and Wang Shijie did have to defend the treaty against scattered attacks by unsatisfied delegates. In the end, the deputies backed down and ratified the treaty; well informed sources, such as the Chinese Communist Central Committee, first became aware of the treaty's full text that day. The next day, Wang Shijie officially released the public text to the Chinese and international press. The Chinese press delivered some criticism of the loss of Mongolia, but censorship squelched most opposing voices. As a result, most newspapers followed the not unreasonable government line that retaining sovereignty over Outer Mongolia was unrealistic anyway.[37]

Choibalsang maintained his public posture advocating immediate unification as long as he could. On August 24, the day after Stalin declared war on Japan, he spoke at a victory celebration in Sükhbaatar Square. On a podium festooned with the flags of Mongolia, the Soviet Union, the United States, Great Britain, and even China, and posters showing the Red Army crushing Germany and Russia and Mongolia destroying Japan, Choibalsang gave vent to the exhilaration of victory. He announced that "Our famous People's Revolutionary Army, accomplishing the desire of the Mongolian people, shoulder to shoulder with the Red Army, has liberated native Mongolian land from the Japanese invaders and fought for the freedom and independence of the Mongol peoples living on the territory of South Mongolia and Bargu."[38]

In the strange days of Mongolia's war on Japan, ambitious territorial claims in Inner Mongolia and an exuberant nationalist euphoria were accompanied by the most respectful treatment of China that the Outer Mongolian media had seen in many years. The last public reference to the unification aims of Mongolian participation came on August 26 with the reprinting of Choibalsang's address of two nights before, and an editorial reference to the "many Mongol peoples."

On August 28, in the foreign news section, *Ünen* carried a translation of an interview with Chiang Kai-shek. In it, Chiang justified recognition of Outer Mongolian independence by invoking the Nationalist Party's principles of nationalism. Under these terms, Tibet could also be granted high-level autonomy, and the other border peoples—presumably including Inner Mongolia—would be allowed to practice self-rule.[39]

To discerning Mongolian readers, this small item must have been an inkling that Outer Mongolia's southern policy was changing. The next day, a massive front-page editorial hailed the Sino-Soviet Friendship Treaty and the two notes detailing the status of Mongolia. From this day forward, the sacred cause of freedom for Inner Mongolia disappeared from the pages of *Ünen* as abruptly as it had appeared on August 10. Editorial comment emphasized how recognition from China would open the way to equality with all the other peoples of the world. The editorial even quoted the interview with Chiang Kai-shek, and expressed the Mongolian people's satisfaction with the attitude of the Chinese government, as embodied in Wang Shijie's note.[40]

Just as important as this policy change, however, was the equally dramatic reappearance of florid praise of the Soviet Union, praise that had normally characterized the Outer Mongolian press. While a strong strain of Mongolian nationalist rhetoric had overshadowed the Soviet-Mongolian alliance during the celebration of the unification of the Mongolian peoples, the accustomed veneration of the Soviet Union now reappeared in a massive way. It is hard to avoid the impression that the Soviet embassy had expressed its concern not only with continuing public support for Mongolian unification, but also for the unexpectedly neglectful stance toward its long-time patron.

On August 30 at 1:00 p.m., Choibalsang, together with Mongolia's President G. Bumtsend, the MPRP General Secretary Yu. Tsedenbal, and Deputy Foreign Minister M. Namsrai, all trooped over to the Soviet embassy. There, in a meeting with the Soviet ambassador I.A. Ivanov, they expressed their gratitude for Stalin's unflagging interest in Mongolia's welfare as shown by the notes exchanged by Molotov and Wang. At a mass meeting that night at the Choibalsang factory, the working people caught on quickly to the new line, extolling Mongolia's independence and ignoring in eloquent silence their Inner Mongolian brothers.[41]

The Aftermath to Mongolian Independence

The disappearance of Inner Mongolia from the public life of Mongolia and the damping down of the temporary nationalist euphoria did not mean Mongolia or the Soviet Union would not play a future role in Inner Mongolian nationalist politics. It did, however, mean that their policies would change radically. In the month of September and early October, the military occupation turned from encouraging the direct unification of Inner Mongolia with the MPR and instead to setting up and to supporting autonomous governments in Khölön Buir and the Chakhar-Shili-yin Gool region. Meanwhile, the students and representatives who had come to Ulaanbaatar to seek unification were put off indefinitely, until they were either returned to Inner Mongolia to work with the Chinese Communists or made their adjustment to living in the MPR permanently.

In Khölön Buir, setting up a new autonomous government was easy, since the old administration of the Khinggan North Province had not been dissolved. Sanjimitub and Gonggorjab, the two official Khölön Buir representatives, met Choibalsang and Bumtsend in early September. Meanwhile, at their Nökhdiin Am compound (modern Yaarmag ward in Ulaanbaatar), Shirendew explained to them Mongolia's policy in Inner Mongolia.[42]

The two returned home with Lhamsüren, Mongolia's representative to Khölön Buir, while the local Soviet commander in Khailar, identified simply as Colonel "Hershof," sent a deputation to bring Erkhimbatu back from the steppe. Under Soviet and Mongolian direction, Erkhimbatu proclaimed on October 1, 1945, a new Autonomous Province of Khölön Buir, with an administration largely based on that of the Manchurian regime's Khinggan North Province.

Soon afterward, Erkhimbatu, the chairman of the autonomous province, announced the formation of his new government in telegrams to Stalin and Chiang Kai-shek. In an October 5 letter to Choibalsang, however, he expressed his hope that Khölön Buir, with its low population and military weakness, might still be able to unite with the MPR.[43] While the new government preserved Soviet and Mongolian influence, it did not openly deny Chinese sovereignty in Inner Mongolia.

In the more chaotic area of Chakhar and Shili-yin Gool, however, the new policy worked far less successfully. First of all, the Mongolian authorities considered Danzangombo, a one-time counterrevolutionary refugee, to be most inappropriate as a leader of Inner Mongolian autonomy. So, sometime in late August or early September, a team led by Colonel B. Düinkherjaw, Deputy Minister of the Interior and chairman of the Office of State Security, and his Soviet adviser Artamanov, called the Narobanchin Lama to Dolonnuur and told him: "You were a counterrevolutionary in the 1930s, so you are not fit to do this sort of thing," and bundled him off into a plane for Ulaanbaatar, blind-folded and with his hands tied behind his back.[44]

Meanwhile, the delegates whom Danzangombo had mobilized to go to Sönid Right Banner continued to arrive. Lamjaw, head of the Mongolian government delegation, arrived on September 9, and the next day the Inner Mongolian delegates opened a "People's Congress of National Liberation." On September 15, they passed an organic law for the "Provisional Government of the People's Republic of South Mongolia." The delegates clearly had Soviet and Mongolian support for the formation of some form of *de facto* government, but calling it a new People's Republic may have been as much a local initiative as one from Mongolia or the Soviet Union. In any case, Choibalsang honored the new government with a personal tour of inspection in Sönid Right on September 16-18.[45]

Such implicit support from both Soviet and Mongolian authorities for a fully independent state constituted an open challenge to the territorial integrity of China, and a clear violation of the Sino-Soviet treaty. It is unclear whether the Soviets, in particular, thought they would be able to finesse the issue as they had done that of the MPR itself for so long, or whether they were only temporarily tolerating the action of a local coterie before imposing a compromise more like that in Khölön Buir. In fact, there is no evidence that the Chongqing government was ever aware of this challenge to its sovereignty in Inner Mongolia. For a month or so, the new People's Republic government, which was never much more than an empty sign-board, dwelt in complete obscurity as its delegates lobbied in Ulaanbaatar for a favorable decision on unification.

Eventually, it was the Chinese Communists who objected to this new government and obtained its abolition. The CCP's Shanxi-Chakhar-Hebei Bureau in Zhangjiakou knew something about the regime in Sönid Right and its character since at least September 29. Knowing of the support it had from the USSR, and the degree to which Inner Mongolian nationalism looked north, the Chinese Communist leaders were extremely anxious to settle the matter peacefully, both with the Inner Mongolian nationalists and their Soviet patrons. The party center thus dispatched its main Mongol member, Yun Ze (Wulanfu) with a few comrades to Sönid Right in mid-October. While attempting to win over the younger members of the government, Yun Ze eventually also had to confront a local Soviet commissar who claimed that national self-determination was a Mongol right.

To resolve this issue, Yun Ze travelled into the Mongolian People's Republic and appealed directly to the command of the Soviet-Mongolian Army. Shirendew recalled: "When so many Inner Mongols were going to Outer Mongolia [to appeal for unification], Mao got angry. He sent Wulanfu who said, 'Thank you, but please withdraw your troops. We will establish an autonomous region [for the Mongols.']"[46] But, Choibalsang and others in the Mongolian government still strongly desired unification. Lamjaw, for example, closed the political section of his October 9 report with the following comment: "In view of this desire [for unification] being expressed to us by the people and political figures of Inner Mongolia and its difficult situation economically, I feel it is important for our government to place it before the appropriate countries and help the liberation of our brothers, the Inner Mongolian people."[47]

But the appropriate countries, in particular the Soviet Union, saw the situation differently and Mongolia had to bow to their demands. Having received a Soviet agreement to drop support for the Chakhar and Shili-yin Gool secessionists, Yun Ze returned to Sönid Right and brought the movement under Chinese Communist control.[48] It eventually became the nucleus for a Communist-controlled front organization, the Federation of the Inner Mongolian Autonomous Movement.

Despite this delicate issue, Moscow-Yan'an relations over Mongolia differed significantly from those that Moscow had with Chongqing. The Chinese Communists valued their relations with the Soviet Union and avoided any semblance of a public breach. The Soviet Union evidently appreciated this awareness of the correct etiquette of relations with fraternal parties, as expressed, for example, in sending Yun Ze to Sönid Right with only a small deputation and no armed escort. Subsequently, neither the Soviet Union nor the MPR ever directly challenged the Chinese Communists' control in Inner Mongolia.

Choibalsang's treatment of another delegation of nationalist Inner Mongols seeking unification confirmed this change in policy. East of the Khinggan Range, among the Khorchin, Daur, and Juu Uda Mongols, a strong nationalist movement developed in September and October of 1945. Located in an area solely under Soviet control, this movement had neither any contact with the MPR nor any Soviet encouragement to unify with Mongolia. When a delegation finally came to Ulaanbaatar to ask for inclusion in the MPR, they were kept largely in isolation and then told by Choibalsang personally to dissolve their party and unite with the Chinese Communists.[49] The days of Mongolia's active Inner Mongolian policy were over.

Indeed at the very time of these events, the Mongolian party and government were generating a new frenzy over the plebiscite that would fulfill the terms of the Sino-Soviet treaty. Conducted on October 20, in the presence of Li Fazhang, Chongqing's Deputy Minister of Interior, the eventual results were reported to Li as 483,281 votes for independence, 0 for China. Li acknowledged the results as legitimate and departed for China. On January 5, the Chinese government officially issued a statement that it recognized the independence of Mongolia.

On February 8, a Mongolian mission reciprocated Li's visit and arrived in Chongqing to establish diplomatic relations with China. Five days later, the head of the Mongolian delegation, Politburo member Sürenjaw, and China's Foreign Minister, Wang Shijie, exchanged notes marking China's formal recognition of Mongolia. Ironically, it was just at this time that the allied governments finally published the full text of the Yalta agreement, the text that had begun Mongolia's long struggle for recognition.[50]

Inner and Outer Mongolian Unity and Separation

The two week furor over Inner and Outer Mongolian unification had seemingly achieved nothing. Outer Mongolia had at long last achieved a recognized independence, but only at the price of definitively repudiating any claim on Inner Mongolia. From the beginning, the whole process had been held hostage to Sino-Soviet diplomacy. As it turned out, the rapid deterioration of these relations after the brief post-war alliance soon destroyed any hope of a normal international life for Mongolia. No other country but China and the Soviet Union recognized the new nation until 1948, nor did it enter the United Nations until 1963. Despite Sürenjaw's mission, Mongolia and the Republic of China never established regular diplomatic relations. They did not exchange ambassadors and the complex question of border delineation later erupted into armed clashes over the Baytag Bogda area on the border of Xinjiang and Mongolia. Even while observing the plebiscite and declaring Outer Mongolia's independence, the Chinese government made clear their view that Mongolian independence was primarily a concession to the Soviet Union.

The failure to unify Inner and Outer Mongolia embittered Choibalsang's relationship with his mentor, Stalin. Angry over the betrayal of his dream to unify Mongolia, he refused to attend Stalin's December 21 birthday celebration. When he did visit Moscow again, just after the formalization of Chinese recognition, he took a train rather than an airplane, perhaps in recognition of how his relations with Stalin had deteriorated; trains were safer.[51] At this celebration of Mongolia's new independent status, Stalin told his Mongolian guests, without any discernable irony, that T.V. Soong had protested that recognizing Mongolian independence would lead to the independence of Tibet or Inner Mongolia, but in the end, thanks to Stalin's firmness, the Chinese were forced to accept this independence. Choibalsang's reply is not recorded.[52]

Eventually Choibalsang's relations with Stalin improved and as Sino-Soviet relations deteriorated, Stalin even encouraged Choibalsang in his dream of unifying both Mongolias. In 1947, at a dacha at Lake Ritsa in the Caucasus, where Choibalsang had gone for a rest cure, Stalin concluded an informal exchange about Mongolian affairs with a toast to the unification of all the Mongols under the leadership of Marshal Choibalsang. And on September 29, 1949, at another informal meeting at Sochi on the Black Sea, Stalin tested Choibalsang's reaction to Mao Zedong's recent request to Moscow that Inner and Outer Mongolia be unified as an autonomous part of China. Choibalsang protested that he supported unification but only with the resulting united Mongolia as an independent state. Stalin agreed, but asked Choibalsang to be patient; Lenin had allowed Finland and Poland to become independent, but Mao Zedong was no Lenin. In any case, he assured the Mongolian leader, the Bolsheviks would always stand for the unification of nations.[53] The idea of unification had become just another topic of idle political speculation.

For the Inner Mongolians the results of this episode were somewhat ironic. The very fact of Mongolian and/or Soviet occupation stimulated the Inner Mongolian nationalist movements and gave them space in which to develop their forces. Yet it was the Chinese Communists who were eventually able to saddle and ride these nationalist movements and channel their ambitions into an autonomous region firmly under Beijing's own control.

The strongest nationalist movement, however, eventually became the eastern Inner Mongolian one growing up in the region east of the Khinggan Range; this movement had never received any encouragement from Mongolia. But the Soviet military authorities in the area did sympathize with the Mongols' struggle against Nationalist Chinese rule and as late as January 1946, were accepting from Mongols petitions for aid and unification. In February, the introduction to a folder of such petitions from Mongols in the eastern Inner Mongolian area, collected by the Political Department of the Soviet 17th Army, noted that all but a "numerically insignificant and sinicized Mongol elite" supported unification with the MPR. It also observed with considerable complaisance how the nationalists were "striving to establish the closest possible ties with the USSR and MPR and to get their support for the Mongolian autonomy movement."[54]

Yet little concrete aid was forthcoming, and the Soviet Union remained a neutral observer, at least, of Communist efforts to co-opt the Mongolian nationalist movement. Despite the rebuffs, Mongolia remained a major cultural influence on Inner Mongolia throughout the 1950s and Inner Mongolian nationalists, many of them now cadres in the new regime, still looked to the MPR as a model, especially after it established diplomatic relations with the People's Republic of China.

Finally, the Soviet Union revealed in this whole venture its thoroughly opportunistic approach towards policy on its borders. Convinced that China's national government could never control its borderlands, Stalin's government was used to supporting "autonomous governments," whether in Inner Mongolia or Xinjiang, but constantly rebuffed them in their desire for full independence. Keeping a hand in the game meant that contacts and groups had to be cultivated, but Moscow's relations with China demanded that both its own actions and those of its clients had to be kept within strict limits. This tried and true pattern broke down in Inner Mongolia when the Chinese Communists were able to thoroughly co-opt and atomize Inner Mongolia's nationalist movements, and use its campaigns of land reform to solidify its control over the border. Unable any longer to control Inner Mongolian events indirectly, the Soviet policy of opportunism bequeathed an irritating legacy to Moscow's relations with the Chinese Communists.

Notes

1. Research for this article was supported in part by a grant from the International Research & Exchanges Board (IREX), with funds provided by the National Endowment for the Humanities, the United States Information Agency, and the U.S. Department of State, which administers the Russian, Eurasian, and East European Research Program (Title VIII).

2. Li-fu Ch'en, *The Storm Clouds Clear Over China: The Memoir of Ch'en Li-fu, 1900-1993* (Stanford, 1994), p. 163; John W. Garver, *Chinese-Soviet Relations, 1937-1945: The Diplomacy of Chinese Nationalism* (New York, 1988), pp. 153-81, gives an excellent description of how Chongqing recaptured actual administrative control over Xinjiang.

3. As indicated in one of his famous interviews with Edgar Snow, Mao Zedong had much the same idea, with the exception that victory over Japan and revolution in China would bring about this favorable turn of events. Edgar Snow, *Red Star Over China* (New York, 1968), pp. 110n, 444.

4. *Mongol-Zöwlöltiin khariltsaa, 1921-1974: barimt matérial,* vol. 2, *1941-1974,* pt. 1 (Ulaanbaatar and Moscow, 1981), 129-30. For a discussion of how Stalin and

Roosevelt may have had different definitions of the term *status quo* see Bruce A. Elleman, *Diplomacy and Deception: The Secret History of Sino-Soviet Diplomatic Relations, 1917-1927* (Armonk, N.Y.: M. E. Sharpe, 1997), pp. 231-51.

5. Christopher Thorne, *The Far Eastern War. States and Societies 1941-1945* (London, 1986), pp. 161-72, 181-92, 257-81.

6. Milton J.T. Shieh, *The Kuomintang: Selected Historical Documents, 1894-1969* (Baltimore, 1970), pp. 196, 202.

7. Garver, *Chinese-Soviet Relations*, pp. 212-14, 216.

8. Ibid., pp. 214-17; Odd Arne Westad, *Cold War and Revolution: Soviet American Rivalry and the Origins of the Chinese Civil War* (New York, 1993), p. 37. Westad records this threat on Inner Mongolia from Chinese archival sources, but informed Mongolian personages had long known of Stalin's threats. L. Jamsran (interview, May 23, 1992) remarked that Stalin was said to have warned the Chinese in these negotiations: "Outer Mongolia doesn't want to unite with either China or the USSR, so it ought to be independent. But there are still some people in Outer Mongolia who would like to take over Inner Mongolia. This is very dangerous for China."

9. *Ünen*, no. 154, July 6, 1945; Lhamsürengiin Bat-Ochir, *Choibalsan (Namtryn ni balarkhaig todruulakhui . . .)* (Ulaanbaatar, 1996), pp. 173-74.

10. Shirendew, interview, June 30, 1992; Westad, *Cold War and Revolution*, pp. 40-41; Garver, *Chinese-Soviet Relations*, p. 220.

11. *Ünen*, (no. 157) July 10, 1945; B. Shirendew, *Dalain dawalgaanaar* (Ulaanbaatar, 1993), pp. 172-73; Bat-Ochir, *Choibalsan*, pp. 174-75; Shirendew, Interview, June 30, 1992. *Ünen* lists the other Soviet guests, besides Stalin and Molotov, as L.M. Kaganovich, I.D. Beria, G.M. Malenkov, N.A. Voznesenskii, N.A. Bulganin, V.N. Merkulov, Yu.M. Kaganovich, Lieutenant-General I.G. Rubin, and the Soviet ambassador to Mongolia I.A. Ivanov. In his memoirs, Shirendew says that A.Ya. Vishinskii was present but this seems to be a mistake. The Mongolian guests included only Choibalsang, the Mongolian ambassador, Z. Sambuu, and Shirendew. Shirendew described the exchange about the plebiscite to me in the interview, but does not include it in his memoirs; he does, however, note the provision for thumbprints in *Dalain dawalgaanaar*, p. 175.

12. Westad, *Cold War and Revolution*, pp. 41-43; Garver, *Chinese-Soviet Relations*, pp. 218-20.

13. Bat-Ochir, *Choibalsan*, p. 174; Shirendew, interview, June 30, 1992.

14. *Ünen*, no. 170, July 28, 1945, p. 1; *Ünen*, no. 176, August 4, 1945, p. 1.

15. See Jan Gross, *Revolution From Abroad: The Soviet Conquest of Poland's Western Ukraine and Western Belorussia* (Princeton, 1988). Meeting with Choibalsang at Sochi in 1949, Stalin explicitly compared the possible unification of Inner and Outer Mongolia with the unification of western Ukraine and Belarus' with their Soviet S.S.R.'s. See Bat-Ochir, *Choibalsan*, p. 187.

16. *Daalgawar biyelüülj yawsan on jilüüd* (Ulaanbaatar, 1990), pp. 66-67.

17. D. Darjaa interview, April 1992. L. Jamsran also recalls hearing about the "Benediction on Living Together'" being printed as a leaflet interview, May 23, 1992. D. Darjaa later published another poem on the fraternal unity of Inner and Outer Mongolia, "Jüng biligtü degüü," in *Ünen*, no. 189, August 19, 1945.

18. Central Historical Archives of the State of Mongolia, 11-1-911, no. 96.

19. L. Jamsran, interview, May 23, 1992. J. Tömörtseren, in Chakhar at the time of the war, also recalled finding such a "Letter of Attention"—interview, April 11, 1992.

20. *Ünen*, no. 180, August 9, 1945, p. 1.

21. *Daalgawar biyelüülj yawsan on jilüüd*, p. 67.

22. *Ünen*, no. 181, Aug. 10, 1945. Choibalsang repeated this part of the declaration at a rally on the evening of August 10—the text is reprinted in *Mongol-Zöwlöltiin khariltsaa, 1921-1974: Barimt matérial*, vol. 2, *1941-1974*, part 2, p. 138.

23. *Ünen*, no. 182, August 11, 1945, p. 1.

24. Westad, *Cold War and Revolution*, pp. 52-53; Garver, *Chinese-Soviet Relations*, pp. 226-228. Mongolian text of the notes, as printed in *Ünen*, August 29, in *Mongol-Zöwlöltiin khariltsaa, 1921-1974: Barimt matérial*, vol. 2, *1941-1974*, part 2, pp. 141-42.

25. Ongoing Sino-Soviet negotiations were mentioned in *Ünen*, no. 181, Aug. 10, 1945, and the signing of the treaty in *Ünen*, no. 189, Aug. 19, p. 4. Set amidst *Ünen's* continuing agitation over the impending unification of Inner Mongolia with the MPR, the news release on the treaty merely noted that the text of the treaty would be printed after ratification.

26. *Ünen*, no. 191, August 22, 1945, p. 2.

27. Central Historical Archives, 11-1-888, pp. 24-27.

28. Tömörtseren, interview, April 11, 1992; Central Historical Archives 11-1-888, p. 36; 11-1-912, p. 3; *Daalgawar biyelüülj yawsan on jilüüd*, p. 29. Danzangombo was originally from Mandal *sumu* in Khentii province.

29. Central Historical Archives, 11-1-912, p. 3; 11-1-888, pp. 17-18.

30. Ibid., p. 5b.

31. Ibid., p. 3.

32. Ibid., 11-1-888, p. 22

33. Tömörtseren, interview, April 11, 1992.

34. *Daalgawar biyelüülj yawsan on jilüüd*, pp. 68, 73-74, 7; Shaariibuu, interviews, April 12 and 15, May 15, 1992.

35. Central Historical Archives, 11-1-912; Shaariibuu, interviews, April 12 and 15, May 15, 1992. The Chinese-populated cities of Khailar and Manzhouli were not represented in this assembly. It should be noted that Khölön Buir at this time meant only those areas west of the Khinggan Range. The merger of largely steppe Khölön Buir with the forested Naun Muren province east of the range only occurred in 1949.

36. Central Historical Archives, 11-1-912; Shaariibuu, interviews, April 12 and 15, May 15, 1992; Shirendew interview, June 30, 1992.

37. Emily Yaung, "The Impact of the Yalta Agreement on China's Domestic Politics, 1945-1946," Ph.D. dissertation, Kent State University, 1979, pp. 88-90, 91-95; Ding Shaochun, Ge Fulu, and Wang Shiying, *Dongbei jiefang zhanzheng dashiji* (Beijing, 1987), p. 6.

38. *Ünen*, no. 195, Aug. 26, 1945, p. 3. Choibalsang's speech is reprinted in Kh. Choibalsan, *Iltgel ba ügüülelüüd*, vol. 3, *1941-1945* (Ulaanbaatar, 1953), p. 437.

39. *Ünen*, no. 196, August 28, 1945, p. 3.

40. Ibid., no. 197, August 29, 1945, p. 1.

41. Ibid., no. 198, August 30, 1945, p. 1; Ibid., no. 199, August 31, 1945, p. 3.

42. Shirendew, interview, June 30, 1992; Central Historical Archives of the State of Mongolian, 11-1-912, p. 5.

43. Layi, "'Yisedüger sar-a-yin gurban'-aca qoyisiki Kölön Buyir-un nigen qugucagan-u törü-yin bayidal-un tuqai durasumji," *Kölön Buyir-un soyol teüke-yin matériyal* 3 (1989), 6; Central Historical Archives, 11-1-913; *Hulun Buir Meng qing*, p. 651; Shaariibuu, interviews, April 12 and 15, May 15, 1992.

44. Central Historical Archives, 11-1-888, p. 36; *Daalgawar biyelüülj yawsan on jilüüd*, p. 29; Tömörtseren, interview, April 11, 1992.

45. Ibid., pp. 139-140; *BNKhAU-yin Öwör Mongolyn öörtöö zasakh oron* (Ulaanbaatar, 1081), pp. 43-45.

46. Shirendew, interview, June 30, 1992.

47. Central Historical Archives, 11-1-888, p. 34.

48. Zhongyang dang'anguan, *Zhong-gong Zhongyang wenjian xuanji*, vol. 13, *1945-1947* (Beijing, 1987), p. 186; Hao Yufeng, *Wulanfu zhuan* (Khökhekhota, 1989), pp. 361-367. Given the sensitivity of mission, it is not surprising that the details of it are very vague. While Yun Ze's mission to West Sönid has long been known, no Chinese source has yet published the exact date. Similarly the excursion into Mongolia to meet the Soviet-Mongolian command was edited out of previous accounts of Wulanfu's life, appearing first in Hao's 1989 biography.

49. Christopher Atwood, "The East Mongolian Revolution and Chinese Communism," *Mongolian Studies*, 15 (1992), 37-43. Shirendew and other informed Mongolians knew of the mission but heard little about it, nor is there even the slim archival evidence that is available for those missions from Khölön Buir and Chakhar.

50. *Ünen*, no. 243, Oct. 23, 1945; *Ünen*, no. 6, Jan. 8, 1946, p. 1; *Ünen*, no. 41, Feb. 19, 1946, p. 1; *Ünen*, no. 38, Feb. 15, 1946, p. 3.

51. Darjaa, interview, April, 1992; *Ünen*, no. 44, February 22, 1946, p. 1.

52. Bat-Ochir, *Choibalsan*, pp. 178-79.

53. Ibid., pp. 180-87.

54. Mongolian People's Revolutionary Party, Central Party Archives, 7-1-33, "Predislovie," pp. 1-3.

Mongolia and Japan in 1945-1995:
A Half Century Reconsidered

Ts. Batbayar

The 1990s have brought unprecedented changes to the Mongolian nation and to its relations with the outside world, including the major powers. The magnitude of changes can be compared only to the early period of this century, when in 1911 the Qing dynasty in China disintegrated, which gave Mongolia the opportunity to revive its statehood after several centuries. In a like manner, in the 1990s Mongolia's powerful northern neighbor, the former Soviet Union, disintegrated, giving Mongolia the opportunity to become a full-fledged member of the world community.

At the beginning of the twentieth century, the Urga leaders faced an old dilemma in their search for ways to protect Mongolia from its two neighbors. In order to survive, the Mongols sought Russian help and proclaimed their independence. Tsarist Russia, however, restrained by secret treaties with Japan, was not able to render full support. In the eyes of the Mongol leaders, Japan—which defeated Russia in 1905—was the only country capable of supporting them. The newly created Mongolian government repeatedly appealed to Japan during 1912-14 for help and protection. Although rejected by Japan, these early Mongol attempts to link up with Japan represent the first Mongol attempts to find a third force with which to break Russian and Chinese domination.[1]

In the 1930s, Japan became Mongolia's neighbor through its client state Manchukuo. Suddenly, Japan was knocking at Mongolia's door, using both pan-Mongol propaganda and military pressure. The Soviet Union, the Mongolian People's Republic's only ally, perceived these attempts by Japan as a direct threat to the Soviet Far East and Siberia, and it promptly concluded a mutual defense protocol with Mongolia that allowed Soviet troops to be stationed on Mongolian soil. Negotiations between Manchukuo and Mongolia to resolve peacefully several border disputes ended in failure, largely due to Japanese and Soviet unwillingness to see these disputes settled.

Japan's aggressive posture in the 1930s was used as a pretext by the Soviet NKVD and the Mongolian Ministry of Interior to conduct mass purges among civil servants, army officers, and the Buddhist clergy. Concerned with Mongolia's vulnerability, the Soviet Union was determined to protect the borders of the MPR as if they were its own. Tensions with Japan reached the breaking point in 1939 when a four-month long battle broke out along the Khalkhingol (Nomonhan), a river on Mongolia's eastern border, in which Japan was soundly defeated.[2]

In August 1945, in the waning months of World War II, Mongolia declared war on Japan, and joined Soviet forces in their attack into Manchuria and Inner Mongolia. This state of war between Mongolia and Japan was technically not abolished until February 1972, when the two countries agreed to establish diplomatic relations. A new active period in bilateral relations came at the end of the 1980s when Japan began playing its present leading role in assisting Mongolia in its transition towards democracy and a market economy.

The two immediate bilateral issues which complicated the normalization process up until 1972 were Mongolia's war reparation claims against Japan and the Japanese war prisoner issue. However, these two issues were not key obstacles to the normalization process. If we carefully analyze the situation in the 1960s, Japan's special relationship with the Republic of China (Taiwan) was the primary reason why Tokyo was not able to recognize the Mongolian People's Republic. By the early 1970s, however, when the PRC was admitted to the United Nations, and the United States declared its intention to normalize relations with Beijing, Japan was able to break its one-sided orientation toward Taipei and to open relations, at first with the MPR, and then later with the PRC.

This essay will examine issues of bilateral relations between Mongolia and Japan based mostly on Mongolian sources, particularly hitherto unpublished archival materials. The author will first reveal the origins of these bilateral issues, that is, how these issues emerged in the late 1940s and early 1950s and the period of the early 1960s, when the first unofficial contacts were started through the capitals of third countries, and then the second half of the 1960s, when negotiations were held which opened the way to Mongol-Japanese normalization. This essay also will help readers to understand the current active period of bilateral relations, although the recent rapprochement appears to be a sharp change of course. Throughout the essay, the author will try to emphasize the continuity of Japan as a potential "third force," assisting Mongolia to obtain some relief from the domination of its two neighbors.

The Passive Period in Mongol-Japanese Relations: Bilateral Issues

The MPR declared war against Japan on August 10, 1945, a day after the Soviet Union had done so. About 80,000 Mongolian cavalrymen took part in a massive Soviet military attack on Japanese forces stationed in Chinese Manchuria and Inner Mongolia. This campaign was mainly dictated by the Mongolian leadership's long-standing desire to achieve international recognition by public participation in the U.N. coalition.

Between October 1946, and May 1947, two letters were sent from Kh. Choibalsang, then Prime Minister and Minister of Foreign Affairs, to the Far Eastern Commission, set up in Washington to determine policies of allied countries towards Japan. The first letter dated October 2, 1946, outlined Mongolia's allegations against Japan by citing all major cases when Japan had threatened Mongolia before 1945, and concluded with war reparation claims against Japan.

This letter stated: "During the whole period of the existence of the Mongolian People's Republic, i.e. since 1921, Japanese militarists had threatened the liberty and independence of the Mongol people and of its territory by disturbing its quiet and peaceful life and aiming at the extension of their aggression westwards in order to attack North and West China and the Soviet Union." Then the letter estimated that "as a result of the Japanese aggression against the MPR the Mongolian army lost a total of 2,039 men during the period of 1935-1945. Material damage caused to the MPR by the Japanese aggression amounts to 321,983,000 tugriks." The letter ended with the following statement: "Proceeding from the fact that the MPR has always steadfastly stood guard for the interests of the U.N. and has made a worthy contribution to the cause of the elimination of Japanese aggression in the Far East, the Government of the MPR declares that it has a right to an appropriate share in the reparations from Japan, as a compensation for the material damage caused by Japan to the MPR, and firmly believes that it will receive it."[3]

The answer came from Nelson T. Johnson, Secretary General of the Far Eastern Commission, dated March 20, 1947, which acknowledged the receipt of the cable and informed Mongolia that no decisions had been reached regarding reparation claims.[4] The second letter from Choibalsang to the Far Eastern Commission was sent on May 1, 1947. Choibalsang reminded the Far Eastern Commission about his first letter and declared that if the Commission was going to decide how much compensation each interested country was to receive from Japan, the Government of the MPR was asking 2-3 percent of the entire reparations from Japan.[5]

Choibalsang's second letter probably came at a time when an ambitious program was being drawn up by the occupation authorities to make available, as reparations to the countries Japan had invaded, all of Japan's industrial capacity in excess of its minimum needs. However, the letter was not answered because that program never materialized. Moreover, the reparations issue never came up again until 1966, when Mongolia and Japan officially began to negotiate a normalization.

The second issue—Japanese war prisoners—emerged in January 1954, when the then Prime Minister Tsedenbal received a letter from the Japanese Red Cross inquiring about the fate of about 100 Japanese war prisoners who by some accounts were still held in Mongolia. According to archival sources, Tsedenbal made an immediate inquiry to the Mongolian Ministry of Interior on when and how many war prisoners were brought to Mongolia and when and how many of them were repatriated.[6]

The official response was dated January 30, 1954, and stated that between November 20 and December 10, 1945, 12,318 Japanese war prisoners were brought into Mongolia in six installments from Soviet military authorities in the Far East. These Japanese were used mostly as construction workers in Ulaanbaatar, and Central and Sükhbaatar provinces. During the two years between 1945-47, 1,613 of them died, most of them by various diseases. All remaining 10,705 Japanese were shipped back to the Soviet Union in October 1947.[7]

At the same time, a letter came from a Japanese woman inquiring about the fate of her husband, Yosito Koyama, who she said was still detained in Ulaanbaatar. According to the response of the Ministry of Interior on April 20, 1954, to the inquiry made by the Ministry of Foreign Affairs, there were four Japanese still being held in prison at that time. They were not prisoners of war, but were captured as spies in August 1945 in the midst of Mongolia's military campaign in Chinese Inner Mongolia, and were then brought to Ulaanbaatar before being sentenced to various terms. An official letter was sent from the Mongolian Red Cross to the Japanese Red Cross on January 17, 1955 that stated that no Japanese prisoners of war remained in Mongolia, but that there were four people in prison sentenced for spying and that they would be handed over to the Chinese authorities soon.[8]

A Japanese reporter named I. Yorioka, a representative of "Kyodo News Service," first visited Mongolia in April 1956 and interviewed Tsedenbal. Using this opportunity, Mongolia's leadership expressed its strong willingness to establish official relations with Japan for the first time. He said: "We will [all] be congratulated if diplomatic relations between our countries will be established. It will certainly contribute to mutual cooperation of all nations. We are ready to work together in trade, and cultural spheres on the basis of mutual usefulness and equality."[9]

In May 1957, following the visit of a high-level party and state delegation to Moscow, a Joint Mongol-Soviet statement was released. The statement expressed the Mongolian Government's desire to establish relations with Japan. It said: "The Government of the MPR views positively the establishment of diplomatic relations between the USSR and Japan and declares its readiness to enter into negotiations with the Government of Japan on the normalization of relations between the MPR and Japan."[10]

Parallel to and even preceding these repeated appeals of Mongolia were a number of unofficial contacts between Mongolian and Japanese public organizations. Between June 13-16, 1956, a twelve member delegation of Japanese Committee for Solidarity with Asian countries visited Ulaanbaatar. In September 1956 the deputy chairman of the Mongolian Trade Unions was invited by the Sohyo labor federation to Japan to attend its meeting. Since then Japan has invited non-governmental delegations on various occasions, such as the annual atomic bomb memorial meetings at Hiroshima, large international expositions, the Congress of Asian and African Writers, and Buddhist conferences.

The First Japanese Response in the Early 1960s

In the early 1960s, the Japanese government started to seriously consider the possibility of normalization of its relations with Mongolia. It even entered into unofficial contacts with Mongolian diplomats through its embassy in Warsaw. Not surprisingly, these contacts coincided with similar efforts made by the American State Department at the same time. Two officials from the Japanese Ministry of Foreign Affairs were sent for a one-month fact-finding mission to Mongolia in October 1961.

According to Mongolian sources, Japanese chargé d'affaires Akira Okada approached his Mongolian counterpart on May 8, 1961, to ask whether it would be possible to set up a trade representative in Ulaanbaatar which could be turned into an Embassy when the MPR joined the United Nations.[11] Okada responded that it was better to use a similar negotiation pattern with Mongolia to that which had helped Japan establish diplomatic relations with Romania, Bulgaria, and Hungary after Japan had first set up its Embassy in Warsaw. Okada met Mongolian ambassador Bat-Ochir again on June 5, and unofficially asked what conditions would be attached if he asked his government about Mongolia's intention to end the state of war and enter into diplomatic relations with Japan.[12]

About two weeks later, on June 21, Japanese chargé d'affaires Akira Sigemitsu met Mongolian Ambassador Luwsan in Moscow. It turned out that the unofficial exchange of opinions in Warsaw had opened the way to more serious dialogue in Moscow. Sigemitsu firstly reminded Luwsan that the Japanese officials had never yet visited the MPR in their official capacity. Therefore, he requested that if the Mongolian government agreed, the Japanese government would like to send two officials to the MPR as the first step prior to the two sides opening negotiations.[13]

After one month, Ambassador Luwsan met Sigemitsu in Moscow and said that the government of the MPR was ready to enter into negotiations with those Japanese officials who have full authority to conduct such negotiations on the issues of ending the state of war and establishing normal relations between the MPR and Japan. Luwsan suggested a preliminary exchange of opinions at Ambassador level before such negotiations started.[14]

The Japanese were not interested in such Ambassador level talks. They continued to insist on sending two officials to Mongolia on a fact-finding mission. When Sigemitsu met his counterpart he strongly requested visas for two officials. The Mongolian government decided to grant visas for two Japanese officials on the condition that they would be allowed to visit Mongolia as tourists and during their visit, Mongolian officials would not enter into any contact with them.

The two Japanese officials, Mitsutaka Akiho (the third secretary at the Japanese Embassy in Moscow) and Takeshi Muto (the third secretary at the Japanese Embassy in Holland), visited Mongolia as tourists in October 1961. During that month they visited Ulaanbaatar, Choibalsang, Sainshand, Arwaikheer, Bayankhongor, Tsetserleg, Altanbulag, and Sükhbaatar City. However, no important diplomatic changes occurred following that fact-finding mission.

The major question was recognition. Speaking at the parliamentary session in January 1963, the Japanese Prime Minister Ikeda announced that Japan *de-facto* recognized the Mongolian People's Republic in 1961 when it did not oppose the latter's entry into the United Nations. Furthermore, two important events took place during 1964. In September, the Japan-Mongolia Association was established which included many prominent Japanese public and private figures, and in the following month thirty-six Mongolian athletes took part in the Olympic Games held in Tokyo, for the first time.

Meanwhile, unofficial trade between Mongolia and Japan, which had started in 1959, experienced some growth in the mid-1960s; the trade turnover was

$40,000 in 1960, it became $600,000 in 1963. In 1964, a 19 percent growth over the previous year was registered and trade reached the level of $700,000. This brought so much optimism to both sides that they even started talking about $1 million trade turnover as a desirable goal by 1965.[15]

By August 1965 Mongolian foreign policy planners started to think seriously about how to normalize relations with Japan. Two events helped this process. One was the U.N. seminar on woman rights in Ulaanbaatar scheduled for August 1965. The Japanese government was interested in sending two officials (Kisaburo Sakiyama and Marohito Hanada) with the Japanese delegation to further investigate the possibility of normalizing relations.

The other event was the twentieth anniversary of the Allied victory over Japan, which was a good occasion to make a significant diplomatic move. As an extraordinary step, the Mongolian Ministry of Foreign Affairs instructed its Embassy in Moscow on July 30 to ask Soviet colleagues two questions: 1) How the Soviet Union was going to commemorate the twentieth anniversary of the victory over Japan; 2) Are conditions suitable for the Government of the MPR unilaterally to declare the end of the state of war with Japan? According to Mongolian sources, Soviet diplomats were not against the idea that Mongolia take the initiative by declaring an end to the state of war unilaterally.[16]

At the end of the year, Tsedenbal, Chairman of the Council of Ministers, was interviewed by *Tokyo Shimbun* reporter Kikuzo Ito. Tsedenbal again declared Mongolia's strong interest in normalizing relations. He said: "Our government as early as 1957 expressed its desire to abolish the formal state of war between our two countries and normalize Mongol-Japanese relations. We are now ready to consider that issue if Japan is interested in normalizing relations with us."[17]

The Second Japanese Response in 1966

A Japanese delegation headed by T. Hasegawa, a member of Parliament, visited Ulaanbaatar and Sükhbaatar cities in August 1966, at which time he finally received the long-sought-for permission from the Mongolian authorities to visit the graves of Japanese war prisoners. The visit brought a real breakthrough in bilateral contacts. Mongolian archival sources bring to light several very interesting details about this visit.

Prior to the August 1966 breakthrough, Japanese ambassador Toru Nakagawa had paid a visit to Mongolia's ambassador Luwsanchültem in Moscow on April 11, 1966, and asked for permission to send a ten-member delegation to visit Mongolia to attend the graves of Japanese prisoners of war. At the same time, he handed over a letter from Aiichiro Fujiyama, Chairman of the Japanese Society on Repatriation of Prisoners of War, addressed to Tsedenbal, Chairman of the Council of Ministers.[18] He also emphasized how important this issue was for the Japanese people and expressed his hope that Mongolia would consider positively Japan's humanitarian request. In his words, about 1,700 Japanese prisoners of war died in Mongolia and twenty-seven of them were still missing.

The Japanese request to visit graves did not come as a complete surprise to Mongolian diplomats. Following the visit of two Japanese officials as tourists in October 1961, Mongolian authorities ordered that work be carried out to beautify these graves; sixteen sites where 1,615 Japanese were buried were cleaned up. In early 1966, an inspection of these graves was carried out by Mongolian local government authorities in order to check to see whether everything was in order.

According to archival materials, by April 1966, the Mongolian Ministry of Foreign Affairs formulated its policy approach toward Japan. It was as follows: 1) if the government of Japan expressed officially its desire to establish diplomatic relations, Mongolia would enter into negotiations with them on the Ambassador level; 2) if the Japanese were ready to publish a joint Statement about the establishment of diplomatic relations and the end of the state of war Mongolia would accept it, but would point out that the issue of prisoners of war would not affect further bilateral relations and that issue would be resolved by issuing a Joint Statement, and also it should be pointed out that the war reparations issue would be settled separately at another time.[19]

In Moscow, Luwsanchültem met Nakagawa on May 25, 1966, and told him that a ten-member Japanese delegation would be welcome to visit Mongolia. A day earlier, a reply from Tsedenbal to Fujiyama's letter was handed to Nakagawa. After a month, Nakagawa again visited Luwsanchültem and introduced the members of the Japanese delegation, consisting of eight persons representing relatives of prisoners of war, three officials, two parliamentary members, and one interpreter. At the same time, Nakagawa told the Ambassador that a Japanese Foreign Ministry official, included in the delegation, would like to exchange opinions with his counterparts on the issue of establishing official diplomatic relations between the two countries.[20]

In August 1966, what was now a fifteen-member delegation visited Mongolia with the announced purpose of attending to Japanese graves. The delegation included two members of Parliament, Takeshi Hasegawa (Liberal Democratic Party) and Sinkichi Ukeda (Japan Socialist Party). Accompanying the delegation were two officials from the Ministry of Foreign Affairs, Mitsutaka Akiho (Deputy director of East European Department) and Marohito Hanada.

Two very substantive exchanges of opinion took place between Akiho and Tserentsoodol (Director of the Department). At the first meeting Akiho explained the position of the government of Japan by suggesting that the two countries use the simplest method to establish official relations (i.e., they exchange diplomatic notes). In his words, Japan did not think that a state of war existed between the two countries. His argument was that Japan never fought a war with the MPR, since it regarded the MPR as a part of China before World War II, so there was no need to abolish a state of war which did not exist.[21]

At the second meeting, Tserentsoodol explained Mongolia's position. Mongolia did not think that issues such as a Peace Treaty with Japan and war reparations would disappear automatically with the establishment of diplomatic relations. Mongolia would retain a right to raise those issues at an appropriate time.

However, the government of Mongolia did not want to link those issues with the main issue—the establishment of official relations.[22]

In response, Akiho again referred to the issue of war reparations. In his opinion, if the government of Mongolia claimed war reparations right after the establishment of diplomatic relations, the government of Japan would feel very uneasy. Akiho explained that the government of Japan would prefer normalization on the basis of an agreement stating that the two countries would not make any preconditions (i.e., mutual non-conditionallity). Akiho in conclusion stated that if Mongolia agreed to drop its war reparations claim, both sides could promptly conduct negotiations and exchange diplomatic notes.

At the last meeting during a lunch on August 28, Tserentsoodol conveyed to Akiho a softer Mongolian position. He made it clear that the issues of the Peace Treaty and war reparations were very complicated and that it was probable that they could not be negotiated in the near future. However, if such a Treaty could be concluded the government of Mongolia would be willing to participate in it. The war reparations issue was primarily a government-to-government issue between the two countries. Therefore, that issue could be settled in a proper manner at some point after the establishment of diplomatic relations.[23]

The Establishment of Diplomatic Relations

D. Adilbish, Chairman of Mongolia's Peace Committee, visited Japan on February 13-16, 1968, to attend the opening ceremony of the Japan-Mongolia Friendship Association.[24] Adilbish met Heishiro Ogawa, Director of the Asian Affairs Bureau, Japanese Ministry of Foreign Affairs, on February 24. According to a Japanese source, a very interesting conversation took place between Hasegawa (who had visited Mongolia before in 1966), a member of the Parliament, and Adilbish. Hasegawa told his visitor:

> As we all know, the Mongolian government notified the Far Eastern Commission on October 18, 1946, about war time losses of 2,039 persons and $80 million of damage caused by the Japanese army between 1935 and 1945. As a precondition for establishing diplomatic relations, Mongolia always asked for the payment of war reparations. Do you still insist on it? We are aware that there was the Khalkhin Gol battle. However, after World War II Mongolia, by blatantly ignoring international law, forced Japanese war prisoners to work for two years. As a consequence, about 1,686 of them died. Such a one-sided request by Mongolia is not acceptable to us. If you agree to drop such claims and start talking with us about economic cooperation, then we can enter into negotiations with you.[25]

Following the Adilbish visit to Japan, the Politburo of the Mongolian People's Revolutionary Party made some important decisions regarding Japan: 1) to formulate a new tactical government policy in order to bring about the establishment of official relations between Mongolia and Japan; 2) to create the Mongol-Japan Friendship Association; 3) to receive a Goodwill mission from Japan in July 1968; and 4) to inform the Japanese side that Mongolia was ready to receive a delegation of influential LDP leaders.[26]

Since 1967, ambassadors of both countries stationed in Moscow had started to meet frequently and exchange opinions on the issue of normalizing relations. On April 30, 1969, Toru Nakagawa, Japanese Ambassador to the USSR, told Luwsanchültem, Mongolian Ambassador to the USSR, that the government of Japan thought that it was appropriate to conduct negotiations if the two parties agreed to acknowledge the non-existence of the issue of war reparations. At the same time, Japan was ready to respond if Mongolia would suggest a concrete project of economic and technical cooperation which would be acceptable to Japan.

At the next meeting on June 16, 1969, Luwsanchültem told Nakagawa that to ignore completely the state of war between two countries was not reflective of reality. Mongolia has full rights to claim war reparations. Luwsanchültem suggested that a meeting of official government delegations be held in the near future to settle the issue of the establishment of official relations. In his opinion, as a result of such meeting a Special Protocol (under which Japan would take a obligation to render economic assistance to Mongolia) could be signed, and at the same time a short announcement could be released announcing the establishment of official relations. Luwsanchültem handed Nakagawa draft proposals of both the Protocol and the press release.[27]

On August 20, 1969, Nakagawa again met Luwsanchültem in Moscow. In his words, the views of both sides had become closer but principal disagreement still remained. Japan still thought that the state of war between the two countries did not exist. However, even without official relations, Japan treated the MPR as a country with which economic and other cooperation could be maintained on an equal basis as with other countries with which Japan had opened formal diplomatic relations.

According to this principle, the Japanese government invited a delegation from Mongolia to attend Expo '70. A delegation headed by B. Gombojaw, Deputy Chairman of the Council of Ministers, visited Japan in August 1970 for the first time. During the visit, Gombojaw met Kiichi Aichi, the Minister of Foreign Affairs of Japan. Aichi asked his guest whether Japan could be sure that Mongolia would drop its war reparations claim. Gombojaw explained his government's position that it is better not to link those two issues: the establishment of relations and war reparations. He again suggested setting aside the war reparations issue so that it could be solved afterward. He added that Mongolia was even ready to reconsider the size of its claims.[28]

It became evident that all of the negotiations held since 1966 had ended in deadlock. This was acknowledged by the two Japanese officials—Kisaburo Sakiyama and Marohito Hanada—who visited Mongolia in August 1968. In their opinion, the issue of normalization had not been settled properly even though more than twenty years had passed since the end of World War II. Negotiations between foreign officials and embassy people had failed to produce tangible results. Therefore, they admitted, this issue should be discussed at higher levels between high-ranking political party or government leaders.[29]

Similar information was provided by Matsuzaki, President of the Japan-Mongolia Association, who visited Ulaanbaatar in July 1971, to attend the fiftieth Anniversary of the People's Revolution of Mongolia. When Matsuzaki met Foreign Minister Aichi (Kiichi Aichi was replaced by Takeo Fukuda on July 5) before his departure to Mongolia, Aichi told him that Japan already recognized the MPR. Now the question was how to exchange Ambassadors. This issue, he said, should be settled as soon as possible.[30]

In the opinion of Matsuzaki, there were at least three influential people in the LDP who felt very favorably toward Mongolia. One was Zentaro Kosaka, who was the chairman of the Political Affairs Research Committee (*Seimu Chosakai*) at that time. He had been the Minister of Foreign Affairs in the second Ikeda cabinet when the MPR was admitted to the United Nations in 1961. In the words of Matsuzaki, Kosaka was willing to visit Mongolia in 1968 to investigate the possibility of economic assistance toward Mongolia.

The second person was Toshio Kimura, who became the Director of the Economic Planning Agency just before Matsuzaki's visit to Mongolia. Kimura told Matsuzaki that he would do his best to accomplish the establishment of diplomatic relations with Mongolia before the term of the Sato government expired. The third person was Takeshi Hasegawa, a member of the House of Representatives, who had visited Ulaanbaatar in 1966 as the head of the graves visiting mission. In the words of Matsuzaki, all three LDP leaders understood Mongolia's position regarding war reparations and all three also shared the view that economic assistance should be rendered to Mongolia in an appropriate form.[31]

During the following September, 1971, the Japanese Good-Will Mission, headed by Shigeki Nakashima, a member of the House of Representatives, visited Mongolia. L. Rinchin, Minister of Foreign Affairs, met Nakashima and his delegation on September 11. The Japanese delegation was not authorized to conduct negotiations. However, they conveyed important messages from the Mongolian side back to the Japanese government and to LDP leaders.[32]

A very important breakthrough took place when Tserentsoodol, Director of the Department, Ministry of Foreign Affairs, visited Japan between November 5-13, 1971. During this visit, Tserentsoodol met Hogen, Deputy Foreign Minister, and Sunobe, Director of Asian Affairs Bureau. Sunobe told Tserentsoodol that Japan was not willing to pay war reparations, but that Tokyo would be willing instead to contribute $20-30 million to finance the construction of a particular plant.[33]

Thereafter, a very important meeting took place on November 9, when Tserentsoodol met seven LDP members of the Parliament, including E. Tanaka,

K. Shoji, H. Yamada, and Y. Sakurauchi. They promised Tserentsoodol that they would meet Prime Minister Sato immediately and solve this issue (of normalization) today or tomorrow. A similar thing occurred when he met Ukeda, member of the Parliament. Ukeda said: "I realized today that only Prime Minister Sato is delaying the establishment of diplomatic relations. I will meet him. If the government does not make a decision this time, we will create a pressure group and raise this issue at the next Parliamentary session."[34]

Three days later (in the evening of November 12), Kisaburo Sakiyama, officer of the Ministry of Foreign Affairs, told Tserentsoodol : "Those LDP members of the Parliament certainly met Foreign Minister Fukuda. Maybe they even met Prime Minister Sato. Now the issue is going to be finally solved positively. One more meeting is needed. The Ministry of Foreign Affairs was asked to prepare opinions how the embassy will be set up and how economic cooperation project will be implemented."[35]

During the morning of November 13, before their departure, Sakiyama handed Tserentsoodol several newspapers, including *Yomiuri* and *Tokyo Shimbun.* Sakiyama said: "It is a gift from our Ministry for you." The November 13th edition of *Yomiuri* carried a report entitled: "The establishment of diplomatic relations with Mongolia: The real intention of the Government." According to the report, the Prime Minister made it clear on November 12 his intention to decide positively the issue, of the establishment of diplomatic relations with the government of the MPR, and a Foreign Ministry source said that there was nothing which could be an obstacle to the establishment of diplomatic relations. The only decision remaining was when the formal establishment should take place.[36]

It is interesting to note that both Japanese and Mongolian parties wanted to announce the establishment of official relations before such relations were established between Japan and China. When Tserentsoodol met Japanese Ambassador Niijeki in Moscow on his way back to Ulaanbaatar, Niijeki told him that he had just received a telegram from Nakagawa, the permanent representative to the United Nations, that the government of Japan had decided to establish diplomatic relations with the MPR well before Japan would do the same with China.

Based on the information provided by Tserentsoodol, the Ministry of Foreign Affairs in Ulaanbaatar recommended that the Great People's Khural, Mongolia's Parliament, issue an edict abolishing the state of war with Japan. At the same time, the Mongolian Ambassador to Moscow Luwsanchültem met his counterpart Niijeki on December 28, 1971, and suggested that they jointly draft an official communique announcing the establishment of diplomatic relations.

Two months later, on February 11, 1972, an edict ending the state of war with Japan was promulgated by the Great Khural and a few days later, on February 24, the two countries entered into formal diplomatic relations. It took, however, another five years for the two countries to agree on the terms of economic cooperation. Eventually, an agreement was signed for Japanese grant aid to be used in the construction of a plant producing cashmere goods. The amount totaled 5 billion yen, worth $17 million at that time.

Following the establishment of diplomatic relations, permanent contacts were set up between the two Parliaments and the two Ministries of Foreign Affairs. Mutual visits by foreign office officials have been ongoing since 1974. The Japan-Mongolia Parliamentary Commission was set up in the upper house of the Japanese Parliament in 1975, and in the lower house in 1978. The Mongolia-Japan Parliamentary Commission was set up in the Great Khural in 1977. A joint delegation of both houses of the Japanese Parliament visited Mongolia in 1978.

The development of bilateral relations after normalization in 1972 was largely dependent on the position of the former Soviet Union. The Soviet leaders were sure that Mongol-Japanese relations would not develop in the political field, but they were concerned about some progress in the economic and trade spheres and constantly warned the Mongolian leaders not to get any closer to the Japanese. Mongolia, in turn, kept assuring the Soviet Union that it would not work energetically with Japan on matters impinging on Mongolia's defense and security. There was one case when Japan became interested in developing the copper deposit at Tsagaansuwarga and even proposed making a feasibility study of that deposit at its own expense. Mongolia at first agreed, but after consulting with the Soviet Union, refused permission. Japan was very much surprised and disappointed by this turn of events.[37]

The Active Period in Mongol-Japanese Relations: A New Beginning

By the latter half of the 1980s new developments within Mongolian society brought about significant changes in its diplomatic relations with Japan. Domestic as well as external factors worked in favor of such changes. Domestically, an economic "open door policy" was promulgated and mutually beneficial economic and trade links with developed countries were strongly encouraged during the 1960s and 1970s. Major changes were made in the priorities of industrial policy. This policy had originally been based on a division of labor among the CMEA countries, whereby Mongolia was to specialize in agricultural raw material processing. But then came the recognition that Mongolia needed to develop entirely new branches of industry like metallurgy, machine building, electronics, and chemicals.

Mongolia's foreign policy priorities also shifted significantly. Following Gorbachev's Vladivostok initiative of July 1986, a withdrawal of Soviet troops from Mongolia began. The Soviet Minister of Foreign Affairs, Eduard Shevarnadze, made a very important visit to Ulaanbaatar in January 1986, during which a number of very sensitive issues, including Mongolia's relations with the United States, Japan, and other countries, were discussed. In the aftermath, negotiations between Ulaanbaatar and Washington were sped up, and in January 1987, the two countries opened diplomatic relations. Undoubtedly, Shevarnadze's visit also favorably influenced subsequent relations between Mongolia and Japan.[38]

Mongol officials working in economic planning and foreign trade were the first to become interested in expanding relations with Japan. In December 1987, a working group was established to formulate concrete recommendations to the government on the kinds of progress that could be achieved with Japan. By April 1988, this working group came up with several concrete proposals. Some top officials, however, opposed these proposals as going too far. After a few month's hesitation, during which time arguments and counter arguments were exchanged, the proposals were enthusiastically supported by T. Namjim, who at that time was the first deputy chairman of the powerful State Committee of Economic Planning. Finally, in October 1988, the new positive course toward Japan was endorsed by Prime Minister D. Sodnom.[39]

In the fall of 1988, Namjim visited Japan, where he raised a number of new issues relating to the promotion of economic and trade contacts between the two countries. He explained his government's basic policy priorities of developing industries that could process Mongolian raw materials with high technology and turn that into finished goods for the world market. Specifically, Namjim suggested the construction of a steel mini-mill, the installation of copper relining equipment, production of communications equipment, a joint study of rare earth elements, and the development of small and medium-size enterprises in Mongolia. The two sides also exchanged opinions on how to exploit more fully Mongolia's tourist potential and how to attract more Japanese tourists to Mongolia.[40]

Political relations between the two countries have also been raised to higher levels. In May 1987, the Mongolian Minister of Foreign Affairs visited Japan, and his Japanese counterpart reciprocated in May 1989 with an official visit. It marked the first time since 1972 that the two countries exchanged visits by their foreign ministers. Responding to a request made by Mongolia, the Japanese government agreed to send a special mission in order to investigate the future potential of bilateral economic cooperation. The mission, headed by former Japanese ambassador to Mongolia, T. Akiyama, visited the country in August 1989, and made a report to the Japanese government outlining certain areas where Japanese assistance should be applied in the near future.[41]

The Mongolian Prime Minister D. Sodnom paid an official visit to Japan in February 1990, during which a trade agreement was signed. In addition, Japan granted Mongolia the most-favored-nation (MFN) status enabling it to promote its trade within a convertible currency area. Later that year, the President of Mongolia, P. Ochirbat, participated in the inauguration ceremony of Emperor Akihito during November 1990.[42] This goodwill visit clearly demonstrated Mongolia's strong willingness to strengthen friendly and mutually beneficial relations with Japan.

The year 1991 was an important one for Mongolia's relations with developed countries, particularly with the United States and Japan. The primary reason was Mongolia's peaceful transformation, as manifested in July 1990 by its first free elections since 1921. Mongolia's transition was complicated when the Soviet Union, its sole creditor and major trade partner, cut its aid and was no longer willing to subsidize Mongolia. By early 1991, Mongolia had to approach a number of Western countries to request emergency aid programs to counteract imminent shortages of essential goods.

By that time, the developed countries began to react more positively, largely due to the Mongolian government's commitment to democracy and a market economy. In February 1991, Mongolia was admitted to a number of international organizations, like the IMF, the World Bank, and the ADB. In January 1991, the U.S. Congress granted Mongolia MFN status. At the end of July of that year, the U.S. Secretary of State, James Baker, made a brief visit, which actually was a follow-up to his previous visit, interrupted in August 1990 by the Iraqi invasion of Kuwait. The July 1991 visit demonstrated to the world the support of the Bush administration for Mongolia's reforms in a difficult period of transition to democracy.[43]

The August 1991 visit of Toshiki Kaifu to Mongolia was the first by a leader of a leading industrialized democracy and showed the Japanese government's firm intention to organize broad-based economic assistance to Mongolia from the world community. Kaifu not only declared his readiness to organize in Tokyo an international meeting for the support of Mongolia, but also communicated the decision of the Japanese government to grant an interest free-loan worth 2 billion yen for the structural reform of the Mongolian economy. During the Kaifu visit, the two sides reached an understanding on the further development of bilateral cooperation. In 1991, total Japanese aid to Mongolia jumped more than tenfold, from 640 million yen the previous year to 8.2 billion yen.

In the following month, September 1991, the first Mongolia support group meeting was organized in Tokyo at the initiative of the Japanese government and in cooperation with the World Bank. Four international organizations, the IMF, the World Bank, ADB, and the UNDP, as well as delegations from fourteen countries, took part. The participating organizations and states supported the activities of the Mongolian government and pledged a total of about $150 million, in which Japan's share alone equaled $55 million.

Japan's role has been very instrumental in organizing Mongolia support group meetings, which were held six times in Tokyo since 1991. Japan is also Mongolia's largest international donor, with aid pledges in each of the last five years running at about $70-90 million.

Japan's firm support for Mongolia's transition process in the 1990s was underscored in July 1999 by the Japanese Prime Minister Keizo Obuchi's visit to Mongolia, the second since the Mongolian democratic revolution began in 1990. Japanese Prime Minister Obuchi pointed to this visit as beginning a new stage of bilateral relations, based on shared values of freedom and democracy, and reiterated Japan's active support of Mongolia's efforts in reform and renovation. A number of agreements, including grant aid for food production and cultural facilities, and a new aviation agreement, were signed during Obuchi's visit.[44]

Trade and Economic Assistance

Improvements in Mongol-Japanese relations have been most noticeable in international trade. Trade between Mongolia and Japan grew by over thirty times between the 1970s and the late 1980s; the trade turnover between the two countries was $1.13 million in 1972, and it reached its highest level, $31.4 million, in 1989. Still, Mongolia's share in Japan's total trade remained negligible, and Japan's share was just over 1 percent of Mongolia's total trade in 1990.

Mongolia's trade with Japan has increased since 1992 because the Mongolian government started to export copper to Japan in addition to its traditional export item—cashmere goods. In 1992, 49,000 tons of copper were shipped, and in 1994, 43,000 tons (see Table 1); this was equal to 10 percent of Mongolia's 1994 copper exports.

Table 1: Mongolia's trade with Japan (in million $)

	1990	1995	1996	1997	1998
Exports	7.6	46.7	35.0	37.7	12.2
Imports	9.8	45.3	77.8	34.8	55.2
Total	17.4	92.0	112.8	72.5	67.4

Source: *Mongolian Statistical Yearbook 1998* (Ulaanbaatar, 1999), pp. 139-141.

The major project financed by Japan is a two-furnace mini electric steel-refinery which was built and put into operation in May 1994. The facility was financed by loans provided by Export-Import Bank of Japan totaling $57.8 million with 6 percent interest per year. It was estimated that Mongolia spends $40 million every year to purchase about 100,000 tons of steel for domestic consumption. Therefore, the mini-mill was planned with a 100 thousand ton capacity per year, sufficient to cover Mongolia's needs. But, there are a number of problems concerning the efficiency of this mini mill. The Mongolian government is worried about overestimation of Mongolia's domestic demand, its competitiveness with Russia's cheap steel, and the sufficiency of iron scrap and other raw materials.

Since 1990, the amount of grant aid allocated by Japan has increased sharply. It was decided to bring Japanese medical equipment to rural hospitals in two installments, each worth 450 million yen. In order to improve Mongolia's communications with the outside world, an Intelsat ground station was built with a Japanese grant of 950 million yen. During Prime Minister Jasrai's visit in November 1993, the Japanese government extended 2 billion yen in aid to help Mongolia cut its balance of payments deficit. Grant aid also included emergency food supplies and other equipment for education and cultural organizations.

As regards loans, following commodity loans worth a total of 7,295 million yen in 1991 and 1992, sizeable loans were provided for railway transportation development in 1993 and 1994, rehabilitation of the No. 4 thermal power plant in Ulaanbaatar in 1995, and mining development in 1996 and 1997 (see Table 2). The Japanese government provided a total of 10,125 billion yen of soft loans for the two-stage renovation work of Baganuur and Shivee-Ovoo coal mining.

Table 2: Japan's Official Development Assistance to Mongolia (1993-1997)

Year	1993	1994	1995	1996	1997	Total
Grant Aid	18.51	44.71	54.95	48.91	46.10	261.35
Technical Cooperation	16.91	23.04	30.18	24.78	19.18	127.37
Loans	22.12	2.33	14.80	30.05	12.70	118.66
Total (US$ mil.)	57.53	71.08	99.93	103.75	77.98	507.40

Source: The Japanese International Cooperation Agency.

Finally, there has been technical assistance in the form of training Mongols in Japan, bringing Japanese experts to Mongolia, and shipping small equipment for specific projects. The number of Mongols going to Japan for training has steadily increased from twenty in 1990, to ninety-nine in 1995, to one hundred and seven in 1996. Technical assistance is conducted by a government agency called the Japanese International Cooperation Agency (JICA). When the biggest power plant in Ulaanbaatar was about to break down, JICA sent a group of experts to make an on-site inspection. It also carried out a study of the Erdenet copper mine with a view toward its modernization and development, and is currently conducting several other feasibility studies.

The Future of Mongolian-Japanese Relations

How people perceive each other is of considerable importance for any bilateral relationship. Until recently, the Japanese considered Mongolia a closed country with pro-Soviet leanings; they probably never thought that this could change so quickly. This situation has changed radically, especially owing to the democratic reforms in Mongolia. It is well-known that since 1990 the Japanese media started to cover changes in Mongolia. Japanese citizens now have a much greater knowledge of Mongolia and its people compared with only a few years ago.

The image of Japan as "an enemy" and of Japanese people as "samurai warriors" were cultivated very strongly in the minds of ordinary Mongols during the last several decades. This was done by the government through all of its means of ideological apparatus (i.e. literature, movies, and TV programs). Each year, in August, the anniversary of the victory over the Japanese militarists was celebrated with a big propaganda campaign. The sudden rapprochement with Japan since late 1980s was received with confusion by the populace, and especially for those middle aged people who grew up in post-World War II Mongolia. A polarization of opinions has occurred.

There are two extreme views expressed by some Mongols regarding Japan and that country's present active role in Mongolian affairs. One view was expressed by a journalist, who said that Mongolia should be brought into a confederation with Japan. The other view was expressed by a historian, who argued that the present policy of Japan very much resembles the Japanese expansionism of the 1930s.

Overall, however, Mongols are learning more and more about Japan and the Japanese people. In October 1992, an interesting opinion poll was conducted by the Japanese newspaper *Asahi Shimbun* and the Mongolian State University. It revealed that, among other things, there was a growing interest among Mongols, and especially among the younger generation, toward Japan. Not surprisingly, Japan topped the list of countries Mongols would like to visit first. It was also evident that expectations had been raised for Japanese assistance in education and culture, the construction of new plants, and to increase food production.

In sum, how we can explain such an active period in bilateral relations since the late 1980s? In my opinion, there are a number of factors. First of all, the Mongolian government's strong commitment toward democracy and a market economy is creating an entirely new situation for further strengthening bilateral relations, relations which had remained virtually stagnant since 1972. Mongolia's peaceful transition process is supported by Japan because if it succeeds it will have a salutary effect upon Mongolia's two neighbors, and on other Asian countries in transition. Second, Mongolia's search for "a third partner" has been revived again since 1990 and Japan is regarded as an important country in this policy, along with the United States, Germany, and others. Finally, Mongolia is one of the few Asian countries where the Japanese military did not commit brutalities during World War II. At the same time, the Japanese people are sympathetic to Mongolia's economic hardships and are willing to help Mongols in this difficult transition period, which the Japanese people associate with their own period of post World War II reconstruction.

Notes

1. For early Mongol attempts to contact Japan, see Fujiko Isono, "The Bogd's letter to the Japanese Emperor and a Japanese called Kodama," *The Canada-Mongolia Review* 3:1 (1977); Tatsuo Nakami, "Independent Mongolia and the Imperialist Powers: 1911-1914," *Journal of Asian and African Studies* 17 (1979), Tokyo University of Foreign Studies (in Japanese).

2. For a Mongolian view of the events in the 1930s, see Ravdangiin Bold, "The International Relations in the Far East in the 1930s and the Mongolian People's Republic," *Dorno-Örnö* 2 (29) (11-1112) (in Mongolian).

3. The Archive of the Ministry for External Relations (MER), 59-34, pp. 13-15.

4. Ibid., p. 18.

5. Ibid., p. 21.

6. Ibid., 59-42, p. 78.

7. Ibid., pp. 73-77.

8. Ibid., 59-42, p. 97.

9. Ibid., 59-43, p. 10.

10. *Ünen*, May 17, 1957.

11. The Archive of the MER, 59-47, pp. 22-23.

12. Ibid., pp. 29-33.

13. Ibid., pp. 35-38.

14. Ibid., p. 49.

15. Ibid., 59-50, p. 51.

16. According to the External Ministry Archive, the Mongolian Councellor Sumiyaa met N.E. Torbenkov, the Councellor at the Soviet Ministry of Foreign Affairs on August 4, 1965. Torbenkov supported the idea that Mongolia take the initiative and declare an end to the state of war.

17. *Ünen*, December 20, 1965.

18. The Archive of the MER, 59-51, pp. 14-18.

19. Ibid., pp. 37-40.

20. Ibid., pp. 48-49.

21. Ibid., pp. 161-69.

22. Ibid., pp. 170-79.

23. Ibid., pp. 180-83.

24. It should be noted that two different Mongolia friendship associations were established in Japan. In 1964, the Japan-Mongolia Association (*Nippon Mongoru Kyōkai*) was established with Yo Matsutaka as the first president; this organization included many LDP people. In 1968, the other Japan-Mongolia Friendship Association (*Nippon Mongoru Shinzen Kyōkai*) was created with Kenjyu Kato as the president which included more JSP people.

25. *Mongoru Nyumen* (Tokyo: Sanseido, 1993), p. 261.

26. The Archive of the MER, 59-54, pp. 52-53.

27. Ibid., 59-63, pp. 53-66.

28. Ibid.

29. Ibid.

30. Ibid., 59-61, pp. 7-11.

31. Ibid.

32. According to a private Japanese source, Nakashima later had over a one hour-long meeting with Prime Minister Sato briefing him about Mongolia. However, Sato was silent and he pronounced only two words, "First China," at the end of the meeting.

33. The Archive of the MER, 59-61, pp. 19-25.

34. Ibid.

35. Ibid.

36. *Yomiuri Shimbun*, November 13, 1971.

37. S. Dambadarjaa, "The Fruitful twenty years," *Dorno-Örnö*, 1 (1992), p. 28.

38. The former Ambassador of Mongolia to the USSR (1984-1990), Ts. Gurbadam in memoirs published in Ulaanbaatar in 1994, gives a very interesting account of this important period of Mongol-Soviet Relations. See Ts. Gurbadam, *Yu. Tsedenbal: Thoughts about the historical truth* (Ulaanbaatar, 1994), pp. 100-106.

39. A working group was composed of the Chairman of the State Planning Committee, the Minister for Foreign Trade, and others. Information about the activities of the working group is based on the author's personal interview with an official from the Mongolian Ministry for External Relations.

40. The January 13, 1990 edition of the newspaper *Ünen* published a long interview with T. Namjim titled "New Perspectives of Mongol-Japanese Relations."

41. On February 3, 1990, *Ünen* published an interview with the Japanese Foreign Minister Taro Nakayama, in which he emphasized the special mission to Mongolia headed by Teruji Akiyama.

42. The speaker of the Mongolian Parliament took part in the funeral of Emperor Hirohito.

43. During the author's trip to Washington, D.C. in July 1991, he was told by American academics that there were discussions between Tokyo and Washington about who should be the chair of the Mongolia support group. Although Tokyo wanted to be co-chair, it was James Baker who persuaded Japan to be the sole chair.

44. For a western reporter's view on Jasrai's visit to Japan, see Charles Smith, "Helping hand: Mongolia Finds a Patron in Japan," *Far Eastern Economic Review*, (9 December 1993), p. 20.

Part III

Mongolia Today

In 1990, Mongolia broke with the USSR, eliminated one-party rule, and embarked on a revolutionary path of political and economic liberalization. Mongolia declared a policy known as the "open door" in order to strengthen trade and economic ties with Japan, the United States, and western Europe. Soon after adopting a new constitution, the democratic government of Mongolia also instituted privatization, financial reform, and trade liberalization.

The Mongols today inhabit an enormous swath of the Asian continent, ranging from Buriatia to the north and northwest of Mongolia, to Uriankhai (Tuva) to the west, parts of Xinjiang and Qinghai to the southwest, large portions of Inner Mongolia to the south and southeast, and various areas in Manchuria, especially the Bargu district of Heilungjiang province, to the east. A linguistic map of Mongol areas would approximate in size all of western Europe.[1]

As A. Hurelbaatar discusses in his essay, one of the largest groups of Mongols outside Mongolia—approximately 5 million—can be found in China. Although the bulk of these people inhabit China's northern regions and provinces—with almost 3.5 million in Inner Mongolia, almost 1 million in Manchuria, and perhaps a quarter million to the west in Xinjiang and Qinghai—people who claim Mongol heritage can be found in all of China's thirty-two autonomous regions, provinces, and municipalities.

In China, there has been an ongoing process of cultural assimilation throughout the twentieth century, as the Mongol people have gradually adopted agriculture, learned to speak Chinese, inter-married with other nationalities, and settled in Han-dominated urban areas. However, since the end of the 1970s the Mongols in China have endured the painful process of readopting their traditional culture, in part by teaching their children how to speak, read, and write Mongolian. This linguistic revival holds out the hope for the Mongols in China of preserving the distinctive cultural and ethnic identity they have formed while being a part of China.

* * *

Even while Mongols in China are undergoing an important cultural revival, Mongols in Mongolia are also attempting to reclaim their heritage. Most importantly, during the MPR's so-called state socialist era under Soviet tutelage, Mongolia's nomadic herders were organized into some 300 collective and state farms; while most of these collectives continued to rely on herding, about fifty devoted their energies to agricultural production.[2] Following the adoption of Mongolia's economic reforms in the early 1990s, however, these collectives and state farms were privatized, and most of the land in Mongolia has once again come under individual management.

Decollectivization was not accomplished without extensive economic disruption. Wages plummeted and it is estimated that a quarter of the Mongolian population was pushed under the official poverty line. There has also been considerable demechanization, a result of the rising price of imported oil (mainly from Russia) and the difficulties inherent in locating spare parts; this process has led to a further decline in productive capacity.

As David Sneath discusses in his essay on pastoralism in Mongolia, the changes which are currently being carried out in Mongolia have led to smaller and more diversified herds, to less extensive pasturelands, and to a sharp decrease in the slaughter rate of the herds. These changes in many ways parallel similar pastoral changes during the 1920s following Mongolia's last great economic upheaval—the adoption of state socialism.[3] Therefore, Sneath challenges the assertation that the ongoing market reforms are destroying Mongolia's traditional pastoral system. Instead, he points to patterns below the formal level of institutions that embody power relations and longer-term shifts.

* * *

Nationalism is without a doubt one of the most important currents in Mongolia today. Arguably, it was the Mongolian nationalist movement that led to the repudiation of communism and the creation of a democratic government. Mongolian nationalism is not a wholly new development, however, and has in fact played an important role during much of Mongolia's twentieth century history. Perhaps the most important symbol of Mongolian nationalism is Chinggis Khan.[4]

The question of Mongolian nationalism became especially important during the early 1960s, when the MPR government was forced to consider what kind of ceremony it should adopt to celebrate the eight-hundredth anniversary of Chinggis Khan's birth.[5] This question proved to be both politically and culturally sensitive. Chinggis Khan was a feudal ruler—and therefore anathema to Marxist-Leninist modern developmentalism. Furthermore, the unified Mongol state that he created had conquered and ruled the MPR's socialist mentor—the USSR—and its less friendly neighbor to the south—the People's Republic of China.[6]

In his essay on the eight-hundredth Chinggis Khan anniversary, J. Boldbaatar discusses the importance of this celebration to the Mongolian nationalist movement by explaining how the celebration's official date—May 31, 1962—was also the thirty-eighth anniversary of the May 31, 1924 Sino-Soviet treaty that had simultaneously guaranteed Mongolian autonomy from China and had also denied Mongolia its true independence. Picking this day to celebrate Chinggis Khan's anniversary was perhaps a sign of Mongolian resistance to the stewardship of the USSR, and the Chinggis monument erected in Khentii province boldly proclaimed: "Let my body be tired, but my state never be exterminated."[7] Although the incipient Mongolian nationalist movement was soon repressed on orders from Moscow, it continued to exist in the hearts of the Mongol people.[8] The Chinggis monument, which the MPR government ordered destroyed but which was protected from harm by local officials in Khentii, outlived its opponents.

* * *

The driving force behind the reform movement in Mongolia may have been nationalism, but the reflection of this nationalism can perhaps best be seen in Mongolia's foreign policy, which has been carefully designed to counteract the dangers inherent in Mongolia's geopolitical position, trapped as it is between the unstable Russian Federation to the north and the Chinese empire to the south. Mongolia's foreign policy emphasizes good relations with Western and Asian capitalist countries, a non-aligned and nuclear-free policy, and the decision to demilitarize Mongolia by prohibiting the stationing of foreign troops on its territory.

In his essay investigating nationalism, the elites, and the transformation of Mongolian society, Tom Ginsburg shows how a relatively small group of intellectual and government leaders—perhaps 300 total—has been largely responsible for the enormous changes that Mongolia has undergone. This governing elite shares many similar characteristics: male, born mainly in the 1940s and 1950s, educated primarily in the former USSR or Eastern Europe, and most often trained in technical fields. Below the governing elites are two other groups—intellectuals and technocrats—who have aided their leaders in formulating and implementing the reforms. Finally, the organizations through which the elites express their opinions include various political parties that have been forming and reforming coalitions at a dizzying pace.

Ginsburg concludes that the single most important concern of all of the governing elite, whether they be intellectuals, technocrats, or members of the numerous political parties, is the so-called China threat. It is that perceived threat that ensures the continued cooperation of these otherwise diverse and divisive groups.

Notes

1. Robert Rupen, *The Mongolian People's Republic* (Stanford, CA: Hoover Institution Press, 1966), pp. 16-17.

2. Collectivization in Mongolia was started in 1929, abandoned in 1932, and then carried through to conclusion some twenty-five years later. Robert Rupen, *How Mongolia is Really Ruled: A Political History of the Mongolian People's Republic, 1900-1978* (Stanford, CA: Hoover Institution Press, 1979), pp. 53-57.

3. Simukov, "Materialy po kochevomu bytu naselenia MNW," *Sovremennaia Mongolia*, No. 2 (15) (1936), p. 49.

4. By the early 1970s, the official line was that Chinggis Khan's "unification of

the tribes was a boon to the land, while his military campaigns . . . brought only devastation and misery to the conquered lands and peoples. Mongolia herself suffered both culturally and economically, and her people were dispersed over a large part of the sprawling empire. Thus, the country's own development was seriously retarded by its Most Mighty King." Albert Axelbank, *Mongolia* (Tokyo, Japan: Kodansha International Ltd., 1971), pp. 24-25.

5. C.R. Bawden, *The Modern History of Mongolia* (New York, NY: Frederick A. Praeger, 1968), pp. 417-19.

6. Elizabeth Endicott-West, *Mongolian Rule in China: Local Administration in the Yuan Dynasty* (Cambridge, MA: Harvard University Press, 1989), p. 112.

7. The Central Archives of the MPRP (CAP), FIW. t-D. h-1, hn-4-22.

8. A visitor to Mongolia in the early 1990s commented: "Yet while the outside world has grown accustomed to using Genghis Khan's name as a synonym for destruction, war, and cruelty, inside Mongolia I was beginning to find that Genghis Khan was being accorded the status of a national hero, even a god." Tim Severin, *In Search of Genghis Khan* (New York, NY: Atheneum Macmillan Publishing Company, 1991), pp. 12-14.

15. Election of Officers for the *Bag*, the Lowest Unit of Rural Administration, near Shili-yin Khota City, Inner Mongolia. *Source*: Photograph courtesy of Christopher P. Atwood (1987).

16. The Mausoleum of Chinggis Khan, Ejenkhoroo banner, Yekhe Juu league, Inner Mongolia, constructed in 1963. *Source*: Photograph courtesy of Christopher P. Atwood (1986).

17. Tents Traditionally Attributed to Chinggis Khan's Three Empresses, Central Chamber of the Mausoleum of Chinggis Khan. *Source*: Photograph courtesy of Christopher P. Atwood (1986).

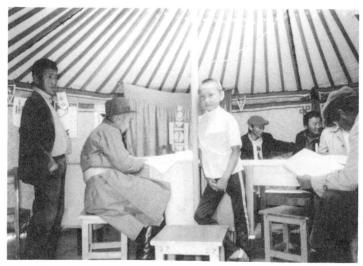

18. Electoral Headquarters for the Democratic Party in the 1992 Parliamentary Elections, Mörön City, Khöwsgöl Province. *Source*: Photograph courtesy of Christopher P. Atwood (1992).

19. Voting in the 1992 Parliamentary Elections, Töw Province. *Source*: Photograph courtesy of Christopher P. Atwood (1992).

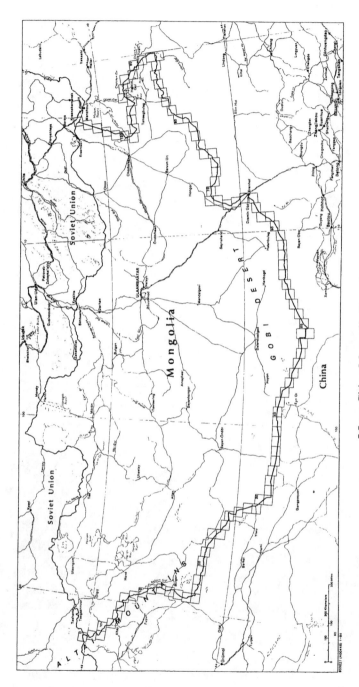

Map: China-Mongolia Boundary

*Source:*United States Department of State, Bureau of Intelligence and Research, *China-Mongolia Boundary* No. 173 (August 14, 1984).

A Survey of the Mongols in Present-Day China: Perspectives on Demography and Culture Change

A. Hurelbaatar

There are 4,800,000 Mongols in China, possessing a variegated and rich culture. Mongolian culture contains many unique and vital elements, a full understanding of which is indispensable for effective research in Mongolian studies. This essay will present a brief introduction into some aspects of Mongols in China, particularly with reference to demography and cultural geography. At the same time, the data will be applied to develop specific conclusions about the four cultural areas in Inner Mongolia, as well as future trends in the culture of the Mongols in China.

Historical Background

Since the rise of the first united imperial regime in China, the Qin-Han empire, Inner Mongolia—here including the adjacent areas of Northeast China and Hebei, which historically have been considered to be a part of Inner Mongolia—has been a border region between the plains of Northern China and the more distant steppes of Outer Mongolia. In this border region, regimes based in the more ethnically homogenous areas in the north and south have contended both for influence and for living space for their own people. As a result, Inner Mongolia's history and population have shown a constant fluctuation between periods when the influence of the Han Chinese to the south has been dominant, and other periods when the steppe peoples of the north have exercised political and cultural dominance.

During the Western Han reign, for example, household registration data indicate that about 1 million Han Chinese settlers from Northern China lived in Inner Mongolia, forming perhaps half of the total population. The rest was made up of the dominant Xiongnu people and their slaves, along with the Wuhuan and Xianbi people in the eastern part of Inner Mongolia. By the time of the Eastern Han dynasty, however, the Han Chinese population of Inner Mongolia and neighboring regions of North China had decreased dramatically. Thus the population of the Wuyuan Commandery, situated on the great bend of the Yellow River, decreased from 231,328 in 2 B.C. to only 22,957 in 140 A.D. At the same time the population of non-Han origin, particularly Xianbi and other proto-Mongolic peoples increased, eventually pushing south even into areas of neighboring Shanxi province. This decrease of the non-Mongol population continued through the period of North and South Dynasties in China but was partially reversed during the Tang dynasty.

In the year 742, the present-day territory of Inner Mongolia is estimated to have had 1.5 million inhabitants, of whom approximately 113,000 were settled residents governed under the commandery and county system, and thus presumably Han Chinese. During the succeeding Liao, Jin, and Yuan dynasties (907-1368), the sedentary population of Inner Mongolia underwent a new period of expansion, even though political power was fully in the hands of Kitan, Jurchin, and Mongol peoples. From the Han to the Tang, Inner Mongolia's sedentary population was focused primarily in the west, around the Yellow River. This pattern changed during the Liao dynasty as the sedentary population near the Kitan capital grew dramatically.

By the year 1000, more than 625,000 sedentary people were registered as living in Inner Mongolia under the Liao dynasty, out of a total Inner Mongolian population estimated at 2 million. Despite a brief decrease during the Jin dynasty, military farms under the Mongol-dominated Yuan dynasty led to a renewed increase of the sedentary population, most of which was Han Chinese. Chinese control of the southern parts of Inner Mongolia continued during the early part of the Ming dynasty. But during the middle of the Ming dynasty (1368-1644), particularly after the Tumu incident in which the Ming emperor was captured by Esen Taishi, the imperial government lost control of almost all of modern Inner Mongolia which was resettled by Mongol tribes immigrating from the north. The Mongols thus established a political and demographic dominance in Inner Mongolia which lasted roughly from the middle of the fifteenth century into the nineteenth century. Still, many Han Chinese remained in Inner Mongolia, particularly in the southwest, around the Yellow River, and in the southeast, in the hill country north of Liaoning.

In 1570-82, the area within the modern frontiers of Inner Mongolia had a population of about 1,795,000, of which Mongols were about 1,090,000. By the opening of the nineteenth century, Han Chinese immigration had increased the Chinese population in Inner Mongolia to perhaps 1,000,000 out of a total of 2,150,000. Mongols are estimated at 1,030,000 with the remainder comprising Manchus, Hui, Daurs, Ewenkis, and other smaller nationalities.[1]

Given this extensive history of nomadic-sedentary interaction in Inner Mongolia, it is not surprising that the non-Han peoples in this area have never been exclusively pastoral nomads in their lifestyle. Particularly in the eastern part of Inner Mongolia, in the watersheds of the Sungari and Liao rivers, the indigenous peoples have long practiced agriculture, combining it in various degrees with pastoralism. Particularly during times of Han Chinese immigration and settlement, the non-Han peoples would often also undergo a process of semi-sedentarization. The Kitans had an early history of practicing agriculture, a tendency that during the tenth century expanded into a semi-pastoral/semi-agricultural economy.[2]

Envoys from the Han Chinese regimes of the Song and the Ming record in both the thirteenth and the sixteenth centuries that the Mongols included not only the classic nomadic pastoralists in the northern and drier regions, but also populations pursuing at least a partially agricultural economy.[3] These reports, separated by more than 300 years, each described Mongolian farming as if it were a recent innovation. During the Yuan dynasty, many Kitans who welcomed

Chinggis Khan as rescuing them from the oppression of the Jurchin rulers seem to have assimilated into the Mongolian people, presumably bringing with them aspects of their semi-agricultural/semi-pastoral lifestyle.[4]

The Daurs, a people who are closely linked to the Mongols but also seem to be descendants of the Kitans, have to this day preserved a fully agricultural lifestyle in the forests of northeast Inner Mongolia.[5] Thus while the Mongols until the twentieth century were primarily pastoralists, they and related peoples of the plateau also have a long tradition of agriculture lifestyle when natural conditions were favorable.

For most of the Qing dynasty, which ruled Inner Mongolia from 1636 to 1912, the Mongols were treated by Beijing as a military reserve. Cavalry soldiers from Mongolia played a major part in the Manchu rulers' campaigns in Inner Asia and China proper. To protect this military reserve and ensure the support of the Mongol elite, the Manchus protected the authority of the Mongol aristocracy from encroachment by the Han officials of China's Central provinces. At the same time they also prohibited permanent immigration of Han Chinese into Inner Mongolia.

During the nineteenth century, however, such regulations were largely ignored and Han immigration steadily increased, just as it did elsewhere along the Inner Asian borderlands of China, such as Northeast China and Xinjiang. Up to the eve of the twentieth century, however, the local Mongolian administration, called banners, were able to preserve their traditional titles to pasture and farming land and could force Han Chinese settlers to pay rent, either to individual Mongol landlords or to the banner administration as a whole.

In 1902, as part of the reformist New Policies, the Qing dynasty began to support and subsidize Han immigration into Inner Mongolia in order to develop the frontier economically and guard against Russian aggression. In tracts designated for cultivation, Mongols lost any right to the land. The result was a rapid expansion of Han Chinese settlement into virtually all the well-watered areas of Inner Mongolia, particularly those south of the Yinshan and east of the Khinggan ranges.

Where the Mongols were traditionally pastoral, such as in Chakhar in central Inner Mongolia, or Yekhe Juu in southwest Inner Mongolia, they were mostly pushed back from the most fertile grasslands into desert areas, while a small number turned to farming. In eastern Inner Mongolia, large numbers of Mongols changed to a semi-pastoral/semi-agricultural or even a purely agricultural lifestyle as Chinese immigration increased. Even so, many of these sedentarized Mongols were unable to defend their land titles and were pushed off fertile farmlands into desert areas. Subsidizing Han Chinese colonization continued to be the main government policy throughout the Republic period.[6]

As a result of this heavy immigration, the Han Chinese population of Inner Mongolia underwent a sharp increase as the Mongol population declined. Table 3 shows changes in Inner Mongolian population through the modern era:

Table 3. Population of Inner Mongolia by Major Nationalities, 1570-1947

Year	Total	Han	Percent	Mongol	Percent
1570-82	1,795,000	705,000	39.00	1,090,000	61.00
1800	2,150,000	1,000,000	47.00	1,030,000	48.00
1912	2,428,894	1,550,948	63.85	877,946	36.15
1937	4,583,542	3,719,113	81.14	864,429	18.86
1947	5,617,000	4,696,000	83.60	832,000	14.81

Source: Song Naigong, ed., *Zhongguo renkou (Nei Menggu fence)*, (Beijing: China Finance and Economy Publishing House, 1987), pp. 46, 50-54.[7]

The chaotic period of the Japanese conquest and Chinese resistance, the Soviet invasion of 1945, and the Chinese Civil War caused great hardship in Inner Mongolia, as the region was a battlefield in all three conflicts. Indiscriminate looting and confiscations hurt the civilian population, while Mongol soldiers fought and died on virtually all sides of these struggles. Outbreaks of bubonic plague from 1945 on caused much death in eastern Inner Mongolia and neighboring areas of Northeast China.

With the reestablishment of peace in 1949, however, Inner Mongolia's population, both Han and Mongol began a major surge of growth. Improved health care and other modern services, sparked a population boom among the Mongols all through Inner Mongolia, as well as elsewhere in China. Han Chinese immigration continued, but changed somewhat in its character.

Whereas previous immigration was almost entirely agricultural and usually resulted in pushing out the Mongols entirely, now immigration often took the form of founding new cities and towns in the heart of the steppe. Many of them, such as Shili-yin Khota, took shape as political centers and would become administrative, economic, and cultural centers for the Mongol populations around them. In these towns, skilled and white-collar Han Chinese from coastal provinces would rub shoulders with Mongol cadres and intellectuals drawn from Inner Mongolia's countryside.

Other new towns on the steppe, such as Bayan'oboo, were founded to service the mining industries in Inner Mongolia. Such towns were essentially purely Han Chinese in population and culture and had few or no links to the surrounding countryside. The creation of these towns marked the final stage in the formation of Inner Mongolia's present-day nationality and demographic composition.

Population and Distribution of Mongols in China

According to China's fourth national census, conducted in 1990, 4,802,407 Mongols lived within the borders of the People's Republic of China. Although persons registered as Mongols can be found in all of China's thirty-two autonomous regions, provinces, and directly administered municipalities, substantial native populations of Mongols are distributed mainly in China's northern provinces and autonomous regions (see Table 4).

Table 4. Han Chinese and Mongol populations in China (in thousands)

	1953	1964	1982	1990
Total population in China	586,303	694,581	1,008,175	1,133,682
Han	547,283	654,565	940,880	1,042,482
Total minority	35,320	40,008	67,290	91,196
Mongol	1,462	1,973	3,416	4,806
Percentage of minorities	6.06	5.76	6.67	8.04

Source: "Guojia minwei jingji si and Guojia tongji ju zonghe si," *Zhongguo minzu tongji, 1949-1990* (Beijing: China Statistics Publishing House, 1991), p. 41.

Thus, 3,379,738 Mongols live in Inner Mongolia, 587,311 in Liaoning province, 156,488 in Jilin province, 139,077 in Heilongjiang province, 138,021 in the Uighur Autonomous Region of Xinjiang and 71,510 in Qinghai province. These areas contain not only the largest populations of Mongols but also the largest population of Mongolian language speakers (see Table 5).

The Inner Mongolian Autonomous Region was officially established on May 1, 1947. In its present frontiers, the region runs along a full 4,221 km of China's northern border, touching on Russia and Mongolia. To the east it borders on Heilongjiang, Jilin, and Liaoning provinces, while it adjoins Gansu and Ningxia in the west and Hebei, Shanxi, and Shaanxi in the south. This region is the third largest province-level unit in China with a territory of 1,183,000 square km, and has rich mineral, coal, and forest resources along with a vast extent of steppe grassland suitable for husbandry.

Currently, the Inner Mongolian Autonomous Region (IMAR) is administratively divided into 8 "leagues" (Chinese *meng*, Mongolian *aimag*), and 4 directly administered municipalities. At the county level, the region consists of 51 "banners" (Chinese *qi*, Mongolian *khoshuu*), 18 counties, 3 autonomous banners, 12 county-level cities, and 16 municipal districts. According to the PRC's fourth census (1990), there were 49 nationalities in the IMAR with a total population of 21,456,798. Among them, Mongols numbered 3,375,230 or 15.73 percent, while the Han, who numbered 17,298,722 or 80.62 percent, formed the vast majority.

Animal husbandry is still the mainstay of the IMAR economy, while agriculture functions as an auxiliary. The livestock industry, with 42,541,000 head of livestock, has developed on a basis of 88,000,000 hectares of natural grassland, 75 percent of the region's total land area (1990 figures).

Table 5. Distribution of Mongols in China, 1990

Total	4,802,407
Inner Mongolian Autonomous Region	3,379,738
Northeast China	
Liaoning	587,311
Jilin	156,488
Heilongjiang	139,077
North China	
Beijing Municipality	16,833
Tianjin Municipality	2,991
Hebei	141,833
Shanxi	2,845
Shandong	2,878
Henan	66,015
Northwest China	
Shaanxi	2,989
Gansu	8,135
Ningxia Hui Autonomous Region	2,281
Qinghai	71,510
Xinjiang Uighur Autonomous Region	138,021
Central, Eastern, and Southern China	
Hubei	5,632
Hunan	1,468
Shanghai Municipality	1,939
Jiangsu	2,749
Zhejiang	652
Anhui	759
Fujian	2,383
Jiangxi	1,199
Guangdong	1,129
Hainan	159
Guangxi Zhuang Autonomous Region	731
Southwest China	
Sichuan	27,303
Guizhou	24,107
Yunnan	13,148
Tibet Autonomous Region	104

Source: *Guowuyuan renkou pucha bangongshi and Guojia tongji ju renkou tongji si*; *Zhongguo 1990 nian renkou pucha ziliao* (Beijing: China Statistics Publishing House, 1993), Vol. 1, pp. 300-01.

Table 6. Population of Inner Mongolia by Major Nationalities,
1947-90

Year	Total	Han	Percent	Mongol	Percent
1947	5,617,000	4,696,000	83.60	832,000	14.81
1949	6,081,000	5,154,000	84.76	835,000	13.73
1953	7,584,000	6,493,000	85.61	985,000	12.99
1964	12,334,138	10,729,407	86.99	1,384,455	11.22
1982	19,274,281	16,277,616	84.45	2,489,378	12.92
1990	21,457,000	17,289,995	80.62	3,379,738	15.73

Source: Ibid., Song Naigong, p. 349.

The Mongol population within the current frontiers of the IMAR grew by 299 percent between 1947, when it numbered approximately 832,000, and 1982, when it reached 2,489,000. If we break this growth down into various stages, by 1949 the Mongol population had increased only 0.36 percent over that in 1947, an annual growth rate of only 0.18 percent. By 1953, however, the number of Mongols had grown by 17.96 percent of that in 1949, an average annual increase of 4.22 percent. While the population grew by 8 percent in 1953 alone, the subsequent rate of population growth slowed. By 1964, the Mongol nationality had increased by 42.44 percent compared with 1953, yielding an average annual increase of 3.27 percent. In 1982, it had grown by 79.81 percent over that of 1964, an annual rate of 3.31 percent.

In the first half of 1982, the Mongol population had increased by 309,300 persons over what it would have otherwise been at the average annual growth rate of 2.55 percent from 1964 to 1981. This sudden jump in 1982 was due not to natural increase, but to a wave of people switching their nationality registration to "Mongol" from other nationality designations. These newly registered Mongols equalled a full 12.44 percent of the Mongol population as per the 1982 census. This reregistration movement was a contributing factor to the reversal of the previous trend for the percentage of Mongols in the IMAR's population to decline; the percentage of Mongols in the IMAR's total population had fallen from 14.81 percent in 1947 to 10.71 percent in 1974, but by the end of 1982 it had jumped to 12.92 percent and in 1984 reached 13.50 percent.

The Mongols of the IMAR constituted 72.97 percent of the total Mongol population of China (1982 census figure). Rural Mongols of Inner Mongolia are found in all of the region's rural economic zones—purely agricultural, semi-pastoral/semi-agricultural, and purely pastoral areas—as well as in the cities and towns. Contrary to the stereotype of Mongols as being found only in dry steppes, a full 31.50 percent of the Mongol population was distributed in irrigated agricultural areas.

Table 7. Regional Distribution of Han and Mongols in IMAR(1982)

League (L.) or Municipality (M.)	Percent of IMAR's Han	Han Percent of Local Population	Percent of IMAR's Mongols	Mongol Percent
Total	100.00	84.45	100.00	12.92
Höhhot M.	6.61	89.68	3.39	7.02
Baotou M.	9.28	95.91	0.96	1.51
Wuhai M.	1.45	94.64	0.20	1.98
Khölön Buir L.	12.33	87.48	5.13	5.56
Khinggan L.	5.23	62.32	18.83	34.33
Jirim L.	9.13	61.03	35.62	36.39
Juu Uda L.	19.60	86.81	16.40	11.10
Shili-yin Gool L.	3.49	70.87	8.43	26.14
Ulaanchab L.	18.51	97.22	2.63	2.12
Yekhe Juu L.	5.84	88.35	4.96	11.47
Bayannuur L.	7.88	94.76	2.08	3.82
Alashan L.	0.63	70.78	1.39	23.76

Source: Song Naigong, p. 351.

In examining the occupational structure of the Mongol population (see Table 8), we see that among Mongols the percentage of those making a living from agriculture, forestry, animal husbandry, or fishery is higher than that of the Han, while the proportion of those in mining, utilities, manufacturing, construction, or transportation and communications is in all cases less than half that of the Han. In the sphere of non-material production, or services, particularly in education, culture, art, and in political offices (government, party and mass organizations) Mongols are represented at a rate nearly double that of the Han Chinese.

Administrative Divisions and Minority Autonomy

Since the late 1940s, with the establishment of the Inner Mongolian Autonomous Region, traditionally Mongol-inhabited areas have been administered by a form of regional autonomy within the limits of the leadership of the Chinese Communist Party and of central economic command. These autonomous regions occur at all levels corresponding to those of the ordinary administrative hierarchy, from "autonomous regions" which are on the same level as provinces, down to "autonomous villages" which are townships, the smallest administrative unit.

In order of size, these units include the following: 1) autonomous regions; 2) autonomous prefectures (A.P.); 3) autonomous counties (A.C., *xian* in Chinese) or banners (*khoshuu* in Mongolian) in primarily Mongol-inhabited areas of Inner Mongolia; and 4) autonomous townships (*xiang* in Chinese) and autonomous *sumus* in primarily Mongol-inhabited areas of Inner Mongolia.

Table 8. Occupations of Han Chinese and Mongols in
Inner Mongolia, 1982

Occupational Type	Whole Area	Han	All Minorities	Mongol
Total	100.00	100.00	100.00	100.00
Farming, forestry, animal husbandry, side-line production, and fishery	68.49	68.34	69.48	75.18
Mining and wood transportation	2.73	2.94	1.35	0.90
Utilities production and service (electricity, gas,running water)	0.45	0.47	0.30	0.21
Manufacturing	9.72	10.19	6.56	4.15
Geological exploration and general investigations	0.32	0.35	0.18	0.12
Construction	2.87	3.03	1.82	1.16
Communications and transportation, post and telecommunication	2.45	2.56	1.74	1.11
Commerce, catering trade, storage of goods and material	4.05	3.96	4.65	3.67
Management of dwellings, utilities, and resident services	0.57	0.57	0.54	0.40
Hygiene, sports, social and welfare services	1.07	0.99	1.60	1.48
Education, culture, and art	3.67	3.32	6.00	6.03
Science, research, and technical staff	0.25	0.24	0.31	0.27
Financial and insurance services	0.34	0.30	0.58	0.58
Government official, political party and mass organizations	2.92	2.64	4.83	4.68
Other	0.10	0.10	0.07	0.06

Source: Song Naigong, p. 359.

In addition to the Inner Mongolian Autonomous Region, which contains almost two-thirds of China's Mongol population, the Chinese government has created three autonomous prefectures for relatively concentrated Mongol populations found outside of Inner Mongolia: one lies in Qinghai (Mongolian, Kökenuur) province, the Haixi Mongolian and Tibetan A.P., while two lie in the Xinjiang Uighur Autonomous Region, the Bayangol Mongolian A.P. and the Bortala Mongolian A.P. The PRC has eight Mongolian autonomous counties distributed in several provinces and autonomous regions, often adjacent to either Inner Mongolia or to the above mentioned autonomous prefectures.

Those autonomous counties found along the eastern and southeastern borders of Inner Mongolia include Fuxin Mongolian A.C. and Kharachin Right Mongolian A.C. in Liaoning province, South Gorlos Mongolian A.C. in Jilin province, Dörbed Mongolian A.C. in Heilongjiang province, and Weichang Manchu and Mongolian A.C. in Hebei province. Three autonomous counties are found in China's northwestern provinces and regions of Gansu, Qinghai, and Xinjiang: Subei Mongolian A.C. in Gansu province, Henan Mongolian A.C. in Qinghai and the Hobogsair Mongolian A.C. in Xinjiang A.R.

Economic and Cultural Patterns

Mongols are often considered to live purely as classic nomadic herders, but the ways of life of the Mongols in China are diverse. To simplify, these life-ways can be divided into four basic economic-cultural types: the pastoral, the semi-pastoral/semi-agricultural, the agricultural, and the city/town. We also can divide each of these major types or patterns into many sub-types.

Most areas heavily inhabited by Mongols are dominated by either a fully pastoral economy or a semi-agricultural economy. If we classify the over 100 county-level units in Inner Mongolia according to their agricultural output, 54 are officially classified as pastoral economic banners or counties and 21 of them as semi-agricultural counties or banners. Outside of Inner Mongolia, a roughly similar pattern prevails. The Mongols of Xinjiang, Heilongjiang, Gansu, and Qinghai predominantly practice animal husbandry, while those of Liaoning and Jilin mostly pursue either a semi-agricultural economy or a purely agricultural economy. Rural Mongols in other provinces generally practice a purely agricultural economy. Mongols in cities and towns make their living either in the "tertiary sector" or as government officials and staff.[8]

Pastoral regions in Inner Mongolia present a fairly typical case of current developments in the animal husbandry of pastoral regions in China as a whole. From the late 1970s and early 1980s, patterns of pastoral land-use and economic activity have undergone dramatic changes in pastoral areas. Most of the steppe has been divided and allocated to households. Only in certain areas such as Old Bargu banner in Khölön Buir league, where ecological limitations and natural resource conditions make the territory inappropriate for division by households, has this change not occurred. But even in those areas, the local government is still trying to find some suitable way to divide the pastoral land by household. Despite this division, the right of ownership over steppe land still belongs to the state, and herdsmen have rights only to use and manage the land. The herds themselves, however, are solely the property of the herdsmen.

Economic development in the IMAR is taking place quite quickly, even if its rate is not comparable to that in China's more developed coastal provinces. However, nearly all pastoral areas in Inner Mongolia are facing rapid ecological degeneration. Historically, Inner Mongolian herdsmen practiced extensive livestock husbandry in most areas, but contemporary Inner Mongolian pastoralism has had to adapt to a changing world hostile to nomadism. At present, Inner Mongolian herdsmen have almost all sedentarized and have adopted measures to adjust to changing local conditions and promote a more diversified economy.

Mongol herdsmen no longer make long-distance migrations as in the past. According to field investigations, in two areas classified as purely pastoral, Alashan Left Banner in Alashan league, a dry desert and gobi pastoral area, and Üüshin banner in Yekhe Juu league, a desert pastoral area, 100 percent of herdsmen have settled down. In Old Bargu banner, a typical steppe area in Khölön Buir league, 80 percent of the herdsmen have settled down, and the local government aims to have 100 percent of them settled down by the end of this century. Even if Mongol herdsmen wanted to migrate over long distances, there simply would not be enough space for them to do so.

In recent years, the policies of the autonomous region have included many new development strategies, such as intensification of animal husbandry, high-results animal husbandry, combining herding with farming, animal husbandry based on crop cultivation, commercialization of animal husbandry, and specialization within animal husbandry. As a result, some households or areas have started to raise only one type of domestic animal.

Others have begun town and township enterprises or so-called tertiary sectors, such as services and small-scale enterprises, or have become involved in the construction of herdsmen's settlements, and so forth. Other developments have been observed in Yekhe Juu League, such as starting "household ranches";[9] fencing or enclosing all pastures; using "air pasture";[10] building enclosures and supplying them with sufficient amount of hay; using various constructions to improve the water supply, primarily by digging wells to exploit underground water; and planting vegetation cover to guard against erosion.

Some herdsmen are changing from a pastoralist lifestyle to either arable agriculture or to managing tertiary industry under the new development strategies encouraged by some local governments. In the purely pastoral Alashan League, for example, the local government has advocated a "three-ways labor restructuring," with one-third of the present pastoral labor force continuing to herd livestock, one-third switching to arable cultivation, and one-third entering urban or township enterprises or tertiary sector. The Inner Mongolian pastoral economy has thus been transformed from a traditional style that depended mostly on adapting to natural weather and grass patterns into the more active livestock management economy now in construction, as herdsmen build fence shades, fence in and irrigate pastoral land, plant grass for haymaking, raise specialized herds, and select new breeds. Some of those who not long ago were managing a purely pastoral economy are beginning to manage sideline productions, such as planting crops and fodder.

To summarize, the changes and developments in the pastoral economy of Inner Mongolia in the last fifteen years are as follows: the pastoral economy has experienced many successful and useful lessons in the changes detailed above, but there are still many unsolved problems which need serious attention. Some of the pastoral areas are currently shifting toward a semi-agricultural economic pattern. If this process is allowed to continue without planning or attention, these areas will follow in the footsteps of some present semi-pastoral/semi-agricultural areas, such as Naiman and Khüriye banners in Jirim League, which have suffered difficult economic and environmental problems largely beyond the capacity of the local people to solve.

In Inner Mongolia's pastoral areas, the gap between rich and poor is becoming steadily more distinct, with many local herdsmen appearing among the ranks of the poor. Almost all of the changes in the traditional pastoral economy have involved a shift to a more management style of herding, but there are relatively few former herdsmen who are able to make the move into other economic forms, such as commerce, or tertiary industry.

Observing these economic patterns and changes in the ways of life of virtually all Mongols in China, we can see two important trends. First, changes in economic patterns and ways of making a living have stemmed not from peoples' voluntary choices, but have depended primarily on ecological and social reasons such as population growth, government policy, and changes in economic and social benefits. Second, these changes have had surprisingly little influence on the ethnic characteristics of the Mongols in China. This could, however, have been predicted by an examination of those Mongols who have traditionally been living in non-pastoral areas. Despite fears of rapid assimilation, Mongols in these non-pastoral areas have indeed been able to preserve their Mongolian identity, sometimes even in purely agricultural areas or in cities and towns.

Present-Day Sociolinguistics of the Mongols in China

The social and political context of Mongolian language use since 1947 can be divided into four general stages: 1) 1947-57, during which the scope of Mongolian written and spoken language widened; 2) 1957-65, during which the scope of Mongolian narrowed under "leftist" political influences; 3) 1966-75, the Cultural Revolution decade, when the use of Mongolian language was prohibited almost completely; 4) 1976 to the present, a period of revival in the use of the Mongolian language.[11]

Students of Mongolian language usually divide Mongolian-speaking areas in China into three main sociolinguistic zones. Zone 1 refers to areas where Mongolian is in full use. The main characteristics of Zone 1 areas are that: 1) Mongols live in compact communities, with Mongols forming a high percentage of the total population. In some areas, the percentage of Mongols might be low in the population as a whole, but high in certain specific areas; 2) most of the Mongols primarily use Mongolian for spoken and written communication; 3) most Mongol students are being educated either with Mongolian as the language of instruction or with Mongolian as a subject; and 4) these areas are usually vast in territory, with a low population density, and are usually agricultural, pastoral, or multi-use.

In Zone 2 areas, Mongolian and Chinese are both used. Zone 2 areas are characterized by: 1) Mongols and Chinese (along with other minorities) living together when viewed on a large scale, but in segregated communities at the more local level. The number of Mongols is low compared to the total population; 2) most of the Mongols or a part of them using Mongolian spoken and written language; 3) some Mongol students learning with Mongolian as the language of instruction and some of them learning Mongolian as a subject; and 4) such areas being mainly *sumu* or banner administrative centers, and as such being political, economic, and cultural centers. As a result, there is frequent contact between ethnic Mongol cadres in administration and the general Mongol public in these small centers.

Zone 3 designates areas where Mongolian has been replaced by Chinese or other minority languages. Its main characteristics are: 1) most Mongols have lost their mother language and mainly use Chinese or some other minority's language; 2) Mongol students study entirely in Chinese. In some places, there are Mongolian-medium classes, but the number of the students is small; and 3) the Mongolian language environment is the worst of the three zones, with virtually no Mongolian being spoken.

According to a survey in 1988, of the 4.1 million Mongols in China, 3.2 million still speak Mongolian as their first language of social communication. Most of these live within the territory of the eight autonomous regions, provinces, and municipalities that formed the *Association for Work in Mongolian Language and Writing* (i.e., Inner Mongolia, Liaoning, Jilin, Heilongjiang, Gansu, Qinghai, Xinjiang, and Beijing). A small number of Mongols in Hebei can also speak Mongolian. As for the rest, some are Mongolian-Chinese bilinguals, while others have lost their Mongolian language entirely.[12]

In Inner Mongolia, forty-six county-level units are classified as belonging to sociolinguistic Zone 1. These banners, counties, and municipalities occupy a total area of 900,000 square km (76 percent of Inner Mongolia's total area), and have a total Mongol population of 2,656,000 (78.7 percent of Inner Mongolia's total Mongol population). Twenty-four banners, counties, and municipalities, with an area of 202,000 square km (17 percent of Inner Mongolia's total area) can be classified as Zone 2. These have a Mongol population of 434,000, representing 12.8 percent of the autonomous region's total Mongol population. Thirty banners, counties, and municipalities, totalling 81,000 square km and 7 percent of Inner Mongolia's total area, fall into the Zone 3 classification. These contain 285,000 Mongols or 8.5 percent of Inner Mongolia's Mongol inhabitants. Direct surveys of Mongolian language use indicate that 2,660,000 or 77 percent of the Mongols in Inner Mongolia primarily use Mongolian, 350,000 or 10 percent use both Mongolian and Chinese, while 450,000 or 13 percent have lost the ability to communicate in Mongolian. The distribution of Mongols and of Mongolian speakers in the various sociolinguistic zones is given in Table 9.

Table 9. Mongolian Sociolinguistic Zones in IMAR

	Total	Zone 1	Zone 2	Zone 3
Area in km^2	1,183,000	900,000	202,000	81,000
(percentage of IMAR's area)	(10)	(76)	(17)	(7)
Mongol pop.	3,460,000	2,723,000	443,000	294,000
(percentage of IMAR's Mongols)	(100)	(78.7)	(12.8)	(8.5)
Population in the zone mainly using Mongolian:				
Total	2,800,000	2,700,000	100,000	0
Mongol ancestry	2,660,000	2,560,000	100,000	0
Ancestry in other nationalities	140,000	140,000	—	0
Population in the zone using Mongolian and Chinese:				
Total	500,000	206,000	290,000	4,000
Mongol	350,000	106,000	240,000	4,000
Ancestry in other nationalities	150,000	100,000	50,000	—
Population in the zone of Mongols unable to use Mongolian	450,000	57,000	103,000	290,000

Source: *Nei Menggu dacidian*, (Höhhot: Inner Mongolian People's Publishing House, 1991), pp. 15-41.[13]

To flesh out these statistics, the sociolinguistic situation of cities and banners typical of each zone will be described:

1. Zone 1, or areas mainly using Mongolian: New Bargu Right Banner in Khölön Buir league, when viewed as a whole, belongs to this sociolinguistic environment. The most important characteristic of this banner is the relatively high population of Mongols, 18,772 or 68 percent in a total banner population of 27,681. Most of the other inhabitants are Han Chinese, 7,054 or 26 percent, with a small population of other nationalities totalling 796, or 6 percent. The Mongol population lives mostly in the vast pastoral zone, while the Han Chinese are mainly distributed in the banner's administrative center, certain of its *sumus* and farms and the four settlements of these *sumus* and farms.

A second distinctive characteristic is that the Mongolian language is the main language used in the banner. Chinese is only the secondary language, one used in some larger settlements of the farms and in Altan'emeel town but not in the vast pastoral zone. The number using Mongolian is about 21,000 (72 percent of total population) and is higher than the number of Mongols in the banner population. The bulk of those of the Daur, Ewenki, and Orochen nationalities as well as some Han Chinese, Manchu, and Hui populations fall in this Mongolian speaking population. Besides the Han Chinese themselves, all of whom can speak Chinese (with or without Mongolian), there about 4,000 people of other nationalities who can speak Chinese. Thus, about 40 percent of the total population of the banner can speak Chinese. But Mongolian is the mother tongue and still the primary language of communication for most of these 4,000 non-Han speakers of Chinese language.

The third characteristic is that the majority of schools use Mongolian as the language of instruction, and teach Mongolian language and literature. Before the "Cultural Revolution" all schools used Mongolian, but in recent years the number of students studying in Mongolian has dropped to about 85 percent.[14]

2. Zone 2, or areas where both Mongolian and Chinese are in common use: Jalaid and Khorchin Right Wing South Banner belong to this zone. There are 51 administrative sub-units in these two banners, with about 80 percent of the two banners' Mongols living in compact communities in 26 of these administrative subunits. The other 20 percent of the banners' Mongols are scattered in the other 25 administrative units. Mongols here mostly use Mongolian in their social communication. An estimated 250,000, or 92 percent of the 270,000 total Mongols in these two banners, speak Mongolian. Only about 8 percent or 20,000 Mongols have lost their mother tongue. This 8 percent is primarily composed of younger Mongols who live in heavily Han Chinese-settled areas. At the same time quite a few of the young Han Chinese who live in more Mongol-inhabited areas can speak Mongolian.

Another sociolinguistic characteristic of these two banners is the use of a distinct mixed Mongolian-Chinese language. Not only are the 20 percent of the Mongols who live in areas where Mongols and Han Chinese live in mixed communities accustomed to using this mixed language, even the 80 percent of the Mongols living in compact communities use the mixed language. In such areas, about 10-20 percent of the vocabulary is formed of Chinese loan words, but most of the loan words have been "Mongolized" to the extent of being often unrecognizable to the Chinese speaker. Mongols in such areas cannot fully understand either standard Mongolian or standard Chinese.[15]

3. Zone 3 comprises areas where Chinese is mainly used. Manzhouli and Khailar cities as well as Butha Banner (currently the city of Zhalantun) are typical of this zone. The primary characteristic of such areas is that the portion of Mongols in the total population is very low. In Manzhouli, there are 1,148 Mongols in a total population of 100,000, or only 1.7 percent of the population. In Butha Banner, there are 5,662 Mongols in the banner's total population of 370,000, comprising only 1.5 percent. In Khailar city, there are 8,000 Mongols among the 1,450,000 inhabitants, making the Mongols 5.52 percent of the population.

A second characteristic is that most of the Mongols live scattered in local communities dominated by Han Chinese. Most Mongols in Khailar and Manzhouli cities are cadres, staff and workers, and their families. They live integrated with Han Chinese in or around their workplaces, so that there are no Mongolian neighborhoods. In Butha Banner, only about half of 5,000 Mongols live in a compact community, the village Wadixiang, while the other half live scattered among the 350,000 Chinese and other minorities. Therefore, Chinese is virtually the only language used in such areas.[16]

Language Use in the Education of Mongols

Since the end of 1970s, Mongolian has again come to be used popularly in education in areas where Mongols live in compact communities. Especially in primary and middle schools, the number of students either learning in Mongolian or studying Mongolian as a subject has increased rapidly. Since this change, education in Mongolian in the IMAR has become systematic and complete from primary school through to universities, and even graduate school. Mongols outside of the IMAR who do not have the opportunity to send their children to a given level of Mongol school may send their children to Inner Mongolia to study.

Despite the expansion in Mongolian-language education after the end of the Cultural Revolution, the number of students either learning in Mongolian or learning Mongolian as a subject has in the most recent years shown a decline in the IMAR. Three main reasons can be advanced for this decline. First, in China, education in Mongolian has not been able to keep pace with the rapid developments in science and technology, at least for the present. Second, for students in Mongolian-language programs the chances of going to a good university and getting a good job are not as high as they are for those learning in Chinese. Finally, as new technology is popularized and the commodity economy develops, the scope for using Mongolian is steadily narrowing. All three of these trends moreover are in turn accelerated by the very decline in the number of students studying in Mongolian. From the point of view of any nationality's future development both in culture and in science and technology, this tendency of a decrease in Mongolian-language education noted above is disadvantageous.

The trends in the years after 1979 are illustrated in the following five tables:

Table 10: Mongol Students in IMAR Learning in Mongolian
or Learning Mongolian as a Subject (1985-86)

	Students in School	Mongol Students	Learning in Mongolian	Learning Mongolian as a Subject
Total	4,122,103	591,241	371,008	43,549
College and university	31,242	6,691	3,405	0
Normal and technical high school	40,184	7,407	4,662	0
High school	188,227	33,602	18,005	7,192
Junior high school	928,419	135,468	74,715	15,640
Primary school	2,548,977	365,336	249,309	18,249
Preschool	164,126	21,674	12,260	238
Kindergarten	81,524	8,796	5,027	1,628

Table 11. Mongol Students Learning in Mongolian in 1986-87

	Students in School	Mongolian Students	Learning in Mongolian
College and university	31,717	6,765	3,423
Technical high school (*zhongdeng jishu xuexiao*)	31,262	4,831	2,417
Normal high school (*zhongdeng shifan zhuanke xuexiao*)	11,755	3,627	2,811
High school	197,403	35,409	18,806
Junior high school	962,600	142,364	80,160
Primary school	2,501,402	366,058	239,444
Kindergarten	295,499	10,836	6,485

Table 12. Mongol Students Learning in Mongolian and Learning Mongolian as a Subject, 1988-89

	Students in School	Mongolian Students	Learning Mongolian	Learning Mongolian as Subject
College and university	32,634	7,367	3,684	0
Technical high school	33,870	6,172	3,259	0
Normal high school	13,023	4,230	3,471	0
High school and junior high	1,126,954	184,318	103,529	13,835
Primary school	2,374,519	369,316	228,871	12,317
Kindergarten	381,245	57,996	32,240	0

Table 13. Mongol Students Learning in Mongolian in Schools in IMAR in 1984-85

	Mongol Students	Learning in Mongolian or Mongolian as Subject	Percentage
Total	567,720	357,296	62.93
Graduate school	45	28	62.22
College and university	6,002	3,297	54.93
Technical high school	7,356	4,580	62.26
Normal high school	159,342	84,680	53.15
Vocational high schools (*zhiye gaozhong xuexiao*)	4,919	2,200	44.72
Primary school	368,403	249,241	67.67
Adult colleges	1,551	122	7.86
Adult technical high school (*chengren zhong-zhuan*)	3,222	1,394	43.96
Kindergarten	16,880	11,704	69.35

Table 14. Changes in the Number of Mongol Students Learning in Mongolian or Learning Mongolian as a Subject

	1979	1980	1982	1983	1984	Percent Change 1984-79	Percent Change 1984-83
1. College and university	2,084	2,414	2,699	2,760	3,297	58.2	19.5
2. Technical high school	1,239	1,433	1,693	1,832	1,821	47	-0.6
3. Normal high school	2,654	2,929	2,331	2,411	2,759	4	14.4
4. High school Total:	23,557	21,705	21,718	23,749	24,365	3.4	2.6
Mongol medium:	15,322 (15,144)	12,499 (12,346)	14,145 (13,962)	15,802 (15,571)	16,398 (16,131)	7 (6.5)	3.8 (3.6)
Mongolian as subject	8,235 (7,359)	9,206 (8,334)	7,573 (6,595)	7,945 (6,928)	7,967 (7,066)	-3.3 (-4)	0.3 (2)
5. Junior high Total:	98,930	94,968	85,542	81,199	85,581	-13.5	5.4
Mongol medium:	73,594 (72,018)	67,358 (65,660)	63,395 (61,944)	61,741 (60,690)	68,282 (67,023)	-7.2 (-6.9)	10.6 (10.4)
Mongolian as subject	25,336 (22,708)	27,610 (23,768)	22,147 (18,833)	19,458 (16,779)	17,299 (15,098)	-31.7 (-33.5)	-11.1 (-10)
6. Primary school Total:	275,030	281,109	286,644	268,976	270,437	-1.7	0.5
Mongol medium:	246,803 (239,349)	250,508 (242,835)	256,106 (249,315)	242,672 (237,601)	249,291 (242,921)	1 (1.5)	2.7 (2.2)
Mongolian as subject	29,227 (24,467)	30,601 (25,102)	30,538 (22,728)	26,304 (19,363)	21,146 (15,939)	-27.7 (-34.9)	-19.6 (-17.7)

Note: Sections 4, 5, and 6 give the total number of students of all nationalities at that level studying either in Mongolian or with Mongolian as a subject. The figures in parentheses gives the number of Mongol nationality in those programs.

Source: Statistics on education compiled by the Educational Department of the IMAR.

The Assimilation of Mongolian Culture

Except in some remote areas which are less settled by Han Chinese, the culture of the Mongols in China has in certain fields been undergoing progressive assimilation by Chinese culture. Early on, the Mongols began to learn agriculture from Chinese immigrants and in many areas gradually turned from herdsmen to peasants. During this process, major aspects of Mongolian culture in these areas underwent concurrent changes. As a result, in purely agricultural areas, and even in Inner Mongolia's semi-agricultural/semi-pastoral areas, it is hard to distinguish Mongolian and Han Chinese culture merely by outward appearance. In their mode of production and way of life the two nationalities in these areas are similar, with their housing, dress, and food showing considerable overlap.

Likewise, linguistic assimilation is a prominent problem for the Mongols. This process can be divided into several distinct stages. At first, where Mongols live in compact communities and with a small number of Han Chinese immigrants, the early immigrants learn to speak Mongolian. But as the Han Chinese population increases and rises in social and economic status, the Han Chinese stop learning Mongolian, while more and more Mongols learn Chinese. If demographic conditions are ripe, then eventually this shift can reach the point where even Mongol children cease to learn Mongolian and the language will then go into rapid decline and, if nothing intervenes, extinction.

We can see this process happening at various times in various places in Inner Mongolia. Let us take as a typical example: New Bargu Right Banner of Khölön Buir League, an area that is both purely pastoral and has had a relatively high Mongolian percentage in the population. In 1945, the banner had little more than 5,000 people, and only 4 percent of them were not Mongols—all of these non-Mongols spoke Mongolian. But by 1979, the total population of this banner had grown to 27,681, while the Han Chinese population had jumped to 6,281. In Altan'emeel, the administrative center and largest town of this banner, the 6,000 Han Chinese form two-thirds of the total population and Chinese has became the main language.[17] An example of the completion of this process of replacing Mongolian by Chinese can be seen in the purely agricultural area of Kharachin banner in Chifeng municipality (former Juu Uda league). In that banner's South Wafang village, 48 percent of the locality's 358 families are registered as Mongols, but not one person in the village could speak Mongolian.

The experience of particular Han Chinese immigrants shows how this switch has occurred. In 1924, when 14 year-old Miao Sheng and his parents came to Fucun village (Ongni'ud Banner), they were the only Han Chinese family in the village. As a result, they had to learn to converse in Mongolian with their neighbors. By 1985, however, only those Mongols over 50 years of age could speak fluent Mongolian, while those from 30 to 50 years old could understand and speak Mongolian but not fluently, and those under 30 could neither understand nor speak Mongolian. A 50 year-old Mongolian woman of this village has two sons and four daughters. Her second son (26 years old) can hardly understand

Mongolian and has married a Han Chinese woman. The grandmother tried hard to teach her two grandsons Mongolian, but in vain, because of the overwhelmingly Chinese language environment.[18]

The decline of Mongolian language in Fucun began in the 1930s. Initially the Han Chinese learned Mongolian, but by the 1950s the Mongols were beginning to learn Chinese. Children born in the 1950s grew up in a Chinese-language environment and while they could understand Mongolian when they spoke with their parents, they used Chinese outside of the home exclusively. As a result, their level of Mongolian-speaking ability is quite poor. In 1970s, as these children became parents in their turn, they could not speak Mongolian with their children, so that Mongolian children born after 1970s even lost the ability to understand Mongolian.

Meanwhile, the earliest Chinese immigrants such as Miao Sheng have followed this new tendency of language assimilation and have gradually forgotten the Mongolian they had learned earlier. Han Chinese children born after the 1950s have neither the motivation nor the linguistic environment necessary to learn Mongolian.[19]

It is a painful process to lose one's own mother language and script and strive, over several generations, to master a new language. Some Mongols have struggled equally painfully to return to their mother language and script again through several generations. The process of losing one's own mother language is also the process of losing one's own traditional culture. Those assimilating learn less and less of the traditional culture that their ancestors had accumulated and passed on from generation to generation, while even after two or more generations of struggle, they can hardly master the culture of the people whose language they are learning. Similarly, even should they desire to revive their mother language, they will still have much less traditional culture to inherit from their parents for some generations to come.

People should not only master their own mother language but also other languages. People can preserve their traditional culture through a thorough mastery of their mother language, while at the same time widening their knowledge and sharpening their intelligence through the study of other languages. The first language skill is a prerequisite for the latter and in no sense an obstacle to it.

There have been many successful examples of this fact among China's minorities. Mongol students who have learned in Mongolian in high school, once they go to Chinese-medium classes in college, have as a rule a rate of success clearly superior to that of either Han Chinese students or Mongol students who have studied only in Chinese. The Mongols in Xinjiang can not only communicate in pure Mongolian, but as a rule can speak several other languages such as Chinese, Uighur, and Kazakh.

Nor does a low percentage in the population necessarily lead to linguistic assimilation. A good example of this is the Korean population in China, a nationality whose educational level is the highest among all nationalities, including the Han Chinese. Except for those in the Yanbian Korean Autonomous Prefecture in Jilin province, Koreans in China are thinly distributed among other nationalities, often constituting an extremely low percentage of the population. Even so, virtually all can speak and write Korean, regardless of the language they study in school. As long as there is any opportunity, parents will send their children to Korean-language classes. Even if there is only one Korean family for many miles around, the parents will insist on teaching their children to speak and write Korean even if they have no choice but to be educated in other languages.

To summarize the sociolinguistic situation of the Mongols in China: Mongols in pastoral areas have been using a relatively pure Mongolian, but at present educated young people in such areas are mostly bilingual in Mongolian and Chinese. The number of Han Chinese in the banners and *sumu* centers is steadily increasing, while the percentage of Chinese in the banner as a whole is also getting higher. As a result, as children come in from the steppe to study in primary and middle schools in these towns and settlements, they are forced to speak at least some Chinese and become bilingual even if their school is conducted in Mongolian.

Even in leagues classified as pastoral, the overall percentage of Han Chinese is sometimes overwhelming. For example, in Shili-yin Gool, Mongols constitute only 254,797 or 28.69 percent out of a total population of 888,047. In Khölön Buir league, the total population is 2,551,763 and Mongols total only 185,400, or 7.27 percent. In Yekhe Juu league in the southwest, Mongols are only 141,021, out of a total population of 1,198,912, thus amounting to only 11.8 percent. All three of these leagues are classic pastoral areas. Because of the low density of these pastoral areas, the Mongolian percentage of the overall population quickly drops with only a relatively small influx of Han Chinese.

Mongols in semi-pastoral/semi-agricultural areas still principally communicate in Mongolian. As they settled down and turned to an agricultural economy, they accepted a large number of Chinese loan-words. The grammar and basic vocabulary still remains clearly Mongolian, however, with which the Chinese vocabulary and phonetic influence has combined to form a unique "mixed language." The Mongols of these semipastoral/semi-agricultural areas in eastern Inner Mongolia mostly communicate in this hybrid tongue even in towns—most Mongols living in these areas still do not fully understand Chinese, even though their language contains many Chinese loan words.

Ethnically and sociolinguistically the situation in these areas seems to have stabilized. Viewed on a large scale (banner or even *sumu*) Mongols and Han Chinese live in mixed communities, but viewed on a smaller scale, particularly that of the village, the two nationalities reside distinctly in compact communities. Villages in these area are as a rule either overwhelmingly Han Chinese or overwhelmingly Mongol in composition. Unlike in pastoral areas, the increase of the Han Chinese population is relatively low. Particularly in Mongolian villages in the countryside, the agricultural population is already so high that the environmental resources are already strained, making it quite impossible to allow further Han Chinese immigration. With Mongols forming a relatively high percentage of the population for the foreseeable future, we can call this resulting situation a "super-steady" ethnolinguistic structure. For example, in Jirim League, the Mongols form 1,160,851 or 42.16 percent of the total population of 2,753,727, while in Khinggan League, the percentage is not much lower—1,524,064 or 38.58 percent out of a total population of 587,929.

The culture of these areas is neither simply a Han Chinese culture, as some observers have mistakenly concluded, nor is it the "classic" nomadic pastoral Mongolian culture. Instead it is a new Mongolian culture that has come into existence under new circumstances, governed by features of the rural economy and demography. Given the continuation of present trends, it may be said that the future of a distinctively Mongolian culture in Inner Mongolia lies precisely in these areas.

Intermarriage Between Mongols and Other Nationalities

One of the results of cultural assimilation is that quite a few Mongols marry partners of other nationalities, mostly Han Chinese. According to a 10 percent sample drawn from the 1982 census materials, the number of Mongols with a spouse equals 86,127, of which 12,909 (14.99 percent) are married to a partner of a different nationality. Among them, 6,360 Mongol men are married to Han Chinese women while 6,018 Mongol women are married to Han Chinese men. Mongol and Han Chinese intermarriage forms the overwhelming majority (95.89 percent) of Mongols' intermarriage with other nationalities (see Table 15).

Within Inner Mongolia as a whole, the regional distribution of intermarriage between Mongols and other nationalities is determined by the distribution of the nationalities concerned, the degree of contact among these nationalities, the overall educational level, and religious beliefs and customs. 75.93 percent of those Mongols married to Han Chinese are found in the eastern part of the IMAR. This concentration in the east primarily reflects the overall concentration of the Mongolian population toward the east.

It also, however, reflects a relatively high rate of intermarriage in some of the eastern leagues and municipalities, in particular Chifeng municipality (former Juu Uda league), and Khölön Buir and Jirim leagues. Intermarriage of Mongols with other minorities (non-Han nationalities) is even more concentrated in the eastern part of the IMAR, accounting for 80.23 percent of such marriages. Like the distribution of the Mongol–Han mixed marriages this reflects the distribution of Mongols as a whole, as well as the other smaller minorities of Inner Mongolia.

Khölön Buir has the highest rate of Mongol intermarriage with other nationalities totalling 25.05 percent. Khölön Buir League has Inner Mongolia's only large populations of the Daurs and Ewenki nationalities, both of which traditionally have had close cultural connections with the pastoral Mongols. Khinggan and Jirim leagues and Chifeng municipality have Inner Mongolia's major populations of Koreans and Manchus.

Table 15. Distribution of Mixed Mongol/Non-Mongol Couples in
Inner Mongolia

League or Municipality	Area's Percentage of Total Mongol-Han Mixed-Marriages	Area's Percentage of Total Mongol-other (Non-Han) Nationality Mixed Marriages
Höhhot M.	7.88	6.97
Baotou M.	0.69	3.39
Khölön Buir L.	5.40	25.05
Khinggan L.	9.93	15.25
Jirim L.	37.49	19.59
Chifeng M. (former Juu Uda L.)	23.11	20.34
Shili-yin Gool L.	2.88	4.71
Wuhai M.	0.69	—
Ulaanchab L.	5.70	—
Yekhe Juu L.	1.72	4.70
Bayannuur L.	1.93	—
Alashan L.	0.82	—

Source: Song Naigong, pp. 372, 374.

A case study on intermarriage between Mongols and Han Chinese in Chifeng Municipality, which alone accounts for 14 percent of married Mongol families, shows a characteristic set of factors influencing rates of intermarriage: 1) among Mongol inhabitants, the intermarriage rate with Han Chinese for young people is distinctly higher than that of middle aged and older people; 2) the rate of Mongols marrying Han Chinese in the southern agricultural areas is higher than that in the pastoral areas; 3) those in a group in the minority among the inhabitants of a given village are more likely to marry the members of the majority group of that village; and 4) highly educated Mongols have more contact with Han, and as a result are more likely to marry Han Chinese.[20]

According to this case study, several common features can be found among most Mongol-Han Chinese couples: 1) most mixed households consist of Mongolian husbands and Chinese wives; 2) the partners in these couples tend to average between 20-40 years old; 3) both partners have higher education; 4) the children of intermarried couples are all officially identified as Mongols; and 5) the household customs (in particular the language of the household) follows those of the Han Chinese, and their children cannot speak Mongolian.[21]

Mongolian Cultural Revival

Mongols in China have been reviving their traditional Mongolian culture in a series of waves since the end of the 1970s. Crucial features such as language, particular customs, religion and beliefs, ethnic consciousness, as well as peculiar ethnic cognitive styles and sentiments, have all been subject to conscious revival. Even in those places where the Mongol population is very small, Mongols have been trying to carry on their traditional lifestyles. A particularly striking example is given by the barely more than 10,000 Mongols in China's capital of Beijing who have been holding a Naadum Fair on a semi-annual basis since 1981. Likewise, the nearly 400 Mongols in Gansu Province's capital of Lanzhou held their own Naadum Fair on July 6, 1991. Mongols in Ürümchi city in Xinjiang have built an *oboo* or cairn near the city and have conducted worship ceremonies there every summer.

The most remarkable aspect of this revival of Mongolian culture has occurred in the sphere of Mongolian language, both written and spoken. As was noted above, there are quite a few Mongols who have lost their mother tongue, because of historical reasons and a change in language-use background. A large part of those Mongols who have lost the ability to communicate in Mongolian language are now trying to revive their Mongolian. This loss of Mongolian language has been particularly noticeable outside of Inner Mongolia. Likewise Mongols in the provinces, autonomous regions, and municipalities outside of the Inner Mongolia Autonomous Region have recently seen widespread efforts to revive their Mongolian mother tongue.

According to the 1990 census, there are 587,311 Mongols in Liaoning province. As the older people remember, although there were less than 90,000 Mongols in Fuxin county before 1949, they could all speak Mongolian. By 1988, however, 20,000 young people out of a total Mongol population of 130,000 in the Fuxin Mongolian Autonomous County could not speak Mongolian. In the Daban village of Daban town in this county, Mongols form the vast majority of the population—712 out of 876. Of these Mongols, more than 300 are young people, but 71 percent of them cannot speak Mongolian. In this village the Mongols have used a variety of methods to revive the use of Mongolian. For example, from 1982 to 1988, 65 Mongolian classes were added to the schools. Adult education has also played a part: from 1984, in more than 20 towns and villages, about 38 special Mongolian-language training classes have been held, directed at Mongol farmers, doctors, and reporters, with an attendance of more than 1,000 people.[22]

Comprehensive information on language loss and the effect of such language revival programs is available for the Mongols in Heilongjiang province, who numbered 139,077 according to the 1990 census. In 1987, a sample investigation of language-use among 33,112 Mongols living in 22 towns and 98 villages of Heilongjiang where Mongolian live in compact communities covered 87 percent of the rural Mongols and 30 percent of the province's total Mongolian population.

Table 16. Mongolian Schools and Students Among Six Provinces and
Autonomous Regions Cooperating in Developing Mongolian (1984)

Province or A.R.	Mongol population (1982)	Type	Technical high school	High school	Junior high	Primary school	Pre-school
Heilongjiang	96,532	schools	0	3	5	79	0
		students	0	747	1,903	8,304	0
Jilin	93,038	schools	1	0	4	24	0
		students	180	0	1,314	2,085	0
Liaoning	428,780	schools	1	6	19	168	183
		students	200	3,520	14,194	37,055	3,254
Xinjiang	117,460	schools	3	12	14	16	0
		students	368	1,777	5,626	17,966	0
Qinghai	50,038	schools	2	2	3	20	0
		students	117	114	612	1,689	0
Gansu	6,226	schools	0	0	1	6	0
		students	0	8	132	614	0
Total	792,074	schools	7	23	46	363	183
		students	865	6,166	23,781	67,731	3,254

Source: "Report on the Fourth Cooperative Meeting on Education of the Eight
Provinces and Regions Cooperative Working Group on Mongolian Lanaguage
and Writing."[23]

According to this survey, 73.4 percent of the Mongols in compact communities
can speak Mongolian, 14 percent can understand but not speak Mongolian, and
12.6 percent do not understand any Mongolian. In written language the situation
is far worse—69 percent of the Mongols in these compact communities cannot
read or write in Mongolian. Analyzed by age, 50.8 percent of children at or
under 7 years of age, 67.9 percent of those 8 to 19, 77.4 percent of those 20 to
39, and 91.1 percent of those over 40 can speak Mongolian. Only 3.2 percent of
the 6,827 Mongols above 40 cannot understand Mongolian, a fact demonstrating
how this generation of Mongols grew up with Mongolian language as their
major language of social communication; even today a part of the older generation
cannot speak Chinese.

But for similar historical reasons, the literacy level of these older Mongols is
extremely low, with 82.6 percent of those above 40 being illiterate in Mongolian.
From the beginning of the 1980s, Mongolian language has generally been taught
in those primary and middle schools of this province designated to serve the
Mongol population. Moreover, from 1984, some Mongolian primary schools in
the Dörbed Mongolian Autonomous County, have begun to use Mongolian as

the major language of instruction, with Chinese in a secondary role. As a result, only 13. 1 percent of the children 8-19 in these schools cannot speak Mongolian and the rate of illiteracy in Mongolian among Mongols has been reduced to 46.7 percent.[24]

Table 17. College Students Sent to IMAR by Participant Provinces and Regions in the Eight Provinces and Regions Cooperative Working Group on Mongolian Language and Writing Mongolian

Years	Total	Xinjiang	Qinghai	Gansu	Ningxia	Liaoning	Jilin	Heilong-jiang
1977-80	267	66	5	0	8	96	22	70
1981	69	30	0	0	0	21	0	18
1982	91	30	0	5	0	30	8	18
1983	79	30	5	0	0	30	6	8
total	506	156	10	5	8	177	36	144

The revival of Mongolian language and writing in these provinces and regions has involved close cooperation with Inner Mongolia, which is the clear center for Mongolian-language higher education in China. Mongols in most of the provinces and autonomous regions outside of Inner Mongolia with significant Mongolian populations have been sending a substantial number of students to study in schools at every level in the IMAR. They have also invited a large number of Mongols from Inner Mongolia to assist in developing Mongolian language work as part of their revival and development of Mongolian culture in their area. The three provinces and regions of Liaoning, Xinjiang, and Heilongjiang, have formally dispatched 177, 156, and 144 students respectively to various colleges in Inner Mongolia during the years 1977-83.

A particularly interesting example of how Mongols outside of Inner Mongolia are developing cultural ties with the region as part of their revival of Mongolian culture and language is provided by the Mongols of Yunnan. According to the 1990 census, there are 13,148 Mongols in Yunnan, descendants of a Mongolian garrison stationed in the area in the thirteenth century. Over time, they changed their predominant occupation from herding to fishing, and subsequently changed from fishermen into peasants and unskilled laborers.

According to scholarly investigation, the vocabulary of the peculiar language designated "special new Mongolian" of Tonghai County's Xin Menggu Dadui or "New Mongolian Brigade," contains 15-20 percent ancestral Mongolian words, 20 percent Chinese words, 20 percent Yi words, with the rest being a mixture of words from Hani, Naxi, Lisu, and other Tibeto-Burman languages spoken in Yunnan. Since 1949, these Yunnan Mongols have been steadily reviving their ancestral Mongolian culture. That only 21 young men have married women of other nationalities in that time shows their strong ethnic consciousness.

As part of this revival of Mongolian culture, the Yunnan Mongols have established close cultural links with the Mongols of Inner Mongolia. In 1957, the Mongols of Yunnan sent two people to Inner Mongolia to learn Mongolian. Subsequently, this contact was broken off due to the incessant political turmoil of this period. Since 1980, however, contact has been reestablished and Yunnan has sent 10 students each year to Inner Mongolia to learn Mongolian. In 1980, a "visiting relatives" (*tanqin*) group of twenty-two members of the Mongol-inhabited New Mongolian Brigade toured Inner Mongolia for more than fifty days and upon returning to Yunnan left nine of their members in Inner Mongolia to learn Mongolian.

In 1981, eight people from this brigade entered the Inner Mongolian Performing Arts School for a half-year course of instruction in Mongolian song and dance. Since 1981, the Yunnan Mongols have annually invited two teachers from Inner Mongolia to teach Mongolian language courses. They have also chosen 21 young students to enter the five-year program in the Mongolian-medium class of the Shili-yin Gool Technical Training School.

The primary school of the brigade now teaches two hours of Mongolian lessons every day and both Mongolian and Chinese are used for broadcasting from the brigade radio station, for both private radios and public loudspeakers. The school and the brigade government now subscribe to Mongolian-language newspapers and magazines, while pictures of Chinggis Khan, Khubilai Kha'an and Möngke Kha'an are hung on the walls both of the brigade government and those of private families. In 1980-81, statues of these three ancestors were made and the Yunnanese Mongols have begun holding ceremonies for worshipping Chinggis Khan every October.[25]

The Tibetanized Mongols in Qinghai furnish another striking example of this phenomenon. Of the 71,510 Mongols in Qinghai (1990 census), more than 50,000 (1986 figure) have been Tibetanized (i.e., they speak only Tibetan). This includes the Mongols in Henan Mongolian Autonomous County as well as smaller populations in the Tibetan autonomous prefectures of Huangnan, Hainan, and Haibei. The Mongols in these areas stopped speaking Mongolian in the last century and except for scattered items of vocabulary, such as place-names and yurt terminology, they principally communicate in Tibetan.

Since 1986, Mongolian language has been undergoing revival in those prefectures and counties where Mongols live in compact communities. For example, the primary school of Huisun *sumu* in Henan Mongolian A.C. changed its language of instruction to Mongolian and decided not to have any classes taught in Tibetan. As part of this Mongolian language revival, Huisun also sent thirty to forty children to Inner Mongolia to study in schools at various levels from primary school to university.[26]

The loss of mother tongue and the recent trend of efforts at language renewal are not restricted to areas outside Inner Mongolia. In Inner Mongolia itself, 450,000 Mongols can no longer speak Mongolian. Some of them are trying to revive their Mongolian. As a typical example, according to 1990 statistics, the

Tümed Left Banner in Höhhot municipality has 30,000 Mongols who have lost their mother tongue completely for more than one hundred years.

However, during the last 15 years they have been undertaking effective measures to revive it. Schools running from primary schools to high schools have been founded to offer a complete general education with Mongolian as the systematic language of instruction. The banner has even created kindergartens with teachers, nurses, and support staff composed purely of ethnic Mongols. The Tümed Left Banner program has been publicly recognized as a successful model for the revival of the Mongolian mother tongue among Mongols who have lost it.

Mongolian has also been actively revived in Liangcheng county where the Mongolian population is only 1,181, or 0.5 percent out of 230,000. Previously, children of the 382 Mongolian families there had no opportunity to have their children study Mongolian, but in 1982-84, a Mongolian primary school was founded in the county seat to address this problem.[27]

The revival of the mother language and spreading education in that language is undoubtedly a positive feature in the overall revival of traditional culture. On the other hand, when older traditions are revived, it is important to be fully conscious of what traditions should be transmitted and how to adapt them to the conditions of the new world environment. Taking religion as an example, Buddhism and shamanism, along with many folk religious practices, have been revived both widely and often blindly. It is important to make sure that the contents of these revived religious traditions contain nothing that contradicts either modern science and technology or is harmful to the development of the Mongol people.

The End of Pastoral Nomadism

By focusing on economic and cultural patterns, change, and assimilation among the 4.8 million Mongols in China, this survey has shown that to be a Mongol in China is far more complex than the picture of Mongols commonly held in the eyes of others. To be a Mongol is not limited to riding horses, living in yurts, wearing traditional Mongolian robes, eating meat and mare's milk, practicing nomadic pastoralism, or speaking pure Mongolian without loan words. Rather it includes Mongols practicing a wide variety of lifestyles, taking on an increasing variety of jobs and careers, and a complex, varied, and rapidly changing culture and language.

As a rough analysis of this diversity, we can divide the Mongols in China into four patterns (i.e., pastoral Mongolian culture, semi-pastoral/semi-agricultural Mongolian culture, agricultural Mongolian culture, and urban Mongolian culture). In drawing conclusions about the Mongol population in China, we cannot afford to ignore any of these patterns. The latter three patterns, which have often been overlooked as being "not truly Mongolian," are indivisible parts of current Mongolian culture, and strongly color Mongolian culture as a whole. The formation, adoption, and development of each of these patterns within the mosaic of Mongolian culture has occurred in distinct social, cultural, and natural environments and in various periods of time. In that sense, they are not only parts of the whole of Mongolian culture but in some respects, the parts which best show the continuing vitality and adaptability of a distinctively Mongolian ethnic culture in conditions of rapid economic change.

Typically, the Mongols of China have either relinquished or will soon begin relinquishing their traditional cultural-historical pastoral nomadism, as pastoralists are everywhere sedentarized, and the phenomenon of semi-pastoral/semi-agricultural economy becomes more common. In this situation, the present question for the Mongols as a nationality is not primarily one of "How do we preserve the traditional culture of pastoral nomadism?" but more importantly, "How can one appropriately develop a sedentarized pastoral, or even more crucially, a semi-pastoral/semiagricultural culture?" In this task, it is important above all to study more fully the cultural and economic forms of, and the experiences and lessons gained by, those Mongols who for more than one hundred years have been travelling along the road of semi-pastoral/semi-agricultural life and who have occupied the majority of the population among the Mongols of China.

From the loss and revival of the Mongolian mother tongue and script among widely dispersed Mongolian communities we can see that preservation of this mother language is the most important condition for the preservation of a distinctive culture and ethnic identity. Nothing in the process of cultural revival is necessarily contradictory to an attitude of openness and willingness to learn other languages and to use those languages for mastering science, technology, and the civilization of the human race as a whole.

Notes

1. Song Naigong, ed., *Zhongguo renkou (Nei Menggu fence)*, (Beijing: China Finance and Economy Publishing House, 1987), pp. 27-50.

2. Zhang Zhengming, *Qidan shilue* (Beijing: China Press, 1979, 6-7), pp. 55-58.

3. See the accounts of Zhao Hong and Xiao Daheng in *Nei Menggu shizhi ziliao xuanbian*, vol. 3 (Höhhot: n.p., 1985), pp. 3, 13, 142.

4. Jagchid, Sechin, *Essays in Mongolian Studies* (Provo, Utah: David M. Kennedy Center for International Studies, 1988), pp. 21-48.

5. *Dawor zu jianshi* (Höhhot: Inner Mongolia People's Publishing House, 1986), pp. 3-10.

6. *Menggu zu jianshi* (Höhhot: Inner Mongolia People's Publishing House, 1985), pp. 269-78, 341-44.

7. Han figures for 1912 and 1937 include all those subject to regular county administration and thus include the Hui population, while Mongol figures for the same years include all those subject to banner administration and thus include the Daur, Ewenki, and Orochen nationalities.

8. The tertiary or "third industry" (*disan chanye*) is a currently popular term which refers to small-scale service or industrial enterprises, particularly those owned either privately or by a township or county-level administration. It is opposed to "first industry"

(*diyi chanye*), or agriculture, and second industry (*di'er chanye*), or large-scale state-owned industry. The growth of third industry is a major feature of the economic liberalization pursued since 1979.

9. "Household ranch" (*jiating muchang/ger büli-yin maljil-un talbai*) is a special status granted by local governments to sedentarized pastoral households which meet certain standards for both the number of livestock, and the application of simple technology, such as fencing, sheds, tractors, and so forth. While the overall standards are set at the national level, local governments actually make the awards so that implementation varies greatly from league to league. In some leagues, other awards are given for households which meet certain criteria in proper supply of water, grass, tree cover, forage, and machinery.

10. "Air pasture" (*kongzhong caochang*) refers to feeding livestock with branches of poplar trees which have been specially grown and cropped to produce a harvest of leaves and thin branches that can feed sheep and goats. Since poplar trees have deep roots, they are able to tap into underground water sources in otherwise desert environments.

11. Damusüring, "Monggol kele bicig-ün ajil kiged onol üiledülge," *Monggol kele bicig,* 1981, no. 3, pp. 1-23.

12. Sénamjil, *Kele kiged oyun-u negegelte* (Höhhot: Inner Mongolian People's Publishing House, 1990), pp. 18-19.

13. Divided approximately according to the 1982 census survey on the use of Mongolian as a written and spoken language in the IMAR, along with several sample investigations. Data on total population and proportion of the IMAR's Mongolian population calculated according to the fourth census of the region (1990).

14. Öbör Monggol-un öbertegen jasaqu orun-u kele bicig-ün jöblel-ün Kölön Buyir-tu ocigsan bayicagaqu duguyilang, "Sin-e Bargu baragun qosigun-u Monggol üge kele üsüg bicig-i surcu kereglegsen bayidal-i bayicagagsan tuqai," in *Kele kiged oyun-u negegelte,* ed. Senamjil (Höhhot: Inner Mongolian People's Publishing House, 1990), pp. 286-300.

15. Öbör Monggol-un öbertegen jasaqu orun-u kele bicig-ün jöblel-ün Kölön Buyir-tu ocigsan bayicagaqu duguyilang, "Jalayid qosigu, Qorcin baragun gar-un emünetü qosigu Monggol kele surcu kereglegsen toyimu bayidal," in *Kele kiged oyun-u negegelte,* ed. Senamjil, (Höhhot: Inner Mongolian People's Publishing House, 1990), pp. 310-23.

16. Öbör Monggol-un öbertegen jasaqu orun-u kele bicig-ün jöblel-ün Kölön Buyir-tu ocigsan bayicagaqu duguyilang. "Qayilar, Manjuur qoyar qota-yin monggol kele bicig surcu kreglegsen bayidal-un tuqai bayicagagsan medegülülte," in *Kele kiged oyun-u negegelte,* ed. Senamjil, (Höhhot: Inner Mongolian People's Publishing House, 1990), pp. 301-09.

17. ÖMÖJO KBJ KBOBD, "Sin-e Bargu baragun . . .", pp. 286-300.

18. Ma Jie and Fan Naigu, "Nei Menggu bannong banmu qu de shehui, jingji fazhan: Fucun diaocha," in *Bianjiang kaifa lunzhu,* edited by Ma Jie and Fan Naigu, (Beijing: Peking University Publishing House, 1993), pp. 82-139. See also Rong Ma, "Migrant and Ethnic Integration in the Process of Socio-economic Change in Inner Mongolia: A Village Study," *Nomadic Peoples* 33(1993), pp. 173-191.

19. Bao Zhiming, "Biandong zhong de Meng min shenghuo–Sanyefu cun diaocha," *Shehuixue yanjiu,* 1991, no. 1, pp. 52-57.

20. Ma Jie and Fan Naigu, "Chifeng nongcun muqu Meng-Han tonghun de yanjiu," *Beijing Daxue xuebao, Zhexue shehui kexue ban,* 1988, no. 3, pp. 76-87.

21. Ma Jie and Fan Naigu, "Nei Menggu bannong banmu qu de shehui, jingji fazhan: Fucun diaocha."

22. Nomuqan and Bulag, "Eke kele-ben aldagsad-tu monggol kele surgaju bayig-a Fusin-u-kin," *Monggol kele bicig*, 1988, no. 3.

23. Mongolian is taught as a subject from the third year of primary school in Heilongjiang province. Liaoning province has a total of 73,000 Mongolian students (this includes those listed above, plus students of Mongol ancestry attending schools not designated for Mongols) of which 51,000 are learning Mongolian as a subject. In Xinjiang, Qinghai, and Gansu, all Mongol students in the Mongolian schools designated above are taught in Mongolian.

24. Oyundalai, "Qaramören muji-yin Monggolcud-un kelen-ü tuqai ögülekü ni," *Monggol kele bicig*, 1990, no. 7, pp. 9-12.

25. Yang Jing-cu, Jai Sheng-de, and Chen Yüng-ya, "Yünnan muji-yin Tüng-qai siyan-u He-si nigedül-ün Sin-e Monggol yeke barigada-yin Monggolcud-i baycagagsan medegülülte," *Monggol kete bicig*, 1984, no. 4, pp. 102-11. Original appeared in Chinese in *Minzu xuebao*, by Yang Jingchu, Zhai Shengde, and Chen Yongya.

26. Bürinbayar, Ci., "Töbedjigsen Monggolcud eke kele-ben sergügejü bayin-a," *Monggol kele bicig*, 1986, no. 11, pp. 5-6.

27. Bagatur, "Liyangceng siyan-du monggol kele bicig-ün ajil-i idebkitei örnigüljü bayig-a ni," *Monggol kele bicig*, 1987, no. 1, pp. 7-9.

Mobility, Technology, and Decollectivization of Pastoralism in Mongolia

David Sneath

Mongolia has rapidly implemented a series of reforms designed to create a competitive market economy based on individuated private property. So far, however, most Mongolians have seen a marked decline in their standard of living. Mobile pastoralism remains the basis of the rural economy of the country, but it has undergone rapid change as a result of the dissolution of the collective and state farms.

This essay briefly examines the pre-collective systems of pastoral movement in Mongolia. Steppe elites, owning large numbers of animals and controlling the labor of subordinates, have long been able to generate extensive, mobile, specialist herding systems, making use of the economies of scale from the management of large herds. These large-scale, complex systems were inextricably linked to administrative structures, and cannot be seen as a subsistence activity that is in some way "natural" to the region.

High mobility requires specialist technology, skills, and knowledge; moreover, in Mongolia it requires political organization that allows access to large areas of land. Paradoxically, it is argued, one can see extensive land-use as an intensification of production. In a given society, long-distance herding strategies require increased labor, greater technical knowledge, more transport animals, and more complex equipment than low-mobility herding of the same-sized flock. But the benefits, according to Mongolian herders, are very real in terms of improved livestock feed provision.

During the collective period, new technology was applied to support mobile pastoralism with some success—such as the mechanized support for pastoral movement and hay supplies. Since the dissolution of the collectives pastoralists have experienced a marked reduction of such transport, hay provision, veterinary support and other services supplied by the collectives, and are being forced to return to older, more laborious techniques. Many pastoral households are struggling to subsist amid rising costs and an increasingly atomized and demechanized pastoral economy.

Sociotechnical Systems

Technological developments have long been seen as both a motor and a product of social change. Social anthropological studies have come to emphasize the importance of studying tools and their use as part of the wider social and cultural systems within which they exist.[1] Pfaffenberger, for example, following Lemonnier and Hughes,[2] argued that instead of trying to analyze technology in isolation we should think in terms of sociotechnical systems—which he defines as the "distinctive technological activity that stems from the linkage of techniques and material culture to the social coordination of labor."[3] This sort of approach shifts the focus from attempting to isolate the technical aspects of society so as to explore their relationships with social change, to an investigation of the change of these sociotechnical systems themselves. Examples of such sociotechnical systems used by Pfaffenberger include the pre-colonial Sri Lankan village irrigation schemes[4] and the Balinese water temple irrigation systems studied by Lansing—in which the temple was central to organization of irrigation. These technologies were lost, he argues, as part of wider political and social changes.

One problem with Pfaffenberger's definition of sociotechnical systems is that it depends upon a certain notion of technology, characterized by Miller as the "systematic exploitation of the range of methods used in order to produce patterned variation."[5] This, however, does not sit well with the distinction that Tim Ingold has sought to introduce between techniques (by which he means skills), and technology (by which he means the corpus of generalized, discursive knowledge capable of practical application). Ingold convincingly argues for rejecting the notion of technology as a universally applicable category. In many societies, practices involve techniques but not necessarily "technology" in the sense that Ingold uses the term.[6] Nonetheless, a modified version of Pfaffenberger's notion of sociotechnical system is particularly well suited to the study of Inner Asian pastoralism.[7] For the purposes of this essay, a sociotechnical system is defined as "a system of activity that links techniques and material objects to the social coordination of labor."[8]

Mongolian pastoralism can be analyzed, in these terms, as consisting of a series of such sociotechnical systems, some of them very old. Although it is a vast and geographically varied country, pastoralism has been practiced over much of Mongolia since ancient times. The climate is fairly dry, average annual precipitation over most of the country is less than 300mm. Much of the land is poorly suited to agriculture, but is used as grazing by pastoralists, most of whom are mobile and use seasonal pastures as part of an annual cycle. The principal domesticated animals are the so-called five types of livestock (*tavan khoshuu mal*)—horses, cattle (including yaks in highland regions), sheep, goats, and camels.

The traditional pastoral dwelling is the characteristic *ger* (yurt)—a sturdy, portable wooden frame covered with layers of felt or canvas. It can be disassembled and packed for movement in a matter of minutes (although in practice *gers* are generally full of belongings and loading them onto carts or a truck usually takes several hours). Another well-known example of Mongolian pastoral technology is the *uurga* pole lasso, used to catch horses and other large livestock. The *uurga* is a gently tapering wooden rod three or four meters in length, with a leather loop at the slender end. Although it can be used on foot, the *uurga* is typically employed by a rider to catch a given animal (such as a horse to be used for riding) by flicking the loop over its head and bringing it to a halt by stopping his or her own steed. It can also simply be used as a long goad to help drive herds of all species out to pasture and back.

Pastoralism involves the utilization of highly-developed series of such artifacts, skills, and techniques, many of which are based in the pastoral domestic group (*ail*) and are generally passed on to children in this context. There is insufficient space to describe all of these constituent elements, but they can be very nominally divided into two loosely gendered and overlapping repertoires. The female sphere includes milking, preparing food products (such as cheeses, yogurt, and blood-sausage), cooking, the making, repairing, and washing of clothes, child care, cleaning the *ger*, making tea, and looking after animals close to the *ail* (Mongolian encampment). Women and children also usually collect the dried dung (*argal*) that is used for fuel. In fact, some of these tasks may be done by men from time to time, but the responsibility for their completion is generally held to be that of the senior woman of the household.

Tasks that are traditionally associated with males include all the activities concerned with herding animals some distance from the *ail*, and finding them if they stray. Apart from this, men and boys are also generally expected to undertake the killing, skinning, and castration of livestock, harnessing animals, and loading *gers* (yurts) onto carts along with other heavy goods, repairing *ger* frames, carts, saddles, and harnesses.

Other pastoral tasks that are usually done by men, although women often help, include lassoing and breaking horses, cutting and transporting hay, and making and repairing enclosures and animal sheds. Many herding tasks are done by family members of both genders, such as penning and counting livestock, shearing sheep, and the combing-out of cashmere from goat fleece. A typical *ail* will include all the equipment needed for everyday pastoral life, everything from combs (*sam*) for the goats to a sewing-machine (*oyodlyn mashin*) and carts (*tereg*) to collect water and, perhaps, move the encampment.

These pastoral techniques and devices, however, are utilized as part of wider sociotechnical systems that include the right to use seasonal pastures, the forms of livestock ownership of livestock, and often—though not always—seasonal movements to different pastures.

During the state socialist era Mongolian pastoralists were organized into approximately 310 collectives (*negdel*) or state farms (*sangiin aj akhui*), each located in a district (*sum*).[9] Although about fifty state farms carried out large-scale crop production, almost all of the other districts were primarily pastoral, organizing seasonal movement and raising livestock in line with state planning. The *sum* generally included a central settlement of a few hundred households and a large area of grassland. Several hundred pastoral households kept the collective or state livestock, as well as a smaller number of their own domestic animals. Most of these herding families lived in *gers* and moved to different seasonal pastures in an annual cycle. They were organized into production brigades and instructed which pastures to go to and when. The collective required households to supply a quota of animal products from the collective livestock—the "*norm*."

Privatization and Pastoralism

In the 1990s the Mongolian government began a vast program of economic reform. In 1991 the assets of pastoral collectives were privatized; most of the livestock and equipment became the private property of the members of the collectives through the issue of share coupons (*tasalbar*) with which the members could "purchase" their share.

By 1993 the distribution of formerly collective assets was completed, and the *negdels* had become companies (*kompan*). In some rural areas these companies were soon dissolved; in other districts they remain principally as marketing organizations. As the formally collective assets were divided some enterprises termed "cooperatives" (*khorshoo* or *khorshoolol*) were formed by members pooling their shares to gain joint ownership of some section of the old *negdel.*

These "cooperatives" either attempted to operate a former collective resource—such as a small vegetable-growing operation—or acted as a marketing organization to sell the produce of pastoral families and deliver the goods they ordered in return. Most of these have gone bankrupt in the last few years, or have become inoperative as a result of financial difficulties. The result is that most pastoral households have to manage independently, relying on their own livestock and labor, selling their products as best they can.

The "Age of the Market" (*zakh zeeliin üye*) as Mongolians call it has led to widespread economic disruption and Mongolians have had to face a marked decline in living standards. Real wages halved between 1990 and 1992, and then declined by a third in 1993.[10] More than a quarter of the population, as of 1994, lived below the poverty line, and that line was very low.[11] Social services have been slashed; for example, the education budget has been cut by around 60 percent.[12] Infrastructure, buildings, schools, and health facilities are all decaying. There has been a loss of the security of basic food provision which the collectives had supplied. The price of flour and other staple foods has increased, in relative terms, much more quickly than the prices paid to pastoralists for their products (wool, meat, and milk). In addition, supplies are often unreliable in remote pastoral districts.

The rapid price increases were, in part, driven by the rising cost of oil and transportation. The Soviet Union had supplied its satellite states with cheap oil, and for Mongolia this meant that mechanical transport, a key factor in such a huge and thinly populated country, was affordable and widely available to local government, national services, and productive enterprises alike. With the collapse of the Soviet empire the price of petrol increased rapidly in the 1990s. The increased cost of transportation has resulted in medical and veterinary treatment being less accessible now than in the past. Health services are also suffering from sever underfunding. Basic medicines are in short supply, and fewer people can now afford to travel to the capital for treatment of serious ailments.

Decollectivization and Reduced Mechanization

We have become familiar with the images of industrial technology spreading into and impacting upon agricultural or pastoral societies. What is perhaps less familiar is the process in reverse. Mongolian pastoralists have seen a process of de-mechanization over the last few years as the vehicles and machinery that were used and maintained by the collectives has been utilized less frequently, diverted to other uses, or have fallen into disrepair.

In the collective period pastoralists were generally moved on the longest legs of the annual migration using trucks supplied by the collective. Hay was generally cut by mechanized units and delivered by truck for pastoralists to use as feed supplement during the crucial winter period. Since these collective motor pools and hay-making units were split-up and sold-off, their new private owners often found it difficult to obtain affordable spare parts or capture sufficient economies of scale to keep the machines running.

In these conditions pastoralists frequently have to make increased use of animal transport, moving with ox, camel or yak—drawn carts. Many herders now find it difficult to continue to make the seasonal moves that the collectives had supported, and in some regions the tendency of pastoralists to stay all year near their best pastures has been exacerbated by insecurity over rights to use pasture land, which used to be regulated and enforced by the collectives. Hay now has to be cut by hand using scythes, an additional exhausting and physically demanding task for pastoralists in late summer. Those households without active adult members, or the money to buy hay, can find it difficult to gather sufficient winter fodder for their animals.

The changes have had a marked effect on pastoral districts, such as Renchinlhümbe and Khankh, two *sums* in Khöwsgöl in the northern region of Mongolia, especially from 1993 through the autumn 1996.[13] It has generally been in the more distant rural areas of Mongolia such as these (i.e., furthest from the markets, supplies, and facilities of the capital Ulaanbaatar), that living conditions have been particularly adversely effected. The dissolution of the collectives rendered large numbers of the service sector unemployed and forced them to rely upon their livestock holdings for subsistence. This changed pastoral practices as many of these new herders still had dwellings in the *sum* center and tended to be much less mobile than the more established herding households which had once been part of the specialized herding brigades in the collective.[14]

A common pattern was for such households from the *sum* center to pasture their livestock relatively near the center during the summer months, and then have some or all of their livestock herded by relatives or friends among the pastoral families in more distant pastures. Many of the pastoral families in these districts had reduced the amount of pastoral movement they undertook since the dissolution of the collectives. Some, for example, had given up the four annual moves that the production brigades had organized and were moving only twice a year—from what had been summer pastures directly to their winter pastures.

Many of the mechanical assets of the collectives have now ceased to be productively used. Livestock gained from privatization could be relied upon to provide some sort of income—even when divided into small herds owned by individual families. Tractors and welding equipment, on the other hand, generally formed part of the motor pools and workshops supported as constituent elements of the collective's overall operation. Without the institutional framework for the employment of machine operators and maintenance staff, the delivery of bulk orders of spare parts and inexpensive fuel, it became much more difficult for the private owners to use these assets.

A typical example of this aspect of decollectivization is the case of one of the Renchinlhümbe families that had recently became pastoralists. Batbayar was a 34 year-old welder who relied on his herd of 200 animals to make a living. He was the youngest of three brothers, and the two others, Pürew and Bat-Erdene, had been tractor drivers for the collective. Since its dissolution they too herded livestock to make a living. Batbayar learned his trade in the army, where he welded for three years before leaving to work for the local collective for seven years. He lost his job, like his brothers, in 1993 when the collective was dissolved. All three brothers secured their equipment from the collective during the privatization process. Batbayar had his welding gear and his brothers had a tractor each—a remarkable set of expensive assets in local terms which, one would have thought, should make them relatively wealthy men.

In fact the tractors stood idle, outside their *gers*, and were hardly ever used. When the author first met the brothers in August 1996, they were preparing to cut hay by hand, despite the fact that they also had the mechanized grass-cutting attachments needed to do this by tractor. The main obstacle, they explained, was the expense and difficulty of running their tractors. Diesel was very expensive, as were spare parts (when they were obtainable at all). When asked why they could not cut enough hay to sell to local families to cover their costs, Pürew laughed at this suggestion: it would be too expensive to get his tractor running.

Furthermore, the really good hay fields were a long way from where they lived, Pürew explained, and the ones used by local families were smallish patches of rather sparse hay, spread out over a large area. This meant that it would be costly to drive all that way and cut a significant amount of surplus hay by tractor, and he would then be faced with the cost of transporting it. Very few local families were wealthy enough to be able to afford such costly hay in any case. Instead, the brothers joined the other local men and spent an exhausting fortnight or so in late August, working dawn to dusk, to cut hay by hand. Some of this hand-cut hay was sold by those families who most badly needed cash. A full truck-load of hay (around 2 tons) sold for about 30,000 tögrögs ($55 U.S.), which although cheap enough to make selling hay unattractive to Pürew and his brother, still represented a considerable expense for most pastoral families, who faced a cash shortage.

An unprecedentedly high number of the residents of Renchinlhümbe *sum* had recently become directly dependent on livestock for their subsistence. In 1996, for example, 1,207 people (over 70 percent of the total sum population of 1,724) were officially classed as *malchid* (herders) by local government in Renchinlhümbe, whereas in the collective period only about half the population would be classed as pastoralists in this way. A further 405 adults (nearly a quarter of the whole *sum* population) were classed as unemployed and mostly were indirectly dependent on the livestock sector, as most of them helped out with odd jobs for family and friends. Indeed, only 6.5 percent of the *sum* population (112 people) were employed in non-pastoral sectors. Most households had found that ownership of animals did not provide sufficient income to compensate them for the loss of salaried employment in collective and government sectors.

Because selling their animal products had become far from easy, pastoral households also faced a cash shortage, and inflation remained high. This meant that herding families were understandably reluctant to retain large amounts of cash, and preferred to have the products that they required instead—principally flour, cloth, candles, tea, tobacco, and salt. This has led to widespread barter trade, whereby traders with trucks would take livestock in exchange for the consumer goods that they brought with them.

Local families complained that opportunities to obtain consumer goods were so rare that they ended up paying very high prices (in livestock) for the traded goods. In the past, the collectives had operated mobile shops—trucks that took goods out to pastoral households who could buy them using the cash credit they had from working for the collective. Without such services and faced by high prices charged by the new private traders, many households have been sliding back to subsistence production, often barely able to supply themselves with basic necessities and quite unable to accumulate savings.

This process of rural demechanization, and demonetarization, illustrates the rationale for adopting the sociotechnical approach. Just as an irrigation scheme requires the operation of both social and material systems, so mobile pastoral techniques form part of larger socio-political systems, which in the collective period included exogenous mechanized components such as trucks and tractors.

From a narrowly technological perspective this would appear to be a return to pre-revolutionary pastoralism; animal-transport instead of trucks; cutting hay by hand instead of by tractor. However, in terms of the sociotechnical system of pastoralism this is not a genuine return to some sort of "traditional" form, but a collapse of large-scale pastoral systems which in many respects resembled structures that are much older than the collectives.

Pre-revolutionary Pastoralism

Popular western images of mobile pastoralists often reinforce stereotypical notions of "fierce and free" nomads; the surviving custodians of an ancient, wandering lifestyle. These sorts of images suggest that the collectives were imposed Soviet structures which restricted the mobility and freedom of innately independent Mongolian nomads.[15] In actuality, however, as early as the thirteenth century, if not before, we find that land, livestock, and even people of the commoner class, were conceived of as constituent elements of an inclusivist socio-political domain under the jurisdiction of an enfeoffed noble. Since the end of the seventeenth century, Mongolia was divided into administrative districts called 'banners' —*khoshuu*—ruled, in most cases, by a hereditary prince the *Zasag noyon* ("ruling lord"), or sometimes by a Buddhist monastery which had been given similar rights over a district. The commoners were tied to the district and were required to render their lord service, both military and civil. In most districts, large numbers of livestock belonged to the ruling monastery or lord, and were herded for them by their subjects.

In Bayanzürkh Uulyn Khoshuu, a district in what is now the Bayankhongor region of Mongolia, at least 70 percent of the population were involved in herding for the Lamyn Gegeen monastery,[16] which governed the banner.[17] These were mostly kept in large single-species herds and moved to different ecological areas by specialist pastoralists who were subjects of the monastery. There was an established system of seasonal movements, with some groups (such as the camel herders, and the horse and sheep herders, trekking 200 kilometers or more each year), and these moves could be enforced by monastic officials. A quota of livestock and animal products was supplied to the monastery, overseen by officials who were responsible for a given number of households.

It becomes clear that these systems of pastoral movement were not the simple subsistence strategies of individual households. Such a complex system required jurisdiction over large numbers of people and areas of land. Long distance seasonal movements required transportation—carts, draught animals, and movable supplies, and poor pastoralists did not generally have the assets they needed to move on their own. They usually had to move with wealthier families for whom they worked—most of whom were herding animals for the monastery.[18]

Paradoxically, perhaps, one can see extensive land-use as an *intensification* of production: long-distance herding strategies require increased labor, greater technical knowledge, more transport animals, and more complex equipment than low-mobility herding of the same-sized flock. Depending on the type of herd and the given ecology, herders using high-mobility strategies will move herds long distances and also relatively frequently within a given seasonal pasture. The benefits of frequent moves to different pastures, according to Mongolian herders, are fatter, stronger animals. It may be difficult to argue that the highly mobile form is more labor-intensive per unit of product, but it is certainly more labor-intensive in terms of the lifestyle of a herder. It also requires more coordination, investment, and wider political authority over land. The Mongolian elite, however, with the ownership of large numbers of animals and the control of subject labor, had long been able to generate extensive, mobile, specialist herding systems of this sort, making use of the economies of scale from the management of large herds by specialist herders.

The *khoshuu* districts tended to take the form of enormous strips of land running north-south, including higher rainfall areas in the north with more arid regions in the south. This reflected the interests of the monastic and noble herdowners who presided over these large-scale sociotechnical pastoral systems. Their jurisdiction over such large areas of ecologically-varied territory allowed the elites to exploit the mobility of their herdsmen to make the best use of available pastoral resources.[19] In Bayanzürkh Uulyn Khoshuu, for example, only the herders of the monastery's horses and camels made full use of much of this territory, moving most of the length of the banner in their seasonal migrations.

This neo-feudal social system was dismantled after the Soviet-style Mongolian People's Revolutionary Party seized power in 1921. In the 1930s a Russian ethnographer named Simukov noted that the collapse of the pre-revolutionary pastoral systems had led to a decline in the amount of pastoral movement—very much as it has since the dissolution of the collectives. Without the institutional drive to make long and arduous annual migrations with their masters' herds, many pastoral households tended to make do by moving their own smaller herds lesser distances.[20]

Another parallel is the increase in the number of livestock in Mongolia after the abolition of the neofeudal systems. The size of the national herd increased from just under 10 million in 1918 to over 25 million in 1940, as pastoralists slaughtered fewer animals. The numbers fell slightly when collectives were introduced in the 1950s, and stayed more or less stable at between 20 and 25 million as the Mongolian state procured large amounts of livestock from the collectives.

Since decollectivization the number of livestock has also begun to increase from about 26 million animals in 1990 to around 27 million in 1994.[21] Pastoralists from many districts have expressed their aim of building up the numbers of their private herds of livestock, but with the cost of staples such as flour rising so steeply it will be difficult for most pastoralists to sell and slaughter fewer animals in the future than they have been in recent years.

When the new revolutionary government of Mongolia had taken power in 1921 it had inherited a society in which pastoralism and the political hierarchy were inextricably combined. This linkage remained as the state eventually imposed new politico-economic structures on pastoralists—the collective and state farms. A new revolutionary political language replaced the earlier aristocratic and Buddhist discourses. But, many elements of the *habitus* of pastoralists and their masters remained. The everyday term used for collective or state animals was "*alban mal*" ("official" animals) and the root of this term translated as "official" is "*alba*"—the feudal obligation owed by pre-revolutionary subjects to their lord. Indeed, in the pre-revolutionary era the term for a common citizen or serf was "*albat*"—"one with duty." In both periods the term referred to the obligations that pastoralists had before their masters. Just as important as the conceptual continuities, many of the practices of pastoralism were retained.

The collectives and state farms also owned most of the livestock in the district, they organized specialist herds of livestock, and enforced movements between seasonal pastures. From this perspective, privatization and the dissolution of the collectives can be seen to have been as radical, albeit less violent, a change as collectivization. As the livestock were divided between individual households there was an end to the specialized single-species herds that the collectives had organized.

Sociotechnical Systems and Elites

So what do we really gain from using this notion of sociotechnical system to analyze Mongolian pastoralism? After all, none of the apparent "insights" it entails are really new, since Weberian sociology and the structural-functionalist modernization theories of the 1960s and 1970s were based on the notion that a technological-economic complex is part of a given social and cultural structure.[22] And Marxist analysis has long emphasized the way in which such systems of production (composed of both the material and the social) produced power and meaning as well as goods. If, in the end, the use of the sociotechnical system approach amounts to the insight that technological activities require a harmonious fit between economic, political, and other social factors as well as the "purely" technical—then are we not simply (to use a technological metaphor) reinventing the wheel? Well, not quite, since the notion of the sociotechnical system permits us to differentiate and describe different complexes of technical activities and their associated social dispositions, and how they coexist and interpenetrate each other, without assuming they constitute "modes of production" in the Marxist sense, and without evoking the Weberian dichotomy between "traditional" and "modern" forms. As such, the term can serve as a useful shorthand to emphasis the socially embedded, systemic nature of what Sigaut would call the "networks of technical action."

One of the problems with the notion of sociotechnical systems as described by Pfaffenberger is—like the explicit holism of structural-functionalist approaches—its emphasis on a harmonious integration of elements, which are described *a priori* as parts of a system. Techniques and aspects of social life must be clearly shown to be part of systems (as this essay has briefly tried to do for Mongolian pastoralism), rather than assumed to be so.

The emphasis upon the seamless and harmonious integration of constituent elements in the sociotechnical system also makes it difficult to account for social change. Apart from the "impact" of exogenous technology and a colonial political system, it is difficult to find a mechanism for the collapse or change of such sociotechnical systems in Pfaffenberger's original model.

Any account of Mongolian pastoralism in this century, however, cannot fail to be an account of systems that have undergone a series of wide-reaching changes. The Mongolian sociotechnical systems that supported pastoral techniques were also hierarchical political formations.[23] These systems "produced power and meaning as well as goods,"[24] and constituted apparatuses of domination. The different and dynamic orientations of elite, subaltern, and subordinate groups strike me as one of the key processes in describing social and technical change.

Indeed, one can trace two discernible constellations of sociotechnical dispositions and orientations in Mongolian pastoralism. One directed toward the local and domestic spheres, and one oriented toward the elite centers of power and ritual. The rural-domestic complex was centered on the family unit, its rituals, values, and small-scale pastoral activities aimed at provisioning its members. This element of the pastoral economy was represented by the private livestock owned by herding families in collective and pre-collective periods for their own subsistence.

The elite-centralist complex was oriented toward political and ritual centers—such as noble, monastic, and later state-socialist structures. As well as the buildings and administrative apparatuses this complex included dispositions and systems of knowledge—duty obligations owed to first feudal and then collective masters. In terms of pastoralism this complex involved the large-scale specialized herding—often of single-species herds (of a thousand or more horses, for example), long-distance pastoral movement, and other activities that first the monasteries and then the collectives organized—including access to land, and hay supplies.

These two sociotechnical subsystems were typically *symbiotically* associated in the monastic or lordly or collective domains described above. We can trace these two interconnected complexes of skills, practices, orientations, and objects back through time. Local-domestic oriented sociotechnical and ritual activity appears to have changed relatively little over the last thousand years or so. The construction of the *ger*—and the organization of domestic space within it—today is virtually indistinguishable to that described by William of Rubruck and Marco Polo in the thirteenth and fourteenth centuries. The high status and ritual part of the space (*khoimor*) is in the northern sector; the low status and workaday area to the south. The public, male area for guests is the western part of the *ger*, and the private, family, and female sector to the east. The *uurga* pole-lasso, the making of *airag* (fermented mares milk), and whole range of other current pastoral techniques date back to the thirteenth century at least.

And yet, the associated objects and techniques of the elite-centralist complex shows a relatively rapid series of changes in the same period. The politico-ritual sphere has seen a change from "Shamanic" to Lamaist Buddhist, and then to State-Marxist faiths. In each case, sacred images were placed in the high-status section at the back the *ger* (on the northern side). The Shamanic *ongon*—small felt idols—were replaced by *burkhan*—Buddhist icons, which were then replaced by State-Marxist political symbols and images such as photographs of Party leaders and certificates showing the occupants had won "production hero" (*üildweriin baatar*) awards. While domestic dwellings have changed little, political buildings changed repeatedly—from great tents for the lords of the Chinggisid period in the thirteenth century (which were often placed on huge carts and pulled by hundreds of oxen), to Sino-Tibetan Buddhist complexes of buildings, and then to first Russian and later Soviet-style edifices and blocks of flats.

When it comes to specifically pastoral techniques—the large-scale pastoral systems were subject to mechanization in the collective period, whereas the domestic systems were not. However, it would be misleading to give the impression that these two complexes are static and contrasting categories of social action—these are inextricably linked features of a continually changing Mongolian culture. And this dynamic relationship between elites and the historical process of ever-changing power centers, provides a means to link the notion of sociotechnical system with a description of social and technological change. In vernacular architecture, for example, one of the central mechanisms for changes in building design has long been taken to be elite emulation.

This is certainly a well-trodden path for the introduction of many mechanical objects, which were at first relatively rare and expensive enough to make them available to the wealthy, initially; but then became more widely found. Finely crafted Buddhist images, for example, were first introduced by the Mongolian nobility. By the nineteenth century almost every Mongolian home, however humble, had a *burkhan* Buddhist icon.

The Free Market

For the second time this century, Mongolia's politico-centralist elite has embraced a new economic and political discourse—first state socialist, now free market. Their latest orientation has led to the dissolution of collectives and state farms. In the new climate the large-scale, politico-centralist, sociotechnical systems have declined, with their particular integration of skills, activities, and machines. The domestic sociotechnical system (or sub-system) has increasingly taken on the primary role in pastoralism, with a noticeable different combination of sociotechnical elements: smaller, multi-species herds, less movement, the slaughtering of fewer livestock, and so on.

But this should not simply be seen as the destruction of some ancient and static traditional system. As far back into the history of Mongolia as we look, the continuity and change of pastoral systems, techniques, and objects provides a commentary on the changes in the nature and orientation of the elites and their relation to subordinate members of their sociotechnical systems.

Notes

1. If, following Lemonnier ("Bark capes, arrowheads and Concords: on social representations of technology," in Hodder, 1. (ed) 1989, *The Meaning of Things: Material Culture and Symbolic Expression,* London) we take technique to mean the system of material resources, tools, operational sequences and skills, knowledge, and specific modes of work coordination involved with the production of material artifacts.

2. Lemonnier points out that technology—the range of known techniques—must be studied as part of the wider social systems whithin which it exists.

3. Pfaffenberger, "Technology and Social Change," *Annual Review of Anthropology,* 21 (1992), p. 497.

4. Pfaffenberger argues that the British administration's obsession with the eradication of multiple claims to land (which, it was assumed, discouraged investment and social progress) undermined the older system of water supply tanks so that these systems decayed and collapsed.

5. Pfaffenberger, p. 505

6. Ingold, T., "Introduction" in K.R. Gibson and T. Ingold (eds), *Tools, Language and Cognition in Human Evolution,* (Cambridge, 1993).

7. Another difficulty with the definifion of sociotechnical system as it stands is that it is predicated, unnecessarily in my opinion, on the notion of material culture.

8. Mauss defined techniques, typically succinctly, as "acts combined to acheive a known goal."

9. The collectives were established in the fifties, although there had been an unsuccessful attempt to collectivize pastoralism in the late 1920s.

10. For declining real wages see World Bank Report No. 13612-MOG. "Mongolia Country Economic Memorandum: Priorities in Macroeconomic Management." Country Operations Division, China and Mongolia Department, East Asia and Pacific Regional Office. October 31, 1994, p. iii.

11. World Bank, p. 35

12. Robinson, B., "Mongolia in transition: a role for distance learning?" *Open Learning*, November 1995, pp. 3-15.

13. The general situation was very similar in Ikh Tamir *sum*, Arkhangai *aimag* (province), Sumber *sum*, Gowi-Sümber *aimag*, and Dalanjargalan *sum*, Dornogowi *aimag*. The general conditions were better in Töw aimag—the district in which the capital Ulaanbaatar is located.

14. These brigades—*brigad*—have now been officially renamed bag—the pre-revolutionary name for the subdivisions of a *sum.*

15. A study of the history of Mongolia shows, by way of contrast, the antiquity of a steppe aristocracy ruling bounded domains of persons, territory, and livestock. (These forms are at least 800 years old, and probably more than 2,000.)

16. Lamyn Gegeen was the title of the reincarnate high lamas (*khutagt*) who was the head of the monastery that also bore this name. Brown and Onon's map of the Bogd Khaan period (1976: 880) names this as the banner of the subjects of Erdene Bandid Khutagt. Their map for 1925 gives the new (secular) name of the district as Bayanzürkh Uulyn Khoshuu. Today the territory of the hoshuu is included in six sums of Bayankhongor aimag: Bayangowi, Bayanlig, Bogd, Jinst, Ölziit, and Erdenetsogt.

17. Simukov ("Materialy po kochevomu bytu naseleniia MNW ['Materials concerning the nomadic life of the population of Mongolia'], in *Sovremennaia Mongoliia,* [Contemporary Mongolia] No. 2 (15) (1936), p. 49) notes that at its height the monastery owned more than 10,000 camels, as well as large numbers of other species of livestock.

18. Simukov, p. 50 and Bawden, C.R., *The Modern History of Mongolia*, (London, 1968), p. 90. Where there was any choice rich pastoral families and their dependents generally moved further in their annual migrations than the poorer households. See Simukov 1936:53 and Hell, C. and Quéré, P., "Le system d'élevage de la banniere Ujumchin de l'Ouest, Mongolie interieure, Chine," *Études Mongoles et Siberiennes*, vol. 24 (1993), pp. 237-90.

19. There is no reason to suppose that the elites simply took-over pre-existing pastoral systems that were somehow established in an earlier and somehow more "egalitarian" era. There is ample evidence as to the control exercised by the emperor and

his lordly officials over all aspects of steppe life as early as the thirteenth century. John of Plano Carpini noted in his eyewitness account, "all things are in the hands of the emperor ... The chiefs have like dominion over their men in all matters, for all Tartars are divided into groups under chiefs ... not a man of them is free ... in short, whatever the emperor and the chiefs desire, and however much they desire, they receive from their subjects' property." Dawson, C., *The Mongol Mission,* New York, 1955, p. 28. William of Rubruck, another observant Franciscan who travelled to the Mongolian capital in the 1250s noted the way in which Mongol lords had specified areas of territory: "Every captain, according to whether he has more or fewer men under him, knows the limit of his pasturage and where to feed his flocks in winter, summer, spring and autumn," Dawson, p. 94

20. Simukov, p. 54.

21. See State Statistical Office of the MPR, 1981. *National Economy MPR for 60 years 1921-81* (Ulaanbaatar, State Publishing House), p. 46.

22. That is, western economic development was the result of an economic-technological complex that is part of a social and cultural structure that can be termed "modern." To develop a society's economy was not simply a question of introducing some new items of technology, but required the emergence of a whole range of appropriate social and cultural institutions so as to support the necessary techno-economic complex.

23. A cruxial aspect of such systems that Pfaffenburger mentions but does not explore is the importance of hierarchy and power relations.

24. Pfaffenburger, p. 502.

The Eight-hundredth Anniversary of Chinggis Khan: The Revival and Suppression of Mongolian National Consciousness

J. Boldbaatar

Mongolia experienced a particularly difficult period during the late 1950s and early 1960s, as an atmosphere of unpredictable self-criticism appeared following Stalin's death. Various views were aired on how to eliminate the ill affects of Stalin's and Choibalsang's so-called cult of personality, how to democratize Mongolian society, and how to further the economic development of the country.[1] During this era there was a revival of Mongolian national consciousness. Major Mongolian leaders, including Prime Minister Yu. Tsedenbal, were worried by this unexpected revival, because it threatened to grow into a national movement. The government's concern was best shown by the renunciation of the ideas and decisions of the fourth Mongolian People's Revolutionary Party Central Committee Plenary Meeting (1956), which had suggested developing democracy and encouraging creative activities among the populace.[2]

The Mongolian government thereafter sought ways to suppress the national movement toward pluralism. For example, Tsedenbal first invited scholars and intellectuals from city, state, and public organizations, as well as from the universities and research institutions, to share their ideas on the MPR's future development. After labelling their views as "intellectual confusion,"[3] however, the MPRP CC Politburo condemned these recommendations as "views incompatible with our Party policy," a decision that was then later "praised" at the fifth Party Central Committee plenary meeting.[4] As a result, the thirteenth MPRP Congress also announced that these views were incompatible with Marxism-Leninism and proletarian internationalism and condemned them as a "revisionist ideology" aimed at undermining the party's long-time policies.[5]

Although the national consciousness movement suffered a severe setback, especially when the MPRP CC passed a resolution blaming several well-known scholars—including writers and artists—for their "non-class" approach to Mongolian nationalism, it was revived in 1962 when the question arose of how to celebrate the eight-hundredth anniversary of Chinggis Khan. Using Chinggis as their symbol, Mongolian intellectuals and artists sought to reawaken a sense of national consciousness among the Mongolian people.

The Conception of the Chinggis Anniversary

With the approach of the eight-hundredth Chinggis anniversary, Mongolian scholars and intellectuals began to debate how to celebrate the great khan's anniversary. It was unclear whether the government would agree to a public celebration, since that smacked of pan-Mongol nationalism, but during the summer of 1961, J. Tsedenjaw, Head of the MPRP CC Ideological Department, informed the historian, Sh. Natsagdorj, that a public celebration of the khan's anniversary had been approved. It then became possible for this question to be openly discussed among historians, journalists, and linguists.

In December, 1961, the eight-hundredth anniversary was discussed at a meeting of the Learned Council of the Institute of History, the Academy of Science. Several speakers noted that the celebration was both of historical and political importance, since it would promote proper appreciation of the Mongols' contribution to world history. Thus, the Council of the Institute of History passed a resolution to mark the anniversary during August 1962, drafted a plan, and handed it to President of the Academy of Sciences, B. Shirendew.

On January 8, 1962, D. Tsedew, the Director of the History Institute, wrote to Tsedenjaw, the then Head of Party CC Department, requesting a rapid resolution on the celebration of the Chinggis anniversary. The MPRP CC Ideological Department nominated B. Liguu and Tsedew to draft a Politburo resolution, which they soon did. After this draft resolution was issued, Tsedenjaw proposed an amendment to the resolution by attaching the MPRP CC Politburo's decision from October 27, 1949, entitled "The Teaching Situation of MPR History and Literature in Schools," which clarified that Chinggis was a feudal leader, and so not an appropriate role model for the MPR. Tsedew argued against this amendment, and at a February 8, 1962 Politburo meeting the following exchange occurred:[6]

Yu. Tsendenbal:	The erection of a Chinggis monument in Ulaanbaatar should be eliminated.
L. Tsend:	It is advisable to include into the agenda the reason for celebrating the Chinggis' anniversary, by explaining state policy at that time, his wars, and other questions.
D. Tömör-Ochir:	The Academy people think that it is best to show equally both the good and bad sides of Chinggis.
Yu. Tsendenbal:	They should be included.
N. Jagwaral:	There was an idea to define the party's view about Chinggis. During the meeting D. Tömör-Ochir read us the October 27, 1949 resolution of the Politburo.
Yu. Tsendenbal:	We should note the party position when passing a resolution on the eight-hundredth anniversary. But we should also say that the 1949 resolution was faulty.

B. Liguu: We should pass the recently proposed resolution. It would be better to give our assessment after exchanging views with scholars.

N. Jagwaral: The present resolution contradicts the 1949 resolution.

D. Tömör-Ochir: It should be mentioned that Chinggis was a founder of the Mongolian unified state who fought to overcome the disjointed feudal situation.

Yu. Tsendenbal: I think the ideological department should be assigned to make appropriate amendments to the previous resolution.

In this manner the MPRP CC Politburo approved the resolution entitled "On Celebrating the Eight-hundredth Anniversary of Chinggis." This resolution included provisions on the date of the anniversary—June 10, 1962—and on the erection of a monument in Chinggis's birthplace.

The ideological department was also requested to submit to the Politburo its views on amendments to the MPRP CC PB resolution No. 56/104 from October 27, 1949 on how to teach the history of Chinggis in schools. The anniversary program adopted at this meeting included the organization of a scientific conference, the creation of a monument in Delüün Boldog palace, the issue of a special series of "Chinggis Khan" postal stamps, and the printing of books and articles, etc.[7]

The actual celebration, however, clearly depended on prior approval from the Soviet Union and, to a lesser degree, the agreement of the People's Republic of China. This was because both countries had formerly been invaded and dominated during the thirteenth century by the Mongols under Chinggis Khan; in Russian history this period was often referred to as the "Mongol yoke," while in China it was called the Yuan dynasty.

Tsedew, the director of the Institute of History, contacted his counterpart in Moscow's Institute of Oriental Studies, S.D. Dylykov, to inquire whether the USSR was planning to celebrate the Chinggis anniversary. Soon afterward, the academician Sh. Bira was sent to Moscow to study the situation. He discovered that most Soviet scholars, including the Academician L.M. Maiskii, Professor N. Ya. Merpert, V.T. Pashuto, and L.V. Cherepin, were against celebrating the Chinggis anniversary, and considered Chinggis simply as a conqueror and oppressor. Only L. Gumilev came out in support of the anniversary, but his views were generally suppressed.[8]

Ch. Dalai, the secretary of the Institute of History, traveled to China to assess their views. He discovered two prevalent opinions: 1) Chinggis and his successors were responsible for oppressing Asian people;[9] and 2) the period of Mongol rule in China had hindered progress within Chinese society.[10] Still, other opinions suggested that Chinggis had helped break down national boundaries, and by creating an enormous international empire, had played a positive role in Chinese history.

The government of the PRC quickly authorized a celebration of the Chinggis anniversary. It had a political goal, however, and this goal was discussed during February-April 1962 in China's principal historical journal "Lishi yanjiu." In one article, Shao Xunzheng, for example, argued that celebrating the Chinggis anniversary reemphasized China's and the MPR's historical relationship, and in so doing reaffirmed that the territory of Mongolia was "an inseparable part of China."

Although the PRC's interpretation of the Chinggis anniversary no doubt caused great concern among Soviet and MPR officials, refusing to celebrate the Chinggis anniversary in the MPR—while the PRC supported such celebrations in Inner Mongolia—was now out of the question. Therefore, planning moved forward and an Organizing Committee was soon formed to implement the resolutions of the MPRP's Central Committee.

Planning and Preparation for the Chinggis Anniversary

The Organizing Committee convened its first meeting on March 28, 1962, and determined that the Ministry of Culture should make a documentary about Chinggis's life, and that copies should be distributed internationally with subtitles in Russian, Chinese, English, and French.[11] The next day, it was decided that a commemorative stamp should be issued.[12] Finally, after an exhaustive study by Mongolian historians and astrologers at the Gandan monastery, who had collected documents in Mongolian, Chinese, and Tibetan, it was determined that Chinggis was really born on May 31, 1162, and the Politburo agreed that the formal celebration should be changed to May 31, 1962.[13]

The dating controversy was taken so seriously that both Tsedew and Dalai were upbraided for allowing the Institute of History to issue the wrong date. In fact, May 31 was an important anniversary in its own right, since it was on this day in 1924 that the USSR and China had formally opened diplomatic relations by agreeing that Mongolia might retain its autonomy, even though officially Outer Mongolia remained a part of China. Although it is difficult to know for sure, perhaps the MPR sought to remind Moscow and Beijing that Chinggis had already achieved Mongolian independence centuries before the Sino-Soviet treaty.

Once the date for the celebration was set, it was then necessary to determine what political spin the events would promote. This responsibility was initially given to the Academician Natsagdorj, who wrote a draft speech entitled "Chinggis: The Founder of the Mongolian National State." When the first draft was discussed it was decided to emphasize mainly the progressive characteristics of Chinggis, and simultaneously deemphasize his vicious personal nature. Later, additional changes were made to include more information about the Mongolian people who lived at the time of Chinggis's rule.

The final draft of this important document was discussed on May 22, 1962, just a week before the celebration. Most of the Politburo and government members, including L. Tsend, Ts. Dügersüren, Tsedenjaw, and Tömör-Ochir, agreed that the tribute should be published, but Tsedenbal—perhaps concerned about possible Soviet or Chinese criticisms—warned: "No doubt Chinggis was a great political figure of Mongolia, a capable leader and a founder of the Mongolian Unified State, but we shouldn't forget about his vicious activities. We should not forget that he caused hardships for people and destroyed human civilization. You should pay special attention to this in the article."[14]

As late as May 29, 1962, the Politburo was still fine-tuning the Chinggis tribute in an effort to temper anything that might embarrass or upset Russia or China. Thereafter, on the morning of May 31, just one hour before the speech was to be broadcast, the Soviet embassy passed on last minute changes that had just been received by radio from Maiskii in Moscow. According to Natsagdorj's account: "I made notes on the phone from Yondon [Tsendebal's secretary], including some ideas in my article although most of it was similar to mine."[15]

The tribute was finally ready. When it was published in the newspaper *Ünen* it bore the title "Chinggis Khan: Founder of the Mongolian Unified State." The title alone proclaimed to the USSR and China that Mongolia's independence dated back some eight hundred years. More importantly, in addition to timing the celebration exactly on May 31, 1962—the thirty-eighth anniversary of the Sino-Soviet Treaty—the final section of the tribute pointedly ignored this treaty by referring instead to the Mongolian revolution of 1921: "Forty years have passed since the establishment of a new socialist Mongolia, [which] owes its principles of peace, friendship, and justice to the people's revolution instead of to the feudal state first founded by Chinggis. The Mongolian people are strengthening and developing unbreakable friendship and unity with the brotherly socialist countries with the same ideology and the same goals [based] on principles of Marxism-Leninism and proletarian internationalism. They are fully determined to build socialism and communism in their Motherland."[16]

The Scientific Conference

A second major issue during the anniversary celebration was where to hold the scientific conference honoring Chinggis. Three possible plans were discussed. The first was to hold the conference in the enormous hall of the Great Khural [Parliament], an act that implied government sponsorship of the event. The second proposal was to hold it in the public library in Ulaanbaatar, which implied a grass-roots campaign to honor Chinggis. The final proposal, and the one that was eventually carried out, was to hold the conference in the public library, but to have the Academy of Science be the official sponsor of the conference.

Shirendew, the President of the Academy of Sciences, formally opened the conference and his speech discussed how it was the responsibility of the conference participants to determine the true historical role of Chinggis. Natsagdorj, the director of the History Institute, then presented his tribute, in which he described Chinggis as wise, daring, an excellent organizer and leader, and an impressive military commander. However, Natsagdorj made it clear that even though the history of Chinggis was linked forever in the minds of Mongols with Mongolian independence, Chinggis was a feudal lord whose primary support came from the noble class; therefore, Chinggis should not be considered a true national hero.[17]

Even though the official line at the conference was that Chinggis supported Mongolian independence without necessarily supporting pan-Mongol nationalism, this distinction became somewhat blurred during the rest of the conference. For example, when Bira, a history Ph.D., presented a paper entitled the "Great Law of Chinggis," he made it clear that not only did this legal code include many different laws, but that these laws were compiled from a great number of sources: "[The] thirteenth century Mongolian unified state was a well-organized, civilized feudal state, with strong laws not only [from] Mongolian tribes."[18]

Later, Dalai, a senior researcher at the Institute of History, discussed how the historiography of the Mongol state under Chinggis encompassed a vast range of literature, including books written in Mongolian, Chinese, Arabic, and Persian.[19] Academician Ts. Damdinsüren, in his speech on historical accounts of Chinggis, criticized several Russian historians for their generally negative accounts of Chinggis; in particular, he questioned one Russian historian's view that Chinggis was unclean, rode poor quality horses, and had married an ugly wife![20] Meanwhile, N. Ishjamts, who later became an Academician, criticized China's claim that when Chinggis wanted to live longer, he turned to a Chinese doctor for help. Instead, Ishjamts said that this was merely a ploy to help extend Mongol rule over China: "When Chinggis invited the Chinese alchemist, the Daoist Changchun, [it was] not aimed at extending his life, [but was] only aimed at using his political authority and knowledge of all of China and to draw him to his side."[21]

Finally, the well-known historian and writer H. Perlee presented a paper on the importance of folk tales in studying the Chinggis legend. Since the conference professed to be a scientific meeting, even discussing folk tales smacked of Mongol nationalism. Perlee cautioned that historians needed to be careful when using folk tales, but if what the tales reported corresponded to actual traditions and beliefs then they could be an important source of historical information.[22]

Soon after the conference was over, it was attacked by various groups as supporting Mongolian nationalism. One of the first criticisms came from the Soviet Embassy, which accused Natsagdorj of having said that Mongolia had been admitted to the U.N. not because of Soviet support, but because of Chinggis; Natsagdorj later defended himself by explaining that his speech never said this, but merely stated that once Mongolia was in the U.N. many countries' representatives knew that Mongolia's independence could be traced back to Chinggis. Other criticisms were leveled at Damdinsüren, because he had referred to specific Russian historians and to their biased descriptions of Chinggis. Perhaps the best proof that the MPR government considered the scientific conference to be subversive was that publication of the conference materials was forbidden.

The Chinggis Monument

Soon after planning for the Chinggis anniversary was undertaken, a team of three specialists—the historian D. Gongor, the sculptor L. Makhbal, and the architect W. Awirmed—were sent to Dadal Sum in Khentii province to determine where to build a monument to Chinggis. By this time, the Institute of History had already determined that Chinggis's birthplace was close to the junction of the Onon and Baljy rivers, close to Delüün Boldog, at east longitude 111° and northern latitude 49°. This three-man team's main job was to determine exactly where the monument should be built.

After investigating the area, this team selected a hillside just 2 kilometers from the center of Dadal Sum and only 211.20 meters from the legendary "Chinggis's heart" which was close to the middle of three lakes. The team listed several reasons for chosing this location, including the nearness to a conveniently placed guest house, the natural beauty of the local scenery, and the correspondence of this location to the setting in which local folk tales said Chinggis was born.

On April 9, 1962, the local party committee in Dadal Sum discussed the plans for a monument and passed a resolution entitled "Concerning the Place of Erection of the Chinggis Monument." In this resolution, the local party members noted: "From ancient times, local people have talked about how Chinggis's birth place was near the middle lake of the three lakes in front of Jantsonhoploo mountain. According to local legend and the advice of researchers from the Academy of Science, party members decided to erect the Chinggis monument on the north side of the middle lake and south of the central square of the rest house."[23]

The sculptor Makhbal began the task of erecting the monument. It was not completed by May 31. Instead, it was unveiled at 10:00 a.m. on July 3, 1962. Hundreds of tourists and local people had gathered for the unveiling. Adiya, head of the administration in Khentii province gave the keynote speech, stating that because of Chinggis's abilities as a statesman, commander, and organizer, the various Mongol tribes united under his leadership into the independent Mongolian Unified State. As a result, he said, Chinggis held an "important role in the development of Mongol society and the Mongol nation." After the ribbon was cut, and the monument was unveiled, a plaque in the old Mongolian script on the front was seen to read: "Let my body be tired, but my state never be exterminated." On the other side, the monument proudly proclaimed: "Erected on the Eight-hundredth Anniversary of Chinggis Khan."[24]

The Chinggis monument was the first public acknowledgment of the role Chinggis had played in creating the Mongol state. Not only did it express the Mongols' pride in their long history of nationhood and national independence, but it quickly became a symbol for the revival of Mongolian national consciousness. Later, after the Chinggis anniversary had been condemned, Tsedenbal ordered the monument to be torn down. But the local administrator—Adiya—prevaricated, claiming that destroying the monument might also damage the nearby guest house. As a result, the monument remained unscathed.

The Aftermath of the Chinggis Anniversary

The celebration of the eight-hundredth Chinggis anniversary was a very important event for developing a greater historical understanding of Chinggis and his times. It also contributed greatly to the growing sense among the Mongol people of their own national consciousness, as well as contributing to calls for a pan-Mongol reunification with other Mongols in the Soviet Union and China. This nationalist movement caused great concern in the MPR Politburo, however, since Mongolian nationalism was clearly in conflict with the chief principles of proletarian internationalism, which were challenged by heightening East-West tensions over Southeast Asia, Berlin, and Cuba. As a result, by August 1962, the tide had turned against the Chinggis supporters, and the MPR government began to take firm steps to forestall the nationalist movement.

On August 2, 1962, the MPRP CC Politburo discussed the special Chinggis stamps that had been printed to celebrate the anniversary. Some 25,000 stamps had been printed at a cost of 1,100,000 tögrögs. To avoid accusations from their socialist brethren, it was decided not to distribute the stamps further; stamps that had already been sent to capitalist countries, however, were allowed to remain there to be sold.[25] Tömör-Ochir was blamed for this debacle, and on September 10, 1962, a special MPRP CC Plenary meeting was convened to discuss his responsibility for the nationalist movement.

According to a letter sent out to party members after this plenum, Tömör-Ochir was accused of being a "vanguard" of the nationalist movement. His specific crimes included attempting to erect a Chinggis monument in Ulaanbaatar, wanting to have the conference in the Great Khural's main hall, inviting the Politburo to attend the celebration, and trying to overturn earlier Politburo resolutions, such as the 1949 resolution on how to teach Chinggis history in schools. All of these actions showed that Tömör-Ochir supported "nationalist" ideologies in opposition to the "internationalist" philosophy of the party.[26]

Other culprits were also identified, as the Politburo called in the other major organizers of the Chinggis anniversary to make self-criticisms of their actions. These included Tsedenjaw, the head of the MPRP CC Ideological Department, researchers like Tsedew and Dalai, and the Academician Natsagdorj. Finally, even the speakers at the Chinggis conference, such as Academician Damdinsüren, were questioned with regard to their nationalist sentiments.

The anti-nationalist repression instigated by the MPR sent a clear signal that the era of Mongolian national consciousness was over. This change closely corresponded to the Soviet Union's deepening problems on the international scene, most importantly the Cuban missile crisis in October 1962, and the ever-deepening tensions with China following the Sino-Soviet split. Clearly, the Soviet government felt threatened by the possibility that the Mongolian nationalist movement might also accelerate out of the MPR government's control. In the end, therefore, the energy and effort that were put into the eight-hundredth Chinggis anniversary were squandered.

The Mongolian Nationalist Movement

Although the immediate impact of the Chinggis anniversary was diminished, the Mongolian nationalist movement continued to be a factor of Mongolian life. In 1963, for example, the fifth MPRP CC condemned the CC's second secretary, Tsend, for attempting to apply wrong-headed lessons of the USSR's anti-cult of personality movement in Mongolia. Under the leadership of Tsendenbal, many important Politburo members were pushed out of power, including Tömör-Ochir, the former head of the party, and Tsend, the former second secretary. Tsendenbal clearly used the struggle between nationalism and internationalism to increase his own power.

By the mid-1960s Tsendenbal had overpowered his opposition and put himself firmly in charge of the MPR government. All thoughts of revering the Mongols' unique past ended, and even memories of the Chinggis anniversary began to fade. In the end, however, when the Mongolian government did finally fall, it turned out that the Chinggis monument had in fact outlived its opposition. Even though the nationalist movement in the early 1960s was crushed in infancy, it undoubtedly played a crucial role in keeping Mongolian nationalism alive, so that it could express itself yet again in the tumultuous events surrounding the Mongolian nationalist revival some thirty years later.

Notes

1. Choibalsang was one of the leaders of the Mongolian Democratic Revolution in 1921. He later led the MPR's Ministry of Internal Affairs during the Stalinist political purges of the 1930s. Later, he was Prime Minister from 1939-52, and was called by the Mongol people the "Mass Leader."

2. Until 1990, the MPR only had one governing party. At the 4th plenum of the MPRP CC (1956), resolutions were passed supporting the USSR CP's 20th congress and calling for greater democracy and criticism of the government.

3. The Central Archives of the MPRP (CAP), F-4, D. 23, HM-21A.

4. *Mongol Ardyn khuwisgalt namyn tüükhend kholbogdokh barimt bichgüüd*, Vol. 2, (Ulaanbaatar 1967), p. 404.

5. *Mongol Ardyn khuwisgalt namyn XIII ikh khurlyn material*, (Ulaanbaatar, 1958), p. 104.

6. CAP. Fond of inside work/sorten FIW/HN-7-149, pp. 69-70.

7. CAP. f-4, d-26, hn-4.

8. I.M. Maiskii "Chinggis Khan" *Voprosy istorii*, 1962 (5), pp. 75-85; N.Y. Merpert, V.T. Pashuto, L.V. Cherepin, "Chinggis Khan and His Legacy," *History of the USSR*, 1962 (5), pp. 92-119; R.V. Viyatkin, S.L. Tihvinskii, "Some Questions of Science and History in the CPR," *Questions of History*, 1963 (10), pp. 3-20.

9. *Renminribao*, August 10, 1961; *Guangming ribao*, January 21, 1962.

10. Yu Yan, *Story of Chingis Khan*, (Shanghai, 1956), pp. 85-97.

11. CAP, f-4, d-26, hn-4.

12. CAP. FIW. t-2. hn-7-156, p. 149.

13. CAP. f-4, d-26, hn-5.

14. CAP. FIW. t-2. t-D, h-1, hn4-24.
15. Ibid.
16. *Ünen*, May 31, 1962.
17. CAP. FIW. t-D, h-1, hn-4-9.
18. Ibid., hn-4-10.
19. Ibid., hn-4-11.
20. Ibid., hn-4-15.
21. Ibid., hn-4-12.
22. Ibid., hn-4-16.
23. Ibid., hn-4-19.
24. Ibid., hn-4-22.
25. Ibid., hn-7-68. p. 204.
26. CAP. 4. hn-A1-15.

Nationalism, Elites, and Mongolia's Rapid Transformation

Tom Ginsburg

In 1990, nearly seven decades after Sükhebaatur's revolution re-established an independent Mongol state, modern Mongolia experienced its second great transformation with the end of the one-party system and the launching of rapid political and economic liberalization. As in 1921, the forces mandating drastic change originated far from Ulaanbaatar, and followed the collapse of an empire. Mongolia's first transformation led to communism, the second away from it; but both moves were led by a small group of leaders who sought to ensure national security. The shared, if not always articulated, understanding of Mongolia's delicate geopolitical situation has constrained domestic politics, but also has enabled a peaceful and rapid transition from communism.

The immediate cause of the second transformation was the collapse of communist regimes in Eastern Europe, paralleling the collapse of the Manchu Empire in 1911.[1] Under Soviet leader Mikhail Gorbachev's influence, Mongolia's leaders had experimented with "restructuring" and "openness" in the late 1980s, but continued to maintain a one-party framework until protests first began in Ulaanbaatar in December of 1989. Since then, Mongolians have experienced radical change in both foreign and domestic policies. Long isolated in world affairs, Mongolian leadership has sought broad contacts with the outside world beyond the two immediate neighbors, China and Russia, who have dictated so much of Mongolia's history.

Domestically, political and economic liberalization have proceeded faster and more coherently than in other countries in the region. Several free and fair elections have been held and a new, liberal democratic constitution ratified. The government, initially under the formerly communist Mongolian People's Revolutionary Party (MPRP) and later under the new democratic parties, has initiated privatization, financial reform, and trade liberalization programs that have led to positive economic growth since 1996. There have been severe social consequences from these rapid reforms, but they have not led any coalition of elites to oppose the basic reforms.

Several questions remain outstanding about this second transformation. If the changes were revolutionary, why were they led by the MPRP? Why did all elites turn so eagerly to the West when Soviet aid dried up? After years of double-digit growth, China would seem to have been a natural partner for development aid, trade, and regime support for the MPRP once the Russian support disappeared. But such an option was not apparently considered by the leadership. Another outstanding question concerns why the transition went so smoothly compared with other post-communist countries. This was despite the fact that the economic shock caused by the Soviet pullout was among the most severe ever recorded.[2]

The rapid economic reforms themselves had severe social consequences, but the basic consensus on reform has remained intact. How are we to understand this smooth transition?

This essay seeks to address these larger issues by focusing on the background and worldview of Mongolia's leadership in the transition period. A close look at the leadership highlights continuities with the pre-1990 period. While policy change after 1990 was real and profound, the seeds of the post-1990 reforms lie in the demographic and social changes of the last decades of the Soviet period, combined with the society's deep cultural aversion to China. The late Soviet period saw the creation and expansion of new classes with a stake in the modernization of Mongol society. At the forefront were perhaps a few hundred top cadres and urban intellectuals who shared a cosmopolitan orientation and common formative experiences in the USSR. These technocrats and intellectuals have emerged as the key leaders today.

While there were differences among these leaders regarding the pace of domestic reforms, there was a fundamental consensus on foreign affairs that produced the "open door" policy while constraining domestic politics. The first part of this essay describes the motives behind this consensus, focusing particularly on the central position of China in modern Mongolian nationalism. Next, the essay examines the background and worldview of the top political leaders since 1990.

The picture that emerges is one of complex interaction of domestic and international forces. International forces were perhaps the immediate cause of reform, but the direction of change was dictated by the interaction of these forces with long-held cultural beliefs and motivations. The new leaders sought to transform the country's international orientation, but as children of the communist period their own mindset was inevitably a product of their formative experiences in Russia. Even as the political leadership undergoes continuing generational change, therefore, the geopolitical continuities shape the regime-level choices of Mongolia today.

Mongolia's Cosmopolitan Nationalism

The driving force motivating Mongolia's elites today is the same that pushed Sükhebaatur and his colleagues: the quest for national survival in a changing international environment. This survival is a remarkable achievement when compared with the fates of many neighboring cultures, so that in 1990 Bawden could write "Mongolia is today the one example of an independent, Inner Asian culture . . . systematically adapting itself to the demands of modern international modes of life."[3] Like other small states at the periphery of large empires, Mongolia's survival has depended on giving large powers a stake in its continuing independence. In this regard, Mongolia was fortunate in that its own nationalist ambitions after 1921 overlapped with the imperial interests of the USSR.

The affinity between nationalist goals and internationalist ideology produced a configuration of ideas and rhetoric among the elite that will be referred to here as cosmopolitan nationalism. The overarching goals of the Mongolian leadership are two: continued national independence and modernization of society. Elites are aware of the need for pragmatism in pursuing these goals. Expressions of popular, more conventionally nationalist goals such as pan-Mongolism are constrained by what external actors will tolerate. In the Soviet period, for example, Mongolian nationalism was attenuated in two ways: first, because the USSR imposed constraints on any independent policy, and second, because pragmatism forced Ulaanbaatar to distance itself from the large numbers of Mongols still living in China and Russia.

In the Mongolian People's Republic, cosmopolitan nationalism was exclusively northward-oriented. Despite good relations with China in the 1950s and early 1960s, lingering ambivalence about the Chinese leadership's claims toward Mongolia and the sheer volume of contacts with the USSR ensured that Russia remained central. Indeed, Russia has always been at the center of Mongol nationalism in its modern form. Lattimore's observation provides insight into the implications of this for elites: "the problem has always been not whether to make Russia the most important country in foreign relations, but how to deal with the fact that Russia is the most important country in foreign relations . . . a concomitant phenomenon is the tendency for power in Mongolia to gravitate into the hands of those Mongols who can get on best with the Russia of the time, whatever the time may be."[4]

The reason for the preoccupation with Russia lies in the contrasting character of Mongol-Russian and Sino-Mongol relations. Whereas Soviet policy, like that of the tsars, focused on Mongolia's utility as a buffer state, the southern problem for the Mongols was entirely different. From China came the more serious threats of displacement, colonization, and cultural absorption. Again, Lattimore states the problem clearly: "[T]he most pressing danger was not the 'colonial' control of their country by a few foreigners representing a foreign government, but actual colonizing of the best part of their land by Chinese settlers; not subjection, but displacement, not the fate of India, but the fate of the American Indian."[5]

This old problem drives and constrains Mongolian nationalism today as it did in the 1920s and 1930s. Indeed the centrality of China goes back even further, to the *Secret History* itself.[6] The deep cultural drive to distinguish themselves from the Chinese ensures that Mongolian nationalism is always perfectly consistent with internationalism, as long as internationalism offers hope of a security guarantee vis-a-vis China. Soviet internationalism offered them precisely that.

Lattimore characterized Mongolian reliance on Russia as a deal to ensure national independence in his hypothetical formulation: "Our only defense [against China and Japan] is the revolutionary Russians. We must rely on them while we gain time to train up a new generation of Mongols to run things in a new way. . . The Russians too must feel they are getting something out of it. That is going to mean not only that they will take the lead and we shall have to go along as subordinates in international policy. . . . It is also going to mean that we have to accept their schedule of priorities when it comes to planning their economic development, our economic development, and the relationship between the two."[7]

This captures nicely the Mongolian rationale for the Soviet alliance, and the pragmatism that sublimated domestic initiative to national security concerns. But the late 1980s witnessed a weakening of Soviet-imposed constraints on Mongolia's choices. Russia remains primary today, but Russian weakness and preoccupation with domestic reform mean that Mongolia's leaders now have some room to maneuver internationally and domestically. Their aggressive courting of Europe, the United States, and Asia reflects the search for a "third force" to guarantee national security and support modernization.[8] Cosmopolitanism continues to be the instrument of national survival in the modern Mongol worldview.

Once we understand the Leninist period as a successful nationalist response to fundamental dilemmas of security and modernization, we can understand part of the reason why Mongolia's leaders were reluctant to give up the old system in the late 1980s, and why change was so rapid once the choice was made. With one eye on China, the ruling Mongolian People's Revolutionary Party (MPRP) was slow to initiate *glasnost* and *perestroika*. In foreign policy, Mongolia resisted the warming in Sino-Soviet relations in the mid-1980s, reflecting ambivalence about any reduction in the Soviet security umbrella.[9] Domestically, Mongolia's economic reforms lagged behind even the half-hearted Russian efforts, and there was no hint of gradualist political institution-building within the one-party framework, such as occurred in Poland. Unlike in Eastern Europe there were no potential competing forces in public life after the complete destruction of the lamaist church in the 1930s.

Nonetheless, when protests broke out in Sükhbaatar Square in the wake of Eastern Europe's revolutions, the MPRP responded quickly by sacking its leadership and calling for multi-party elections. With significant advantages in resources, and building on its record as the party of national renewal, the MPRP won the first elections in 1990 handily. Nevertheless, it formed a national unity government including prominent opposition figures in important posts, under the leadership of Dashiin Byambasüren (1990-92).

This transitional government and the newly formed Baga Khural (standing legislature) initiated rapid legislative and institutional change, culminating in the ratification of a new constitution in 1992. The MPRP dominated parliamentary elections in 1992, leading to the formation of the MPRP-only government under P. Jasrai (1992-96). The opposition coalition of the National Democratic Party (MNDP) and the Social Democratic Party (SDP) then secured a victory in 1996 parliamentary elections, leading to the new government under the leadership of M. Enkhsaikhan.

The rapid institutional change since 1990, much of it occurring under the leadership of the MPRP, shows that the Party was able to read the external situation and pragmatically shed its ideology. When MPRP candidate N. Bagabandi won the presidential election in 1997, his Chief of Staff Sanjaagiin Bayar was able to say: "There are no more communists in Mongolia."[10] Despite a perception of Mongolia as one of the world's more isolated countries, Mongols have historically been able to adapt to new conditions and to embrace the world. This cosmopolitan worldview has allowed the post-1990 reforms to occur peacefully.

Mongolia's Foreign Policy Consensus

What has this international pragmatism produced since 1990? Despite several different governments under two party groupings, and vocal disputes over domestic policy, the basic consensus on the open door foreign policy has remained in place.[11] In this section, we outline the broad contours of this consensus, and argue that it is driven by the logic of Mongolia's geopolitical position and the particular character of its cosmopolitan nationalism. Post-1990 foreign policy can be seen as an extension of Mongolia's efforts to secure independence and modernization.

The basic shape of the consensus was already apparent in the very first statement of foreign policy in the new era, namely the MPRP's Basic Policy Direction adopted at the extraordinary party congress in April 1990. This statement committed the MPRP to attract foreign investment,[12] to expand relations with the West and with Asia, to implement a non-aligned, nuclear-free policy, and to prohibit the stationing of foreign troops on Mongolian soil.[13]

This has since been translated into a six-point foreign policy program: top priority is placed on maintaining good relations with Russia and China; other priorities include expanding relations with the developed capitalist countries, Asian countries, international organizations, former partners in Eastern Europe, and developing nations.[14] This rapid switch toward international openness was among the first moves of the MPRP in response to opposition demonstrations.

Indeed, the adoption of the open door policy by the party which had for seventy years been the "quintessential expression of the interests of a foreign power"[15] helped the MPRP to recapture the nationalist ground, as it could present itself as the party best able to preserve Mongolia's status as an independent nation in an era of international uncertainty. Foreign Minister Ts. Gombosüren characterized the policy as a reflection of national interest, rather than the interests of the government or the MPRP,[16] and the minimal controversy over foreign policy since 1990, as well as the continuation of the course under the post-MPRP government since 1996, suggests that he is correct.

Mongolian leaders of all parties differ very little on foreign policy. The consensus is illustrated by the platforms of various political parties for the 1992 parliamentary elections.[17] Several parties did not mention foreign policy issues at all. The two major contenders, the MPRP and the "Coalition" of the Democratic Party, the Party of National Progress and United Party (the three parties who later merged into the Mongolian National Democratic Party), had nearly identical statements.[18]

Newspaper interviews with three major Party leaders in 1993 likewise exhibited a similar consensus.[19] When asked which country ought to receive priority attention, all agreed that Russia and China together were the primary concern. This reflects a pragmatic understanding of the limits of Western interests in Mongolia, as explained by MP and Mongolian National Democratic Party leader D. Ganbold: "(A)lthough we talk about independence and sovereignty, we must face reality. In certain cases, one will have to decide whom to follow and what political choice to make. . . . Let us say that suddenly Mongolia ceases to exist. This will not have the slightest impact on the USA, Germany or any other (non-neighboring) country."[20] Similarly B. Batbayar of the Social Democrats said that "Mongolia, by virtue of its geographical location, will naturally give priority to Russia and China over any other country."[21]

While the elites share pragmatic views about foreign policy, not all Mongolians are willing to sublimate more extreme nationalistic rhetoric. Democratization has complicated matters for Mongolian leaders by allowing the airing of sensitive pan-Mongolist ideas likely to irk the governments of Russia and China, which have large Mongolian minority populations. For example, students calling themselves the Prince Demchugdongrub Association, dedicated to the "spiritual unification of Mongolians," have protested the treatment of Inner Mongolians in China and Buriats in Russia by staging demonstrations at the Russian and Chinese embassies.[22]

This group obviously puts policymakers in a difficult position, especially with regard to China; the leadership must assuage Chinese fears of the spillover of Mongolian nationalism into Inner Mongolia, without abridging the new rights of free association and speech. For the most part, the government has walked this line well. China for its part has refused to allow Inner Mongolians to attend Mongolian cultural meetings in Ulaanbaatar.[23]

What is significant for our purposes is that opposition politicians have not tried to exploit these issues with pan-Mongolist rhetoric. D. Ganbold, for example, noted that independence does not mean "the restoration of statehood which existed under Chinggis Khan, the ideas of pan-Mongolism, and disruption of relations with the former partners. We simply cannot resort from one extreme to the other."[24] Other politicians, including President Ochirbat and former Prime Minister Byambasüren, attended an international Congress of Mongolists in Ulaanbaatar, but none has so far advocated pan-Mongolism as a policy.

Mongolia's Foreign Policy Continuities

This is not to say there are no disagreements about foreign policy. The chief axis of disagreement has been the degree of cooperation with Russia, with some urging a restoration of closer relations and others preferring a more independent path. The most pro-Russian party in the early years was the Independence Party, a group of ardent nationalists originally called the Union of 281.[25] The stance of the Independence Party was formed in response to anti-Russian sentiment in Ulaanbaatar, when there were calls for cancellation of Mongolia's debt to Russia for "reparations" to cover Soviet-caused environmental damage.[26]

In response, the Independence Party took a more pro-Russia stance than other parties, stating that "we condemn any attack on Russia. It would be erroneous to believe that Russia was exploiting Mongolia."[27] Suspicious of China and the West, it cautioned the public to "be on guard in relation to foreign aid, because phenomena alien to Mongolia might come with such aid."[28] This party never won a parliamentary seat, however, and several elites expressed concern over the "irresponsible" rhetoric of the Union.[29]

There is some evidence of a swing back toward closer relations with Russia. Russia remains the leading source of joint ventures, and economic contacts have expanded. Cultural relations are normalizing as well: the Russian language publication *Novostii Mongolia*, published in Mongolia, stopped publication in 1991 but resumed after a three year hiatus.

Foreign Minister Gombosüren expressed disappointment over the poor period of Mongolian-Russian relations in 1992, when disputes over debt repayment and other negative matters dominated the relationship. He asserted that relations with Russia would be the number one priority for 1993.[30] In 1995, President Ochirbat claimed that Russia would continue to be the top priority in Mongolia's foreign policy.[31] And shortly after being elected President in 1997, N. Bagabandi claimed that "Mongolia has always considered and will continue to consider Russia as its most important neighbor."[32]

All leaders assert a desire for good relations with China, but notably absent are voices calling for increased reliance on China. This is true despite continuous improvement in Sino-Mongolian relations since the late 1980s. Several agreements have been signed since the Foreign Ministers met at the U.N. in 1986. Prime Minister Byambasüren traveled to China in 1992, the first visit by a Mongolian premier to China since Tsedenbal's visit in 1962. Since then, Ministerial visits have been frequent. President Yang Shangkun visited in 1991 with Ochirbat reciprocating in 1995.[33] When Li Peng visited Mongolia in 1994, a Treaty of Friendship and Cooperation was concluded.

Despite formal warming, deep cultural mistrust of China lingers among the population. The continuing wariness of China can be seen in the frequency of China-related rumors that circulate regarding the political leadership. In 1994, for example, a disgruntled intelligence officer, Col. L. Sanjaasüren, lost his job in an administrative reorganization. He responded by announcing that he had evidence of corruption on the part of then-Speaker of the State Great Khural N. Bagabandi, Deputy Chair J. Gombojaw, and opposition MPs D. Ganbold and S. Zorig.[34] He also asserted that Bagabandi and Gombojaw had "secret contacts" with Chinese citizens.[35] A parliamentary commission later rejected the charges.[36]

Later that year, the Procurator announced that assertions that Prime Minister Jasrai had "Chinese business interests" were false.[37] Another charge was that Jasrai had issued false passports to Chinese citizens. The accusations continued against the post-1996 government headed by the Democratic Union, specifically Foreign Minister S. Altangerel.[38] These rumors illustrate what insiders describe as a pervasive culture of rumor and gossip that exists in the small world of

Mongolian politics.[39] The character of the accusations themselves is revealing for its resonance with traditional Mongol fears of Chinese colonization.

Furthermore, while not endorsed or articulated by any public figures, rumors circulated in the early years of reform that the opposition-inspired reforms were designed to benefit China by allowing Chinese citizens to buy up Mongolian territory.[40] The heated controversy over the land law in large part resulted from this fear.[41] Anti-Chinese sentiment again came up during discussions of privatization.[42] Some such references are veiled, such as the assertion that private land ownership would "lead to the obliteration of the Mongol nation as foreigners would come and marry Mongolians and their children would own the land of the Mongolian parents."[43] Other references are more explicit such as when one scholar asserted that President Ochirbat was part Chinese.[44] Indeed, Mongol elites who do have Chinese blood take care to hide the fact.[45] Even a new romanization of the Mongolian language was criticized as being too close to the Chinese pinyin system.[46]

Despite its position as the embodiment of the Soviet alliance, even the MPRP has not been immune from China-related accusations. The 1992 formalization of relations between the MPRP and the CCP in 1992 was met by accusations of secret "cooperation" that prompted denials in the press by MPRP Chairman B. Dash-Yondon and Foreign Minister Gombosüren.[47] Dash-Yondon acknowledged the "gift" of 500 tons of newsprint in 1990, but denied any illegal contacts.[48]

The potency of these China-related rumors is rooted in deep cultural antipathy,[49] but not all rumors are without factual basis. In 1992, during nationalist activity in Inner Mongolia, Mongolian officials were forced to respond to allegations of fostering pan-Mongolism. They protested the appearance of a Chinese document, issued by the Inner Mongolia branch of the State Security Bureau, allegedly claiming that the MPR and other Mongol-speaking regions belonged to China.[50]

In 1993, diplomatic controversy erupted over the publication in Beijing of a volume "The Secret Story of Outer Mongolian Independence" (*Wai Menggu duli neimu*) including a 1946 map showing Mongolia as part of China.[51] China's foreign ministry responded with a statement reaffirming the official position that China has always respected Mongolian independence, and the publisher's license was revoked.[52] Nevertheless, suspicions of governmental involvement remained. Another serious incident occurred in 1995, when listening devices were discovered in the Mongolian Embassy in Beijing.[53] Mongolia responded by canceling the scheduled visit of the Minister of Construction to Beijing. China denied allegations of spying and asserted that the Mongolian government would be responsible for any negative consequences in foreign relations. Together, these incidents provide plenty of fodder to those suspicious of Chinese intentions.

Multilateralism and the Search for a "Third Force"

An articulate discussion of Mongolia's current foreign policy thinking is found in a paper by Sanjaagiin Bayar (b. 1956), one of the architects of the 1992

Constitution.[54] Bayar discusses the historic search for a "third force" to offset reliance on the two neighbors. Today, Bayar argues, Mongolia has finally found its third force, not in a single country but in the collective weight of the Western powers, the multinational banks, and Asian countries beyond China.

China is at the heart of Bayar's concern. In attempting to make a case for outside awareness of Mongolia, Bayar emphasizes geopolitics, and makes a veiled reference to China when he noted "Mongolia might seem for some overpopulated countries as a plausible *Lebensraum.*"[55] Later, Bayar addresses the fear of China more directly. Despite formal recognition of Mongolia's independence, "a number of vague statements made by Chinese leaders, and recently published history textbooks, geographical maps, and other documents treat Mongolia as part of China."[56]

Even if such fears are subjective, Bayar also notes that the fear has an "objective quality" as well. Noting that natural barriers prevent expansion to the West and East, and that Southern expansion is inhibited by populated countries, "expansion to the north, particularly to Mongolia, might seem more feasible and beneficial —even the fact that Mongolia is now in a 'power vacuum'—let alone other important factors such as its huge sparsely populated territory and vast natural resources.[57] Furthermore, even though new agreements have been signed to resolve border disputes, Bayar notes that some Mongolians fear that "the disputed territories are still regarded by the Chinese elite as Chinese land."[58]

Distrust of China runs deep in the population. Despite a decade of double-digit growth in China that would seem to render it a natural source of markets and economic cooperation, Mongolians commonly assert that China is an unattractive partner. A 1996 survey conducted by the Mongolian Academy of Sciences asked which country Mongolia should cooperate with to end its economic crisis. The single most frequent response was Russia, garnering 35.2 percent of respondents. In contrast, only 6.2 percent named China, ranking it below Germany and South Korea. The United States, central to Bayar's third force, garnered 28.4 percent, while Japan was mentioned by 25.6 percent.[59]

Official policy also reflects the distrust of China. The main national security documents issued since 1990 are the "Concept of Mongolia's Foreign Policy," and "Concept of National Security," both endorsed by the parliament in 1994. The latter identifies various threats to national security, including massive inflows of migrants from a neighboring state,[60] a sharp increase in the number of resident foreigners,[61] dissemination of false information by outsiders that may sow doubts about Mongolia independence,[62] and assimilation into other cultures as a result of policies of foreign countries and external forces.[63] All of these, and other threats, may be read as emanating from the South.

A third foreign policy document is an undated statement by the Policy Section of the Foreign Ministry, identifying Russia, China, and the United States as the priority relationships for Mongolia.[64] Comparing the language of the paragraphs discussing Russia and China shows some of the key differences in the relationships. The discussion of Russia says that "initiatives will be undertaken in order to ease the procedures concerning the reciprocal travel of citizens." There is no corresponding discussion of allowing Chinese greater access to Mongolia. Instead there are references to "universally accepted norms of international relations," a clear invocation of international law as a basis for Mongolian sovereignty.[65]

Russia has never been hesitant to exploit Mongol fears of China. In a 1991 article, Yuri Kruchkin of the Russian Embassy in Ulaanbaatar asserted that Russia was the only power capable of balancing the Chinese: "[I]t will take some time for the West to realize the threat, hidden in growing dislike by the Chinese of reforms in Mongolia and their attempts to impose economic influence over this country. Russia knows better. . . . Like Mongolia, Russia is doomed to have China as its neighbor and will act cautiously."[66]

Such rhetoric hearkens back to an earlier era, when Russians openly played the China card in Mongolia. For example, Leonid Brezhnev's statement on the signing of the 1966 Treaty of Friendship, Cooperation, and Mutual Assistance is explicitly directed at China: "As is known, China has not renounced its claims toward its northern neighbor, and this is sufficient for both the Soviet Union and Mongolia to be vigilant. . . . The basic sense of the Soviet Mongolian Treaty is that it recognizes the real possibility that the independence of a socialist country can be endangered by another socialist country."[67]

In the one-party period, anti-Chinese sentiments helped to justify the MPRP's rule domestically and the Soviet alliance internationally. These sentiments remain powerful today. Although nostalgia for the relationship with Russia exists, Mongolians are aware that, as Prime Minister Jasrai said, "there is no going back."[68] Given the recent history of domination by the Soviets, and the fear of China, Mongolia's best choice is to search for a third force. This is the logical extension of Mongolia's cosmopolitan nationalism.

Foreign Policy Constraints on Politics

This geopolitical logic has constrained domestic politics significantly. Most obviously, economic policymaking, like that of other transitioning countries, has been conducted under the watchful eye of international donors and development banks. But it is not only *policy* that has been constrained: an awareness of geopolitics has set boundaries on political conflict itself. This is not to say there is no conflict in Mongolian politics. Rather it points out the real constraints on conflict that flow from a shared desire for national independence. As one leader said in 1991, "we Mongols can fight among ourselves, but we must be careful never to give outside powers an excuse to intervene."[69]

Others echoed the spirit of this comment when they asserted there was never any real possibility of the MPRP responding violently to the 1990 demonstrations.[70] Confronted with the protests in Sükhbaatar Square, the Revolutionary Party faced an apparent choice between the Tiananmen-style crackdown and the Russian-style liberalization. The choice of the latter is completely consistent with cosmopolitan nationalism. Had Sükhbaatar Square become a Tiananmen-style bloodbath, the leadership would be inexorably casting its lot with China, a move of doubtful legitimacy domestically. The opposition was also constrained by the need to avoid violent conflict: one advocate of violent resistance to the MPRP's rule in 1989 and 1990, a former intelligence officer named S. Enkhtüwshin, left Mongolia after his view was decisively rejected by other opposition leaders.[71]

The constraints on domestic conflict were also apparent during hunger strikes in 1994.[72] Faced with a parliament almost completely controlled by the MPRP, opposition protestors took to the Square again to protest corruption, and called for the fall of the government. Several persons began a hunger strike, and they were joined by thousands of supporters. As demonstrations continued, they threatened to disrupt the scheduled visit of Li Peng to Ulaanbaatar.

Soon, the MPRP agreed to negotiate under the auspices of President P. Ochirbat, and the leaders of the three major political parties signed an agreement. The MPRP promised to introduce into parliament a law on public demonstrations and a law on media freedom during the next session.[73] This incident illustrates how the need to present a unified face to China played some role in inducing the MPRP to compromise on policy grounds.

If foreign policy has constrained domestic conflict, it has also provided access to a rich source of ideas for restructuring Mongolian society. A central example is the process of drafting the new Constitution.[74] In substance, the Constitution was a victory of modernist international transformation. The drafting committee, which included representatives from all political parties, looked at the drafts of over 100 different Constitutions in preparing the final version.

The political system is modeled partially on fifth Republic France, and includes a delicate separation of powers scheme. A thoroughly modern set of institutions are given traditional Mongol names. There is an extensive set of human rights provisions, and there was extensive and effective input from the United Nations Human Rights Center, Amnesty International, and international academics before the draft was finalized. Many of the rights included in it are drawn from the International Covenant on Civil and Political Rights.

The balance of powers scheme combines aspects of French and German tradition with a unicameral parliament. The Constitution, and political reform more generally since 1990, represent the first time Mongolian political developments preceded those in Russia, and were the most important sign of Mongolia's new latitude. It shows the elite's cosmopolitan impulses in designing the domestic reform process.

The foregoing description of the foreign policy consensus suggests that Mongolia's elite is operating within a cultural environment that forces them to look away from the South. With the Russian option foreclosed to a great extent after 1990, the logic of a cosmopolitan foreign policy was clear. In turn, this foreign policy ensured a consensus on the direction, if not always on the pace, of the domestic reform process. To understand this consensus, it is useful to examine in more detail those who participated in it and what forces shaped their worldview. The next sections examine the political leadership in greater detail.

Inclusive Leninism and the Origins of the Elite

Mongolia enjoyed an exceptionally long period of what Ken Jowitt calls the "inclusion" phase of Leninism.[75] In Jowitt's conception, the first task of Leninist parties is to transform the old social and political structure, a necessarily violent process. Once this task is accomplished the Party must consolidate its rule. Finally, its rule secure, the Party expands and integrates with society, while still maintaining its distinct charismatic identity as the vanguard. The final stage began in the USSR with the ascendance of Khrushchev after the death of Stalin, and was replicated in Mongolia during the long rule of Yumjaagiin Tsedenbal (1952-84), known as Mongolia's Khrushchev and later as Mongolia's Brezhnev.

In Jowitt's view, the inclusion phase is characterized by an expansion of the party and a revival of occupational identities and a rationalization of power relations.[76] The system introduces internal merit-based performance criteria and develops a bureaucratic structure. In the case of Mongolia, party membership expanded dramatically after 1970, outstripping population growth.[77] The economic system emphasized professional identities for the first time.

Urbanization increased rapidly as well during this period, with the urban percentage of the population rising from 21.6 percent in 1956 to 57 percent in 1989.[78] Along with a modern industrial work force and an urban bureaucratic class, socialist development created an intelligentsia.[79] These people represented the modern element of Mongolian society as it set about "bypassing capitalism" and proceeding directly from feudalism to socialism.[80]

These modern classes owed their existence directly to Soviet-funded development. As Bawden noted in 1968, "Mongolia's whole contemporary ethos is something new and originating from abroad. Ideologically, at the official level, she is a Soviet creation."[81] Paralleling the flow of material aid that created entire cities, Soviet oversight mandated the creation of a complete institutional infrastructure to parallel and serve as proxy for that of the USSR itself.

By 1978, over fifty ministries and government departments had direct links with their Soviet counterparts, and the Soviet Ministry of Finance had a permanent representative in its Mongolian counterpart.[82] Tens of thousands of Soviet workers and troops were stationed in the MPR.[83] At the high point, officially reported Soviet military and civilian workers comprised perhaps 5 percent of Mongolia's total population.[84]

Today's elites are entirely a product of this phase of Leninism. Unlike counterparts in other Asian socialist regimes, Mongolia's original revolutionary generation is long since gone. Politics now occur between members of the second and third generations born after the revolution. The oldest major figure active in current politics, Prime Minister P. Jasrai, was born in 1930.[85] While many others currently active may remember the coercive collectivization of livestock in the late 1950s, they could have no personal experience of the bloody 1930s, whose violence established the party as the sole center of public life. Instead their formative experiences were in the post-World War II phase of socialist modernization with its aid-driven programs of industrialization and urbanization. They have well-developed professional and corporate identities, a fact that has had some implications for post-1990 polities.[86] The next generation of those who will have come of age after 1990 has not yet emerged; the key to understanding the politics of the transition lies in the current transitional generation.

Education and the Orientation of the Elite

Mongolia experienced massive Russian cultural influence in the cities and formal institutions of the country, epitomized by the use of the Cyrillic alphabet.[87] Knowledge of Russian was a sign of modernity and a key to social mobility, especially after 1970.[88] Every state employee had to pass a Russian language examination.[89] The cultural integration of Mongolia and Russia became more intense as the inclusive phase progressed, so that in 1982, the People's Great Khural called for Russian language study to begin in kindergarten.[90] Children of elites were sent to Russian schools, with expatriate Russian children, and by 1989 there were 23 such schools, with an enrollment of 1,000 Mongolian children.[91] But even ordinary schools were designed on Soviet models.[92]

By all accounts, education was one of the great success stories of socialism in Mongolia, and was a top priority for the government, constituting 25 percent of government expenditures as late as 1990.[93] Gross enrollment ratios for primary schools were in the neighborhood of 98 percent, and Mongolia virtually eliminated illiteracy.[94] Data from the Ministry of Science and Education (1989) indicate that 10 percent of college-age and 5 percent of university-age persons attended those institutions, producing professionals in ever-increasing numbers.[95]

Total Mongolian enrollments in higher education increased rapidly after 1970. The *Government Statistical Yearbook* reports that in 1970, total enrollments were 8,400 students.[96] By 1980 the total was 23,200. The pre-1990 peak came in 1985 when 24,600 Mongolians enrolled in higher education programs. Of these, 6,110 or approximately 25 percent were enrolled in foreign universities, of whom the vast majority was in the Soviet Union and other CMEA countries.[97] Even at the State University, much of the instruction was in Russian because of the lack of Mongolian language technical texts.[98]

This integration into the Soviet system of higher education is key for understanding today's leadership. While Mongolian elites began to study in Russia as early as the 1920s, their numbers expanded along with gross enrollments after 1970. By the 1980s they numbered in the thousands.[99] A typical pattern was a year of language study followed by three to five years of more specialized study at a so-called *technikom* or university, although some fields such as medicine required more time.[100]

While in later years, Eastern Europe emerged as a desirable place for study in certain fields, others required going to Russia, especially fields with political implications such as security studies or international relations. Moscow was of course the most desirable location, but Leningrad and Irkutsk were also important destinations. Irkutsk was especially important given its proximity to Mongolia and its status as the educational center for much of the eastern USSR. At its peak, roughly 5,000 Mongolians studied there during the early 1980s in a number of institutions, and a consulate was established there.[101]

Beyond the regular higher education system, there were "higher party schools" in the USSR to which mid- and senior level party officials would go, as well as military training academies. Figures from the government statistics on higher education did not include such party- and military-sponsored study abroad, and we can assume that many more Mongolians had opportunities to train in Russia under these auspices. The political schools in particular offered opportunities to return to the USSR as a reward for performance and political loyalty.

What was life like for the Mongolians in Russia? Those interviewed report excitement at the prospect of going to Russia, and young Mongolians were eager to be exposed to the world through Russian lenses.[102] There was a sense in which the modern was "out there" to the North. The Mongolians quickly became integrated into Russian patterns of life, and one person interviewed explained that Mongolia and Russia were so similar that there was no experience of culture shock going from one to the other.[103] Mongolians ate Russian food, spoke Russian, and sometimes lived with Russians.[104]

The thousands of students in Russia each year were true elites. While the selection procedures for travel abroad changed several times, they typically relied on uniform national examinations administered at the end of elementary, middle, and high school levels.[105] Some fields required a specific exam for study abroad. Schools would post announcements of various programs, both in Mongolia and abroad, and students could apply to any school within their chosen field.

While there was some choice over career, students who desired a government fellowship were required to obtain an institutional sponsor. Upon returning from Russia they would return to their sponsor institutions as employees. The period in Russia was formative both in a personal sense, in fostering a cosmopolitan attitude, and in a professional sense, as individuals were functionally sorted into the careers they would remain in for the rest of their lives. They received international training for the task of national development.

Furthermore, the practice of reaching out to the countryside, and the expansion of primary education, meant that even herdsmen's children were part of the system. A herdsman's child from remote regions could progress to the State University and on to foreign study; indeed, most of Mongolia's elites came from outside Ulaanbaatar and followed this path. Thus, the functional integration into the USSR educational system served also as a mechanism of national integration within Mongolia, and a means of recruiting elites from various regions, which appears to have been an important legitimating factor in MPRP rule.[106]

Russian contacts in Mongolia and the higher education system thus fostered cosmopolitan nationalism. Russian language was the *lingua franca*, Moscow the cultural center of the universe. While later some went to Eastern Europe for specialized training, Moscow remained primary.[107] Elites both within and outside of the MPRP shared this Northward-oriented version of cosmopolitan nationalism, entailing a belief in Russia as the power best able to guarantee continued independence, and an equation of Soviet influence with modernization.

At the same time, the seeds were present for a metamorphosing of Northward oriented cosmopolitan nationalism into a more universal form. During the Soviet period, contacts with third countries outside the CMEA regime were limited by Soviet policy, but not by factors internal to Mongolia. In the idealized setting of cosmopolitan nationalism, contacts with third powers would be desirable to the extent they supplemented the two core functions of the Soviets, providing security and supporting modernization. Today students are able to travel to a wider variety of countries, but in smaller numbers.[108] Russian influence has diffused outward, but the search for the modern "out there" continues.

The Mongolian Elites

Mongolia's post-1990 transition reflects the choices of a very small group of elites, perhaps two or three hundred people, who make up the political and economic leadership of the country.[109] Available data on the political leadership are collected below (see Chart 2). The Chart includes all individuals who held cabinet positions in the Byambasüren (1990-92), Jasrai (1992-96) or Enkhsaikhan (1996-98) governments, as well as the Presidents, the Chairmen of the Supreme and Constitutional Courts, parliamentary leaders, and heads of major parties (those parties which won a parliamentary seat sometime during the period).[110]

Several things stand out about the group. Every figure on the list is male. The 1992-96 parliament had only three female members out of seventy-six, and the government had no female Ministers. These figures are in sharp contrast with the previous era in which 20 percent of parliamentary seats were reserved for women.[111] Women constituted half of the work force, and over half of enrollments in higher education, in 1989.[112] But there has been an exodus of women from public life after 1989 as they strive to escape the double duty of professional and home life.[113] As of 1997, women occupied only 7 of 76 seats of parliament, and only 9 of 373 governorships at the local government levels; not a single ambassador, cabinet member, or state secretary was female.[114]

Virtually all of the leaders on our table studied in Russia at one time or another. Of the fifty-five figures on the list, only eleven individuals had no record of advanced study in Russia or Eastern Europe in our sources.[115] Many of these studied at the National University in Ulaanbaatar, which was designed on the Soviet model. Fourteen out of the fifty-five were engineers by training, with another eleven studying economics, and six studying law.

Only thirteen of our group were born in Ulaanbaatar, reflecting the relative importance of the countryside before increased urbanization began in the 1950s. Only five were born before 1940 in the generation that had contributed the senior leadership until 1990.[116] Most were born in the 1940s (22) and 1950s

MONGOLIA'S POLITICAL LEADERSHIP

Name	Position	Born	Province	Field of Study	Higher Education/ Date
P. Ochirbat	President 1990-1997	1941	Zavhan	engineering	Leningrad 1965
D. Byambasuren	Prime Minister 1990-2	1941	Hentii	economics	Moscow (Econ & Stat College) 1964
P. Jasrai	Prime Minister 1992-1996	1933	Gobialtai	economics	Moscow (Econ & Stat College) 1961
M. Enksaikhan	Prime Minister 1996-1998	1955	UB	economics	Kiev 1978
R. Gonchigdorj	Vice-President 1990-92, Chairman of SGH 1996-	1954	Arkhangai	mathematics	UB 1975, Budapest 1992
S. Gunjaadorj	Acting PM 1990	1937	Dornogobi	agriculture	Moscow (Academy of Agriculture) 1959
Ch. Ulaan	Chair, Nat'l Dev. Board 1992-1996	1954	Sukhbaatar	economics	Irkutsk 1972, Russian Institute of Management 1990-2
D. Demberelseren	Chair, Supreme Court 1990-	1952	Overhangai	law	Irkutsk 1976
N. Bagabandi	Chairman of SGH 1992-1996, President 1997-	1950	Zavhan	food tech	Leningrad 1972, Odessa 1980, Moscow (Academy of Social Sciences) 1987
S. Sovd	Chairman, Constitutional Court 1992-1998	1930	Uvs	law	UB 1954; Sverdlovsk 1963
K. Zardykhan	Deputy Chair, Baga Hural 1990-2	1940	Hovd	history	UB 1965
J. Gombojav	Deputy Chairman, SGH 1992-1996	1941	Sukhbaatar	economics	UB 1964, Moscow (Higher Political School) 1974
Ch. Purevdorj	Deputy PM 1990-1996	1948	Arkhangai	engineering	Sverdlovsk 1970
D. Dorligjav	Deputy PM 1990-2, Minister of Defense 1996-1998	1959	Uvs	veternarian	UB 1978
D. Ganbold	Deputy PM 1990-2, leader of MNDP 1992-1996	1957	UB	economics	Moscow (State Univ.) 1979
L. Enebish	Deputy PM 1992-1996	1947	Bulgan	engineering	UB 1970
N. Zoljargal	Head of Stock Exchange 1991-1996	1964	UB	economics	Budapest 1988
B. Dash-Yondon	Chairman of MPRP 1991-1996	1946	Huvsgul	philosophy	UB 1970, Kiev 1979
Ch. Dol	Leader, Free Labor Party, 1990-2	1946	UB	glassmaking	USSR (location N/A) 1960s,Moscow (Inst. Int'l Rel'ns)1973
D. Basandorj	Leader of Green Party 1990-2	1960	Hovd	engineering	Sverdlovsk , 1984
S. Zorig	Leader, Democratic Association 1990-91,MP 1992-98	1962	UB	philopophy	Moscow (State Univ.) 1985
E. Bat-Uul	Leader, Democratic Party 1990-	1957	UB	physics	UB 1981
B. Batbayar	Leader, Social Democratic Party 1990-	1955	Arkhangai	biophysics	UB 1981, In UK for advanced research 1990
J. Urtnasan	MP, Chairman of SGH 1991-2	1942	Hovd	agriculture	UB 1965
D. Radnaaraychaa	Min. of Agriculture 1990-92	1940	Zavhan	economics	UB 1967, Moscow (Academy of Social Sciences) 1978
L. Nyamsambuu	Min. of Agriculture and Industry 1996-1998	1948	Selenge	engineering, economics	UB, Moscow (Higher Political School) 1984
Ts. Damiran	Min. of Construction/Planning 1992-3	1948	Hovd	engineering	UB 1971
N. Enkhbayar	Min. of Culture 1992-1996	1958	UB	literature	Moscow (Gorky Lit. College) 1988
Sh. Jadambaa	Min. of Defense 1990-1996	1940	Gobialtai	military science	Blagoweshenk Mil. College 1964, Moscow (Military Academy) 1970, (Academy of General Headquarters) 1977
E. Gombojav	Min. of Demography Policy/Labor 1992-1996	1950	Huvsgul	economics	Warsaw, Poland 1973, Moscow (Higher Political School) 1979
N. Urtnasan	Min. of Education 1990-2	1951	Overhangai	education	Moscow (Pedagogical Institute) 1977, (Academy of Social Sciences) 1987
Ch. Lhagvajav	Min. of Education 1996-1998	1947	Bulgan	astrophysics	Moscow (State University) 1973
B. Jigjid	Min. of Energy/Geology/Mining 1992-1996	1945	Arkhangai	engineering	Sverdlovsk , 1969
Ts. Adyasuren	Min. of Environment 1996-1998	1951	Arkhangai	engineering	UB, 1975
A. Bazarkhuu	Min. of Finance 1990-92	1948	Gobialtai	finance	Moscow (State University) 1971, Moscow (Inst. Int'l Rel'ns)1984
D. Davaasambuu	Min. of Finance 1992-95	1951	Zavhan	economics	UB 1972, Moscow (Inst. Int'l Rel'ns) 1979
P. Tsagaan	Min. of Finance 1996-1998	1959	Bayan-olgii	law	Moscow (Inst. Int'l Rel'ns) 1985, Washington, DC (George Washington Univ.) 1994
Ts. Oold	Min. of Food/Agriculture 1992-1996	1942	Overhangai	agroeconomics	Moscow (Ag Academy) 1966;Moscow (Ag Academy) 1977
Ts. Gombosuren	Min. of Foreign Affairs 1987-1996	1943	Overhangai	engineering	Moscow 1966, Moscow (Higher Political School) 1976
Sh. Altangerel	Min. of Foreign Affairs 1996-1998	1951	UB	linguistics	Moscow (State University) 1975
D. Tsogbaatar	Min. of Geology/Mining 1992-93	1954	UB	geology	UB 1977?
P. Nyamdawa	Min. of Health 1990-1996	1947	Selenge	medicine	UB 1970, East Berlin (Humboldt), 1977;Moscow (Inst of Medical Sciences), 1989
L. Zorigt	Min. of Health and Social Care 1996-1998	1958	Huvsgul	medicine	Moscow (Medical University) 1982
R. Sandalkhan	Min. of Infrastructure 1992-1996	1943	Bayanolgii	engineering	Irkutsk 1967
G. Nyamdavaa	Min. of Infrastructure 1996-1998	1958	Hovd	engineering	Moscow (Energy Institute, 1983)
J. Amarsanaa	Min. of Justice 1991-92, 1996-1998 Con. Court 1998-	1953	UB	law	UB 1975
N. Luvsanjav	Min. of Justice 1992-1996	1954	UB	law	Irkutsk 1977
Ts. Tsolmon	Min. of Labor 1991-2; leader, Rennaisance Party	1953	Arkhangai	engineering	Irkutsk, 1976
J. Batsuur	Min. of National Development 1990-92	1949	Overhangai	biotechnology	Moscow (State University) 1973
Z. Batjargal	Min. of Nature/Environment 1990-1996	1945	Uvs	engineering	Leningrad, 1969
N. Ulzihutag	Min. of Science/Education 1992-95	1938	Dornogobi	biology	UB 1962, Moscow (Academy of Sciences) 1988
S. Bayarbaatar	Min. of Trade/Industry 1990-92	1956	UB	engineering	Sverdlovsk 1978, Moscow Academy of Foreign Trade 1988
Ts Tsogt	Min. of Trade/Industry 1992-1996	1958	UB	economics	Moscow (College of Economics)1979, Moscow (Foreign Trade Academy) 1990
B. Chimid	Secretary, Baga Hural 1990-2, MP 1992-1996	1934	Huvsgul	law	UB 1966
Ts. Elbegdorj	Prime Minister 1998	1963	Hovd	journalism	Lvov 1988

Key: SGH: State Great Hural, PM:Prime Minister, MNDP: National Democratic Party, UB: Ulaanbaatar
NOTE: Ministries have been reorganized several times since 1989; all Ulaanbaatar studies completed at National University unless noted

Chart 2: The Mongolian Elites,
1990-98

(24), a generation with less experience of nomadism.[117] Thirteen out of eighteen *aimag* are represented, with the greatest number of leaders coming from Arkhangai (7) and Hovd (6). But there is no evidence of factions based on regional origin or study cohort among the leaders.

The fifty-odd leaders listed in the table represent only the top level of Mongolia's political leadership. Below them are several hundred other important leaders, including members of parliament, the supreme and constitutional courts, the political party apparatuses, banks, ministries, the media, the private sector, trade unions, and other important organizations. An unscientific selection of biographical data from this "second-tier" group indicates roughly the same patterns: nearly all had studied in Russia, quite often in technical fields.[118]

The Intellectual Elites

Broadly speaking, these elites fall into two groups, intellectuals and technocrats. Note that in the parlance of the Mongolian class system, both groups are part of the intellectual class, which includes anyone with advanced education.[119] For example, *The Mongol Messenger* reported in June 1992 that 98 percent of the eighty-eight candidates for parliament in Ulaanbaatar were intellectuals, including lawyers, writers, teachers, and economists.[120] A job profile, however, showed that 45 percent of these candidates were employed by government organizations, with another 10 percent employed by political party organizations.

This paper distinguishes between the two groups mainly by occupation at the time of the reforms. Intellectuals are those individuals who were working at a university or think tank during 1990; in contrast, technocrats worked for party or government organizations. Both groups shared the common experience of being in Russia. Despite the similarities in the two groups, technocrats were more cautious about change than those at universities and research institutions. They were the Mongolian *nomenklatura*, insiders with a great deal vested in the old system, in contrast to outsider intellectuals.

The attitude of the regime toward intellectuals had always been ambivalent.[121] On the one hand, the traditional position of the intellectual in Mongolian society had been as a vehicle for importing foreign knowledge: just as Buddhist lamas had been keepers of sacred Tibetan texts, the Soviet-era intellectuals played a key role as translators of Socialist values and "modern" know-how. On the other hand, for the communist party to claim to be the vehicle of Mongolian nationalism, it needed to suppress independent proponents of that nationalism.

Once the lamas and nobles were eliminated, the greatest threat in this regard came from urban intellectuals, such as historians who wanted to write about the purges and those involved in the celebration of the eight-hundreth anniversary of Chinggis Khan's birth in 1962.[122] Many of them had been targets of abuse and oppression. "Mongolian intellectuals always resisted the MPRP," said one scholar who gave up his party membership after 1990, and many of them were exiled for pushing the boundaries of what was "acceptable" Leninist scholarship.[123]

In 1990, Mongolia's intellectuals continued the tradition of critiquing the Communist regime, and in doing so utilized both nationalist and cosmopolitan tools. The nationalist argument stemmed from the regime's subservient position vis-a-vis the Soviet Union, and the opposition called for a withdrawal of Soviet troops and a reassertion of an independent foreign policy. This dovetailed with their cosmopolitan perspective, as the opposition ideologies were exclusively drawn from international sources. The Greens and Social Democrats, for example, received support and inspiration from counterpart parties in Germany, Sweden, and elsewhere. The Free Labor Party and the Party for National Progress ran on liberal economic platforms that owed an intellectual debt to Thatcherism.

Many of the leaders of the democratic forces taught together. When parties became legalized in April 1990, they formed around clusters of academics. The National Progress Party, for example, was led by a group of economists; the Social Democrats were drawn from Physics and Math departments of the State University. This is testimony to the successful development of corporate professional consciousness in the waning years of Soviet power.

Four parties took seats in the Baga Khural elected in summer 1990: the MPRP, the Democrats, the Social Democrats, and the Party for National Progress. Two others, the Greens and the Free Labor Party, competed and failed. Like the other new parties, the Greens were also led by an academic, Dawaagiin Baasandorj (b. 1960), who was a herdsman's son from Khowd Aimag. A hydroengineer, he taught at the Polytechnic University in Ulaanbaatar. With an environmental platform and ties with international Green parties, the Green Party was more an adoption of an international label than an effort to resolve the core dilemmas of security and modernization that confront Mongolia, and the polls showed this.[124]

Besides leading the opposition in 1990, intellectuals had also criticized the party from within during the waning days of the *ancien regime*. K. Zardykhan is an example of a prescient and courageous agitator for reform within the Party, most notably in a crucial 1988 article in the Party magazine *Namyn Amidral*.[125] A history Ph.D. and soft-spoken intellectual, he used his position as head of the Council of Trade Unions to call for new interpretations of Marxist-Leninism and an end to one-party monopoly. He was thus well-positioned to play a leadership in crafting the MPRP response to democratic pressures, and became Deputy Chairman of the Council of Ministers in March 1990. After the elections, he was named Deputy Chairman of the Baga Khural, and thus became the highest ranking Kazakh in government.[126] Mongolia's leaders had always been analogized to Russian counterparts, both legitimizing their leadership and describing their rule, and hopeful democrats named Zardykhan Mongolia's Yeltsin.

The Technocratic Elites

If the intellectuals precipitated change and gave it direction through international contacts, it was a group of technocratic elites who implemented the changes in party and government organizations. This would have been inevitable even if the new parties had done better at the polls, for the ranks of the intellectuals were thin. There was little option but to leave the administration to the professional technocrats who had spent their lives climbing the ranks. In this sense, the 1990 changes were not truly revolutionary, but merely accelerated the transfer of power to a younger generation that would have eventually acceded to it anyway.

The MPRP led the way in this process of generational change in March 1990 when it removed the oldest leaders in response to the protests. In March, Jambyn Batmönkh (b. 1926), the General Secretary of the Party, Prime Minister Dumaagiin Sodnom (b. 1933) and the entire Politburo announced their resignations. Replacing Batmönkh as Head of State was P. Ochirbat (b. 1941) who later became President. An engineer by training, he had worked in the Ministry of Energy and Geology and later Foreign Economic Relations and Supply, eventually becoming Minister. The key moment for Ochirbat came in March 1990 when he was appointed Chairman of the Presidium of the Great Khural, and he was later elected President in 1990 and 1993.

The 1990 shift to Ochirbat may have reflected the priority of ensuring continuing transfer of resources from Russia, for in his capacity as Minister he undoubtedly had close relations with the Soviets. If so, this nicely illustrates Lattimore's observation that power flows to the Mongols best able to maintain relations with Russia. Ochirbat's external orientation may have secured him the job, but his personal abilities enabled him to keep it. Several times during the next few years, Ochirbat's political abilities to forge compromise and forestall confrontation defused potential crises between the MPRP and new parties. Although he represented the MPRP originally, Ochirbat was nominated by the opposition for the 1993 Presidential election, which he won (though he later lost his bid for re-election in 1997).[127] Ochirbat's transfer between parties illustrates the lack of ideological differences between the two sets of political forces.

Although the MPRP won the 1990 parliamentary elections, the MPRP invited the opposition to join the government because of the mood of crisis. Three of the top six positions went to opposition figures. Ochirbat of the MPRP was elected President, with Gonchigdorj of the Social Democrats becoming Vice President and the country's senior opposition figure at age 36. MPRP member Dashiin Byambasüren (b. 1941) headed the government, becoming fourteenth and final Prime Minister of the MPR.

An economist, Byambasüren had previously served as head of the State Statistical office and of the Institute of Management. He had suffered a political demotion with the fall of Tsedenbal in 1984, but had made a comeback and had become Deputy Chairman of the Council of Ministers in 1989. Byambasüren is typical of a group of more conservative communists in the Batmönkh-Sodnom regime who were pragmatic enough to change their outlook in the new era.

There were three Deputy Prime Ministers in the Byambasüren government. Representing the old line technocrats in the MPRP was Deputy Prime Minister Choijilsürengiin Pürewdorj (b. 1948), whose portfolio included industrial issues such as power and technology. He was a longtime cadre who had served as

Deputy Minister of Fuel and Power in 1983. Later, he joined the staff of the Council of Ministers in May 1990, and also became a Member of the Presidium of MPRP Central Committee during the transitional state.

The opposition was represented by two Deputy Prime Ministers. Dambyn Dorligjaw, 31 years old at the time of his appointment, was a veterinarian trained at the Mongolian State University, and had responsibility for cultural issues. He came from the Democratic Party. Finally, there was Deputy Prime Minister Dawaadorjiin Ganbold (b. 1957) who came from a family of famous economists. He graduated from the Moscow State University Faculty of Economics and later taught economics at the Mongolian State University 1979-84. After defending his higher degree in Russia, he returned to teach at the Party's Higher Political School, where party cadres and technocrats went to receive current political indoctrination and gain skills in public administration. He was the leader of the Party for National Progress, thus ensuring that each major opposition party was represented in the leadership. Ganbold was given responsibility for managing the economy just as it collapsed. The ingenious move by the MPRP of giving the economy to the opposition prompted him to lament later, "we could have let them eat the soup they had been cooking for seventy years. But we didn't and now we take the blame."[128]

The rest of the cabinet was composed primarily of younger technocratic insiders and careerists who had studied in Russia, then patiently worked their way up through the ranks of the party and government bureaucracies.[129] This pattern was repeated with the 1992-96 government, led by P. Jasrai (b. 1930), a political survivor prominent in the Batmönkh regime.

After a career as an elementary school teacher in the 1950s, Jasrai was sent to the Moscow Institute of Economics and Statistics, where he spent five years. A party loyalist, he joined the staff of the Central Committee and eventually became Deputy Prime Minister and Chairman of the State Planning Committee. After the democratic demonstrations forced him to resign, he became head of the Union of Industrial and Service Cooperatives.

This form of economic enterprise was a transitional one created by decree in 1987 as part of the Gorbachev-era economic reform efforts. These private cooperatives eventually became joint-stock companies, and were enormously successful in transforming the rural economy, due in part to Jasrai's competence. Nevertheless, Jasrai was reluctant to return to the political leadership. He was offered a job in the Byambasüren regime but refused, and reportedly did not want the Prime Ministership in 1992. The MPRP asked him several times before securing his acceptance

Jasrai's cabinet had some holdovers from the Byambasüren regime, and continued to be made up primarily of technocrats.[130] The most telling holdover from the Byambasüren cabinet was in the Foreign Ministry, virtually the only important national institution that did not see a change in top-level leadership from 1988-96. Foreign Minister Tserenpiliin Gombosüren was a key figure in crafting the MPRP's response to the democratic pressures in 1990.[131]

Like others of his generation, Gombosüren studied twice in the USSR, once for vocational training as a printer and again after rising in government and party circles at the Higher Political School in 1974-76. Upon returning to Mongolia, he joined the foreign ministry, becoming Deputy Foreign Minister by 1982. After managing the international relations bureau of the Party's Central Committee, he spent 1984-87 as Counselor in the Mongolian Embassy in Moscow. Gombosüren became foreign minister in June 1988, replacing Mangalyn Dugersuren who had dominated Mongolian foreign policy for the previous quarter century.[132]

Gombosüren's tenacity reflects the primacy of international factors over domestic developments in Mongolia's reform process, and illustrates yet again Lattimore's axiom. Gombosüren's ability in this regard was undoubtedly bolstered by his contacts with *perestroika* architects in Russia.[133] In an era of superpower rapprochement, he managed Mongolia's integration with the world beyond, developing contacts with Asia and North America, and joining international organizations such as the IMF, World Bank, Asian Development Bank and the non-aligned movement.

Gombosüren has also managed an ever-warmer relationship with China, after making an important visit to China in 1989. As the most senior government official to visit since Tsedenbal went in 1962, he ushered in an era of expanded high-level contacts. Gombosüren's emphasis on balance and expanded contacts with all nations clearly played a role in his ability to maintain his post from 1988-96.

The coalition of new parties that took power in 1996 was significantly younger than the MPRP group. The average age of the cabinet was 43, compared to the average age of 50 in the Jasrai cabinet. The ranks of the first cabinet of the new parties was primarily technocratic, in part because of a controversial Constitutional Court decision, rendered immediately after the coalition's parliamentary victory, that prevented members of parliament from serving in the cabinet.

With the top coalition leaders (the intellectuals who started the 1990 demonstrations) having run in parliamentary elections, the court decision forced the coalition to fill the cabinet with second-tier leaders. In academic and career background, they were similar to those whom they replaced, with the possible exception of Finance Minister P. Tsagaan, who stood out as being the only political leader on the list to complete an advanced degree at a western university. In this, he was the forerunner of Mongolia's future leaders, and received high marks from international donors for his macroeconomic management.[134]

Foreign Policy and Cosmopolitan Nationalism

The story of Mongolia's post-1990 reforms reflects the primacy of foreign policy in influencing domestic politics. Mongolia's historic wariness toward China meant that it would look outward for a security guarantee. With Russia weak, the natural choice in 1990 was to look for a benevolent third force in the form of the international community to guarantee Mongolia's security and survival. Political and economic liberalization bolsters Mongolia's ties with the world beyond its two neighbors, and thus helps secure a collective third force to at least partially offset the influence of China and Russia. But it is clearly the China threat that is most stark in the eyes of the Mongolian people and their leaders.

This perspective helps explain the puzzle of how political liberalization proceeded through 1996 under the continuous leadership of the former communist party. Underneath the ideological veneer, the MPRP was a nationalist party, and the party had little difficulty in staking out the open door foreign policy. Domestically, the MPRP transferred power to a younger group of technocrats who knew their intellectual counterparts. Post-1990 domestic politics has been limited to a small group of people who knew each other and shared a common background, including formative experiences in the Soviet bloc. A key legacy of these non-native experiences was a cosmopolitan orientation, fostered in part by socialist rhetoric, as well as the very real sense in which Soviet domination paradoxically opened up the world to Mongolia.

While the modernization of Mongolia will continue with the support of the international community, the way of life that created the current political elite is gone. In the future, dropout problems will make it less likely that herdsmen's children from rural districts can rise to the highest levels. Nomadic families, subsidized in the one-party period so that they could send their children to school, have begun keeping their children home to work. Roughly 10 percent of the school population dropped out in a single year, 1992.[135] It is likely that class stratification will increase with the market economy and may lead to greater rural-urban differentiation in politics. Education is likely to be a scarcer commodity, and the proportion of urban-born elites will rise.

Nevertheless, our argument suggests that the driving forces dictating policy are likely to remain the same even as new generations take over. Mongolia has always been adept at integrating foreign influences when useful. While from a Western perspective, Mongolia is one of the world's more isolated countries, in fact foreign influences have always been important. The adoption of Tibetan Buddhism and the Chinese influence over the economy during the last century are but two historical examples. The post-1990 adoption of a market economy and democratic institutions is but another chapter in the long quest for national survival in a strategically important location.

The real driving force in Mongolia today is a pragmatic cosmopolitan nationalism, itself reflecting the ambivalence toward China that drove the Mongols to look North in the first place. This nationalism is cultural rather than overtly political in character, and has survived despite the collapse of the ideological overlay which MPRP provided. If there was any lingering doubt that this nationalism drove ideology and not the other way round, it ought to have been laid to rest by events since 1990, the second great turning point in modern Mongolian history.

Notes

1. Ts. Batbayar, *Modern Mongolia: A Concise History* (Ulaanbaatar, 1996), p. 104 [hereafter, Batbayar, *A Concise History*].

2. Peter Boone, et al., "Mongolia's Transition to a Democratic Market System" in W. Woo, S. Parker, and J. Sachs, eds. *Economies in Transition* (Cambridge: MIT Press, 1997), pp. 103-104.

3. C.R. Bawden, "Mongolia and the Mongolians" in S. Akiner, ed. *Mongolia Today* [hereinafter Akiner, *Mongolia Today*] (London: Kegan Paul, 1991), p. 31. This statement was written before the collapse of the Soviet Union and the emergence of new nation states in Central Asia.

4. Owen Lattimore, Introduction to Gerard M. Friters, *Outer Mongolia and its International Position* (Baltimore: Johns Hopkins, 1949) p. xix.

5. Owen Lattimore, *Studies in Frontier History* (New York, Oxford, 1962), p. 276.

6. David Morgan, "Prelude" in Akiner, *Mongolia Today*, p. 3.

7. Owen Lattimore, *Nationalism and Revolution in Mongolia* (New York: Oxford, 1955) p. 39. Lattimore contrasted this formulation with the more radical pan-Mongolism of the Inner Mongolian nationalists. In support of his contention, he notes that unlike other Soviet satellites, Outer Mongolia never experienced a serious revolt against the Soviet alliance, even when Japan in the 1930s offered a real potential counterweight. He also analyzes Mongolian language texts to demonstrate the apparent sincerity of Mongolian leadership in dealing with Russia.

8. A thoughtful discussion of this problem by one of the architects of Mongolia's 1992 Constitution is found in S. Bayar, "Mongolia's National Security Challenges" (San Francisco: Center for Asian Pacific Affairs, Report No. 16, September 1994).

9. See William Heaton, "Mongolia in 1986" XXXVII *Asian Survey* 1 (January 1987).

10. *Mongol Messenger* (hereinafter MM), May 21, 1997, p. 3.

11. MM 8/12/91, p. 1; MM 1/5/93, p. 2.

12. A Foreign Investment Law had been passed only two weeks before on March 23, 1990. This law has since been replaced.

13. This version of the statement comes from S. Akiner, *Mongolia Today*, at xxxiii.

14. Interview with J. Od, Embassy of Mongolia, 2/15/96. See also MM 9/22/92, p. 1.

15. H. Hulan, "Mongolia's Political Transformation" in *Economic Reform and Political Change in Asia* (San Francisco: Center for Asian Pacific Affairs, 1993).

16. MM 1/5/93, p. 3.

17. See, for example, MM 5/12/92, 5/19/92, 5/26/92, and 6/2/92.

18. Compare the MPRP's promise to "consistently continue a foreign policy designed [at] developing friendly relations and equitable and mutually beneficial cooperation with the neighboring states and other countries of the world" with the Coalition's assurance that "active cooperation will be developed with all countries on the principles of respecting equality and independence." More specifically, the Social Democratic Party indicated that it would pursue an open-door foreign policy and "work to develop traditional relations with the Northern neighbor."

19. MM 1/19/93, p. 2.

20. Ibid.

21. Ibid.

22. For reports on the protests at the Chinese Embassy, see MM 11/4/91, p. 1. On

the protest at the Russian Embassy regarding treatment of Buriat nationalists, see *Economist Intelligence Unit* (hereinafter EIU) 1993(3) p. 38. Prince Demchigdomrov is the Mongol name for Inner Mongolian nationalist Te Wang. See Lattimore, *Studies in Frontier History,* pp. 433-35.

23. EIU, 1993(3), p. 38.

24. MM 1/19/93, p. 2.

25. Most Mongolians asked were unable to explain the source of the number "281 " although one person indicated that this number is of some kind of mystical significance.

26. Interview, L. Jargaisaikhan, Soviet Desk, Foreign Ministry, 6/92. Another sensitive issue has been revelation of crimes committed by Soviet soldiers in the previous era. See Dashpurev, *Reign of Terror,* p. 73 quoting the newspapers *Shin Toli* 8/27/90 and *Aradchlal* 8/1-10/90.

27. MM 3/24/92, p. 3.

28. Ibid., 4/7/92.

29. Interview H. Hulan 6/19/92; S. Zorig 6/12/92.

30. MM 1/5/93, p. 3.

31. See letter to Yeltsin published in *Ardyn Erkh,* 12/13/95.

32. MM 10/22/97, p. 5.

33. *Far East Economic Review Asia,* 1995 Yearbook.

34. EIU 1994(l), p. 36.

35. Interview with G. Ganzorig, Supreme Court of Mongolia, 12/30/95.

36. EIU 1994(l), p. 36.

37. Ibid., 1994(4), p. 37.

38. "Allegations Made Against Foreign Minister Prove Unfounded," *E-mail Daily News,* Ulaanbaatar, January 31, 1997.

39. Urban Mongolian society remains a small community, and insiders report extensive gossip and a pervasive flow of rumors. Gossip and rumor, of course, play an important role in creating and enforcing norms in small communities, and may be particularly characteristic of Leninist societies where politically inspired truth manipulation sharply constrained public discourse for so long.

40. Interview with Mr. Sükhebaatur of the Center for Northeast Asian Studies, Ulaanbaatar, 7/93.

41. Robin Meams, "Community, Collective Action and Common Grazing: the Case of Post-Socialist Mongolia," 32:3 *Journal of Development Studies,* p. 297, at n. 13.

42. Peter Montagnon, "State Assets to be Auctioned" *Financial Times,* Sept. 17, 1997 quotes Oleg Gorelik, advisor to the State Privatization Committee as saying Chinese dominance of the privatization program would be politically unsustainable. In 1997, "(r)esponding to public concern that many Chinese individuals and companies were behind the new Mongolian owners, [Head of State Property Committee] Mr. Enkhbold said, 'The Chinese can't carry these objects away." MM 9/10/97, p. 1.

43. Editorial, MM 5/25/93, p. 2.

44. Interview with Mr. Sükhebaatur of the Center for Northeast Asian Studies, Ulaanbaatar, 6/93.

45. While for obvious reasons specific names will not be cited, this came up in the course of several interviews and conversations with Mongolians.

46. O. Corff, "In Defense of the New Romanization," MM 3/17/92, p. 3.

47. Interview with Ts. Gombosüren, *Unen* 6/24/92.

48. MM 7/7/92, p. 1.

49. See generally Lincoln Kaye, "Faltering Steppes: China looms large in ethnic upsurge among Mongols," FEER April 9, 1992, p. 16.

50. MM 5/12/92, p. 1; FEER *Asia 1993 Yearbook*, p. 169.

51. EIU 1993(3), p. 40; See also *Il Tovchoo*, June 1-10, 1993.

52. Ibid.

53. EIU 1995(3), p. 47.

54. Bayar was head of the Committee on State Structure of the Constitutional Commission. Born in 1956, Bayar studied law at Moscow State University before becoming a journalist. In 1990 he stood for election to the Great Khural and was selected by the MPRP to serve in the Baga Khural, where he became chair of a Standing Committee on State Structure. He is currently Chief of Staff to the President.

55. S. Bayar, "Mongolia's National Security Challenges" (San Francisco: Center for Asian Pacific Affairs, Report No. 16, September 1994), p. 1.

56. Ibid., p. 2.

57. Ibid.

58. Ibid., p. 4; For a concurring view that details the history of Chinese policy toward Mongolia see Henry G. Schwarz, "The Security of Mongolia," *Mongolian Journal of International Affairs* 77 (1996); Schwarz maintains that the nine categories of Mongolian national security found in the government's 1994 Concept of Mongolian National Security are directed implicitly toward China.

59. *The Mongols in a Sociological Survey*, Vol. 1, (Ulaanbaatar, Mongolian Academy of Sciences, Institute of Philosophy, Sociology and Jurisprudence, Sociological Sector, 1997), p. 12. Russia was named by over half the respondents in a similar survey in 1994, so its support among the population appears to be declining, although it is still the strongest. China was named by 5.6 percent of respondents in 1994, as in 1996 the sixth most common response.

60. *Concept of National Security,* Art. 21 (11).

61. Ibid., Art. 35 (8).

62. Ibid., Art. 41 (1).

63. Ibid., Art. 45 (1).

64. Both documents are translated into English in *Mongolian Journal of International Affairs* 1995(2).

65. *Foreign Policy Section,* 1997, p. 1.

66. MM 10/14/91, p. 3.

67. Quoted in Ram Rahul, *Afghanistan, Mongolia and the USSR* (New Delhi: Vikas Publishing, 1987) p. 65.

68. MM 7/14/92.

69. Interview with D. Ganbold 7/93. Similar sentiments were expressed in interviews with a number of diplomats.

70. Interview with G. Ganzorig, 12/30/95.

71. Interview with S. Enkhtüwshin, 6/95.

72. This incident is described in Sheldon Severinghaus, "Mongolia in 1994," XXXV *Asian Survey* 70-5, (January 1995).

73. While the law on demonstrations was passed, the media law has been delayed several times since 1994, and has still not been passed.

74. This section relies on interviews with B. Chimid 6/2/93, P. Tsagaan 6/10/93, and S. Bayar 2/92, and draft comments on the constitution provided to the drafting commission by Amnesty international, the UN Human Rights Center, and the Asia Foundation.

75. Kenneth Jowitt, *New World Disorder* (Berkeley, CA: University of California Press, 1990), p. 88.

76. Ibid.

77. For statistics, see Ts. Batbayar, *A Concise History*, p. 94.

78. See *National Economy of the MPR for 70 years* (Ulaanbaatar: State Statistical Office, 1991), p. 15.

79. There was a small intelligentsia even before the socialist period, formed out of younger lamas and certain elements of the princely classes. Most of this group was destroyed in the 1930s. But the intelligentisa was revived in the later years of the MPR, with the percentage of urbanites with higher education rising from 5.2 percent in 1979 to 7.5 percent in 1985. Ibid., pp. 15, 19-20.

80. This was Mongolia's unique contribution to socialist theory. See C.R. Bawden, *The Modern History of Mongolia* (London: Kegan Paul, 2nd ed. 1989) p. 9. [Hereinafter Bawden, *The Modern History*.]

81. Ibid., p. 421.

82. *Ibid*, p. 426; Asian Development Bank, *Mongolia: A Centrally Planned Economy in Transition* (New York: Oxford, 1992), p. 16.

83. One of the most common cultural reactions to the changes was to blame the Russians. Individual Russians were regularly insulted and occasionaliy attacked in the streets in 1991 and 1992, before the vast majority of them left the country.

84. Sanders estimates that the number of Soviet civilian workers in Mongolia reached 32,000 in the early 1980s, with an equal number of dependents (Bawden, *The Modern History*, pp. 426-27). In addition, there were roughly 55,000 Soviet troops "temporarily" stationed in Mongolia in 1984. (*Far East Economic Review, Asia 1985 Yearbook*, p. 204.) Taking these two figures together, there were roughly 119,000 Soviet citizens in Mongolia, compared with a Mongolian population of 1.9 million. Worden and Matles report that in the early 1970s, over 100,000 Soviet troops were stationed in Mongolia, which would represent a higher percentage of the total population, R. Worden and A. Matles, eds., *Mongolia: A Country Study* (Washington, D.C.: Library of Congress, 2nd ed, 1991). A Russian newspaper, *Krasnaia zvezda,* reported the maximum figure as 80,000 Soviet troops. *BBC World Broadcasts,* 11/28/95. Despite the range of available figures, the 5 percent figure is probably slightly low if one accepts Sanders' estimate of the civilian population.

85. Biographical data on file with author. *The Far East Economic Review, Asia Yearbook 1993,* reports that Jasrai was the oldest MP.

86. One important cleavage has been between younger academics who agitated for more rapid change and professional technocrats employed in the MPRP and government bureaucracies, who by and large are a more cautious group. Beyond this, there has been some institutionalization of politics since 1990, reflected in the number of inter-institutional disputes sent to the Constitutional Court. Constitutional Court statistics, on file with author.

87. Bawden, *The Modern History*, p. 426; The Cyrillic script was adopted in 1941.

88. Worden and Matles, *Mongolia: A Country Study,* p. 97; Ts. Batbayar, *A Concise History*, p. 96.

89. Ibid.

90. Ibid., p. 110.

91. MM 10/7/91, p. 4. At least two important political figures, S. Zorig and S. Bayar, are known to have attended such primary schools.

92. See Derek Pritchatt, "The Development of Education in Mongolia" in S. Akiner, *Mongolia Today*, p. 211.

93. Shelia Smith, "Human Capital Formation under Conditions of Acute Resource Scarcity" in Keith Griffin, ed. *Poverty and the Transition to a Market Economy* (London: St. Martin's 1995) [hereinafter, Griffin, *Poverty*], p. 65.

94. Ibid.

95. Kim Bing Wu, "Mongolia: Financing Education During Economic Transition," *World Bank Discussion Paper #226*, p. 46.

96. *Mongolia Economy and Society: Annual Statistical Yearbook* (Ulaanbaatar: State Statistical Office, 1993).

97. These figures come from R. Bat-Erdene, Director of Higher Education at the Ministry of Education, interviewed 2/19/96.

98. Worden and Matles, *Mongolia: A Country Study,* p. 110.

99. Pritchatt, p. 207.

100. Interview with J. Od, Embassy of Mongolia, 2/15/96.

101. Ibid.

102. Interviews with J. Od, 2/15/96, G. Bilgee 2/10/96, G. Ganzorig 12/30/95, and R. Bat-Erdene 2/18/96.

103. Interview, R. Bat-Erdene, 3/10/96.

104. Interviews with Sh. Sandag, 3/1/96 and L. Jargaisalkhan 7/93. At the same time, communities with many Mongolians allowed more interaction with countrymen, although there were few community organizations. One such organization was the Revolutionary Youth League, which had chapters in cities where large numbers of Mongolians studied. Several persons reported meeting their future spouses in Russia. Interviews with G. Ganzorig 12/26/95, L. Jargalsaikhan 6/17/93, E. Tüwshin, 9/30/95.

105. This section relies on interviews with R. Bat-Erdene, 2/26/96, 3/10/96; J. Od, Embassy of Mongolia, 2/15/96; and G. Ganzorig, Supreme Court of Mongolia, 12/30/95.

106. A member of the Supreme Court says that the unofficial criteria for selection to that body included some attention to the geographical origin within Mongolia as a way of ensuring balance. Interview, G. Ganzorig, 12/28/95.

107. Jowitt, *New World Disorder*, pp. 164, 212, describes Moscow as "politically sacred space" in the "Leninist centered regime world." It is unclear whether such a quasi-religious connotation is appropriate to attribute to the Mongolians, whose national consciousness provided enough incentive for their participation in the socialist project.

108. By 1995, gross enrollment ratios in higher education had dropped silghtly. Wu, *Financing Education*, p. 47. A total of 32,777 students were enrolled at undergraduate and graduate levels as of 1995. However, only 41 new students went to the Soviet Union in 1995. A number of fellowships have been offered by foreign govemments of China, Japan, Hungary, Turkey, Australia, and Russia, and hundreds of students have privately enrolled in short and mid term courses in the United States and elsewhere. The Government of Mongolia has been unable to keep statistics on this group but plans to start in 1998. As of 1996, the Washington Embassy estimated they probably number in the hundreds in the U.S. alone. At least 25 were then studying in the San Francisco area. Another trend is private universities, of which there are now over 50 in Mongolia. Interview with R. Bat-Erdene 2/19/96. For a partial list of private universities and some figures on tuition rates see G. Chingis, "Pay! If You Want to be Educated" MM 10/20/92, p 2.

109. This section draws on a variety of sources on contemporary Mongolia, including interviews with Mongolians conducted in Ulaanbaatar in 1993 and 1997, and in the

United States in 1995 and 1996. In addition, the author's informal interviews in Ulaanbaatar in 1991 and 1992 were used for context.

Until the advent of the *Mongolia Monthly* (published from 1995 through 1998) and E-mail Dally News from Ulaanbaatar (ganbold@magicnet.mn) sources of information available to the U.S.-based non-Mongolian-speaking researcher were few and difficult to obtain. For current affairs, the English language *Mongol Messenger*, published since 1991 in Ulaanbaatar, is an invaluable source, along with newer English newspapers such as the *UB Post*. Although published by the government-owned Montsame News Agency, the Messenger has offered what appears to be a balanced perspective, including anti-MPRP editorials, essays by and interviews with opposition figures, and probing questions of government officials. The Economist Intelligence Unit's China/Mongolia Country Reports contain good summaries of recent events. The annual reports in the Far East Economic Review's Asia Yearbook and the scholarly summaries in Asian Survey's January/February Survey of Asia provide accounts of the year's main events.

The Internet has dramatically improved the situation since this essay was first drafted. Two excellent umbrella sites on Mongolia are Mongolia Online at www.mol.mn and the United Nations site at www.undp.org/missions/mongolia.

Biographical information on Mongolian elites was drawn from three principal sources. The *Mongol Messenger* occasionally publishes biographical summaries of leading figures in Mongolia, with uneven but useful information. This was supplemented by the author's file of biographical information obtained during field research in Ulaanbaatar in 1993 and 1997. Finally, some Mongolian figures are listed in the annual volume *Who's Who in the World* (Chicago: Marquis Who's Who, 1997), and in a 1991 volume *Who's Who in Asian and Australasian Politics* (London: Bowker-Saur, 1991).

110. Two notes on selection criteria. There has been a rapid proliferation of political parties, and several alliances, merges, and splits among opposition parties. As an effort to identify major parties from the 19 registered for the 1992 elections, only party leaders from parties who won a parliamentary seat in 1990, 1992, or 1996 national elections are included.

There are three other groups of senior leaders who are not included. First is private businessmen and heads of state enterprises, on whom very little information exists either in English or Mongolian language and in any case are not "political" leadership in the conventional sense of the term. Nevertheless, their role in policy may grow. A second group includes leaders of institutions such as the Central Bank and Mongol TV and Radio. The final omitted group is rural governors. While this is due in part to a lack of information, this omission is arguably justified in that the national level policies which are the focus of this chapter are made and implemented in Ulaanbaatar, with little direct input from local government or party figures.

There are two omissions of persons for whom biographical data were unavailable. First is N. Urtnasan, Minister of Education 1990-92, and second B. Dashbalbar, Member of Parliament and leader of the United Traditional Party. J. Gombojaw, included in the table, was the presidential candidate of this party in 1997.

111. Worden and Matles, *Mongolia: A Country Study.*

112. See Barbara Skapa, "Mongolian Women and Poverty During the Transition," in Griffin, ed. *Poverty,* p. 93 and Ministry of Science and education statistics given in Wu, pp. 49-50.

113. For an account of Mongolian women in recent years, see Barbara Skapa, "Mongolian Women and Poverty During the Transition," in Griffin, ed. *Poverty,* p. 90-103.

114. *Human Development Report 1997* (Ulaanbaatar: UNDP, 1997), p. 26.

115. It is possible that these persons did study in Russia at a political institute, but did not graduate or otherwise did not see a need to include that fact in their biographical data.

116. The table intentionally does not include the pre-1990 leadership such as Batmonh (b. 1926), head of the MPRP 1984-90 and premier 1974-84, and D. Sodnom (b. 1933), premier 1984-90, both of whom retired in 1990. But former Prime Minster P. Jasrai (b. 1933) who was Deputy Premier until 1990, is a survivor from this group. For another generational categorization, see Batbayar, *A Concise History*, p. 94.

117. Batbayar, *A Concise History*, p. 98.

118. The *Mongol Messenger* biographical series includes a number of MPs, heads of State companies, and other figures.

119. See State Statistical Office, *National Economy of the MPR for 70 Years.*

120. MM 6/92, p. 3.

121. See Batbayar, *A Concise History*, p. 94.

122. The controversy surrounding the anniversary is discussed by Bawden in *The Modern History,* pp. 417-18. Suppression of intellectuals during the Tsedenbal period (1952-84) is discussed in Dashpurev and Soni, *Reign of Terror*, pp. 54-84.

123. Interview Sh. Sandag, 2/12/96.

124. The only opposition party in 1990 whose leadership did not come from academia was the Free Labor Party, founded by one of the country's first businessmen, Choidogiin Döl (b. 1946). Döl was an old party technocrat who had studied in the Soviet Union twice, once as a glassmaker in the 1960s and again at the Moscow Institute for International Relations in the early 1970s. After the second stint, he joined the State Committee for Foreign Economic Relations, serving as trade representative in Moscow in 1979-86. After 1989 he renounced his MPRP membership and became a free-trade advocate (a position not shared or understood by many of his countrymen if the poor electoral showing of his party is any indication). It is probable that he drew the name of his party from a Russian party with the same name, identified in M. Steven Fish, *Democracy from Scratch: Regime and Opposition in the New Russia* (Princeton, NJ: Princeton University Press, 1995), p. 49.

125. See A.J.K. Sanders "Restructuring and Openness," in S. Akiner, *Mongolia Today*, pp. 72-74.

126. In 1991, Zardykhan led a fight to rename the MPRP the Mongolian People's Party, the name originally adopted by Sükhebaatur and his band of revolutionaries. See MM, 12/91 passim. When the faction leadership was excluded from preparations for the 21st MPRP Party Congress, they broke away during the Great Khural's Constitutional debates to form the Mongolian Party of National Renaissance. This was clearly an attempt to spur the breakup of the MPRP.

The gamble failed. Despite attracting young MPRP leaders like the Minister of Justice J. Amarsanaa and Baga Khural Legal Affairs Committee Chairman L. Tsog, the party failed to develop much mass support, and all its candidates failed in the Summer 1992 parliamentary elections.The timing of the decision to break away from the MPRP hurt Zardykhan's political prospects, as the constitutional debates involved an ultimately successful process of integrating disparate views. He later served as the Ambassador to Uzbekistan.

127. Ts. Batbayar, "Mongolia in 1993" XXXIV *Asian Survey* (January 1994).

128. Interview, D. Ganbold, July 1993.

129. MM 8/5/91 reports that the average age was 43.

130. P. Nyamdawaa remained Minister of Health until 1996. For more on Nyamdawaa, see MM 11/19/91. The Minister of Defense, S. Jadambaa, also remained in place until 1996. See MM 11/11/91.

131. See MM 10/28/91. From March 1990 through March 1991 Gombosüren served as a member of the post-Batmönkh Central Committee of the MPRP.

132. See Alan Sanders, "Mongolia in 1988," XXXII *Asian Survey* (January 1989).

133. See Frank Viviano, "Investors Welcome in New Mongolia" (interview with Gombosuren), *San Francisco Chronicle*, 10/13/90.

134. Interview, William Bikales, Ulaanbaatar, Dec. 6, 1997.

135. C. Harper, World Bank Discussion paper #229, *An Assessment of Vulnerable Groups in Mongolia,* 1994, p. 27. See also *Human Development Report 1997*, p. 20.

Epilogue

Mongolia's Foreign Policy Revisited: Relations with Russia and the PRC into the 1990s

G. Tumurchuluun

Mongolia is a vast and landlocked country, entirely surrounded by Russia and China. It covers an area of over 600,000 square miles and has 4,450 miles of borders, 2,500 of which are with China and 1,850 with Russia. That is among the reasons why strong relations with Japan and the United States are seen as so crucial. Ultimately, however, there is no escaping Russia and China.

"When Two Elephants Fight Each Other"

In the twentieth century, Mongolia has constantly been the focus of discord between Russia and China. The Mongols' favorite slogan was, to paraphrase Mackinder, he "who conquers Mongolia, conquers the world." To Mongolians this constant struggle was like the well-known African tale about two elephants: when they fight the grass suffers. Mongolia suffered deeply because of its two elephant-like neighbors, but neither Russia nor China ever succeeded in annexing Mongolia. The main reason for this was that Mongolia served both Russia and China equally well as a buffer by protecting critical points along the Chinese and Russian borders that would otherwise be in close proximity to each other. Yet although Mongolia never faced outright conquest, it was generally forced to submit to one of its two neighbors. As history has shown, dramatic changes in the geopolitical environment—caused by dynastic decline, revolutions, and war—could easily shift this precarious balance from one elephant to the other.

During the twentieth century, Mongolia's foreign policy can be divided into three major periods: 1911-45, 1945-90, and since 1990. The main goal of the country's foreign policy during the first period was to be recognized as an independent state by Russia and China. The Soviet government, in a treaty signed with the Mongolian government in 1921, was the first to recognize officially the independent status of Mongolia. Finally, after many diplomatic ups and downs, the Chinese government followed suit in 1945. It was the Yalta agreement's secret clause on the conditions for Russia's entry in the Far Eastern war, which stated that "the status quo in Outer Mongolia should be preserved," that finally allowed Russia to push China into making this irreversible decision.[1]

Thus, from Mongolia's viewpoint, the year 1945 marked the beginning of a definitive change in its international status. The USSR and China announced during August 1945 that China would recognize the independence of Mongolia only after the Mongols' desire was confirmed by a plebiscite. The plebiscite was held in October 1945, and 98 percent of the electorate expressed a desire for independence. China officially recognized Mongolia on January 5, 1946. A month later an agreement on the establishment of diplomatic relations was signed, with the Chinese government agreeing to "recognize Outer Mongolia with the existing boundary as its frontier."[2]

Following the Communists' overthrow of the Nationalist government in 1949, in an exchange of notes following the signing, in February 1950, of the Sino-Soviet Treaty of Friendship, Alliance and Mutual Assistance, the Soviet Union and China appeared to confirm the independence of the MPR by establishing diplomatic relations with the Mongolian government. Although China continued to seek the return of Mongolia to its sphere of influence, between 1955 and 1961 Mongolia carried out an active campaign for U.N. membership. This long-sought-after goal was achieved in 1961, with 9 votes in favor and 1 abstention (the United States). The Security Council subsequently recommended the admission of the MPR to the U.N.; Nationalist China, which claimed that the 1945 Sino-Soviet Treaty had been invalidated by Soviet violations, took no part in the proceedings.

During the post-war era, Mongolia's international position was enhanced in January 1963, when the UK became the first western nation to establish diplomatic relations with Mongolia. But Mongolia's foreign policy during this period was characterized by an extreme unilateralism vis-a-vis the USSR. In Owen Lattimore's words, Mongolia was a Soviet "satellite state" or, according to some analysts, Mongolia was trapped in a center-periphery relationship (*Galtung*). In accordance with this view, any variations within the dominant—center—state are promptly reflected in the satellite—periphery—state.

Indeed, the Mongolian People's Republic came firmly down on the side of USSR on every major foreign policy issue during this period—including Albania, Yugoslavia, and the Soviet split with China. Under Soviet guidance, Mongolia's ties with Central and Eastern European communist nations strengthened. It became a *de jure* member of COMECON, a *de facto* member of Warsaw Treaty, and a close Soviet ally following the signing of an Alliance Treaty in 1966. Such one-sided diplomatic conditions, of course, made it very difficult for Mongolia to aspire to diversify its foreign ties. This opportunity only became available beginning in the 1980s, during the so-called Gorbachev era, and full diplomatic independence was achieved by Mongolia only after the dissolution of the Soviet Union in 1991.

Russia and China: The Honeymoon

One of the most important changes in Asia after the Cold War has been the dramatic improvement of Sino-Russian relations, including in such delicate spheres as the military. No foreign policy is made in a vacuum, and during the Cold War China's biggest foreign policy headache was first and foremost the Soviet Union. The dissolution of the USSR, therefore, played a decisive role in the improvement of China's external environment, both in terms of its neighbors and the new balance of power in its favor in Asia. The Soviet collapse meant, first of all, Soviet "encirclement" of China ceased to exist. This encirclement was represented by the enormous Soviet military presence in the north—Mongolia—in the west—Afghanistan—in the south—India—and in the southeast—Vietnam.

During the 1980s, Sino-Soviet relations began to improve, leading to Gorbachev's visit in 1989 and Yeltsin's visit in late 1993; over twenty agreements were reached during these visits. In 1993, China and Russia decided to open twenty-one border crossings, paving the way to a free-flow of people and goods. Sino-Russian economic cooperation and bilateral trade grew rapidly. According to the *Mainichi* daily newspaper, in 1993 Sino-Russian trade had grown to $7 billion; even during the height of cooperation during the 1950s, there had never been a period of such active Sino-Soviet trade. Military cooperation was also deepened, as Russian military equipment began to be shipped into China.

During his 1993 visit, Yeltsin signed a joint declaration on the basic principles governing Sino-Russian bilateral relations. Mongolia's national security was touched on by article 3, which stated: "Neither party should resort to force or threat of force in any form against the other party, including the use of the territorial land, water and air space of a third country bordering the other party."[3] Article 4 proclaimed that "neither party should join any military or political alliance against the other party, sign any treaty or agreement with a third country prejudicing the sovereignty and security interests of the other party, or allow its territory to be used by a third country to infringe on the sovereignty and security interests of the other party."[4]

The provisions of this joint declaration laid down the legal basis of Mongolian-Russian and Mongolian-Chinese treaties signed soon afterwards. The security provisions of all three documents are similar, since they prohibit resorting to force and using the territories of bordering states and/or a third country. By third country, of course, China and Russia especially mean Mongolia, which has the longest common border with both Russia and China.

Legally speaking, a declaration does not have the same legal force as a treaty, but Mongolia did receive some reassurance that its territory cannot be used as a threat against either Russia or China. This declaration is very important for Mongolians, therefore, since the strong resort to power, and the weak to principle; the current Sino-Russian declaration is a far cry from past Sino-Russian and Sino-Soviet agreements and treaties—such as those signed in 1913, 1915, and 1924—in which Mongolia was obliged to fall under Chinese suzerainty.

Mongolia and Russia: Stagnation

Faced with changing Sino-Russian relations, Mongolia could not avoid the process taking place around her, especially in the former USSR; as the center changes, the periphery must change too. Mongolia's status as Moscow's close ally began to change in the late 1980s due to the *glasnost* and *perestroika* policies pursued by Gorbachev, the breakdown of the socialist system and, finally, the collapse of the USSR. The ongoing revolutionary changes in the former USSR and Eastern Europe had two basic domestic and international consequences for Mongolia.

Domestically, Gorbachev's *glasnost* policies led to Mongolia's peaceful revolution of 1990, culminating in the first democratic elections in Mongolia in seventy years. Following elections, a new state structure was put in place, the foundations of a democratic society were laid down, the initial steps toward a market economy were made, and a new constitution was promulgated that legally guaranteed democracy, freedom, human rights, and the continuity of democratic reforms. Mongolia, unlike other Asian-Leninist societies, had followed the USSR's and Eastern Europe's model by beginning thorough political reforms, instead of undertaking economic reforms while maintaining the one-party political system.

Internationally, the breakup of the USSR left Mongolia in a power vacuum. That vacuum—political, economic, and ideological—produced two results. For the first time in the last seventy years it gave Mongolia a chance to pursue an open and relatively independent foreign policy, aimed at protecting her genuine national interests, in the process enhancing ties with the United States, Japan, and other democracies. Second, Mongolia's business links with Russia dramatically declined, while trade with China increased faster than with any other country.

Many outsiders thought that the Mongolian government would swing toward China to seek political protection, but that shift never happened for several reasons. First, once a market economy and democracy were proclaimed as the paramount goals of Mongolia, the country's policymakers shifted their foreign policy toward the West; the western powers, in turn, reacted promptly. Second, Mongolia declared she would pursue a non-aligned foreign policy, something that the Soviets would have never previously allowed, since such a step would have eroded the unity of the socialist bloc. Third, Mongolia declared she would pursue a course of balanced relations with Russia and China.

These political changes had to be embodied in legal agreements before they could take effect. In January 1993, the Mongolian President visited Russia and the two signed a new treaty outlining friendly relations and cooperation to replace the 1966 Alliance Treaty. Three very important elements in this treaty require discussion. First, the new treaty, unlike the old 1966 alliance does not have a so-called security clause. So, it is not a treaty of alliance. Second, Russia recognized Mongolia's nuclear free zone status and agreed to respect the policies of Mongolia not to allow foreign troops. Third, Russia accepted that Mongolian territory shall not be used against neighboring state; article 4 of the treaty states: "The Parties shall not enter any military-political bloc, directed against each other and are committed not to conclude with third parties and treaties and agreements contradicting the interests of sovereignty and independence of the other Party." Furthermore, article 5 states: "Upon the request of one of the Parties, which considers that his security interests may be threatened, the Parties shall carry out prompt consultations."[5]

Although other documents related to bilateral relations were also concluded, the two Presidents failed to solve the debt problem; the Mongolian side argues that the MPR's total debt to Russia is around 10 billion rubles, while the Russians claim that the total is 18 billion. Some scholars and political parties in Mongolia even argue that there is no debt at all, since Mongolia's natural resources were sold to the USSR at artificially low prices. Nevertheless, the debt problem is one of the most urgent issues requiring attention in the future.

Bilateral economic cooperation between the two countries is now in a period of stagnation, due to the domestic crisis in Russia and the current financial difficulties that both sides are experiencing. In 1992 the Mongolian and Russian governments held their first meeting on trade, economic, scientific, and technological cooperation. During these talks, the sides signed a protocol on trade and economic cooperation, and an agreement on payments. They also agreed to normalize and further boost trade and economic cooperation. Russia has agreed to provide $38.6 million in loans for construction.

Agreements on trade, economic, and cultural cooperation were signed with neighboring Buriatia and Tuva, and also the Chita region, which marked the beginning of a new kind of pan-Mongol economic relationship. The sides have started working together to create free economic zones in Mongolia's Selenge province and Kiakhta district of Buriatia. Mongolia has also signed an agreement on opening outlets to the sea via Russian territory and using twenty Russian ports. In the three years after these agreements, nearly fifty joint industries and enterprises were built and Russian contributions to their budgets is estimated at $12,242,000.

Diplomatic relations with Moscow, however, remain troubled. In April 1995, the Mongolian Prime Minister P. Jasrai visited Russia in an attempt to improve bilateral relations. The two sides signed a number of documents related to Russian investments in Mongolia, tariffs on Mongolian export products, the reconsideration of old agreements and treaties, science and technology, and education.[6] During the visit, the two prime ministers agreed that the Mongolian debt question should be considered within the framework of historical traditions of cooperation between the two countries and is therefore to be considered mainly a political issue, rather than an economic one.[7]

As for the Russian diplomatic attitude toward Mongolia, it seems that Russian policymakers are in a process of determining new policies in their relations to Mongolia; a dispute between Atlantists and Euroasianists still continues. Some scholars in Mongolia argue that Russia must continue its former cooperation with Mongolia, while others argue that Russian involvement in domestic issues—such as the war in Chechnya or problems in the CIS—allow little opportunity to pay attention to Mongolia.

This passive and even neglectful Russian attitude toward Mongolia will not last. The first reason is that historically Russia—regardless of whether it was the Tsarist government or the Soviets—has always sought to strengthen its position in Mongolia; it is naive to believe that Russia would abandon Mongolia. Culturally, most of the Mongol intelligentsia was graduated from Soviet schools and most educated Mongols speak Russian and are familiar with Russian-Soviet culture.

Economically, during the Soviet period Mongolia was a raw material supplier to the USSR. The economies of the two countries became highly interdependent, albeit asymmetrically. Russia remains Mongolia's leading petroleum supplier, while Russia's position in Mongolia's foreign trade (see Table 18) is still dominant at almost 60 percent. With Soviet assistance, hundreds of enterprises, along with accompanying houses and schools, were built. Russian policymakers are also keenly aware that Mongolia is a country tied to Russia by its 10 million or so ruble debt.

Table 18. Russia and China in Mongolia's Foreign Trade
(1994 in million U.S. dollars)

	Total	Russia	PRC
Export:	324,3	89,8 (27.7%)	62,8 (19.4%)
Import:	221,7	128,3 (57.9%)	21,2 (9.6%))
Total Turnover:	546,0		

Source: Board of Statistics, Mongolia, January 7, 1995.

Finally, Russians are aware of Mongolia's political and military importance. Anatoly Arbatov, former head of the Institute of World Economy and International Relations, a well-known Moscow think tank, wrote: "The neutrality and sovereignty of Mongolia will represent a considerable security element in Asia, given the geostrategic position of China, which is projected toward Russian Transcaucasus, Kazakhstan, and Kyrgyzstan. In the event of a Chinese dominant position in Mongolia the Russian defense needs in this region would triple and communications with the Russian Far East would become more vulnerable"[8]

Mr. Arbatov's argument is remarkably similar to those held by Tsarist government officials (Sazonov) and the Soviet leaders (Stalin): Mongolia should remain a buffer state, protecting Russia and Siberia against China. Yuri A. Nikolaichuk, a researcher at the Russian Institute for Strategic Studies, has argued that Russia is interested not only in a friendly Mongolia, but in a Mongolia strategically allied with Russia. If Mongolia were to be dominated by China or any other nation—he writes—that would represent a dramatic shift in the balance-of-power in the entire region of Asia and Pacific.[9]

Mongolia and the PRC: Challenges and Opportunities

It is a well-known fact that at present China views economic development as the most important national objective. In order to achieve this goal, Beijing stresses the need for reform and liberalization of its domestic economy. At the same time, for this strategy to succeed China needs a peaceful international environment, so the Chinese government is eager to promote peaceful diplomatic policies. But it should not be ignored that China also desires to become a powerful country politically and militarily; Beijing has claimed that only a powerful China can prevent renewed militarism in Japan. Therefore, the world cannot easily ignore China, a country with nuclear weapons.

Since the collapse of the USSR, China's leadership has taken a very pragmatic approach to the world: they no longer view the world from the viewpoint of class struggle, but from the viewpoint of power politics, where each state must struggle for its survival and power. It almost seems that the Chinese have decided to act on Thucydides' advice: 'the strong do what they want and the weak suffer what they must.' Chinese diplomacy has also changed radically away from world revolution to policies characterized by nationalism or *Realpolitik*. In realist diplomacy, international politics are viewed as a power struggle in which every state pursues its own national interest, especially prosperity and survival, as the most important objective. The definition of "enemy" is not influenced by ideology, therefore, but as Lord Palmerston advised, every state could potentially turn out to be both enemy and friend.

The Chinese need for a peaceful international environment and the Sino-Soviet and Sino-Russian rapprochement allowed Mongolia and China to normalize and improve bilateral relations. Soviet troops were withdrawn from Mongolia, which greatly decreased the threat to China from Mongolian territory. These events, coupled with China's and Mongolia's open door policies, have laid the foundations for improving bilateral ties.

During recent years, the Chinese president as well as prime minister visited Mongolia—the first Chinese visit since Zhou Enlai's in the 1960s. Mongolia's leaders responded in kind. The most important result of this renewed diplomacy was the Mongol-Chinese Treaty on Friendly Relations and Cooperation, signed on April 29, 1994, during the visit of Chinese Premier Li Peng to Ulaanbaatar. By the terms of this treaty, the two sides are committed to not enter any political-military bloc, not sign any agreement with a third party which may threaten the state sovereignty and security of the other party, and not allow the use of each other's territories to harm the state sovereignty and security of the other party.[10]

At the beginning of Mongolia's process of democratization, China initially took a very cautious stand, perhaps fearing the spread of democratization to Inner Mongolia and to the Uighurs in Xinjiang. But this attitude did not last long and China began accepting Mongolian requests for Mongolian exports to use Tianjin's port, for the confirmation of Mongolia's right to transport commodities through Chinese territory, and for other issues. The Chinese also lifted their prohibition of Inner Mongolians to visit Mongolia. This change in Chinese attitude resulted in the Dalai Lama's visit to Mongolia.

Mongolian-Chinese economic relations are growing daily. In 1992, an inter-governmental commission agreed to use 50 million yuan in soft long-term credits from China. As of 1994, the total trade turnover between the two countries amounted to more than $84 million. As a result of these economic changes, in just a matter of three or four years China became Mongolia's second most important trading partner and a number of joint ventures were set up. The two sides agreed to open new border points to ease the exchange of people and border trade. Also, important agreements were concluded on protecting the border environment, transit facilities, and on economic and scientific and technical cooperation. Finally, regional trade and cooperation are growing with the neighboring Chinese provinces of Inner Mongolia and Xinjiang, where a number of border ports have been opened.

It would seem that Sino-Mongolian relations have finally taken the right path. Nevertheless, the rapid improvement in relations has caused great alarm and concern among the Mongols. Among the stated reasons for such concern are: 1) China's economic boom and Mongolia's and Russia's economic stagnation; 2) China's huge excess population; 3) Mongolia's traditional geographic fatalism towards China; and 4) China's increased military budget.

There are even more reasons that do not favor greater Chinese influence in Mongolia. These include: 1) Russia still maintains a strong position in Mongolia; 2) the traditional pro-Russian attitude of most Mongols; 3) the Mongolian government's official policy of relying on the West—especially the United States and Japan—to counterbalance China; 4) Western interest and support for Mongolia's still young democracy; 5) historical mistrust of Mongols toward the Chinese; 6) incompatibility of Mongolian and Chinese culture and civilization; 7) emerging Mongolian nationalism; and 8) Mongols' concern that China might try to exert the same power over Mongolia that it did in Inner Mongolia.

Jawaharlal Nehru once said that in Chinese history, whenever a united and powerful China was established, the rapid development of industry and the enormous increase of population of China would inevitably create an explosive situation. Mongols hope that this will not be the case, and that China will be able to develop its economy while pursuing a disarmament policy intended to make China a peaceful power in Asia.

For Mongolia, the continuation of a stable China is absolutely vital, especially given the fact that Mongolia needs a peaceful environment for the continuation of her own economic and political reforms. For the Chinese, at least according to the Mongols' view of the current Chinese leaders, a stable Mongolia is vital for China's reforms. An essential element of contemporary diplomacy is honesty, but honesty must be bilateral and not unilateral. Therefore, so long as both China and Mongolia uphold their diplomatic agreements, bilateral relations between them will not undergo great change in the near future.

The Issue of Mongolian National Minorities: A View From Mongolia

It is estimated that approximately 6 million Mongols live in Russia and China. According to Chinese statistics, in 1953 the number of Chinese Mongols was 1,400,000, in 1964, 1,900,000, in 1982, 3,400,000, and in 1990, 4,800,000. Most of these Mongols live in Inner Mongolia (3,500,000) and in the Xinjiang Uighur Autonomous Region (1,300,000). The annual growth rate of the Mongol population has been 3.1 percent.[11] One possible explanation for the sudden rise in the number of Chinese Mongols could be that during the "cultural revolution," many national minorities were forced to hide their nationality, fearing repression from the authorities. Therefore, the numbers were underreported. The numbers are smaller in Russia, but still significant. According to Mongolian researchers, in 1989 in the Russian Buriat Republic there lived approximately 700,000 Mongols, in Kalmykia, 174,000, in Tuva, 200,000, and in the Altai region, 61,000 Mongols.[12]

Mongolian national minorities living in Russia and China have had more or less the same destiny: some of them have practically lost their identity as Mongols, while others—to a greater or lesser degree—have had to struggle to conserve their language, culture, and traditions. Nevertheless, one thing is certain about both cases, the Mongol people do continue to have a common culture, language, and traditions. The Mongolian government feels obliged, therefore, to support efforts by these national minorities to preserve their national identity.

As a result of the twentieth century partitioning of Mongolia, the Mongolian national minorities living in immediate proximity to the Mongolian boundaries serve almost as an ethnic and cultural buffer between Mongolia, Russia, and China. This fact deserves greater attention. The Mongolian government's underlying reason behind supporting these minority groups is not only that they are a part of the Mongolian "race," therefore, but because Mongolia profits by preserving and strengthening this buffer zone between Mongolia, Russia, and China. In other words, Mongolia's future security and survival may depend on the continued existence and growth of these minority groups.

Some researchers, and even some Mongolian political leaders have argued that a pan-Mongol revival is underway in Mongolia. However, it is hard to accept such statements since virtually all Mongolian researchers agree that there is no possibility of uniting all Mongols to create a Mongol state. On the contrary, fueling ethnic and nationalistic sentiments might prove to be dangerous for the Mongol minorities in both Russia and China, as well as for Mongolia's own national security. Mongolia and Mongolian national minorities should continue to cooperate, but that cooperation must be carried out without any political or ideological goals in mind. Cooperation should be concentrated in four spheres: economic, trade, cultural-humanitarian, and environmental. These types of cooperation are normal, mutually beneficial, and commonly pursued by people living in different states with common borders. Cooperation should be supported and assisted by the three governments rather than hindered, since interference would lead to greater distrust rather than increased confidence.

In Search of a "Balancer": The Need for Diversification of Foreign Ties

The new trends in global, regional, and subregional levels of Mongolia's international environment and domestic reforms—characterized by democratization and the shift to a market-oriented economy—represent a challenge for Mongolia's foreign policy. Mongolia adapted to the changing international situation by adhering to a foreign policy of interdependence and by handling her foreign relations more pragmatically and more flexibly. Therefore, Mongolia needed a radical shift in foreign policy priorities.

In 1994, the Mongolian parliament approved a new foreign and national security policy. According to this policy, the basic principles, priorities, and decision-making process of Mongolia were changed. Mongolia, according to the new concept, should seek to change its former one-sided foreign policy toward Russia by trying to make it multi-sided and multi-levelled. The first goal, of course, was to improve ties with the West and with eastern democracies like Japan. The second goal was to promote a market-oriented economy to overcome Mongolia's former self-isolation and autarchy. In the period of transition now underway, Mongolia needs capital and technology from the more developed countries, as well as assistance and private investment from multinational companies. An initial breakthrough was achieved when Mongolia concluded a number of trade and economic agreements with Japan, the United States, and other G-7 countries.

Mongolia was quickly admitted to the International Monetary Fund (IMF), the World Bank, ADB and is actively cooperating with them to solidify its reforms. After the implementation of the IMF stand-by agreement, the Mongolian government is now engaged in carrying out the ESAF program. Diplomatic contacts were established with the European Union and Mongolia took steps towards membership in World Trade Organization. Mongolia is also seeking membership in PECC and Asian Pacific Economic Cooperation. With the cooperation of the United States and Japan, a permanent mechanism on the question of donor assistance to Mongolia was set up, and this group has already organized four meetings in Tokyo. During the November 1994 meeting held in Tokyo, representatives from twenty-five nations and six international organizations offered Mongolia $210 million in soft loans and assistance. Japan is playing a key role in Mongolia's economic performance. Tokyo is already Mongolia's biggest donor in terms of economic assistance (around $70 million per annum), followed by Germany, and the United States.

The western democracies not only assist Mongolia economically, they also have been giving political support. A good example of this from the point of view of Mongolia's national security was the following statement of support by the Government of United States: "If Mongolia ever faces a threat and decides to refer the matter to the United Nations Security Council, the United States, along with other members of the Security Council, would consider appropriate steps to be taken."[13] Clearly, statements like this one would make Russia and China think twice before interfering in Mongolia.

Even though direct government-to-government contacts are important, it seems that the decision makers in Mongolia are aware of the necessity to attract western capital into the country as the most important way of securing the sovereignty of Mongolia. At present, the most important national goal is the development of the domestic economy. With the emergence of a new group of nations that are willing to support Mongolia politically, the country's destiny is no longer an exclusive object of dispute between Russia and China. Instead, economics are increasingly the dominant force in its international relations. In the early 1990s, the Asia Pacific region became the fastest developing area in the world. Only by continuing and extending world and regional economic cooperation can nation-states survive and flourish. As economic activities become more and more interdependent, and as internationalization and regionalization become more pervasive, Mongolia will strive to be a firm member of the international community.

During the last years of economic reforms, Mongolia engaged in exchanges of specialists and advisers as well as commodities. Businessmen, government officials, scholars, and students from many countries visited Mongolia. In view of its geographical location in the so-called "heartland" of Asia, Mongolia faces a unique situation in terms of a vast range of opportunities to pursue economic cooperation with other countries, namely in terms of mineral resources, acting as a bridge between the European and Asian markets, a strong government commitment to a market economy, and political stability.

With all of these advantages, Mongolia hopes to pursue even greater regional economic cooperation. Mongolia's abundant supply of natural resources and raw materials is certainly one of the most attractive features. A secure supply of natural resources is regarded as the most critical issue for developed economies, such as Japan and Korea. Mongolia could soon become such a supplier, but the most pressing problem is the lack of capital and technology. Joint development projects should be based upon the principle that the developed economies would supply the equipment, machinery, and materials required for development on a long-term deferred payment basis, and in turn would be provided with longterm guaranteed quantities of natural resources developed in Mongolia.

Together with large-scale projects for exploiting natural resources, such as coal, oil, and copper, establishing new fields of industry should be considered. For example, the manufacturing industry should be promoted on the assumption that the market economies of North East Asia (NEA) could import semi-processed goods from Mongolia with the intent of adding more value to them prior to resale. The potential for cooperation between Mongolia and other countries in the service sector is also emerging. In particular, the entrance of foreign companies into Mongolia is creating a huge demand for office buildings, show rooms, exhibition halls, and distribution centers.

The most common form of regional cooperation between Mongolia and its neighbors may include the importation of plants and equipment, with payments in end-products, contracting, and joint production. While under Soviet domination, the importation of plants usually took the form of the delivery of complete plants, equipment, or production lines against payment in manufactured products or raw materials extracted by means of this equipment. In these cases, the supplier would undertake not only to deliver the production machinery and equipment, and to assemble it, but would also provide advisers to teach the Mongolians how to operate the plant. Joint production could also be facilitated through the extensive transfer of technology and in the form of purchasing licenses, which might include purchasing a supply line or an entire factory.

One of most challenging problems that the Mongolian economy faces is poor infrastructure, communications, hotel and banking facilities, and transport network, which are all relics of the Soviet era. Geographically, access to Mongolia is possible only through Russia or China. Thus, export commodities from NEA countries would almost certainly arrive at a Chinese or Russian port by sea and then be transported to Mongolia by rail, a distance of about 2,000 kilometers. Such a situation, of course, can and must be improved and the transportation network should be diversified so that neither Russia nor China could exert a stranglehold over the Mongolian economy.

In this light, Mongolia has expressed its desire to join the Asian Highway project. This project is intended to link the roads of Asian countries with those of Europe and Middle Eastern Highway systems. This project is also geared to assist the development of international trade and tourism, stimulate economic cooperation, and further cultural exchanges between nations of the region.

Another important aspect of the transport problem is how to connect Mongolia with Japan, North Korea, and South Korea by rail. There are many suggestions, such as one proposed by a researcher at the East-West Center in Hawaii that the Chinese Baicheng-Arxan railway could be connected with eastern Mongolia in order to shorten the railway distance to a suitable port. A Chinese scholar named Jiang Daming from Northeastern Normal University presented a similar plan at an international meeting held In Ulaanbaatar in 1991. In 1992, the Governor of Jilin province proposed that a railway should be constructed from the Chinese city of Tumen, through Yanji, Changchun, Baicheng, Arxan, and then on to Mongolia. Future railway construction could also improve the Zamyn-Üüd and Erlian (Erenhot) railway, as well as rebuilding the national railway network.

Mongolia's Future Security

In the future, Mongolia will face greater challenges than ever before in achieving the basic goals that form its national interests, namely the survival of the nascent Mongolian democracy, the enhancement of the nation's wealth, and the furtherance of economic development along capitalist lines. The present international environment can be compared to the 1950s, when Mongolia, the USSR, and the PRC enjoyed relatively friendly relations, and were guided by the same ideology of world revolution, but in the current situation there are widely different values and ideological incongruities between the various political systems.

As before, Mongolia's security will depend first of all on whether diplomatic relations between Russia and China are good or bad; currently, Sino-Russian relations appear good, but if Russia becomes progressively weaker, China may decide that a perfect opportunity has arisen to extend its geopolitical interests in Mongolia with little threat of Russian interference. Secondly, the domestic situations prevailing both in Russia and China will play a large role; both China and Russia are presently looking inward, with Russia occupied with nation-building, which could take many more years to complete, and with China occupied with economic reforms and its continued opening up to the outside world. Fortunately, both countries desire a peaceful international environment to achieve these goals, thus providing Mongolia with greater security.

In the present era of Russian and Chinese reform, there is no tangible military threat to the security of Mongolia. The security of the nation has especially been strengthened by Mongolia's diplomatic negotiations, which have resulted in a series of Sino-Russian, Mongolian-Russian, and Mongolian-Chinese treaties. So long as there are no unforeseen dramatic changes in Sino-Russian relations, the military threat to Mongolia should remain low.

Nevertheless, Mongolia's primary goal is to retain friendly and balanced relations with both Russia and China. Today's Mongolia is totally different from the Mongolia of yesterday and the Mongols are convinced of one thing: Mongolia will never go back to the Orwellian days of 1984. In this regard, the Mongolia of today is no longer a "mare nostrum" of Russia or of China. Its international position has been enormously enhanced, particularly since its democratization. One Western diplomat was quoted as saying of the Mongols that in the thirteenth century they conquered half of the world, but now they have conquered the heart of the world by their enthusiasm and energy to change the face of the nation. To paraphrase Oscar Wilde: 'A map of the world that doesn't include Mongolia is not even worth glancing at.'

Notes

1. *BNMAU-yn gadaad khariltsaany barimt bichgüüdiin emkhtgel*, vol. 1, pp. 278-79.

2. Ibid., p. 280.

3. *Izvestiia*, December 20, 1993.

4. Ibid.

5. *Ardyn Erkh*, January 23, 1993.

6. *Ardyn Erkh*, April 6, 1995.

7. Ibid., April 8, 1995.

8. *MEMO*, August/September 1994.

9. Paper presented to the international conference "Mongolia's Geopolitics: Past, Present, and Future," organized by the School of Foreign Service, March 20-21, 1995 in Ulaanbaatar, pp. 4-5.

10. *Ardyn Erkh,* January 30, 1994.

11. *Chinese National Annual of Statistics* (Beijing, 1994), p. 150.

12. *Oros dakhi Mongolchuud* (Mongolian national minorities in Russia), (Ulaanbaatar: Institute of International and Oriental Studies, Academy of Sciences, 1995), p. 30.

13. *Ardyn Erkh*, October 18, 1993.

Selected Bibliography

The following bibliography includes materials cited in the notes and is intended to facilitate use of this volume. Further references can be found in many of the books listed. Comprehensive bibliographical work in all appropriate languages remains an unfilled task in Mongolian studies.

Archives

Archives of the Russian Ministry of Foreign Affairs, Moscow (AVPR).
Central State Historical Archives in St. Petersburg.
Central Historical Archives of the State of Mongolia.
Central Historical Archives of the MPRP.
The National Palace Museum in Taipei.
The First Historical Archives of China (referred to below as FHAC).
Russian Center for the Storage and Study of Modern History Documents (RTsKhIDNI).

Books, Articles, Unpublished Manuscripts

Akramov, N.M. *Vydaiushchiisia russkii vostokoved V.V. Bartol'd: Nauchno-biograficheskii ocherk* (Dushanbe, 1963).
Akiner, S., ed. *Mongolia Today* (London: Kegan Paul, 1991).
Arbatov, G.A. *The Soviet Viewpoint* (London: Zed Books, 1983).
Asian Development Bank, *Mongolia: A Centrally Planned Economy in Transition* (New York: Oxford, 1992).
Atwood, Christopher P., "The East Mongolian Revolution and Chinese Communism," *Mongolian Studies* 15 (1992).
————. "A Buriat Agent in Inner Mongolia: A. I. Oshirov (c. 1901-1931)," in Edward H. Kaplan and Donald W. Whisenhunt, eds., *Opuscula Altaica.* (Bellingham: Western Washington University Press, 1994).
————. "A Romantic Vision of National Regeneration: Some Unpublished Works of the Inner Mongolian Poet and Essayist Saichungga," *Inner Asia* 1.1 (1999).
Baddeley, John F., ed. *Russia, Mongolia, China; being some record of the relations between them from the beginning of the XVIIth Century to the Death of the Tsar Alexei Mikhailovich A.D. 1602-1676* 2 vols. (London: Macmillan, 1919).

Ballis, William. "Soviet Russia's Asiatic Frontier Technique: Tana Tuva," *Pacific Affairs*, (14, March 1941).

Bartol'd, Vasilii V. *Istoriia izucheniia Vostoka v Evrope i Rossii* (St. Petersburg, 1911; 2nd ed. Leningrad, 1925).

Batbayar, Ts. *Modern Mongolia: A Concise History* (Ulaanbaatar, 1996).

Bawden Charles. *The Modern History of Mongolia* 2nd ed. (London: Kegan Paul International, 1989; first issued 1968).

Beloff, Max. *The Foreign Policy of Soviet Russia* (New York: Oxford University Press, 1949).

———. *Soviet Far Eastern Policy Since Yalta* (New York: Institute of Pacific Relations, 1950).

———. *Soviet Policy in the Far East, 1944-1951* (New York: Oxford University Press, 1953).

Boikova, E.V., ed. *Vladimirtsovskie chteniia* (Moscow: Institut vostokovedeniia RAN, 1995),

———. "Creation of Database on Russian Expeditions to Mongolia at the End of the XIX-in the Beginning of the XX Century," unpublished paper presented at the Seventh International Congress of Mongolists, Ulaanbaatar, August, 1997.

Brandt, Conrad. *Stalin's Failure in China* (New York: Norton, 1958).

———. Benjamin Schwartz, and John K. Fairbank, eds. *A Documentary History of Chinese Communism* (Cambridge: Harvard University Press, 1952).

Burdukov, Aleksei V. *V staroi i novoi Mongolii: Vospominaniia, pis'ma* (Moscow, 1967).

Cameron, Merideth E. *The Reform Movement in China* (Stanford: Stanford University Press, 1931).

Campi, Alicia Jean. "The Political Relationship Between the United States and Outer Mongolia, 1915-1927: The Kalgan Consular Records" (Indiana University Dissertation, 1988).

Ch'en Li-fu. *The Storm Clouds Clear Over China: The Memoir of Ch'en Li-fu, 1900-1993* (Stanford: Stanford University Press, 1994).

Chimitdorzhiev, Sharap B. *Rossiia i Mongoliia* (Moscow: Glavnaia redaktsiia vostochnoi literatury, 1987).

Circautas, Arista Maria. *Nicholas Poppe: Bibliography of Publications from 1924 to 1977* (Seattle: University of Washington Press, 1977).

Chiang Kai-shek. *China's Destiny* (New York: Roy Publishers, 1947).

The China White Paper, August 1949 (Stanford: Stanford University Press, 1967).

Chu Chi-hsien. "The Sino-Soviet Conflict in Turkistan" (Northeast Missouri State University M.A. Thesis, 1980).

Cleaves, Francis W. *The Secret History of the Mongols: for the first time done into English out of the original tongue and provided with exegetical commentary* (Cambridge, MA: Harvard University Press, 1982).

Clubb, Edmond O. *China and Russia: The "Great Game"* (New York: Columbia University Press, 1971).

Carruthers, Douglas. *Unknown Mongolia: A Record of Travel and Exploration in Northwest Mongolia and Dzungaria,* 2 vols. (London: Hutchinson, 1914).

Dallin, Alexander, ed. *Soviet Conduct in World Affairs* (New York: Columbia University Press, 1960).

Dallin, David J. *The Rise of Russia in Asia* (New Haven: Archon Books, 1971).

Damdinsüren, Ts., ed. *Öwgön Jambalyn yaria* [Reminiscense of Old Jambal], (Ulaanbaatar: Shinjlekh ukhaan, deed bolowsrolyn khüreelengiin erdem shinjilgeenii khewleliin gazar, 1959).

Day, Alan J., ed. *Border and Territorial Disputes* (Detroit: Gale Research Company, 1982).

Degras, Jane, ed. *Soviet Documents on Foreign Policy: Vol. 1, 1917-1924* (New York: Oxford University Press, 1951).

————. *Soviet Documents on Foreign Policy: Vol. 2, 1925-1932* (New York: Oxford University Press, 1952).

————. *The Communist International: 1919-1943* (New York: Oxford University Press, 1956. two volumes).

Dennis, Alfred L.P. *The Foreign Policies of Soviet Russia* (New York: E. P. Dutton, 1924).

Dirlik, Arif. *The Origins of Chinese Communism* (New York: Oxford University Press, 1989).

Doolin, Dennis J. *Territorial Claims in the Sino-Soviet Conflict* (Hoover Institution Studies, No. 7. Stanford: Stanford University Press, 1965).

Duus, Peter, Ramon H. Myers, and Mark R. Peattie, eds. *The Japanese Informal Empire in China, 1895-1937* (Princeton: Princeton University Press, 1989).

Ewing, Thomas. *Between the Hammer and the Anvil? Chinese and Russian Policies in Outer Mongolia, 1911-1921* (Bloomington: University of Indiana Press, 1980).

Eudin, Xenia Joukoff, and Robert C. North. *Soviet Russia and the East, 1920-1927: A Documentary Survey* (Stanford: Stanford University Press, 1957).

————. *M. N. Roy's Mission to China: The Communist-Kuomintang Split of 1927* (Berkeley: University of California Press, 1962).

Fairbank, John King, ed. *On the Chinese World Order* (Cambridge: Harvard University Press, 1968).

————., ed. *The Late Ch'ing, 1800-1911,* Part I, vol. 10 of *The Cambridge History of China* (Cambridge: Cambridge University Press, 1978).

Feigon, Lee. *Chen Duxiu: Founder of the Chinese Communist Party* (Princeton: Princeton University Press, 1983).

Fletcher, Joseph. *Studies on Chinese and Islamic Inner Asia* (Brookfield, VT: Varorium, 1995).

Flynn, John T. *The Lattimore Story* (New York: Devin-Adair, 1953).

Forsyth, James. *A History of the Peoples of Siberia: Russia's North Asian Colony, 1581-1990* (Cambridge, UK: Cambridge University Press, 1992).

Fritters, Gerard. *Outer Mongolia and Its International Position* (Baltimore: Johns Hopkins, 1949).

Garver, John W. *Chinese-Soviet Relations, 1937-1945: The Diplomacy of Chinese Nationalism* (New York. 1988).

Geyer, Dietrich. *Russian Imperialism: The Interaction of Domestic and Foreign Policy, 1860-1914* (New Haven: Yale University Press, 1987).

Gibson, Michael Richard. *Chiang Kai-shek's Central Army, 1924-1938* (George Washington University Dissertation, 1985).

Glinka, G.V., ed. *Atlas Aziatskoi Rossii* (St. Petersburg: Izdanie Pereselencheskogo upravleniia glavnogo upravleniia Zemleustroistva i zemledeleniia, 1914).

Gol'man, Mark I. *Problemy noveishei istorii Mongol'skoi narodnoi respubliki v burzhuaznoi istoriografii SSHA* (Moscow, 1970).

Goncharov, Sergei N., and John W. Lewis, Xue Litai. *Uncertain Partners: Stalin, Mao, and the Korean War* (Stanford: Stanford University Press, 1993).

Gorokhova, G.S. *Ocherki po istorii Mongolii v epokhu man'chzhurskogo gospodstva* (Moscow: "Nauka," 1980).

Grum-Grzhimailo, G.E. *Zapadnaia Mongoliia i Uriankhaiskii krai*, vol. 1 (St. Petersburg, 1914), vol. 2 (Leningrad, 1926).

Grimm, E.D. *Sbornik dogovorov i drugikh dokumentov po istorii mezhdunarodnykh otnoshenii na Dal'nem Vostoke [1842-1925]* (Moscow, 1927).

Hangin, John G. and Urgunge Onon. *Analecta Mongolica: Dedicated to the Seventieth Birthday of Professor Owen Lattimore* (Bloomington: The Mongolia Society, 1972).

Hasiotis, Arthur Christos, Jr. "A Study of Secret Political, Economic, and Military Involvement in Sinkiang from 1928-1949" (New York University Dissertation, 1981).

Haslam, Jonathan. *The Soviet Union and the Threat from the East, 1933-41: Moscow, Tokyo and the Prelude to the Pacific War* (Pittsburgh: University of Pittsburgh Press, 1992.)

Heissig, Walther. *Ein Volk sucht eine Geschichte: die Mongolen und die verlorene Dokumente ihrer grossen Zeit* (Dusseldorf: Econ Verlag, 1964).

———. *A Lost Civilization: The Mongols rediscovered* (London: Thames and Hudson, 1966).

———. *Geschichte der Mongolishcher Literatur*, 2 vols. (Wiesbaden: Harrassowitz, 1972).

———., ed. *Collectanea Mongolica: Festschrift für Professor Dr. Rintchen zum 60. Geburtstag* (Wiesbaden: Harrassowitz, 1966).

Humphrey, Caroline. *Karl Marx Collective: Siberian Collective Farm* (Cambridge: Cambridge University Press, 1983).

Iakovlena, E. N. *Bibliografiia Mongol'skoi narodnoi respubliki* (Moscow, 1935).

Iriye, Akira. *After Imperialism: The Search for a New Order in the Far East, 1921-1931* (Cambridge: Harvard University Press, 1965).

———. *The Cold War in Asia: A Historical Introduction* (Princeton: Princeton University Press, 1974).

Isaacs, Harold R. *The Tragedy of the Chinese Revolution* (Stanford: Stanford University Press, 1961).

Jacobs, Dan N. *Borodin: Stalin's Man in China* (Cambridge: Harvard University Press, 1981).

Jagchid, Sechin. *Essays in Mongolian Studies* (Provo, Utah: David M. Kennedy Center for International Studies, Brigham Young University, 1988).

Jamsran, L. *Mongolchuudyn sergen mandaltyn ekhen* [The Beginning of the Restoration of the Mongols] (Ulaanbaatar: Soyombo khewleliyn gazar, 1992).

Jelavich, Barbara. *A Century of Russian Foreign Policy, 1814-1914* (Philadelphia: Lippincott, 1964).

Jones, W.L.G., ed. *Pioneer Settlements* (Worcester, MA: Commonwealth Press, 1932).

Jowitt, Kenneth. *New World Disorder* (Berkeley: University of California Press, 1990).

Kabo, Rafael M. *Ocherki istorii i ekonomiki Tuvy. Chast' pervaia: dorevoliutsionnaia Tuva* (Moscow-Leningrad, 1934).

Kaplan, Edward H. and Donald W. Whisenhunt, eds. *Opuscula Altaica: Essays Presented in Honor of Henry Schwarz* (Bellingham: Western Washington University Center for Asian Studies, 1994).

Kara, György. *Knigi mongol'skikh kochevnikov* (Moscow: Glavnaia redaktsiia vostochnoi literatury, 1972).

Kasanin, Marc. *China in the Twenties* (Moscow, 1973).

Kashiwabara Takahisa and Hamada Jun'ichi. *Moko chishi* [A topography of Mongolia] (Tokyo: Tomiyama Bo, 1919).

Kataoka, Tetsuya. *Resistance and Revolution in China: The Communists and the Second United Front* (Berkeley: University of California Press, 1974).

Kennan, George F. *Soviet-American Relations, 1917-1920: Russia Leaves the War* (Princeton: Princeton University Press, 1956).

————. *Soviet-American Relations, 1917-1920: The Decision to Intervene* (Princeton: Princeton University Press, 1958).

————. *American Diplomacy* (Chicago: University of Chicago Press, 1984).

Korotsovetz, Iwan J. *Von Cinggis Khan zur Sowjetrepublik: eine kurze Geschichte der Mongolei unter besonderer Berucksichtigung der neuesten Zeit* (Berlin and Leipzig: Walter de Gruyter, 1926).

Kotkin, Stephen and David Wolff, eds. *Rediscovering Russia in Asia: Siberia and the Russian Far East* (Armonk, N.Y.: M.E. Sharpe, 1995).

Krueger, John R., ed. *Tuvan Manual. Area Handbook, Grammar, Reader, Glossary, Bibliography* (Bloomington: Indiana University, Uralic and Altaic series Vol. 126, 1977).

Lamb, Alastair. *British India and Tibet, 1766-1910*, 2nd ed. (London: Routledge & Kegan Paul, 1986).

Lattimore, Eleanor Holgate. *Turkestan Reunion* (New York: John Day, 1934).

Lattimore, Owen. *The Desert Road to Turkestan* (Boston: Little Brown, 1929).

————. *High Tatary* (Boston: little Brown, 1930).

————. "Mongolia Enters World Affairs," *Pacific Affairs* (7:1, 1934).

————. "The Geographical Factor in Mongolian History," *Studies in Frontier History* (1938).

————. *Inner Asian Frontiers of China* (New York: American Geographical Society, 1940).

————. "The Inland Crossroads of Asia," *Studies in Frontier History* (1944).

————. *Pivot of Asia: Sinkiang and the Inner Asian Frontiers of China and Russia* (Boston: Little, Brown, 1950).

————. "Inner Asia: Sino-Soviet Bridge," *Studies in Frontier History* (1952).

————. "The New Political Geography of Inner Asia," *Studies in Frontier History* (1953).

————. *Nationalism and Revolution in Mongolia* (Leiden: E.J. Brill, 1954).

————. "Satellite Politics: The Mongolian Prototype," *Studies in Frontier History* (1956).

————. *Studies in Frontier History: Collected Papers, 1928-1958* (New York: Oxford, 1962).

————. *Nomads and Commissars: Mongolia Revisited* (New York: Oxford, 1962).

Lederer, Ivo J., ed. *Russian Foreign Policy* (New Haven: Yale University Press, 1962).

Ledovsky, A. *The USSR, the USA, and the People's Revolution in China* (Moscow, 1982).

Lensen, George Alexander, ed. *Revelations of a Russian Diplomat: The Memoirs of Dmitri I. Abrikossow* (Seattle: University of Washington Press, 1964).

————. *Russia's Eastward Expansion* (Englewood Cliffs, NJ: Prentice-Hall, 1964).

————. *Japanese Recognition of the U.S.S.R.* (Tokyo: Sophia University Press, 1970).

Leong, Sow-Theng. *Sino-Soviet Diplomatic Relations, 1917-1926* (Canberra: Australian National University Press, 1976).

Li Yushu, *Mengshi luncong* (Taipei: Liwen shuju, 1990).

Magsarjav, N. *Mongol ulsyn shine tüükh* [A New History of Mongolia], (Ulaanbaatar: Instituti Historiae Academiae Scietiarum Mongolici, 1994).

Mänchen-Helfen, Otto. *Reise ins Asiatische Tuva* (Berlin: Der Bückerkreis, 1931).

————. *Journey to Tuva. An Eve-Witness Account of Tannu-Tuva in 1929*, trans. from the German by Alan Leighton (Los Angeles: University of Southern California, Ethnographics Press, 1992; originally published in German in 1931).

Mancall, Mark. *Russia and China* (Cambridge: Harvard University Press, 1971).

Maiskii, Ivan. *Sovremennaia Mongoliia* (Irkutsk, 1921).

————. *Mongoliia nakanune revoliutsii* (Moscow, 1960).

Mao Peizhi, comp. *Bianfa zhiqiang zouyi huibian* (1901; reprint, Taipei: Wenhai chubanshe, n.d.).

McCormack, Gavan. *Chang Tso-lin in Northeast China, 1911-1928* (Stanford: Stanford University Press, 1977).

McLane, Charles, *Soviet Policy and the Chinese Communists, 1931-1946* (New York, 1958.)

MacMurray, John V.A. *Treaties and Agreements with and Concerning China, 1894-1919* (London: Oxford University Press, 1921).

Mineev, A., ed. *Agrarnyi vopros na Vostoke* (Moscow, 1933).

The Mongols in a Sociological Survey, Vol. 1, (Ulaanbaatar, Mongolian Academy of Sciences, 1997).

Moskovskaia Torgovliaia Ekspeditsiia v Mongoliiu (Moscow: Publishing House of P.P. Riabushinskii, 1912).

Murphy, George G. S. *Soviet Mongolia, A Study of the Oldest Political Satellite* (Berkeley: University of California Press, 1966).

Nakami Tatsuo. "A Protest Against the Concept of the 'Middle Kingdom': The Mongols and the 1911 Revolution," in Eto Shinkich and Harold Z. Schiffrin, eds., *The 1911 Revolution in China: Interpretive Essays*, (Tokyo: University of Tokyo Press, 1984).

————. "Mongoru-no dokuritsu to kokusai-kankei," *Ajia-kara kangaeru (3): Shūen-karano rekishi* (Tokyo: Tokyo daigaku shuppankai, 1994).

————. *Nairiku Ajia: Chiiki-karano sekaishi 6* [Inner Asia] (Tokyo: Asahi shinbun-sha, 1992).

Nawaannamjil G. *Öwgön bicheechiin ügüülel* [Reminiscence of an Old Clerk], (Ulaanbaatar, Ulsyn khewleliyn gazar, 1956).

Newman, Robert P. *Owen Lattimore and the "Loss" of China* (Berkeley: University of California Press, 1992).

North, Robert C. *Kuomintang and Chinese Communist Elites* (Stanford: Stanford University Press, 1952).

————. *Moscow and Chinese Communists* (Stanford: Stanford University Press, 1953).

————. *Chinese Communism* (New York: McGraw-Hill, 1966).

Oberländer, Erwin et al., eds., *Russia Enters the Twentieth Century, 1894-1917* (London: Temple Smith, 1971).

Okada Hidehiro, *Sekaishi no tanjō* (Tokyo, Japan: Chikuma shobo, 1992).

Onon, Urgunge, ed. and trans. *Mongolian Heroes of the Twentieth Century* (New York: AMS Press, 1976).

Onon, Urgunge and Derrick Pritchatt, *Asia's First Modern Revolution: Mongolia Proclaims Its Independence in 1911* (New York: E. J. Brill, 1989).

Paine, S.C.M. *Imperial Rivals: China, Russia, and Their Disputed Frontier* (Armonk, NY: M. E. Sharpe, 1996).

Pavlovsky, Michel N. *Chinese and Russian Relations* (1949. Reprint, Westport, CT: Hyperion, 1981).

Phillips, G.D.R. *Russia, Japan, and Mongolia* (London: Frederick Mueller, 1942).

Pipes, Richard. *The Formation of the Soviet Union: Communism and Nationalism, 1917-1923* (Cambridge: Harvard University Press, 1964).

Popov, A. "Tsarskaia Rossiia i Mongoliia v 1913-1914gg." *Krasnyi arkhiv*, Vol. 6/37/ (1929).

Poppe, Nicholas. *Reminiscences* (Bellingham: Western Washington University Center for East Asian Studies, 1983).

————. "Mongol'skaia narodnaia respublika," *Vestnik Instituta po Izucheniiu Istorii i Kul'tura SSSR* [Munich] (No. 4:11, July-August 1954).

————. "Mongolovedenie v SSSR," *Institut zur Erforschung der Geschichte und Kultur der UdSSR*, (1:14, 1955).

———. "The Buddhists," in *Genocide in the USSR: Studies in Group Destruction* (New York: Scarecrow Press, 1958).

Pozdneev, Aleksei M. *Mongoliia i mongoly*, 2 vols. (St. Petersburg, 1896-98).

———. *Mongolia and the Mongols* (Bloomington: Indiana, 1975).

———. *Religion and Ritual in Society: Lamaist Buddhism in Late 19th-Century Mongolia*, ed. by John R. Krueger, trans. from the Russian by Alo Raun and Linda Raun (Bloomington: The Mongolia Society, 1978).

———. *Mongolia and the Mongols*, ed. by John R. Krueger and Fred Adelman, trans. from the Russian by John Roger Shaw and Dale Plank (Bloomington: Indiana University, Uralic and Altaic Series Vol. 61, 1971).

Prescott, J. R. V. *Map of Mainland Asia by Treaty* (Melbourne: Melbourne University Press, 1975).

Price, Don C. *Russia and the Roots of the Chinese Revolution, 1896-1911* (Cambridge: Harvard University Press, 1974).

Price, Ernest Batson. *The Russo-Japanese Treaties of 1907-1916 Concerning Manchuria and Mongolia* (Baltimore: The Johns Hopkins Press, 1933).

Puntsagnorov, Ts. *Mongolyn awtonomit üyeiin tüükh* [A History of the Mongolian Era of Autonomy] (Ulaanbaatar: Ulsyn khewlel, 1955).

Quested, R. K. I. *Sino-Russian Relations: A Short History* (Winchester, MA: George, Allen, and Unwin, 1984).

Rinchen, B. *Mongol bichgiin khelnii züi. Udirtgal* (Ulaanbaatar: Shinjlekh ukhaany akademiin khewlel, 1964).

Romanov, B. A. *Russia in Manchuria*, trans. Susan Wilbur Jones (Ann Arbor, Mich.: American Council of Learned Societies, 1952; reprint, New York: Octagon Books, 1974).

Rossabi, Morris. *China and Inner Asia: From 1368 to the Present Day* (London: Thames and Hudson, 1975).

Rupen, Robert. *How Mongolia Is Really Ruled: A Political History of the Mongolian People's Republic, 1900-1978* (Stanford: Stanford University Press, 1979).

———. *Mongols of the Twentieth Century*, Vol. 1 (Bloomington: Indiana University Press, 1964).

Saich, Tony. *The Origins of the First United Front in China: The Role of Sneevliet (Alias Maring)* (Leiden: E. J. Brill, 1991).

Sanders, A. J. K. *The People's Republic of Mongolia: A General Reference Guide* (London: Oxford University Press, 1968).

———. *Mongolia: Politics, Economics, Society* (London: Francis Pinter, 1987).

Sanjdorj, M. *Manchu Chinese Colonial Rule in Northern Mongolia*, trans. from the Mongolian by Urgunge Onon (New York: St. Martin's Press, 1980).

Sandag, Sh. *Mongol ulusyn töriin gadaad khariltsaa, 1850-1919* [Foreign Relations of Mongolia, 1850-1919], Vol. 1 (Ulaanbaatar: Shinjlekh ukhaan akademiin khewlel, 1971).

Schiffrin, Harold Z. *Sun Yat-sen and the Origins of the Chinese Revolution* (Berkeley: University of California Press, 1968).

————. *Sun Yat-sen: Reluctant Revolutionary* (Boston: Little, Brown, 1980).
Schwarz, Henry G., ed. *Studies on Mongolia: Proceedings of the First North American Conference on Mongolian Studies* (Bellingham: Western Washington University Center for Asian Studies, 1979).
————. *China's Policies towards Minorities* (Bellingham: Western Washington University, 1971).
————. *The Minorities of China: A Survey* (Bellingham: Western Washington University Center for Asian Studies, 1984)
————., ed. *Mongolian Publications at Western Washinaton University* (Bellingham: Western Washington University Center for Asian Studies, 1984).
Shieh, Milton J. T. *The Kuomintang: Selected Historical Documents, 1894-1969* (Baltimore, 1970).
Sheng, Yueh. *Sun Yat-sen University in Moscow and the Chinese Revolution: A Personal Account* (Center for East Asian Studies, University of Kansas, 1971).
Shinkich, Eto and Harold Z. Schiffrin, eds. *The 1911 Revolution in China: Interpretive Essays* (Tokyo: University of Tokyo Press, 1984).
Sinor, Denis. "Central Eurasian" in *Orientalism in History* (Cambridge: Cambridge University Press, 1954).
————. *Inner Asia: A Syllabus* (Bloomington: Indiana University Press, 1969).
————. "Introduction: The Concept of Inner Asia," in *The Cambridge History of Early Inner Asia* (Cambridge: Cambridge University Press, 1990).
Snell, John L., ed. *The Meaning of Yalta* (Baton Rouge: Louisiana State University Press, 1956).
Snow, Edgar. *Red Star over China* (London: Gallienz Press, 1938).
Sokolsky, George. *The Story of the Chinese Eastern Railway* (Shanghai, 1929).
Sovetsko-Mongol'ski otnosheniia, 1921-1947. Dokumenty i materialy, V. 1 (Moscow. 1975).
Stephan, John J. *The Russian Far East, A History* (Stanford: Stanford University Press, 1994).
Tan P'ing-shan. *The Path of Development of the Chinese Revolution* (Moscow, 1927).
T'ang Leang-li. *The Inner History of the Chinese Revolution* (London: G. Routledge and Sons, 1930).
Tang, Peter S. H. *Russian and Soviet Policy in Manchuria and Outer Mongolia, 1911-1931* (Durham: Duke University Press, 1959).
Thorne, Christopher. *The Far Eastern War. States and Societies, 1941-1945* (London, 1986).
Tian Zhihe and Feng Xuezhong. *Minguo chunian mengqi "duli" shijian yanjiu* [A study of the independence events of the Mongolian banners in the early years of the Republican period] (Huhe haote: Neimenggu renmin chubanshe, 1991).
Tsedenbal, Yu. *Izbrannye stat'i i rechi,* V. 2. (Moscow. 1962).
Tuchman, Barbara W. *Stilwell and the American Experience in China, 1911-45* (New York: Macmillan, 1971).

Uhalley, Stephen. *A History of the Chinese Communist Party* (Stanford: Hoover Institution Press, 1988).

VKP(b), the Comintern and the National-Revolutionary Movement in China, Documents, Vol. 1 (1920-1925) (Moscow, 1994).

Vainshtein, Sevyan. *Nomads of South Siberia. The Pastoral Economies of Tuva*, trans. from the Russian by Michael Colenso (New York: Cambridge University Press, 1980).

van de Ven, Hans, J. "The Founding of the Chinese Communist Party and the Search for a New Political Order, 1920-1927" (Harvard University Dissertation, 1987).

————. *From Friend to Comrade: The Founding of the Chinese Communist Party, 1920-1927* (Berkeley: University of California Press, 1991).

Vernadsky, George. *A History of Russia. Volume 3: The Mongols and Russia* (New Haven: Yale University Press, 1953).

Vucinich, Wayne, ed. *Russia and Asia* (Stanford: Hoover Institution Press, 1972).

Wei Chao. "Foreign Railroad Interests in Manchuria: An Irritant in Chinese-Japanese Relations (1903-1937)" (St. John's University Dissertation, 1980).

Wei, Julie Lee, Ramon H. Myers, and Donald G. Gillin. *Prescriptions for Saving China, Selected Writings of Sun Yat-sen* (Stanford: Hoover Institution Press, 1994).

Weigh, Ken Shen. *Russo-Chinese Diplomacy* (Westport, CT: Hyperion, 1981).

Westad, Odd Arne. *Cold War and Revolution: Soviet-American Rivalry and the Origins of the Chinese Civil War* (New York: Columbia University Press, 1993).

Whiting, Allen S. *Soviet Policies in China, 1917-1924* (New York: Columbia University Press, 1954).

Wilbur, C. Martin. *Sun Yat-sen: Frustrated Patriot* (New York: Columbia University Press, 1976).

———— and Julie Lien-ying How. *Documents on Communism, Nationalism, and Soviet Advisers in China 1918-1927: Papers Seized in the 1927 Peking Raid* (New York: Columbia University Press, 1972).

———— and Julie Lien-ying How. *Missionaries of Revolution: Soviet Advisers and Nationalist China, 1920-1927* (Cambridge: Harvard University Press, 1989).

Worden, R. and A. Matles, eds. *Mongolia: A Country Study* (Washington: Library of Congress, 2nd ed, 1991).

Wu Fengpei, comp. *Qingmo menggu shidi ziliao huicui* (Beijing: Janguo tushuguan wenxian suowei fuzhi zhongxin, 1990).

Yakhontoff, Victor A. *Russia and the Soviet Union in the Far East* (New York: Coward-McCann, Inc., 1931).

————. *The Chinese Soviets* (New York: Coward-McCann Inc, 1934).

Yigu, *Kenwu zouyi* (reprint, Taipei: Wenhai chubanshe, 1974).

Yamane Yukio, ed. *Gendaishi kenkyū bunken mokuroku* (Tokyo, 1971).

Zhao Erxun, ed. *Qingshi gao* (Beijing: Qingshi guan, 1928).

Zlatkin, Il'ia. *Mongol'skaia narodnaia respublika—strana novoi demokratii* (Moscow, 1950).

Index